# ANDY WARHOL
## A RETROSPECTIVE

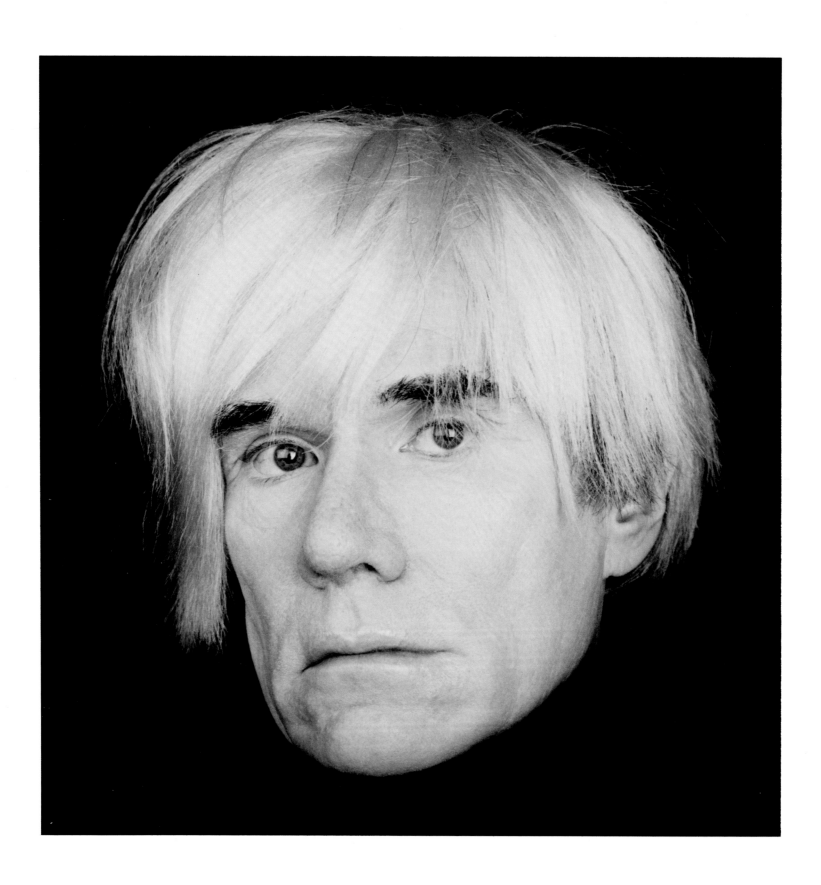

# ANDY WARHOL
# A RETROSPECTIVE

EDITED BY KYNASTON McSHINE

WITH ESSAYS BY

KYNASTON McSHINE

ROBERT ROSENBLUM

BENJAMIN H. D. BUCHLOH

MARCO LIVINGSTONE

THE MUSEUM OF MODERN ART, NEW YORK

DISTRIBUTED BY BULLFINCH PRESS/LITTLE, BROWN AND COMPANY, BOSTON

Published on the occasion of the exhibition
*Andy Warhol: A Retrospective*
organized by Kynaston McShine, Senior Curator
Department of Painting and Sculpture
The Museum of Modern Art, New York
February 6–May 2, 1989

Library of Congress Catalogue Card Number 88-63474
ISBN 0-87070-680-2 (hardcover edition)
ISBN 0-87070-681-0 (paperback edition)
ISBN 1 85332 035 8 (British paperback edition)

Edited by Harriet Schoenholz Bee and James Leggio
Designed by Steven Schoenfelder
Production by Tim McDonough
Composition by Graphic Technology Inc., New York
Color separations by Spectra II Separations, Inc., New York
Printed by Eastern Press, Inc., New Haven, Connecticut
Acetate jacket printed by Hopp Press Inc., Newark, New Jersey
Hardcover binding by Horowitz/Rae, Inc., Fairfield, New Jersey
Paperback binding by Sendor Bindery, New York

The Museum of Modern Art
11 West 53 Street
New York, New York 10019

Frontispiece: Robert Mapplethorpe. *Andy Warhol*. 1986

# CONTENTS

The exhibition *Andy Warhol: A Retrospective* has been supported
by a generous grant from Knoll International.

Additional funding has been provided by
the Henry J. and Drue Heinz Foundation,
The International Council of The Museum of Modern Art,
and the National Endowment for the Arts.

An indemnity for the exhibition has been received from
the Federal Council on the Arts and the Humanities.

This publication has been supported by a
grant to The Museum of Modern Art from
an anonymous donor.

# *FOREWORD*

This book is published on the occasion of the exhibition *Andy Warhol: A Retrospective,* which marks the first full-scale critical examination of this remarkable American artist's career. At a time when we may appropriately begin to assess his contributions to twentieth-century art, this book and exhibition span the wide range of his creativity, from the earliest work of the fifties to works executed just before his untimely death, in February 1987. Through his art, ideas, and style, Andy Warhol left a lasting imprint on the history of modern art and on our culture. We hope that this book, and the exhibition it accompanies, will contribute significantly to understanding his vision and originality, his influence and legacy.

That we have been able to mount this retrospective is due in large part to the cooperation of The Estate of Andy Warhol and its executor, Frederick W. Hughes. We are also most appreciative to the trustees of The Andy Warhol Foundation for the Visual Arts, Mr. Hughes, John Warhola, and Vincent Fremont, as well as its General Counsel, Edward W. Hayes. Their assistance and enthusiasm have been unfailing sources of encouragement.

On behalf of the trustees and staff of The Museum of Modern Art, I wish to express our deep appreciation to Marshall Cogan and Knoll International for their generous and farsighted support of this exhibition. We also owe particularly warm thanks to Drue Heinz and to the Henry J. and Drue Heinz Foundation for their thoughtful commitment to this project. Similarly, the generous support received from the National Endowment for the Arts and from The International Council of The Museum of Modern Art continues their long and distinguished records of furthering contemporary art.

Warm thanks are also due to an anonymous donor, who generously provided a grant toward the publication of this book. Additional funding was graciously given by Lily Auchincloss. We are most appreciative of their support.

The Federal Council on the Arts and the Humanities, through the Art and Artifacts Indemnity Act, provided insurance coverage for foreign loans, which was essential to the realization of this exhibition.

An enormous amount of thought and effort has gone into the organization of this exhibition and the publication of this volume. To all those who have given so unsparingly of their time, and especially to the writers of the essays and the contributors to the Collective Portrait in this book, the Museum is deeply grateful.

I should also like to thank the staff of The Museum of Modern Art, almost all of whom contribute in some degree to the realization of an exhibition of this scope. The individual most responsible for this ambitious undertaking is Kynaston McShine, Senior Curator in the Department of Painting and Sculpture and director of the exhibition. He deserves our great admiration as well as our warm thanks.

Finally, the most essential element of any exhibition is necessarily the generosity of lenders. Without their cooperation, no exhibition, however well conceived, can be realized. In this instance, their response has been extraordinary and represents a high tribute to the work of Andy Warhol. To all our lenders, individuals and institutions, we express our profound gratitude.

Richard E. Oldenburg
*Director*
*The Museum of Modern Art*

# *ACKNOWLEDGMENTS*

On a summer evening in 1962 I was invited by my friend Henry Geldzahler to visit the studio of an artist whose work he thought might interest me. To my surprise the studio was not in Lower Manhattan, and upon arrival at a small Upper East Side brownstone we entered a wonderfully crowded room cluttered with canvases stretched and unstretched, piles of photographs and magazines and art supplies. I do not remember all of the paintings that the reticent but friendly artist showed us, but an indelible memory is *Do It Yourself (Sailboats)*. I remember believing that it had a natural inevitability and an extraordinary contemporaneity.

This was my first encounter with Andy Warhol. For the next twenty-five years I saw a great deal of his extraordinary output and saw him fairly regularly in the New York scene until his unexpected death, in February 1987. It is incumbent upon us now to present fully his remarkable and serious achievement. The daunting task of organizing the exhibition and this accompanying publication has been, despite the complexity of the project, a lively and exciting one. But Warhol's absence from the venture has been very deeply felt.

The full and generous cooperation of many people and institutions in several countries attests to the extent to which his life and work have been significant both to those who knew him well and to many who never met him. On behalf of the trustees of The Museum of Modern Art, I wish to express my deepest gratitude to all who have participated in preparing the exhibition and its accompanying publication.

I extend my personal thanks to Marshall Cogan and to Mrs. Henry J. Heinz II. Their wholehearted support of this exhibition and their recognition of its significance are acknowledged with profound appreciation.

The International Council of The Museum of Modern Art, a unique group of dedicated individuals, under whose auspices the exhibition will travel to Europe, has from the outset offered encouragement and provided crucial assistance. I owe them a great debt of gratitude.

I also acknowledge the contributions of the National Endowment for the Arts, which has very generously assisted contemporary art in the United States over the years. An indemnity for the exhibition has been gratefully received from the Federal Council on the Arts and the Humanities. It is a vital contribution to the realization of an exhibition of this scope.

This publication received generous support through an anonymous gift to The Museum of Modern Art, for which we are grateful. I would also like to thank Lily Auchincloss for her contribution and acknowledge the kindness of John C. Davis, President of CTI Industries.

This endeavor would have been impossible without the enthusiastic and thoughtful support of Frederick W. Hughes, the executor of The Estate of Andy Warhol and a trustee of The Andy Warhol Foundation for the Visual Arts. He has unstintingly given of his time and graciously assisted us in innumerable ways, beyond being a generous lender. My personal debt of gratitude to him is immeasurable. This project has benefited from the full cooperation of the other trustees of The Andy Warhol Foundation, Vincent Fremont and John Warhola, as well as its General Counsel, Edward W. Hayes, and I thank them. Through them, information and documentation have become available that have given all connected with this project new insights into Warhol's oeuvre and biography.

A special debt is owed to the entire staff of the Warhol studio and especially to Steven Bluttal, Timothy Hunt, Margery King, and Jay Shriver. I have depended on them greatly and I deeply appreciate how they readily, skillfully, and with good humor coped with the various demands and countless details that this project entailed.

To the authors of the essays in this volume, to the many who contributed to the Collective Portrait, and to those who provided elusive information go special thanks for enriching our understanding of Warhol.

For Andy Warhol as well as for many of the people associated with this project, Dominique de Menil's vision, astute judgment, and enthusiasm have always been an unfailing source of encouragement. We also thank her for the wholehearted participation of The Menil Foundation in Houston. They have been extraordinarily helpful. Walter Hopps, a much valued friend and colleague, has been a source of essential advice and aid. Neil Printz (a contributor to this publication) and Susan Davidson, both of The Menil Foundation, as well as other staff members have provided valuable assistance. The Dia Art Foundation was most crucial to this project and is owed our gratitude.

Many friends and associates of Warhol went to much trouble to facilitate the research for this project, and I specially thank the following: Thomas Ammann, Heiner Bastian, Irving Blum, Andreas Brown, Leo Castelli, Ronnie Cutrone, Ronald Feldman, Henry Geldzahler, John Giorno, Nathan Gluck, Samuel Adams Green, Jed Johnson, Billy Klüver, Charles Lisanby, Dr. Peter Ludwig, Gerard Malanga, Robert Mapplethorpe, James Mayor, Mary Adeline McKibbin, Robert Miller, Gene Moore, Paul Morrissey, Billy Name, Glenn O'Brien, Philip Pearlstein, Paige Powell, Charles Saatchi, Rupert Smith, Geraldine Stutz, John Wallowitch, James Warhola, and Paul Warhola.

I am also grateful for the cooperation and assistance received from Todd Alden, Doris Ammann, Martha Baer, Carl Belz, Michael Boodro, Hilary Borow, John Cheim, Hugh Davies, Julia Ernst, Trevor Fairbrother, Robert Felner, Michael Findlay, Gary Garrels, Christopher Gibbs, Manuel Gonzalez, Eric Goode, Anthony Grant, Peggy Jarrell Kaplan, Stephen

Koch, Kasper Konig, Erika Lederman, Anders Malmberg, Jason McCoy, Susan Meng, Andrew Meyer, John Neff, Anthony d'Offay, Howard Reed, Stephen Shore, Morgan Spangle, Dr. Dierk Stemmler, the Ströher family, Charles Stuckey, Alexander Vreeland, Angela Westwater, and Charles B. Wright.

At The Museum of Modern Art this project has had enthusiastic cooperation from the entire staff. Several colleagues have contributed essential and much valued advice. They have been fully supportive and I deeply thank them all for their help.

Richard E. Oldenburg, the Director of the Museum, has lent encouragement and made every effort toward the realization of this project. I am grateful. Particular thanks are due to the directors of the curatorial departments of the Museum, especially William Rubin and Kirk Varnedoe. The success of this project has depended on them greatly. I also especially acknowledge Riva Castleman, Deputy Director for Curatorial Affairs and Director of Prints and Illustrated Books.

My personal indebtedness to Marjorie Frankel Nathanson, Jennifer Wells, and Daniel Schulman of the Department of Painting and Sculpture is incalculable. Every aspect of this publication and exhibition has been enriched by their careful and considered judgment, their unflagging thoroughness, extraordinary resourcefulness, and above all their memorable generosity of spirit.

In the Department of Painting and Sculpture thanks are also due Matthew Bank, who handled the voluminous correspondence and many related tasks for this exhibition and publication. Indeed, the success of any undertaking such as this depends on the cooperation and participation of the entire department. I thank each of its members for their goodwill.

A debt is owed the Department of Publications for producing this volume. I particularly acknowledge the valued contribution of Harriet Bee and James Leggio, who have expertly edited this book with rigor and thoroughness. I would also like to specially thank Maura Walsh. Tim McDonough oversaw the printing and complex production of this volume with exemplary patience and skill. I deeply appreciate their splendid teamwork.

I most warmly thank Steven Schoenfelder, for he has given this complicated book an appropriately elegant, lively, and colorful design.

For their assistance in various ways that facilitated the publication of this book, I wish to thank: Maria Brassel, Doug Bressler, Patricia Brundage, Susan Brundage, Sarah Cooke, Suzanne Donaldson, Shelley Dowell, Anita Duquette, Gudrun Erhard, S. Jeffrey Figley, Ken Heyman, Patricia Koch, Rebecca Lincoln, Joshua Mack, Maureen McCormick, Adam Reich, Helene Rundell, Martina Schneider, Harry Shunk, Matthew Siegal, Lillian Singer, David White, and Dee Weldon-White. I also want to acknowledge the photographers who have provided the essential material for this book and especially, for their extraordinary effort, Kate Keller and Mali Olatunji, the Museum's photographers. Richard Tooke and the entire staff of Rights and Reproductions are specially thanked. The Museum's Library has been the source of much useful documentation; Daniel Starr of its staff has contributed the bibliography included in this volume.

The Department of Film and its director, Mary Lea Bandy, are to be thanked for facilitating the selection of films of Andy Warhol to be presented in conjunction with the exhibition. Jon Gartenberg has been very helpful. We are especially grateful for the kind cooperation of John G. Hanhardt, Curator of Film and Video at the Whitney Museum of American Art, who is director of the collaborative project with The Museum of Modern Art to preserve and catalogue Warhol's films.

Richard L. Palmer, the Museum's Coordinator of Exhibitions, has my heartfelt thanks for his customary patience and deep commitment to the exhibition program. He has expertly guided us through many budgetary difficulties arising from the loans, both national and international, and has coped with the insurance problems an enterprise such as this creates. I am grateful to Jerome Neuner for his untiring attention to detail in the complicated installation of the exhibition in galleries on two floors of the Museum. Special thanks are owed the Registrar's office, particularly to Lynne Addison, who has efficaciously dealt with the various challenges posed by the assembly and disassembly of the works. The special cooperation of the Conservation staff is gratefully acknowledged. They have manifested their usual professionalism, extending advice and assistance whenever needed.

I have benefited from the measured advice, astuteness, and knowledge of Beverly M. Wolff, the Museum's General Counsel. I am deeply appreciative. The Department of Public Information and especially Jeanne Collins are warmly thanked for their essential efforts on behalf of this project.

The Museum's International Program, its director Waldo Rasmussen and his associate director Elizabeth Streibert, deserve our gratitude. Their commitment to international exchange will enable this exhibition to be shown in England, Germany, Italy, and France. Their advice and assistance have been welcomed.

Many other members of the Museum's staff have contributed in many ways, and I wish to specially cite the following: Guillermo Alonso, Anny Aviram, Rosette Bakish, Eleanor Belich, Karl Buchberg, Jennifer Carlson, Mikki Carpenter, Louise Chinn, James Coddington, Carol Coffin, Fred Coxen, Sue Dorn, William P. Edwards, James Gara, Gregory Gillbergh, Michael Hentges, Patricia Houlihan, Joan

Howard, Susan Jackson, Ruth Janson, Laurence Kardish, Susan Kismaric, Nancy Kranz, Maria Martin, Donald McLeod, Karen Meyerhoff, Terry Myers, James Snyder, Andrea Stone, Kristin Teegarden, Daniel Vecchitto, and John L. Wielk.

I want to express my personal gratitude to the lenders to *Andy Warhol: A Retrospective*. Their kindness, graciousness, and enthusiasm have been memorable. Particular thanks are due them for extraordinary generosity in sharing their works with a wide audience for a long exhibition tour, as well as for giving liberally of their own time. It is indeed a special tribute to the artist.

Many friends have assisted me during the months this volume and exhibition have been in preparation. I wish to express my deepest appreciation to them. I specially acknowledge Peter Freeman and Elizabeth Cunnick, George Montgomery and Dan Wagoner. Nothing would have been possible without the extraordinary kindness of Sylvia Guirey and Ann Lewis.

Finally, a personal comment. In the last few years, we have suffered the loss of many people of creativity and imagination. Some were close friends, others known only from their work. I wish they could have seen this volume and the exhibition.

K. McS.

In this volume, the dimensions of works of art are given first in inches, then in centimeters, height preceding width, and followed in the case of sculpture by depth.

Since Andy Warhol worked on many different projects concurrently, it is impossible to determine an exact sequential order for his oeuvre. Therefore, the works in the plate section are arranged not in a strict chronological order but rather in groups established primarily by subject.

A number of the works included in the plate section are not on view in the exhibition that this publication accompanies; a checklist of the exhibition is available from The Museum of Modern Art.

# INTRODUCTION

BY KYNASTON McSHINE

"JE est un autre."

—Arthur Rimbaud

"Andy has fought by repetition to show us that there is no repetition really, that everything we look at is worthy of our attention. That's been a major direction for the twentieth century, it seems to me."

—John Cage

Very few artists achieve the level of recognition that secures for them a place in the public imagination. Andy Warhol was an artist who did. However, this very celebrity of Warhol's, his sheer, inescapable fame, has often disguised the fact that he was one of the most serious, and one of the most important, artists of the twentieth century. He quite simply changed how we all see the world around us. He also had an uncanny ability to select precise images that still have great resonance today. The straightforward, shockingly simple images—usually culled from the pages of newspapers and magazines or discovered in photographs—found their way to a new authorship, becoming timeless, potent signs that are indelible in the minds of most of us.

Despite this, many would want to remember Andy Warhol for a glamorous reputation, for his ability to be at all the right places at seemingly all the right times. However, even though he was constantly in one spotlight or another, he nonetheless managed to hide from most of us, to maintain both public and private personas. In part this is so because as an artist, Warhol erased himself in favor of subject matter, a strategy that encouraged the more active participation of viewers but one that also distanced him, on an emotional level. This notion has been expressed often, not only by Warhol himself, as when he acknowledged that he wanted to be a machine, but also by historians and critics alike.[1] From the beginning his work exploited a similar, paradoxical

sense of disguise. The flashy surface of mass-media publicity, and the multiple, mutually cancelling images (figure 1), concealed another, more subtle, complex, and private set of concerns.

1. Andy Warhol. *Photo-Booth Self-Portrait*. c. 1964. Gelatin-silver prints; two strips, each 7¾ × 1⅝" (19.7 × 4.1 cm). Collection Robert Mapplethorpe

The first recorded "scandal" of Andy Warhol occurred during his senior year at Carnegie Institute of Technology, in 1948–49, when his provocatively titled painting *The Broad Gave Me My Face, But I Can Pick My Own Nose* (figure 2) was rejected by the jury of the Associated Artists of Pittsburgh annual exhibition.[2] The painting, which shows Warhol himself, is not simply a gesture of youthful rebellion; it is an act of self-definition. The jokey title assumes an artist's freedom, the possibility of revising nature, even if only through the artifice of choosing his own nose. With the aid of hindsight, knowing Warhol's history of dissatisfaction with his appearance (and knowing of his eventual, and for him unsatisfactory, cosmetic facial surgery in 1957), we can perhaps see the work as an early instance of the artist's characteristically ambiguous sense of self, and of a wish to change himself.

The nature of his background and upbringing also suggests some of his personal concerns. Born of immigrant, Roman Catholic Czech parents at the beginning of the Depression, Warhol grew up near the mills of Pittsburgh. From an early age, he seems to have been interested in adopting another identity, having experienced the problems of being himself—of being linguistically, culturally, and religiously different. Warhol yearned to be someone else. He wanted to be some physically and socially different person, to transcend the limitations of his family and partake more fully of what that almost foreign country, America, had to offer—the glamorous America portrayed in the movies, on the radio, in magazines and newspapers. Simply put, Warhol wanted most of all what he lacked by birth: beauty, wealth, or any other obvious avenue to fame.

After graduation from Carnegie Tech in 1949, he and his friend Philip Pearlstein as well as other classmates moved to New York, 13 where Warhol began to satisfy his need for financial security by working as a commercial illustrator. The ambivalent nature of his self-image, his sense of being at a remove from what he did, which would ultimately affect his art, can be seen in his remarks concerning these early activities: "I loved working when I worked at commercial art and they told you what to do and how to do it and all you had to do was correct it and they'd say yes or no."[3]

Warhol's fascination with beauty and stardom is also evident in his work of the fifties, both commercial and private. By their very nature, his works for department stores served the commodities associated with fashion and beauty, promoting women's clothing, accessories, perfume, and cosmetics by embodying in them an idea of the glamorous. The shoe drawings for I. Miller, which appeared in the society pages of the *New York Times,* were a theme Warhol expanded, for himself, to include "celebrity shoes," personifying such stars as Mae West, Zsa Zsa Gabor, Elvis Presley, Julie Andrews, and Kate Smith. And with the same lyrical line used to portray his friends in the more private drawings, he celebrated Truman Capote, Greta Garbo, and James Dean (plates 70, 71).

In the later fifties Warhol began to develop an interest in the works and the careers of Jasper Johns and Robert Rauschenberg. And his own ambitions as an artist came to the fore. He seems to have thought of an artist as someone whose "aura" could transform ordinary things. As Charles Lisanby has said of Warhol and Matisse: "What interested Andy in Matisse was not, I think, so much the work but the fact that . . . all Matisse had to do was tear out a little piece of paper and glue it to another piece of paper and it was considered very important and very valuable. It was that aspect of Matisse. It was the fact that Matisse was recognized as being so world famous and such a celebrity."[4]

The celebrity of the artist confers upon him the power to make the ordinary extraordinary. It is the alchemy of fame. And so Warhol now wanted above all to be a famous artist, and that meant being accepted and shown in a gallery, selling his works, and seeing them enter museum collections. That would be his new identity, his way of transforming himself.

Warhol's first works in what became his

2. Andy Warhol. *The Broad Gave Me My Face, But I Can Pick My Own Nose.* 1948–49. Tempera on masonite, 37 × 18″ (94 × 45.7 cm). Collection Paul Warhola family

new mode suggest that he looked for a subject in which he was most interested, by which he could define himself as an artist, and found it in the banal world of pulp: in the fan magazines he read to follow the lives of the stars he adored, and in the tabloids, with their ads, their comics, and their screaming headlines. It was "easy," it was what he loved and found somehow deeply satisfying, and it was ground just then being explored by a generation of new artists.

Warhol's first major appearance as an artist came in 1961. He exhibited five paintings as a backdrop to mannequins sporting the latest fashions in a display window at Bonwit Teller (plate 77). The imagery of all five works, whether drawn from the comic strips or from the advertisements printed in the newspaper, reflects his desires and deficiencies, for all traffic in vernacular metaphors of metamorphosis and self-transcendence. Of the three works from the comics, two show characters who change dramatically: Superman (plate

113), who emerges from his secret identity of Clark Kent, and Popeye (plate 122), who is made a new man by spinach (so much so that in Warhol's painting he seems to be punching the picture plane). Even The Little King (plate 124), from a comic strip more limited to the sight gag, is nonetheless representative: the victory of the little guy.

Warhol's cartoon-derived images (which also include *Nancy,* two versions of *Dick Tracy,* and *Batman* [plates 110–112, 126]), were not the first of their kind. He was preceded by Philip Pearlstein, who in 1952 created a personalized *Superman* (figure 3) soaring in the skies above Metropolis, painted in a style derived from the heavily impastoed paintings of some of the Abstract Expressionists. Johns's *Alley Oop,* 1958 (figure 4), showed the comic strip hovering in an orange field, not unlike his earlier Flags, and masked by strokes of the brush. Rauschenberg, too, used comic images from the newspapers in the fifties. But it was Roy Lichtenstein who was the closest to Warhol in the use of comic-strip imagery, as can be seen, for example, in his 1961 *The Engagement Ring* (figure 5). When Warhol came face to face with Lichtenstein's work, while visiting the Leo Castelli Gallery in 1961, encountering comic-strip paintings by an artist then unfamiliar to him, he was surprised.[5] But he conceded that Lichtenstein's elegant humor and his ingenious appropriation of the look of mechanical printing methods, including the Benday dot, surpassed his own work in this vein. Lichtenstein's presence also seemed to preempt Warhol's more worldly ambition of exhibiting at what he considered *the* gallery of the New York avant-garde. Warhol appears to have abandoned the cartoon, not wanting to share the subject with a competitor. However, he had already grasped the larger implications of using such popular subject matter—and of the comic-strip structure, grounded as it is in serial imagery—for his budding aesthetic.

The images in the other two works in the Bonwit's window, *Advertisement* and *Before and After* (plates 78, 81), draw on newspaper material that is starkly nonfictional. The subject of both works is physical self-improvement. Promoting devices and products promising improved posture and silhouette, fuller hair, broader shoulders, and bigger

3. Philip Pearlstein. *Superman*. 1952. Oil on canvas, 40⅛ × 35⅞″ (101.9 × 91.1 cm). Private collection

4. Jasper Johns. *Alley Oop*. 1958. Oil and collage on composition board, 22⅞ × 18⅛″ (58.1 × 46 cm). Collection Mr. and Mrs. S. I. Newhouse, Jr.

5. Roy Lichtenstein. *The Engagement Ring*. 1961. Oil on canvas, 67¾″ × 6′ 7¾″ (172.1 × 202.6 cm). Collection Mr. and Mrs. S. I. Newhouse, Jr.

arms, these ads touch the core of Warhol's physical insecurities. They also provide the impulse for much of his painting over the next several years.

The newspaper ads that most interested Warhol were graphically crude and terribly direct—aimed at the lowest common denominator, and delivered with maximum force and economy (the marketing imperative of getting the most impact for the dollar). As he worked on the paintings, he avoided "improving" these images, or any vestige of his personal handwriting. The rather un-sexy advertisements for such household items as pots and pans, kitchen appliances, hardware, and a television set, on the one hand, and self-improvement ads for nose jobs, trusses, and wigs, on the other, gradually give way to those for simple food and drink: Coca-Cola and Pepsi, and such products as Del Monte peach halves and Campbell's soup (see plates 78–101).

The newspaper suggested other avenues, which Warhol pursued simultaneously. It is of course a major medium for advertising, a means of proffering objects of desire in a way that Warhol, a veteran of print ad campaigns, understood as creating, as much as satisfying,

15

6. Barnett Newman. *Cathedra*. 1951. Oil and synthetic polymer paint on canvas, 7' 10½" × 17' 10" (240 × 543.6 cm). Stedelijk Museum, Amsterdam. Purchase, with the support of the Vereniging "Rembrandt" and the Theo van Gogh Stichting and an anonymous gift

the needs of the consumer. But more than this, the tabloids were seen as a source of sensational news and gossip, a vehicle for fame. Following the lives of glamorous celebrities provided the artist, hungering for recognition and starved for beauty, with a nourishment as essential as food.[6] In two major canvases of 1961–62, *Daily News* and *A Boy for Meg* (plates 134, 135), Warhol lifts the format of the front page whole, giving the works a rigid formal order as well as ready-made imagery and content. The headlines of both concern the intimate lives of "royal" celebrities, Elizabeth Taylor and Princess Margaret. Even in the fifties Warhol had experimented with the newspaper format (plates 127–133). But then, the "news" he reported on the page had usually been imaginary, some items featuring friends, such as Charles Lisanby.

The graphic immediacy of the tabloid format, with bold headlines and photos, appealed to Warhol's developed sense of style. The format is perhaps most effective in the reporting of catastrophe. The first of what would come to be called the Disaster paintings, *129 Die in Jet (Plane Crash),* 1962 (plate 136), was also one of his last hand-painted works. (This dramatic and affecting painting was of an air-

plane en route to the United States crashing on takeoff at the Paris airport. It was an "art world" disaster, for many of those who died were patrons of the High Museum of Art, in Atlanta.) Warhol had been experimenting with mechanical means of reproduction (such as rubber stamps and silkscreens prepared from drawings) to produce works based on printed "currency," like the S & H Green Stamps, Airmail Stamps, and Dollar Bill paintings (plates 137–151). Now he went further toward removing the traditional sense of the artist's "touch" by utilizing silkscreens prepared by a photo-mechanical process. This was the beginning of a new phase in the manipulation of his images taken from the mass media, images of disasters, celebrities, and products.

One of the first paintings produced by means of the photo-silkscreen process was *Baseball* (plate 198), dating from late July or August 1962. His choice of Roger Maris as the subject is an interesting meditation on the ambiguity of fame, since Maris, after breaking Babe Ruth's home-run record in 1961, was awarded both glory and scorn. Following *Baseball,* two major thematic groupings appear in the

work: the Disasters, and another that can loosely be termed celebrity icons—Marilyn Monroe, Elvis Presley, Natalie Wood, Elizabeth Taylor.

The Disaster pictures, derived from news photographs, cover a broad range, from common accidents to global tragedy (plates 256–286). Automobile crashes predominate, but we also see images related to mental illness (in *Bellevue*), fatal food poisoning (*Tunafish Disaster*), fire (*Black and White Disaster*), capital punishment, and nuclear holocaust; even birth trauma is included (*Hospital*). In most of the works, Warhol uses repeated images to reinforce the obsessive way our thoughts keep returning to a tragedy, and to stress the flash of fame that these little-known victims achieve in death, as their pictures are repeated in thousands of copies of newspapers. The sense of being at an extreme, of seeing things in a dislocated way, is heightened in certain of the paintings by the use of vivid and strangely juxtaposed colors. As a group, these paintings represent one of the most compelling series produced in our era.

Warhol's Electric Chairs (plates 278–285), a series within a series, deal with a specifically American instrument of execution. Addressing the controversial issue of the death penalty, they also provoke in the viewer a feeling of helplessness in the face of such a nondescript, seemingly harmless object, whose function is betrayed only by the word SILENCE visible in the background, a startling reminder that the condemned has an audience. It was in one of these Electric Chair paintings (plate 284) that Warhol used a blank panel for the first time. While the suggestion of a large expanse of solid color may have come from the monumental paintings of Barnett Newman, such as *Cathedra* (figure 6), the blankness also conveys directly a sense of obliteration and void consistent with the image on the adjacent panel, making these paintings iconic, almost religious, in their otherworldly reference. The blank, second panel suggests a metaphysical "before and after."

It has to be noted that Warhol, who seemed to be politically neutral throughout his life, created not only these Electric Chairs, but also several works about racial unrest in the American South, specifically in Birmingham (plates 275–277), paintings that can be interpreted as indictments of bigotry, violence, and brutality, a presentation of the visual evidence. In their way, these works make powerful aesthetic statements, delivering their message in one case (plate 275) through seemingly pointed choice of colors (red, white, and blue) and of (flaglike) composition.

The celebrity icons Warhol started to produce by means of the photo-silkscreen technique in the late summer of 1962 are tinged by the same awareness of catastrophe. The mass media, upon which he drew for both series, are not just a conduit of violent and tragic news but a catalyst for dreams of glory and glamor, encouraging in many the belief that the impossible is possible—that even the ordinary child from ordinary surroundings can become a star.

This is a sense of Warhol that we begin to get from his painting of Robert Rauschenberg, whom, in the early days in New York, Warhol admired, as he did Jasper Johns, for his art and for its acceptance. He became the subject of a painting in 1962, *Young Rauschenberg #1* (plate 225). The painting has the wonderful sepia tones of an old photograph, which immediately sets it off from its time. Indeed, it

not only is a portrait of an artist, an apotheosis of the glamorous young man, but also suggests his triumph after the drawback of being brought up during the Depression years. It is a picture of someone rising from an impoverished background to fame and fortune. Along with other portraits of Rauschenberg and his family—such as *Let Us Now Praise Famous Men* (plate 226), named after the book by Walker Evans and James Agee—it is quietly symbolic of Warhol himself and his childhood.

From childhood, Warhol believed in the myth of stardom. His attraction to the persona of the youthful and famous motivates some of the first silkscreen paintings, based on images of Troy Donahue, Elvis Presley, and Warren Beatty (plates 193–196). Warhol's identification with them is twofold, both as objects of desire and as role models. In contrast to the later versions of Elvis and of Marlon Brando, who are depicted by more than just their faces (plates 233, 234, 253–255), these first works

project an appeal that is wholesome, intimate, and attainable. Executed in much the same idiom as *Troy Donahue* and *Warren, Natalie* (plate 197) was their female counterpart; Natalie Wood had recently been Warren Beatty's co-star in the film *Splendor in the Grass.*

But it was when the Disasters' theme of death coincided with his fascination with stardom and beauty that Warhol found the subjects of his best-known groups of celebrity portraits: Marilyn Monroe, Elizabeth Taylor, and Jacqueline Kennedy. The ironic implication of doomed beauty produced a number of strong, memorable paintings. Initiated shortly after the actress's suicide in August 1962, the Marilyn series constitutes some of the key images of our time. He created the *Gold Marilyn Monroe* (plate 199) as a gilded Byzantine icon. However, the object of veneration here is not a Blessed Virgin but a slightly lewd seductress, the image of whose face is still suffused with erotic magic. This sensuous

7. Willem de Kooning. *Woman, I.* 1950–52. Oil on canvas, 6′ 3⅞″ × 58″ (192.7 × 147.3 cm). The Museum of Modern Art, New York. Purchase

radiance transforms the unhappy Marilyn Monroe of real life—the victim of abuse, failed marriages, affairs, and finally suicide. In Warhol's paintings of her, the very human and vulnerable Marilyn becomes a symbolic image of the need for love and to be loved. The dramatic, and not very tender, painting devoted to rows of her lips (plate 203) celebrates the absurdity of mere desire. Reducing Marilyn to an anatomical fragment, to a kind of endlessly repeating osculation machine, it dispels any romantic illusions about the idea of a kiss.

Well informed throughout his life about the contemporary art scene, Warhol was aware of the precedents set by depictions of Marilyn before her death. He said in an early interview, "De Kooning gave me my content and motivation,"[7] and it can be pointed out that in Willem de Kooning's Women series (figure 7), begun in 1947, he incorporated a somewhat alarming cutout of a woman's mouth from a cigarette advertisement in one of the studies.[8] De Kooning's *Marilyn Monroe,* 1954, seems to be her first appearance in fine art.

An attraction to luxury and spectacle, along with his voyeuristic interest in the brightest stars, led Warhol to another love goddess of the screen. Liz Taylor, whose private life, her affairs and marriages, fueled the publicity of her public career, epitomized Warhol's attraction to the star who is of such magnitude as to become a divinity as well as a product. As with Marilyn, he painted Liz for the first time (plate 135) under the aspect of mortality, when she was critically ill. But then he was so intrigued by her infinite variety that he painted not only the virginal child star she had been, in *National Velvet* (plate 228), but also the voluptuary in her sensational role as Cleopatra (plate 232), wherein she became not only Queen of the Nile but also Queen of Hollywood through a highly publicized romance (on-screen and off) with her Marc Antony, Richard Burton.

But it remained for another kind of star to be the subject of some of his strongest works. Warhol was deeply moved, as were most in the United States and the world, by the assassination of John F. Kennedy on November 22, 1963. From this came another series of paintings, based primarily on that event and on the President's widow, Jacqueline, who, in

her dignified bearing, assumed the role of tragic queen.

It was during that long November weekend that television became a unifying force for the whole country, assuming a pervasive new role in defining the national consciousness. And it is in these paintings that Warhol's use of repetition and serial imagery became something more than a simple aesthetic device derived from Muybridge or Marey. His multiplied images of those days offer the viewer an obsessive reenactment, since the actual events had already been repeated ad infinitum on television; their inescapable repetition had itself become a part of everyone's consciousness of that time.

This, and the harsh disjointedness of the images that Warhol assembled in paintings such as *Jackie (The Week That Was)* (plate 241)—a very jarring title, juxtaposing her name with part of the name of a political-satire television show—helped a wider group of people to comprehend his visual strategy. It became more possible to see what he was trying to accomplish through his choice of subject matter and techniques, as well as through the seeming mass production of many works on a specific theme.

In November 1964, Warhol had his first exhibition at the Leo Castelli Gallery, a marker that he had set his sights on early in his career. He chose to exhibit the Flowers, a recent series of works based on an image taken from a magazine. But barely six months later, during an exhibition of the same works at the Galerie Ileana Sonnabend in Paris in May 1965 (plate 306), Warhol made the declaration that he was going to retire from painting. Nonetheless, he had his first institutional exhibition, at the Institute of Contemporary Art at the University of Pennsylvania in Philadelphia, in the fall. The opening of the exhibition became the subject of intense publicity, culminating in a frenzied fracas in which the crowd reached such proportions that all the paintings had to be removed from the walls of the galleries. The event was widely reported in the national press and confirmed once and for all Warhol's celebrity status.[9]

With the coming of true recognition, changes began to be felt in his life and in his work. The shy, reticent, yet sociable persona

of the artist who seemed to be constantly receiving visitors in the studio, or as it aptly began to be called, the Factory, disguised an immense capacity for work. Buoyed by the exhibitions and publicity that he had engendered, Warhol was being propelled into a new mode. Now that his ambition to be famous, to be wealthy, and to be recognized in the visual arts was actually being realized, Warhol was at an impasse. There seemed little left to accomplish.

Prior to his "retirement," activity at the Factory had accelerated. As early as 1963 his studio had become a total environment, his own *Merzbau* of aluminum foil; life inside the silver screen, as it were. Employing assistants, Warhol had been able to achieve the end results he desired in the variants and versions of such signature series as the Brillo Boxes (plate 185) by producing in the Factory's "assembly-line" style.

In addition to serving as a studio, the Factory became Warhol's own Hollywood set, and the maestro found himself surrounded by a coterie of acquaintances and friends: *jeunesses* (some *dorées,* some tarnished), glamorous transvestites, eager dealers, avid collectors, avant-garde matrons of New York society, prescient young curators, precocious poets, and the cunning curious. This cast became the subject of his films.

While other artists, for example Claes Oldenburg, Allan Kaprow, and Jim Dine, decided to involve themselves with the live, hybrid theater of happenings, Warhol leapt naturally onto the more mechanical medium of film, which allowed for more of his basic aesthetic. He viewed his filmmaking (begun in 1963) as complementary to his painting and installations. To the temporal medium of film he brought the unique sense of dislocation and repetition that had been part of his formal innovations in painting. Through the highly humorous and loose narrative film *The Chelsea Girls,* with its projection of two separate reels of film simultaneously, Warhol in 1966 achieved another level of attention from the national press. But perhaps more important, film allowed him, with the flick of a switch, to create something, a work of art.

Surrounded by "the beautiful people" and intrigued by his own drawing power, Warhol regarded himself as director and impresario, both within and outside the Factory, with the power to invent "superstars."

During 1967–68, he was at his coolest, in both his creative and his social lives. The unceasing activities ranged from multimedia presentations with the music group The Velvet Underground to extensive travel and miscellaneous other projects. The frenetic night-and-day life continued until the afternoon of June 3, 1968, when Valerie Solanis, an occasional extra in Warhol's films, casually appeared at the Factory and shot him.

After the near-fatal assault Andy Warhol's life was never the same. But from the experience he did seem to salvage some motivation to return to painting.

His first work during recuperation was a commissioned portrait of Mrs. Nelson A. Rockefeller. He subsequently did a few more portraits, and traveled to the increasingly frequent exhibitions of his work, especially in Europe. However, it was not until 1972, with his series of paintings of Chairman Mao (plates 348–363), that he again received the approbation of the exigent art world.

If Warhol can be regarded as an artist of strategy, his choice of Mao as a subject—as the ultimate star—was brilliant. The image of Mao, taken from the portrait photograph reproduced in the Chairman's so-called Little Red Book, is probably the one recognized by more of the earth's population than any other—a ready-made icon representing absolute political and cultural power. In Warhol's hands, this image could be considered ominously and universally threatening, or a parody, or both.

The Mao series is important, too, for its announcement of a new freedom in the way Warhol would handle paint and color in the seventies. In some works bold and lush while in others astringent and cold, the paint on the surface competes with the screened image. Especially in the large paintings of Mao, Warhol used a mop to get wide swathes of color; in the smaller works, he often painted over the screened image.

The Maos were done in as large a variety of sizes as the Flowers series had been. For their exhibition in Paris in 1974 (plate 347), Warhol installed a large number of them on a specially created Mao wallpaper, which added a bold-

ness and dramatic tension that was startling in its symphonic complexity.

In the seventies, portraiture took over as Warhol's primary theme, and source of income. As others have remarked, more than any other artist of the past thirty years he revived the portrait as a major genre. Portraits, both of himself and of others, were a staple of his oeuvre from the very beginning. Many of the private "boy drawings," drawings of glamorous women, and the elegant, gold portraits of the later fifties depict close

8. Publicity photograph of Watson Powell used by Warhol as a source for his painting *The American Man—Watson Powell*, 1964. The Estate of Andy Warhol

companions and other acquaintances (plates 42, 43, 55–61, 63–69, 72).

The advent of the photo-silkscreen technique in 1962 had strongly affected Warhol's portraiture. A striking feature is the detachment between artist and subject involved in the making of a portrait. Warhol's "hands off" (or do-it-yourself) approach is best exemplified by one of his earliest commissions, that of Ethel Scull, 1963 (plate 325). Here, pose and expression are almost completely controlled by the sitter, in her encounter with a totally mechanized camera. From a large number of the resulting photographs, Warhol selected those to be screenprinted on thirty-six small canvases, painted with vivid and pastel colors, and mounted together. The ensemble is not unlike the multipanel Jackie pictures.

In contrast to the lively Ethel Scull portrait, *The American Man—Watson Powell* (plate 324) was made from a single, reduplicated image (figure 8), repeated thirty-two times in muted and bland colors. It is a comment on the American corporate executive.

When Warhol's portrait commissions increased enormously following the critical success of the Mao paintings, he accepted commissions from heads of state, politicians, royals, powerful industrialists, women of international society, athletes, rock stars, dancers, a veritable cast of hundreds—a whole spectrum of people of our time transmogrified into their own and Warhol's dream of themselves. It becomes a curious social phenomenon that because of his powerful iconic paintings of Marilyn, Liz, and Jackie (and himself, in the long run), others yearned for a similar status—for the stardom, beyond their own special and privileged standing, to be conferred by a Warhol portrait.

The process of making these portraits has been well documented.[10] They are almost double portraits, with their two layers giving them something of a dual identity. The first layer is an abstract evocation of the individual, defined exclusively by the juxtaposition of colors (ranging from the shockingly electric to warm and subtle combinations), while the second layer is the photographic image, a more precise representation of the individual (although even these were almost always touched up by Warhol). Despite what appears to be a somewhat formulaic approach to picture-making, there is great stylistic range, from hard-edge to more gestural, expressionistic representations. In works such as *Liza Minnelli, Truman Capote,* and *Lana* (plates 338–340), for example, Warhol presents people in their element, as "public" figures whose faces appear to be lit by the frozen glare of the flash camera. The women's lips, eyes, and hair are accentuated almost to the point of becoming generic. In contrast are, for example, portraits of David Hockney and Henry Geldzahler (plates 332, 337), where the paint is thick and applied wet on wet, in broad, sweeping strokes. As a result, the image of the face is almost lost.

If the photo booth had been his original self-focusing camera, the Polaroid camera, used as a first step for the portraits, proved even more suitable, with its simplicity and instant results. From now on, Warhol was rarely without a camera. Constantly taking pictures, many of which were published in *Interview,* the magazine he founded in 1969, or in his 1979 book *Exposures,* as voyeur he documented his own life as well as the lives of those with whom he was in close social contact.

In the general whirl of the production of portraits, Warhol was capable of minor digressions from the work at hand. As a counterpoint to his fancy commissions, he decided to paint *Ladies and Gentlemen* (plate 333), part

the Ladies and Gentlemen with ever bolder experimentation in color. Most of all the series serves as a profound summation of the nature of portraiture—the skull is Everyman. Within the continuum of the history of art, the Skulls are the *memento mori* of our time.

Warhol painted *Self-Portrait with Skull* (plate 12) in 1978. We find him using the skull humorously—the vulnerable Andy as Hamlet. For someone who had nearly experienced death, it is a rather casual meditation on mortality, as it is not, for example, in the otherwise comparable self-portrait by the

self-portrait image used, as a "wanted" poster, for the announcement of that artist's 1963 retrospective exhibition at the Pasadena Art Museum (figure 10), an event coincident with Warhol's exhibition of Lizes and Elvises in Los Angeles.

In another portrait from 1964 (plate 3) Warhol makes use of the photo-booth pictures (such as figure 1) in which he hides behind sunglasses and pantomime gestures.

The Self-Portrait series of 1967 (plates 4–10), originally made for the American Pavilion (a huge geodesic dome designed by Buckminster Fuller) at Expo '67 in Montreal, con-

9. Arnold Böcklin. *Self-Portrait with Death.* 1872. Oil on canvas, 29½ × 24″ (74.9 × 61 cm). Staatliche Museen Preussischer Kulturbesitz, Berlin

10. Poster for Marcel Duchamp's retrospective exhibition at the Pasadena Art Museum, 1963

11. Max Beckmann. *Self-Portrait in a Tuxedo.* 1927. Oil on canvas, 55 × 37½″ (139.7 × 95.2 cm). The Harvard University Art Museums (Busch-Reisinger Museum), Cambridge, Massachusetts. Purchase

of a series, with a double entendre title, of portraits of black transvestites, for example. Exhibited in depth only in Europe, so far, this group revealed anew his fascination with the mysteries of identity: "It's hard work to look like the complete opposite of what nature made you and then to be an imitation woman of what was only a fantasy woman in the first place."[11] In these paintings, the color is purposely garish and the images seem obscured by the paint. Difficult and unsympathetic, they are among the most melancholy portraits he produced.

Warhol's Skull series of 1976 (plates 364–366) is a wonderful achievement: it seems to take the best from the Mao series and follows

nineteenth-century Swiss painter Arnold Böcklin (figure 9).

The self-portraits document Warhol's entire life, from drawings of his youth (plate 1) to the startling paintings of 1986 of him in various wigs (plates 16–19, 460).

The first of his mature portraits to engage us is the double self-portrait of 1964 (plate 2). The cool and detached expression is matched by the doubling of the image, which has the effect of denying the individuality for which we search in either image. It is Warhol perceiving himself as a pair of mass-produced objects, related to the impersonality of Johns's sculptural Ale Cans. Its mug-shot character is inspired, perhaps, by the Marcel Duchamp

stitutes the images by which Warhol is best known to the public. They came at the point in his career when he had the confidence to accept his status as star and celebrity, as their large, six-foot-by-six-foot scale confirms. They are Warhol's most archetypal projection—as iconic now as his portraits of Marilyn. Yet Warhol still insisted, for himself, on a certain obscurity. Posed with his fingers against the mouth (long a received symbol of contemplation), his face half hidden in shadow, it is Warhol-as-observer par excellence: he sees us more clearly than we are allowed to see him. The mottled paint accentuates the notion of the picture as an impenetrable surface. In their detachment, these 1967 self-portraits avoid direct, self-confident confrontation with the viewer, such as Max Beckmann's full form presents (figure 11).

The distanced, uncommitted observer had always been a principal persona of Warhol, whether distanced by the photo booth, the camera (movie, television, or Polaroid), or the tape recorder. Warhol as a product of the media, and of his own studio, is as elusive as The Shadow (plate 14), but in the vain acceptance of himself as a star places his image among those of others in *Myths* (plate 387). It is not quite a pantheon of Olympian deities but, rather, a directory of demotic idols.

In the series of self-portraits with camouflage (plates 16, 17, 460) we not only see Warhol being amusing, as he uses Polaroids of himself in a wig. We also see camouflage of various colors deployed to obscure more than ever the artist and his personality. These are not the paintings of some reticent, evasive young innocent but of ravaged maturity. The camouflage does not disguise their sadness and poignancy. The intense gaze of the artist/voyeur is directly on the viewer.

In the education of an artist, reproductions— slides, photographs, or the images printed in books and magazines—are a fundamental source of visual information. For someone who is also interested in the possibilities of the commercial graphic world, as Warhol was, the mechanical reproduction—the copy, the duplicate, and the multiple—becomes raw material.

There was, therefore, a natural affinity with the art of Marcel Duchamp, especially as seen in that touchstone of modern art, *L.H.O.O.Q.* (figure 12), as well as in *Belle Haleine, Eau de Voilette* and *Wanted/$2,000 Reward*.

Stolen from the Louvre in 1911 (a case in which the poet Guillaume Apollinaire was wrongly arrested), and later adorned with Duchamp's notorious moustache and beard, no painting has been so thoroughly appropriated by the twentieth century as the *Mona Lisa*. It came on a state visit to the National Gallery in Washington and to The Metropolitan Museum in New York, sent by Charles de Gaulle to honor President and Mrs. Kennedy. It was inevitable, given the extraordinary "celebrity" status conferred on this paint-

ing—which not only has been one of the most frequently reproduced of all works of art but which is a cross-cultural talisman, rather than a mere painting by Leonardo da Vinci—that Warhol should impose on it his own vision and style. Remade in the image of the commercial world (plate 238), it takes on the coloring of the four-color reproduction process. It becomes a grand summation of his aesthetic in *Thirty Are Better Than One* (plate 237).

For Warhol the interest in art about art arose as an issue not just from the expected traditional and academic sources. It was also part of the New York vocabulary of the early fifties, when Old Master reproductions were being used in collages and assemblages in work such as Rauschenberg's, reflecting the ongoing debate about how to reintroduce subject matter, how to escape the domination of the Abstract Expressionists and their critical advocates.

It was the work of Larry Rivers that captured the imagination of several contemporaries. The exhibition of his *Washington Crossing the Delaware* (figure 13) in December 1953 and its acquisition by The Museum of

12. Marcel Duchamp. *L.H.O.O.Q.* 1919. Rectified Readymade; pencil on reproduction, 7¾ × 4⅞″ (19.7 × 12.4 cm). Private collection, Paris

13. Larry Rivers. *Washington Crossing the Delaware*. 1953. Oil, graphite, and charcoal on linen, 6′ 11⅝″ × 9′ 3⅝″ (212.4 × 283.5 cm). The Museum of Modern Art, New York. Given anonymously

Modern Art a year later represented for young artists the transformation of the banal into a non-anecdotal, highly sophisticated painting. This explicit elevation of a trivial nineteenth-century academic machine into high art was the hopeful signal for artists of Warhol's generation; it showed the way, as did much of Rivers's work, to many new possibilities, notably the Pop art of the early sixties.

While this spirit informed a good deal of Warhol's earlier work, it is in the eighties that, with his characteristic susceptibility to suggestions from dealers, collectors, and friends, he found himself making works derived from, among others, Giorgio de Chirico, Edvard Munch, Sandro Botticelli, and Johann Heinrich Tischbein (plates 401–407). However, it is in Leonardo's *Last Supper* that Warhol finds his last grand theme and series (plate 454). Contemporaneous with this series, Warhol also uses the majestic and eloquent *Sistine Madonna* (figure 14) of Raphael for some large paintings, on occasion purposely adding to works on both of these subjects logos from advertising, to emphasize his secularization of the images and to reemphasize that his source is from commercial reproduction. Warhol photographed a three-dimensional, kitsch version (figure 15) of the Leonardo for his collages and paintings rather than beginning with any

14. Raphael. *Sistine Madonna*. Oil on panel, 8′ 4½″ × 6′ 5¼″ (255.2 × 196.2 cm). Gemäldegalerie Alte Meister, Dresden

of the refined lithographic reproductions that exist in such plenitude.

During the eighties the output of work was considerable and the renewed productivity admirable. It is exemplified by large-scale paintings, especially those of the Retrospective and the Reversal series (plates 382–385).

Besides the portraits, there were many commissions, and requests for work and for exhibitions in many places. Demands were made for work in honor of anniversaries and commemorations, as well as for marketing campaigns. While some of this may not have been his primary interest at the time, he tried to keep the products interesting. His passive acceptance in producing series such as Campbell's Soup Boxes, Guns, Knives, Lenins, Cars, Vesuviuses, Beethovens, Frederick the Greats, and the Zeitgeist series showed how much the world demanded Warhols in various forms.

In the middle of all this he was also experimenting with various mediums and techniques, as is seen in the Oxidation paintings and in works that employ diamond dust. There was in addition a great deal of print activity, and his early interest in advertisements and self-improvement was renewed in several of his later drawings and paintings.

A concern for abstract art as well reappears in the eighties. One of the results is the Rorschach series (plates 422–424), a "found" abstraction evoking not only the more psychological Jackson Pollocks such as *Portrait and a Dream*, 1953, but also the ready-made adventures of the Dadaists. Warhol extended the idea even further in the Camouflage series of 1986 (plates 442–445), which also has the effect of concealment, especially in the very large-scale works having several layers. A number of the Camouflage paintings—because of a palette quite different from the standard military colors, and because of their size—become ambitiously environmental (plate 444), reminiscent of Monet's grand, enveloping mural series of Water Lilies.

During the last decade Warhol traveled extensively and maintained his active social life, adding his presence to special events of all of the *mondes* of New York and further afield. But life centered very much on the studio, where he received a continuous stream of visitors. It was a time when a whole new group of artists emerged who sought his approbation, believing they had learned not only from his art but from his strategies in the world of art and commerce.

His availability did allow for some special friendships, some kept very private, as throughout his life, but also some others more directly related to the art world, primarily with several talented young artists. The two friendships that were especially of meaning to

22   15. Warhol's studio, 1987

the work of the last few years were with Jean-Michel Basquiat and Francesco Clemente. With Basquiat, who died in August 1988, Warhol tried to encourage a prodigious talent shadowed as it was by drugs. With both Basquiat and Clemente, separately and collectively, he entered into his only significant collaborations (plates 408, 409). The lightheartedness and the confusion of the styles of the artists led to some very spirited paintings wherein each contribution remains specific but the painting as a whole becomes one entity.

At the time of his death, in February 1987, many projects and commissions, some art and some not, were under way; the activity was what it had always been. Given the mythologizing of Warhol, there has been speculation about which was the last painting or drawing he was working on. It is salutary, and in the true spirit of his obscurity, that the question may never be answered. Perhaps the sentimental would like to believe that it was a Last Supper, but it could as easily have been *Moonwalk* (plate 459), one of the prints from a series on the history of American television.

After his death, it was revealed that he had been an obsessive collector of many things: books, photographs, artworks, watches, jewelry, folk and popular art, furniture. Surprisingly, he had found time to pursue many beautiful, exquisite, and exotic objects. As a collection, they were as remarkable as the collection of people he had known in his lifetime.

But Warhol's own work remains the greatest collection that he could have amassed—a serious body of work that redefined art and moved its boundaries. Warhol eliminated, almost by himself, the venerable distinctions between the "avant-garde" artist and the general public, between the commercial graphic world and the world of fine art. He thus became a major cultural and aesthetic reality of the twentieth century. And having already altered the idea of modernism, he is now a major influence on another generation.

Without his own dramatic and stylish presence, Andy Warhol's work remains great art, a monument impossible to ignore. It has changed the reflections of other artists, the considerations of poets, and the deliberations of philosophers. The camouflage cannot conceal a celestially cool and catholic art.

16. Duane Michals. *Andy Warhol.* 1958

# NOTES

1. "I think everybody should be a machine. I think everybody should like everybody." Andy Warhol, in an interview with G. R. Swenson, "What Is Pop Art?: Answers from 8 Painters, Part I," *Artnews* 62 (November 1963), p. 26. Many have written on the subject of Warhol's emotional detachment, most recently discussed in Bradford R. Collins, "The Metaphysical Nosejob: The Remaking of Warhola, 1960–1968," *Arts Magazine* 62 (February 1988), pp. 47–55.

2. A more detailed account of the controversy is in Patrick S. Smith, *Andy Warhol's Art and Films* (Ann Arbor: UMI Research Press, 1986), p. 14. Two works now in the Paul Warhola family collection fit the title's description. Both are reproduced in the present volume—one in this Introduction, the other on page 403, in the Chronology.

3. Warhol, *The Philosophy of Andy Warhol (From A to B and Back Again)* (New York: Harcourt Brace Jovanovich, 1975), p. 96.

4. Interview by Patrick Smith with Charles Lisanby in *Andy Warhol's Art and Films,* p. 373.

5. Warhol first saw Lichtenstein's work in the back room of the Leo Castelli Gallery in 1961. *See* Warhol and Pat Hackett, *POPism: The Warhol '60s* (New York: Harcourt Brace Jovanovich, 1980), pp. 6–7; *see also* interviews in Smith, *Warhol's Art and Films,* with Ted Carey (p. 254), Leo

Castelli (p. 266), and Ivan Karp (p. 360).

6. Walter Hopps has described his first visit to Warhol's studio in 1961 in Jean Stein with George Plimpton, eds., *Edie: An American Biography* (New York: Alfred A. Knopf, 1982), p. 192: "What really made an impression was that the floor—I may exaggerate a little—was not a foot deep, but certainly covered wall to wall with every sort of pulp movie magazine, fan magazine, and trade sheet, having to do with popular stars from the movies or rock 'n' roll. Warhol wallowed in it. Pulp just littering the place edge to edge."

7. "Andy Warhol," an interview with G. R. Swenson, in John Russell and Suzi Gablik, *Pop Art Redefined* (New York: Praeger, 1969), p. 118.

8. The most recent article to discuss the relationship between Warhol and de Kooning is Thomas Crow, "Saturday Disasters: Trace and Reference in Early Warhol," *Art in America* 75 (May 1987), pp. 128–36.

9. Warhol's account is in *POPism*, pp. 131–33.

10. *See also* David Bourdon, "Andy Warhol and the Society Icon," *Art in America* 63 (January/February 1975), pp. 42–45; Smith, *Warhol's Art and Films,* pp. 186–89; and Charles F. Stuckey, "Andy Warhol's Painted Faces," *Art in America* 68 (May 1980), pp. 102–11.

11. *The Philosophy of Andy Warhol,* p. 54.

# WARHOL AS ART HISTORY

BY ROBERT ROSENBLUM

Despite his maxim, Andy Warhol's own fame has far outlasted the fifteen minutes he allotted to everyone else. During the last quarter-century of his life, from 1962 to 1987, he had already been elevated to the timeless and space-less realm of a modern mythology that he himself both created and mirrored. And now that he is gone, the victim of a preposterously unnecessary mishap, the fictions of his persona and the facts of his art still loom large in some remote, but ever-present, pantheon of twentieth-century deities.

On the popular level alone, the evidence for his secular sainthood is everywhere. What other artist could have covered the entire front page of the *New York Post* not once, but twice? (On June 4, 1968, the day after he almost died; and on February 23, 1987, the day after he did die.) For how many others do we remember the exact moment and place we first received the jolting news of their untimely death, as if it were a personal trauma? (If we are old enough, for Marilyn Monroe, John F. Kennedy, and Elvis Presley—all, ironically, Warhol subjects.) Like Marilyn and Elvis, Andy, too, was referred to and recognized by his first name alone, a modern variation upon the affectionate, prayerful ways classical gods or Christian saints could be addressed, beings both close to our hearts and close to heaven. And in more earthly terms, who but Warhol could have inspired, just after his death, a limited edition of 2,500 counterfeit commemorative postage stamps, privately printed in Paris by Michel Hosszù, then affixed to letters sent all over our planet, and honored, albeit illegally, by countless postal clerks who apparently recognized the image of Warhol's 1967 *Self-Portrait* (plates 4–10) and his name and dates inscribed below?[1] And in these days of *glasnost*, what better relic of Western modernity could be treasured by a willfully hip young Muscovite painter and rock musician than a can of Campbell's tomato soup with a mock Warhol signature?[2]

Warhol's lofty role in our modern Olympus is recognized not only by the world at large, but by his own artist-contemporaries, young and old, at home and abroad. Two examples of the many symbolic portraits of Warhol poignantly bracket the date of his death. The earlier one, painted in 1986, the last full year of Warhol's

1. Carlo Maria Mariani. *Andy Warhol*. 1986. Oil on canvas, 28 × 24″ (71.1 × 61 cm). Courtesy Sperone Westwater Gallery, New York

life, is by the Italian neo-neoclassicist Carlo Maria Mariani, and represents him as a resurrected Davidian image of Napoleon as Emperor (figure 1). Bewigged, cloaked in ermine, decorated with imperial eagles, and holding a laurel-wreath crown, Warhol gazes sternly down at us. Even within the context of Mariani's other allegorical portraits of artists, which include mythic re-creations of Francesco Clemente, Jasper Johns, and Julian Schnabel, Warhol is clearly the reigning deity, as the painting's golden tonality affirms.[3]

The later example, painted in 1987, is by the American artist-duo David McDermott and Peter McGough (figure 2). Working here in their neo-Victorian mode, they offer a memorial tribute to the just-deceased Warhol that would take him and us on a time-trip to exactly a century ago, when his Christian name would have been properly recorded as Andrew, not Andy, and his dates given as 1828–1887. A winged putto, seated on a crescent moon inscribed in a star-studded globe, mourns the passing of this many-faceted genius whose multiple accomplishments, radiating outward from this heavenly sphere, are defined in eight Victorian categories: ART, MUSIC, JOURNALISM, THEATRE, SOCIETY, PHOTOGRAPHY, PHILOSOPHY, LITERATURE. (To avoid anachronism, FILM is not included.)

Moreover, Warhol's universality in the art world united the conventional factions of modernist and avant-garde versus conservative or hopelessly square. Just as he exhibited with LeRoy Neiman and with Jamie Wyeth (who painted Warhol's portrait, as Warhol painted his, in 1975),[4] so, too, could he join forces in 1984 on the same canvas as Jean-Michel Basquiat (plate 409), thereby covering all bases and toppling all hierarchies of elite and populist image-making. Similarly, although museums of conventionally "modern" art throughout the world have collected and exhibited his work, Warhol was equally at home with the more neoconservative or, put more positively, postmodernist establishment. After all, the New York Academy of Art, which opened in 1980 to promote the revival of traditional instruction in drawing from life models and plaster casts, can claim Warhol as one of its founding board members.

As for Warhol's own images, from the beginning, they have nourished not only the vast public domain of everything from advertising to gingerbread cookies (as baked in New York by

2. David McDermott and Peter McGough. *Andy Warhol: In Memoriam—1887.* 1987. Oil on linen, 70 × 70″ (177.8 × 177.8 cm). Courtesy Massimo Audiello Gallery, New York

image of Marilyn Monroe (figure 4). Small wonder, then, that the word *Warholism*, originally coined in 1965 to deride the artist's seeming indifference to traditional values,[5] may have become indispensable in defining the ever-expanding mythological mixture of art and public notoriety with which he created, after 1962, a new empire that, in retrospect, may make the last quarter-century be known as the "Age of Warhol."

By now, in fact, the phenomenon of Warholism has covered so many different territories—from the populist to the elite, from old-fashioned drawing on paper to films, performance art, and globally recognized logos—that no single view of Warhol ever seems adequate. Hearing about this or that symposium on Warhol (and since his death, such events have proliferated), one can barely guess which cast of characters will speak on what wild variety of topics. Indeed, Warhol may end up rivaling Picasso himself in providing to all comers the most daunting breadth of approaches.

For one thing, the subject matter of his work, now that we are beginning to see it in full retrospect, covers so encyclopedic a scope of twentieth-century history and imagery that, in this alone, it demands unusual attention. To be sure, in the early sixties, his work could be sheltered under the Pop umbrella shared by Roy Lichtenstein, James Rosenquist, Tom Wesselmann, and others, joining these contempo-

Patti Paige in the form of Brillo Boxes or Campbell's Soup Cans), but—the sincerest form of flattery—the work of other artists. As early as 1963 Bill Anthony offered a penciled gloss on a then one-year-old Campbell's Soup Can that was clearly an instant icon (figure 3); and thereafter, not only have fashionable commercial portraitists like Rodney Buice imitated Warhol's formulas (as in a multiple portrait he did of Prince Charles in 1976) but on more conceptually elevated levels, his art has been appropriated and simulated by, among others, Elaine Sturtevant, Richard Pettibone, Mike Bidlo, and his sometime alter ego, Allen Midgette (who impersonated Warhol on lecture tours in the sixties). And, as another memorial tribute to Warhol, Mark Lancaster exhibited in London in 1988 over 179 historicizing varia-

26  tions on the theme of the master's now classic

3. Bill Anthony. *Campbell's Soup Can.* 1963. Graphite and colored pencils on paper, 6¼ × 5⅝″ (15.9 × 14.3 cm). Private collection

4. Mark Lancaster. *Marilyn Aug. 5 '87 (25th Anniversary of Marilyn Monroe's Death).* 1987. Oil on canvas, 12 × 10″ (30.5 × 25.4 cm). Courtesy Mayor Rowan Gallery, London

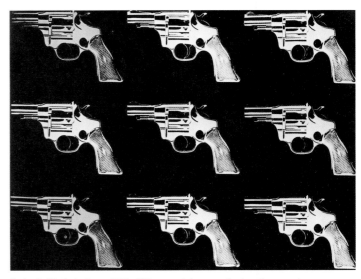

5. Andy Warhol. *Knives*. 1982. Silkscreen ink on synthetic polymer paint on canvas, 52 × 69⅝" (132 × 177 cm). Private collection

6. Andy Warhol. *Guns*. 1982. Silkscreen ink on synthetic polymer paint on canvas, 52 × 69⅝" (132 × 177 cm). Private collection

raries in what can now be seen more clearly as an effort to re-Americanize American art[6] after a period of Abstract Expressionist universals that renounced the space-time coordinates of the contemporary world in favor of some mythic, primordial realm. Within this domain, Warhol quickly emerged as a leader, choosing the grittiest, tackiest, and most commonplace facts of visual pollution in America that would make the aesthetes and mythmakers of the fifties cringe in their ivory towers: advertisements for wigs, trusses, nose-jobs, cut-rate appliances; a comic-strip repertoire that ran through Superman, Dick Tracy, Nancy, and Popeye; packaged food from the lowest-priced supermarket shelves with grass-roots brand names like Campbell's, Mott's, Kellogg's, Del Monte, Coca-Cola; American money, postage stamps, and bonus gift stamps; vulgar tabloids (*Daily News* and *New York Post*); the most popular stars from James Dean and Elvis Presley to Elizabeth Taylor and Marlon Brando.

This alone, if only in terms of inventory, would have been enough to make him the king of Pop art. But what is less obvious is how Warhol's initial inventory of ugly, counteraesthetic Americana expanded to unexpected dimensions. Looking back at his entire output, the sheer range of his subjects becomes not only international (indeed universal in its concern with death) but mind-boggling in its journalistic sweep. What other modern artist's work comes so close to providing a virtual history of the world in the last quarter-century? In terms of the role of the artist as chronicler of his times, Édouard Manet, a full century before Warhol, might be something of a contender. Recording

cross-sections of both the lowest and the highest strata of Parisian society, from beggars to fashion plates, as seen in the streets, in cafés, in parks, or in bed, he painted and drew portraits of every kind of celebrity, starting with the world of his fellow artists (Monet, Morisot, Desboutin), and continuing into literature (Baudelaire, Poe, Zola, Mallarmé, George Moore), politics (Rochefort, Clemenceau), the art establishment (Duret, Antonin Proust), and the stage (Lola de Valence, Faure, Rivière). He also depicted front-page events that ranged from the American Civil War and an execution in Mexico to the barricaded streets of Paris under the Commune and the escape of a leftist politician from a penal colony in New Caledonia, and even threw in, as Warhol would, several disturbingly poker-faced Christian subjects viewed, along with pampered dogs and high-style costume, from the most secular of modern societies. Picasso, too, cut a wide swath, commenting directly or indirectly on every war he lived through, and leaving us a portrait gallery of twentieth-century pioneers, from Gertrude Stein and Igor Stravinsky all the way to Stalin. But Warhol's art is itself like a March of Time newsreel, an abbreviated visual anthology of the most conspicuous headlines, personalities, mythic creatures, edibles, tragedies, artworks, even ecological problems of recent decades. If nothing were to remain of the years from 1962 to 1987 but a Warhol retrospective, future historians and archeologists would have a fuller time-capsule to work with than that offered by any other artist of the period. With infinitely more speed and wallop than a complete run of the *New York Times* on microfilm, or even

twenty-five leather-bound years of *Time* magazine (for which, in fact, he did several covers),[7] Warhol's work provides an instantly intelligible chronicle of what mattered most to most people, from the suicide of Marilyn Monroe to the ascendancy of Red China, as well as endless grist for the mills of cultural speculation about issues ranging from post-Hiroshima attitudes toward death and disaster to the accelerating threat of mechanized, multiple-image reproduction to our still-clinging, old-fashioned faith (both commercial and aesthetic) in handmade, unique originals.

The diversity of Warhol's subject matter is staggering, embracing the kind of panoramic wholeness aspired to in John Dos Passos's *U.S.A.*, a literary trilogy of the thirties that covered the first three decades of our century's history. As for people alone, almost everybody is there: a generic *American Man—Watson Powell* (plate 324) and the *Thirteen Most Wanted Men* (plates 287–300); artists like Robert Rauschenberg, Frank Stella, Joseph Beuys, and David Hockney; stars like Elizabeth Taylor and Mick Jagger, statesmen like Chairman Mao and President Nixon, sports champions like Muhammad Ali, and literary celebrities like Truman Capote. But this encyclopedic Who's Who is only one facet, if a major one, of Warhol's vast image-bank of our age. There is a documentary history of modern catastrophes, both manmade and natural, like the jet crash reported on June 4, 1962, which took 129 lives (plate 136), or the Neapolitan earthquake of November 23, 1980, which may have taken some ten thousand lives (plate 386). There are inventories of modern ways of death, whether by such lethal commonplaces as knives and revolvers (figures 5, 6), car crashes, leaps from highrise buildings, and canned-food poisoning, or by such specialized technological horrors as the atom bomb and the electric chair (plates 256–286). There are anthologies of endangered species, both human (the American Indian) and animal (the giant panda and the Siberian tiger), that right-thinking people concerned with our planet's natural, social, and economic history worry about; and there is a pantheon of mythic beings, from Santa Claus and Dracula to Uncle Sam and Mickey Mouse, that both right- and wrong-thinking people the world over simply know about, much as they would recognize Warhol's international symbols culled from art, money, and politics: *The Last Supper*, the dollar sign, the hammer and sickle. And if one includes the hundreds of even-handed, seemingly effortless drawings that Warhol quietly and continuously produced from the fifties to the eighties, the range of his imagery is infinitely amplified, taking in Christ and Buddha, gay sex and breast-feeding.

Even when looked at in terms of more venerable hierarchies of subject matter, Warhol covers all bases. Although, by earlier standards, he might be classified primarily as a history painter and portraitist, he ventured into other traditional territories as well, translating them into his own language, which as often as not means the language of our times. For instance, he occasionally tried his hand at still life, updating age-old conventions with Space Fruit (plate 314) or an after-the-party mess of empty glasses and bottles, and even metamorphosing flower painting into a repeat pattern of poppy emblems (taken from a photograph) that could be expanded from the dimensions of easel painting to floor-to-ceiling coverage (plates 306–310). He could rejuvenate moribund landscape formulas through the mythic American idyls reproduced in do-it-yourself paint books or by suddenly reviving the unlikely theme of Mount Vesuvius in eruption (figure 7),[8] once a major motif in Romantic nature painting; and he could even venture into animal painting, at times perpetuating earlier traditions with intimate portraits of his own and other people's pet dogs and cats and at times shaking up these traditions drastically, as in his wallpaper pattern of the head of a totally vacuous cow, the most unexpected postscript to the Western pastoral con-

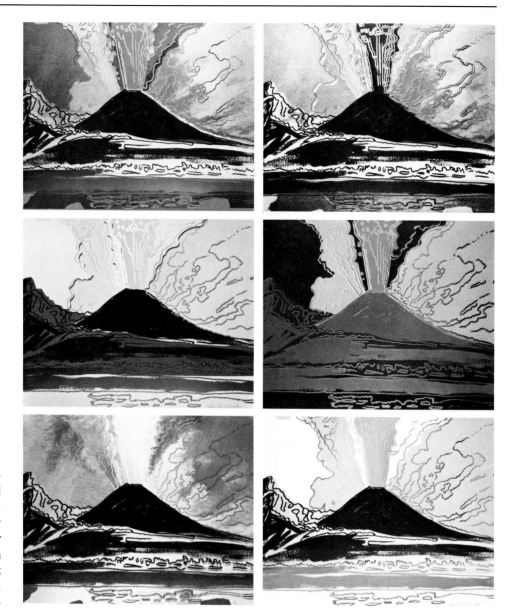

7. Andy Warhol. *Vesuvius*. 1985. Serigraphs on cardboard, each 31½ × 39½″ (80 × 100 cm). Private collection

vention of cattle grazing in a landscape (plates 303–305).

This remarkable breadth might in itself be enough to make Warhol a singular artist of our century, a strange hybrid of major journalist, chronicling the broadest spectrum of public experience, and media master, who can be at once painter, photographer, draftsman, decorator, sculptor, filmmaker, and illustrator. But it also turns out, looking ahead and back across the decades, that Warhol, essential to any account of Pop culture, commands fully as much attention within the more elite world of high art.

From the sixties to the very last months of his life, Warhol's art, in fact, constantly intersected the major concerns of other artists—seniors,

contemporaries, and juniors—casting its glance not only backward to the now remote world of Ad Reinhardt and Mark Rothko but forward to the most youthful activities of the eighties, from the making of art based on reproductions of reproductions, as in the work of Sherrie Levine or Mike Bidlo, to the bald use, in both two and three dimensions, of the most ordinary imagery and commodities from the world of commerce and advertising, as in the work of Jeff Koons or Haim Steinbach. To be sure, in the sixties, when the initial impact of Pop art appeared to threaten the fortified towers of abstract art with a bombardment of visual and cultural pollution, Warhol, like Lichtenstein, was seen on the other side of an unbridgeable gulf that separated a faith in aesthetic purity from the vulgar reality of the life outside the studio door. But in retrospect, this black-and-white antagonism, like the Classic–Romantic, Ingres–Delacroix polarity of the 1820s, has grayed and become a larger whole, making it possible to see forest as well as trees, to see how Warhol, for instance, fully participated in the structural changes conventionally associated with the march of formalist innovation from the late fifties onward.

Already in the sixties, in fact, critics began to notice how Warhol, despite the seeming heresies of Pop imagery, could be located on both sides of the high-art/low-art tracks.[9] In 1968, for instance, John Coplans traced in an exhibition and more expansive catalogue the important genealogical table of serial imagery in modern art from Monet and Mondrian through Reinhardt and Stella, and concluded with Warhol, whose Campbell's Soup Cans and Marilyns may at first have looked like illegitimate heirs in this noble modernist ancestry, but gradually settled firmly into historical place.[10] Typically, Warhol himself, with his customary no-nonsense succinctness (often worthy of Gertrude Stein), later declared his allegiance to this exalted and primarily abstract tradition by claiming, "I like Reinhardt when he began painting those black paintings and they were all the same black paintings."[11] Within this context, we might note, too, how not only Reinhardt's repetitive, rectilinear blackness could provide foundations for Warhol's own version of serial monotony, but how even Rothko's procedures might also be invoked as a precedent from the fifties. For just as Rothko would prune his pictorial world down to the most elemental, head-on format of a few hovering planes, released from the laws of gravity, and then complicate this image with infinitely nuanced chromatic combinations, so, too, would Warhol take his disembodied soup cans, floating frontally on an abstract ground, and embellish their initial fidelity to the crude factory colors of the original product with a series of lurid variations upon a new Day-Glo spectrum of artificial hues, from torrid orange to sultry purple.

In the seventies, another of Warhol's characteristic devices, the grid, generally used by him to evoke impersonal, belt-line replication, began to be recognized and included in rigorous discussions of this format in primarily abstract art, first by John Elderfield[12] and then by Rosalind Krauss,[13] both of whom located Warhol within the more cerebral company of artists like Agnes Martin, Kenneth Noland, and Sol LeWitt. And even more broadly, seeing the aesthetic skeleton as well as the cultural flesh of Warhol's art, Richard Morphet, in 1971, caught Warhol in a wide net of American abstract artists, quickly suggesting many analogies between the variety of structures characteristically employed by Warhol and those explored by artists ranging from Reinhardt and Kelly, Stella and Andre, Judd and Morris, all the way to LeWitt and his wall drawings.[14]

Now, almost two decades later, when the first battles between Pop and abstract art may seem as remote as our century's earlier theoretical conflicts between the partisans of Cubism and the supporters of pure abstraction, such affinities between Warhol's work of the sixties and that of his contemporaries have become far more apparent, to the point where he now looms large as one of the major formal innovators of the period. For instance, he shares with Johns, Lichtenstein, and Stella an attraction to what might be called a bifocal composition, that is, one that obliges the spectator to look side by side, or above and below, at two identical or equally compelling images, whether of the Mona Lisa, a car crash, or Marlon Brando (plates 234, 235, 261). This vision, often transformed literally into a diptych structure, undermines the absolute authority of those unique images so precious to artists of a pre-Warhol era, setting up instead an either/or situation, or else creating a world of multiple replication, where even the artist's self-portrait is doubled as a means of diffusing any one-to-one focus on what might once have been a singular revelation of face and feeling at a particular time and place. In any anthology of this art of the double, so abundant in the late fifties and early sixties (as in Rauschenberg's Factum I and Factum II, 1957; Johns's Ale Cans, 1960; Lichtenstein's Step-On Can, 1961; and Stella's Jasper's Dilemma, 1962–63), Warhol must play a central role, exploring every aspect of the structure of duplication, from a shoulder-shrugging indifference toward direct, unique experience to a tonic visual assault on what had become a tedious formula of seemingly spontaneous compositions.

As for the latter, Warhol again occupies center stage in the history of Minimalism, first as a master of rock-bottom reduction, which, in the case of the single Campbell's Soup Can or the Gold Marilyn Monroe of 1962 (plate 199), could convey an aura of sanctity; and then as a master of modular repetition, which, in the case of Coca-Cola bottles or air-mail stamps, would evoke the endless monotony of mass production and consumption. It is telling that beyond, or underneath, these rich cultural associations, the structure of Warhol's art bears close affinities to the abstract innovations of such contemporaries as Stella and Andre, much as they look backward to the crossword-puzzle patterns of Johns's Alphabets and Numbers of the mid-fifties. And within this context, it should also be noted that like Andre and Morris, Warhol, in the sixties, often polarized his structures into two compositional extremes: an obsessive order and an equally obsessive disorder. As early as 1962 Warhol could arrange eight-by-twenty-four tidy rows of dollar bills in a perfect grid while, at the same time, he could explode this graph-paper regularity with a total disorder of dozens of dollar bills that seem, like a dropped deck of cards, to have landed all over the surface of the canvas (plates 145, 146).

The sense of the rigorously disciplined versus the willfully aleatory (to use the buzzword of the period) was apparent as well in Warhol's three-dimensional art. His Brillo Box (Soap Pads) of 1964 (plate 185), for example, is the supermarket Doppelgänger of Judd's and Morris's ideal cubes, a building-block of almost sacred, elemental clarity. Replicated in more secular quantities, however, and piled up not in neat rows but haphazardly stacked at casual heights and angles, as they were in their first installation at the Stable Gallery in 1964, they subvert their inherent geometries. It is a dialogue of extreme contradiction that was equally explored by Morris and Andre in the sixties, when both artists would switch back and forth between abstract structures of cerebral purity and an elegant chaos of controlled spill and scatter (figures 8, 9), as if the theoretical principles of reason and its negation had been isolated in a laboratory and illustrated with palpable forms.

On other levels, too, Warhol's new structures joined forces with the most audacious explorations of the sixties and early seventies. His exhibition of helium-filled Silver Clouds at the Castelli gallery in 1966 (plate 302), consisting

8. Carl Andre. *Equivalents I–VIII*. 1966. Sand-lime brick. Installation view, Tibor de Nagy Gallery, New York, 1966

art products is an integral part of the history of the many challenges the seventies offered to those earlier prejudices about art as a sacrosanct avowal of a personal world of touch and feeling, a world that reached its apogee in Abstract Expressionism. Here it should be said, too, that Warhol's devaluation of works of art made solely by the hand of the artist-genius has ample historical precedent, of which Jacques-Louis David's faith in the primacy of his images over his personal facture is the most apt. For instance, not one but two versions of his *Bonaparte at St.-Bernard* were first exhibited together; and subsequently many copies, mixing in varying proportions his own hand with the work of studio assistants, were made and signed as "Davids," since the image, being his invention, mattered more than the execution.

The importance of Warhol's art in the sixties, whether for the innovations of Pop imagery, new formal structures, or new relationships to second-degree image-making (in the employment of silkscreen techniques and in

of airborne, ballooning "pillows"—cool but glitzy and festive—once more employed the language of chance and clearly belonged with the kind of imaginative extension of volatile substances as art material that Morris used in his even more ephemeral "steam piece" of 1968–69 (figure 10). And Warhol's Cow Wallpaper (plates 303–305), which reached palatial dimensions as the background for the Whitney Museum's installation of his retrospective in 1971, can now be thought of as a counterpart to LeWitt's wall drawings of the early seventies, which similarly disrupted all our deeply ingrained Western assumptions about the proper boundaries of frame and image or the accepted distinctions between primary architectural elements and secondary interior decoration. Moreover, Warhol's accelerating detachment from what to many began to seem an archaic concept of picture-making—a one-to-one, handmade expression of an individual artist's unique craft and sensibility—prophesied many aspects of Conceptual art, in which the artist conceived images whose material execution could be entrusted to other, anonymous hands (as in the case of LeWitt's wall drawings). Indeed, the metamorphosis of Warhol in the sixties from private artist to the head of a factory of art workers who would manufacture his

9. Carl Andre. *Scatter Piece (Spill)*. 1966. Plastic blocks and canvas bag. Collection John Powers

10. Robert Morris. *Untitled*. 1968–69. Steam

the faith in photography as the most truthful record of reality for the post-fifties generations nurtured on television) has seldom been doubted, even by his sworn enemies. But it has often been assumed that after the sixties or, with more rhetorical precision, after his near-death in 1968, his art drifted further and further from center stage, catering only to the luxury trade or simply repeating, in ever more diluted form, the once fresh ideas of his youth. In 1979 the Whitney Museum's exhibition of Warhol's portraits of the seventies, a glittering gallery of well-heeled celebrities who filled the pages of *W* and *Vogue*, tended to give most visitors, at least, the idea that Warhol, as a painter, had turned exclusively into a society portraitist—a sensational virtuoso, if one admired the likes of Giovanni Boldini and John Singer Sargent, or a trashy sellout to the jet set, if one still maintained the pre-seventies illusions that artists are beings who should take vows of chastity and poverty.[15] But apart from this specialized exhibition, Warhol's art of the seventies and eighties was surprisingly little seen in the United States, and usually only in erratic presentations of a single series rather than in any cohesive scope.

Now that this huge oeuvre, with its daunting quantity and variety, is at last being sorted out and, as often as not, being seen for the first time,

it is slowly becoming clear that Warhol's art after the sixties, far from running on a private and ever more peripheral track, not only intersected the development of his contemporaries (Johns, Lichtenstein, and Stella) but was concerned with the same issues as any number of younger artists, from David Salle to Philip Taaffe. In formal terms alone, Warhol's art of the seventies and eighties followed general patterns of evolution, from the lean austerity of the early sixties—ascetic in color, sharp in contour, frontal and spaceless in structure—to far more intricate period styles. The passages of bravura brushwork that literally surfaced in the seventies over the silkscreened images below them, shared with Stella and Johns, among others, that growing sense of painterly virtuosity as a kind of homeless, disembodied decoration over a pre-existent structure, creating new kinds of spatial layering and transparencies that infinitely complicated the deadpan, frozen lucidity of, say, Johns's first Flags and Targets or Stella's first "stripes." Such visual complexities characterized even more fully Warhol's work of the eighties. For instance, the 1985 paintings of Mount Vesuvius in action (plates 410–412)[16] were both literally and formally eruptive, centrifugal explosions that would be at home with the most flamboyant Stellas of the same

decade. Indeed, Warhol's archetypal forms of the eighties might be the camouflage and Rorschach patterns (plates 16, 17, 422–424, 442–445, 460), ready-made abstractions that provided elaborate surface labyrinths under which a densely concealed imagery could be discerned, the visual opposite of the trumpet-blast clarity of the archetypal soup can of the sixties. In fact, the change from the sixties to the eighties could hardly be seen more clearly than in Warhol's updating of his original Campbell's Soup Cans with a new series of 1985–86 commemorating Campbell's newer product (boxes containing pouches of instant soup; plate 416) and even some new flavors (Won-Ton).[17] These late images offer infinitely intricate variations on the raw, vintage Warhol of the early sixties, with suggestions of spatial illusion and layering in the compression of the cardboard boxes, with occasional croppings that indicate continuities beyond the frame, with conspicuous off-register disparities between color and enclosing contour, and with hues that deviate totally from the harsh, primary clarity of those now "ancient" soup cans.

But apart from the elaboration of Warhol's visual language, there is also a mood of both personal and public retrospection here, which not only captures the period flavor of the eighties but belongs to a mode practiced by some of his most eminent contemporaries. The very choice of a newer Campbell's product recalls the way Johns first followed the American flag's change from forty-eight to fifty stars with the addition of Hawaii and Alaska to the Union in 1959, and then, much later, reverted to forty-eight stars, as if he were recalling in private meditation an earlier point in his life, in his art, and in public history. These rear-view vistas are, in fact, abundant in late Warhol. Not only did he repeat, often with ghostly variations (such as photographic negatives or concealing sweeps of paint) the single images that had made him famous in the early sixties, but he even anthologized his early works in single paintings (plate 383), thereby selecting what amounts to his own mini-retrospectives. This series, of 1979–80, usually executed on canvases of large dimensions, presents surrogate Warhol shows, compiling, for example, self-portraits, soup cans, corn-flakes boxes, flowers, cow's heads, Marilyns, and car crashes. These by now famous Warhol images are often printed backwards and/or in black-and-white reversals, which contributes to a phantom mood of floating memory images that confuses both private and public domains. But no less telling is the fact that in the seventies and eighties Stella, Johns, and Lichtenstein all painted comparable anthologies of their own remembrances of art past. Stella will often pick up his own signature motifs from the sixties and quote them in riotous wholes; Lichtenstein, tongue-in-cheek as usual, will populate Matisse-like domestic interiors with a selection of hits from his own past performances; and in the most intensely private, diaristic terms, Johns will also compile fragments of his artistic autobiography (frequently using, like Warhol, such spectral devices as reversals of shape, tone, and color) in the context of solemn meditations on the passage of time and on the grander cycles of life, love, and death.

Such retrospection, to be sure, may be characteristic of many artists as they grow older. Picasso, for one, accumulated in his last decades what seems an infinity of layers of artistic and biographical self-reference. But it should also be noted that Warhol's personal retrospection has a fully public face, typical of the rapidly escalating historicism of the late twentieth century. It is revealing that Warhol's subjects in the sixties were almost all contemporary, culled from the news of the day, the celebrities of the moment, the supermarket shelves around the corner. When he did a series of artists' portraits in 1967 (plate 317), they were not, after all, past heroes like Picasso, Matisse, and Pollock, but rather a selection of his own peers from the Castelli stable—Stella, Bontecou, Rosenquist, Johns, Chamberlain, and Rauschenberg. But by the eighties, Warhol, like everybody else it would seem, began to look constantly backward, conforming to the century's twilight mood of excavating memories. In a decade that is eager to commemorate almost anything that corresponds to historically retrospective round numbers—from the twentieth anniversary of the student revolutions of 1968 to the two-hundredth anniversary of the French Revolution of 1789; from the fiftieth and twenty-fifth anniversaries of the New York World's Fairs of 1939 and 1964, respectively, to the hundredth anniversary of the completion of the Eiffel Tower at the Paris World's Fair of 1889—Warhol, too, kept looking from present to past. As a one-shot

commemoration, for instance, he could salute the Brooklyn Bridge when its centennial was celebrated in 1983, or the Statue of Liberty, when it turned one hundred in 1986 (plate 442). And for layered nostalgia, in 1985, he could reproduce modern advertisements that included images from decades past of such now archaic film stars as James Dean, Judy Garland, and Ronald Reagan (plates 413–415). But his historical sweep could have epic grandeur as well, continuing in the path of such erratic pre-

11. Andy Warhol. *Franz Kafka* from the portfolio *Ten Portraits of Jews of the Twentieth Century*. 1980. Serigraph, printed on Lenox Museum Board, 40 × 32″ (101.6 × 81.2 cm). Courtesy Ronald Feldman Fine Arts, Inc., New York

cedents from the sixties and seventies as Larry Rivers's *History of the Russian Revolution: From Marx to Mayakovsky*, 1965; Gerhard Richter's 1971–72 series of forty-eight portraits of great men of modern history; or Anselm Kiefer's halls of German fame, such as *The Ways of Worldly Wisdom*, of 1976–77 and 1978–80.[18] Warhol too, began to reach backward in our own century to record, in his later works, such encyclopedically lofty themes as a pantheon of Portraits of Jews of the Twentieth Century (from Sigmund Freud, Albert Einstein, and Franz Kafka [figure 11] to the Marx Brothers), a never-completed history of great moments in American television (plate 459), or, as an industrial commission by Mercedes-Benz, a chronological picture history of their cars (plate 417), a

sequence that provokes the kind of nostalgia we often feel for such forward-looking movements as Futurism.

Here again, Warhol figures large in the mood of the eighties, when the history of art, like the history of everything else, floats about in a disembodied public image-bank where Caravaggio and Schnabel can jostle for equal time in weekly magazines and daily conversations. In this context, Warhol is indispensable to an understanding of the imagery of art about art, or the domain of what is called, more fancily, "simulation" or "appropriation." To be sure, in the sixties, following in the footsteps of Marcel Duchamp (who wanted to desanctify the *Mona Lisa*) and Fernand Léger (who wanted to turn her into a machine-age product), Warhol took on this art icon, transforming her into a hybrid movie star and dime-store art reproduction (plates 235–238) in the manner of Rauschenberg's earlier use of the tackiest postage-stamp prints of museum masterpieces. But by the eighties, his quotations of earlier art belonged to another frame of reference, a postmodern vision in which any citation from any historical time could turn up in a contemporary context. For example, in 1982, in both paintings and prints, Warhol was able to resurrect, on the one hand, a profile portrait of Alexander the Great to coincide with his historical veneration in an exhibition at The Metropolitan Museum of Art and, on the other, a portrait of Goethe (plate 401), excerpted from the most famous painting of the great man, that by Wilhelm Tischbein.[19] And mirroring the constant buckshot barrage of art-history images that bounces off us daily, Warhol could go on switching channels, usually with a shrewd irony that reflects Lichtenstein's own art-about-art choices, which would single out ostensibly the polar opposite of his own style (the painterly nuance and sensibility of Monet's cathedrals, the strident *Angst* of German Expressionism). It would be hard, for instance, to think of anything less compatible with Warhol's mass-produced imagery than precious details from Quattrocento paintings by Botticelli, Uccello, and Leonardo, but that is what Warhol startled us with in 1984 (plate 402), varying these unique, handmade passages by craftsmen from a remote era of image-making with a shrill rainbow of Day-Glo colors worthy of Stella's comparably extravagant palette of the eighties. And it would be no less

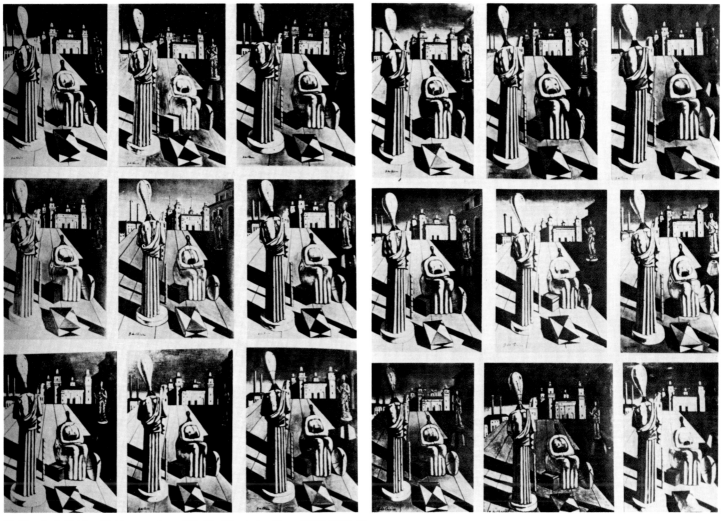

12. Giorgio de Chirico. Eighteen versions of his *The Disquieting Muses* (1917). 1945–62

difficult to find an artist who, in psychological terms, could better symbolize the denial of Warhol's poker-faced emotional anesthesia than Edvard Munch, whom Warhol nevertheless resurrected by redoing his most unsettling images of fever-pitch hysteria (*The Scream*) and engulfing sexual desire (*Madonna*) (plates 406, 407).

Warhol's canny selections from the data bank of art history also reflected, like Salle's borrowings from Yasuo Kuniyoshi or Reginald Marsh, the revisionist thrust of a postmodernist view of twentieth-century art that would no longer accept the party lines still held in the sixties. Nothing could demonstrate this more acutely than his appropriation of imagery from Giorgio de Chirico in 1982 (plates 403, 404),[20] in exactly the same year that The Museum of

Modern Art's retrospective offered the canonic, truncated version of the old master's art, which presumably ended in decades of shame with endlessly diluted replications of his early, epoch-making masterpieces. But Warhol translated the de Chirico story into something appropriate to himself and to the reversals of taste of the last decade, which, in the nostalgic orbit of such three-dimensional re-creations of de Chirico's pictorial theater as architect Charles Moore's Piazza d'Italia in New Orleans (1975–80), began to value precisely those aspects of layered memory and replication so conspicuous in the artist's paraphrases and self-counterfeits of his own glorious, but remote, historical past. Warhol added new angles to these "Chinese boxes," replicating de Chirico's own replications of his earlier works, such as *The Disquiet-*

*ing Muses* (figure 12) and *Hector and Andromache*, and thereby shuffling in this Pirandellian way not only artistic identities, but early and late dates, originals and reproductions.[21] Warhol could also share the eighties' taste for treating abstraction as a kind of *objet trouvé*, a phenomenon familiar to the work of, say, Salle and Taaffe, who can approach the widest vocabulary of abstract imagery—from Jean-Paul Riopelle and Barnett Newman to Ad Reinhardt and Bridget Riley—as if it were simply part of, and interchangeable with, the rest of the visual data around us. In Warhol's case, however, this attraction to what might be called "ready-made abstraction" occurs in a more public and accidental domain: the usually unheeded abstractions created by cast shadows, by the Pollock-like aftermath of urinating,[22] by

13. Performance of *Within the Quota*, Théâtre de Champs-Élysées, Paris, 1923. Produced by Les Ballets Suédois; scenario, decor, and costumes by Gerald Murphy; music by Cole Porter; choreography by Jean Börlin

*York Post*, and the *New York Mirror*, of 1961–62, to *Il Mattino* of Naples, of 1981 (plates 134–136, 386)[23]—have been shown to have a fascinating prototype in a ballet set by Gerald Murphy of 1923 for *Within the Quota* (figure 13).[24] It is within this territory of twenties American modernism that many other Pop previews can be glimpsed, of which the richest may be a small canvas by Stuart Davis, *Lucky Strike* (figure 14), now impossible to look at without Warhol's as well as Lichtenstein's instant intervention.[25] For here, in 1924, Davis compiled a virtual inventory of exactly the same kind of would-be shocking anti-art objects and shocking anti-art style that launched Warhol in 1961–62: the full expanse of newspaper front page (that of the *Evening Journal* sports section, which includes a cartoon, complete with dialogue-filled balloons), and a still life of packaged smoking products, from Lucky Strike roll-cut tobacco to Zig Zag cigarette paper, which replicate the typefaces and logos of their commercial wrappings.

However, such foreshadowings of American Pop have, like Davis and Murphy themselves, a widening international dimension, and Euro-

the elaborate visual subterfuge of camouflage patterns or Rorschach tests (plates 16, 17, 376–381, 422–424, 442–445, 460). And in his last years Warhol arrived at what now look like, in terms of religion and art history, the ultimate appropriations, the supreme Christian icons of Western art that fix forever Jesus and the Virgin—Leonardo's *Last Supper* and Raphael's *Sistine Madonna* (plates 445–454)—quoted in their entirety and in parts, and reaching at times vast pictorial dimensions that, like Schnabel's inflated, scavenged images, echo with a death-rattle irony the mural ambitions and achievements of Renaissance frescoes and altarpieces.

Warhol's connections with art history, however, are not only those of the eighties' quotation-mark eclecticism explored by many of his lively younger contemporaries, but also those of more resonant connections that conjure up a wide range of ancestral charts. In nationalist terms, Warhol, like Lichtenstein, can stir up a protohistory of Pop art in America between the two world wars. His now famous paintings that replicate the front pages of the newspapers—which extended from the *Daily News*, the *New*

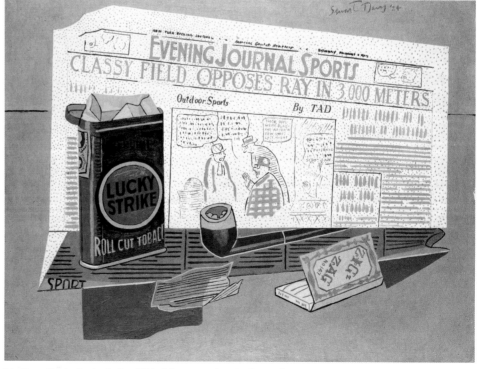

14. Stuart Davis. *Lucky Strike*. 1924. Oil on paperboard, 18 × 24″ (45.6 × 60.9 cm). Hirshhorn Museum and Sculpture Garden, Smithsonian Institution, Washington, D.C.

15. Juan Gris. *Le Paquet de Quaker Oats*. 1915. Oil on canvas, 17½ × 14⅝″ (44.5 × 37 cm). Private collection

16. Francis Picabia. *Portrait d'une Jeune Fille Americaine dans l'État de Nudité*. 1915. Ink on paper. Whereabouts unknown

17. Francis Picabia. *Portrait of Max Jacob*. 1915. Ink on paper. Whereabouts unknown

pean Cubism and Dada can also disclose a multitude of Warhol lookalikes that provide him with a more cosmopolitan pedigree, albeit one that still has American roots.[26] It was, after all, an American product, a box of Quaker Oats cereal, as imported into France, that Juan Gris carefully reproduced (including the cartoonlike emblem of William Penn on the label) in a Cubist still life of 1915 (figure 15). And it was the milieu of New York and American mechanical products that excited the Dadaist spirit of Francis Picabia (whose work caught Warhol's eye)[27] to create, in 1915, such sexually symbolic machine-age portraits as that of a spark plug representing an American girl in a state of nudity (figure 16) or a flashlight representing a phallic Max Jacob (figure 17), a prophecy, incidentally, of the more cryptically erotic implications of Johns's flashlight imagery.[28] In both of these heretical images from the pages of the magazine *291*, Picabia not only embraced the kind of ordinary, machine-age object familiar to the Warhol-Lichtenstein repertoire of the early sixties but, as much to the point, depicted these mundane appliances in the language of the commercial illustrator, flattening them, clarifying them, and isolating them like disembodied icons against a totally blank, spaceless ground. Such weightless and homeless relics of our machine age, seen without context and appropriately rendered in the visual vocabulary of an anonymous image-maker in a technologi-

cal civilization, again strike Warholian chords of recognition.

There are more offbeat areas of twentieth-century art as well that have become recognized as proto-Warhol territory, most particularly, as already noted by Richard Morphet,[29] the later portraits and news images of the British artist Walter Sickert, whose work, whether early, middle, or late, still remains unfamiliar to American audiences. From the twenties on, Sickert based many of his paintings on photographs, such as his portrait of Winston Churchill of c. 1927 (figure 18), first capturing the flash-bulb immediacy of a journalistic snapshot and then embellishing it with the marks of high art, that is, visibly brushed strokes of paint. The unsettling combination of a reportorial photographic image and the conventions of handmade realist painting is one that now prefigures, in many of Sickert's oil paintings of newsworthy people and events (King George V; Amelia Earhart's airplane landing in London), an area that Warhol was to stake out for his own, even if, given the low exposure of Sickert's work outside of England, this must be a question of coincidence.

Such a fusion of artist and reporter, however, has grander roots that, in terms of voyeuristic sensibility, lead back to Manet, who, like Warhol, maintained the stance of an aesthete-observer in the face of any subject, whether a stalk of asparagus or a murder. Flipping

through Manet's oeuvre, one can stumble upon the most unlikely coexistences. For instance, in the early 1880s, he recorded, as Warhol often would do (plates 32, 33, 35–39, 390–392), the fashionable, under-the-table fact of the silhouettes of a pair of chic, high-heeled shoes (figure 19), a rapid glimpse of elegant urban detail that would hardly prepare one for a different kind of look at modern life, a tumbled bed on which is strewn the corpse of a well-dressed gentleman who, revolver still in hand, has apparently just killed himself (figure 20). This morbid vignette, however, is seen through Manet's familiar screen of protective, aesthetic detachment, a coolly painted figure in an interior that, on the face of it, would elicit a response no different from any of his uneventful domestic scenes or, for that matter, from a lemon or a bouquet of moss roses. Like Warhol, Manet might have shrugged his shoulders while saying, "There's a disaster every day,"[30] pausing perhaps to record the disaster of the day as Warhol paused to record, on the one hand, a man leaping from a highrise building and, on the other, a bunch of poppies. The customary accusation that the deadpan coolness of Manet's news-photograph surrogate, *The Execution of Maximilian*, is inadequate as a response to its brutal subject is one that might equally be leveled at Warhol, who also seems to approach the facts of modern death with no apparent shift of emotional tone. And it is revealing as well that Manet could cut up one of his multiple versions of the Execution of Maximilian (as he had earlier cut up his no less nominally horrific scene of death in a bull ring) into fragmentary, undramatic parts that totally cancel the would-be shock of the gory narrative. Warhol's use of electric chairs or car crashes as wallpaperlike repeat patterns or as components in larger wholes similarly underscores and contradicts the terror of modern death, the daily statistic that has become so commonplace that the conventional hierarchy of emotional values begins to look like a naive and outmoded support system for cushioning grief and outrage. Following Manet, Warhol would view death as being as ordinary as the front page of the daily newspaper which might one day announce "A Boy for Meg" and another "129 Die in Jet" (plates 134, 136) and as such, demanding, it would seem, an approach no different from the rendering of a dollar bill or a photograph of Elizabeth Taylor. We may all owe a debt to Warhol, as we do to Manet, for reflecting exactly that state of moral and emotional anesthesia which, like it or not, probably tells us more truth about the realities of the modern world than do the rhetorical passions of *Guernica*.

Yet paradoxically, Warhol also clung to what might seem, in the context of the jet-set glamor of his public persona, an archaic piety, maintaining a quiet, surreptitious devotion to the Catholic Church, which had given him spiritual nurture since childhood and which sustained his attraction to the ultimates of life and death. (He was a daily visitor to the church of St. Vincent Ferrer at Sixty-sixth Street and Lexington Avenue—located almost symbolically, for him, halfway between his townhouse and the high-society restaurant Mortimer's—and he never stinted on time or money in his efforts to help, with virtual anonymity, the homeless at the Church of the Heavenly Rest on East Ninetieth Street.)[31] If his approach to the most harrowing images of the American way of death at first seems as reportorial as Manet's, the growing dominance of this morbid leitmotif in his work begins, in retrospect, to take on more personal, obsessive dimensions. It is not only a question of murderers at large and electric chairs, but also the apocalyptic vision of the

18. Walter Sickert. *The Rt. Hon. Winston Churchill.* c. 1927. Oil on canvas, 18 × 12″ (45.5 × 30.5 cm). National Portrait Gallery, London

19. Édouard Manet. *At the Café: Study of Legs.* c. 1880. Watercolor on squared paper, 7¼ × 4⅝″ (18.5 × 11.9 cm). Cabinet des Dessins, Musée du Louvre, Paris

atom bomb and devastating earthquakes. It is not only a question of death on the road or in the air, but of the glaring presence of the skulls and skeletons that haunt all living flesh. Indeed, these constant reminders of our private and public mortality, whether as reportage or through the traditional emblem of the skull, can rival in abundance and impact the persistent theme of death as the overwhelmingly inevitable adversary that casts its dark shadow over the work of Picasso.[32]

No less remarkably, Warhol, presumably the most secular and venal of artists and personalities, has even been able to create disturbing new equivalents for the depiction of the sacred in earlier religious art. His galleries of myths and superstars resemble an anthology of post-Christian saints, just as his renderings of Marilyn's disembodied lips or a single soup can become the icons of a new religion, recalling the fixed isolation of holy relics in an abstract space. Elsewhere, the mute void and mystery of death are evoked, whether through the use of photographic reversals that turn their already impalpable images into ghostly memories or, most startlingly, through the use of a blank canvas, as in the case of *Blue Electric Chair*, 1963 (plate 284), in which a diptych (the form itself recalling an altarpiece) offers, at the left, three times five electric chairs silkscreened in a flat blue plane and, at the right, the same blue ground left numbingly empty.

But there is also the supernatural glitter of celestial splendor, as when the single image of Marilyn Monroe is floated against a gold background, usurping the traditional realm of a Byzantine madonna (plate 199). And even the shimmer of diamond dust, redolent of dimestore dreams and the magic sparkle of Wizard-of-Oz footwear, can waft us to unimagined heights, providing for Joseph Beuys an impalpable twinkle of sainthood (plate 344), like a pulverized halo, or transforming a touristic snapshot of the vertical sweep of Cologne Cathedral's Gothic towers into an exalted vision of Christian eternity. Both ingenuous and shrewd, blasphemous and devout, Warhol not only managed to encompass in his art the most awesome panorama of the material world we all live in, but even gave us unexpected glimpses of our new forms of heaven and hell.

20. Édouard Manet. *The Suicide*. 1877–81. Oil on canvas, 15 × 18½″ (38.1 × 47 cm). Foundation E. G. Bührle Collection, Zürich

## *NOTES*

1. As reported in *New York* 21 (February 29, 1988), p. 38. The birth date "1930," printed on the mock stamp, is incorrect.
2. As illustrated and reported in the American Airlines "in-flight" magazine, *American Way* (May 1, 1988), pp. 66–67.
3. On these portraits, *see* Carolyn Christov-Bakargiev, "Interview with Carlo Maria Mariani," *Flash Art* (April 1987), pp. 60ff.
4. For Wyeth's comments on these reciprocal portraits, *see* Stuart Morgan, Glenn O'Brien, Remo Guidieri, and Robert Becker, "Collaboration Andy Warhol," *Parkett* 12 (1987), pp. 95–96. The exhibitions were *Andy Warhol and Jamie Wyeth: Portraits of Each Other*, Coe Kerr Gallery, New York, June 1976; and *LeRoy Neiman, Andy Warhol: An Exhibition of Sports Paintings*, Los Angeles Institute of Contemporary Art, 1981.
5. By Max Kozloff. On this, *see* the doctoral thesis by Patrick S. Smith, *Andy Warhol's Art and Films* (Ann Arbor: UMI Press, 1986), ch. 6.
6. This viewpoint has been brilliantly argued in the book and exhibition catalogue by Sidra Stich, *Made in U.S.A.: An Americanization in Modern Art, the '50s and '60s* (Berkeley: University of California, 1987).
7. *See* the issues of January 29, 1965, and February 16, 1970.
8. *See* the exhibition catalogue *Vesuvius by Warhol* (Naples: Fondazione Amelio, 1985).
9. I myself made some preliminary suggestions in this direction in "Pop and Non-Pop: An Essay in Distinction," *Art and Literature* 5 (Summer 1965), pp. 80–93.
10. John Coplans, *Serial Imagery* (Pasadena, Calif.: Pasadena Art Museum, 1968). For Warhol, *see* pp. 130–37.
11. Quoted in *Warhol's Campbell's Soup Boxes* (Los Angeles: Michael Kohn Gallery, 1986), p. 28.
12. John Elderfield, "Grids," *Artforum* (May 1972), pp. 52–59.
13. Rosalind Krauss, *Grids: Format and Image in 20th Century Art* (New York: Pace Gallery, 1979).
14. *See* Richard Morphet, "Andy Warhol," in *Warhol* (London: Tate Gallery, 1971), pp. 24ff.
15. I have explored these ideas further in my catalogue essay "Andy Warhol: Court Painter to the 70s," in David Whitney, ed., *Andy Warhol: Portraits of the 70s* (New York: Whitney Museum of American Art and Random House, 1979).
16. *See above*, figure 7 and note 8. In terms of Warhol's historicism, it should be noted that these paintings provide an unexpected postscript to a long Romantic tradition of depicting the spectacle of Vesuvius in eruption, examples of which are illustrated in the Naples catalogue. Warhol's detached approach to this obviously awesome sight is, incidentally, prophesied by Edgar Degas, who, in a monotype of c. 1890–93, coolly recorded Vesuvius erupting. (*See* Eugenia Parry Janis, *Degas Monotypes* [Cambridge, Mass.: Fogg Art Museum, 1968], no. 310.)
17. On these, *see above*, note 11, which includes a particularly informative essay by Michael Kohn.
18. *See* Mark Rosenthal, *Anselm Kiefer* (Chicago and Philadelphia: Art Institute of Chicago and Philadelphia Museum of Art, 1987), pp. 49–51, where a parallel with Warhol's celebrity portraits is discussed.
19. For an excellent account of such images in the context of Warhol's history as a printmaker, *see* Roberta Bernstein, "Warhol as Printmaker," in Frayda Feldman and Jörg Schellmann, eds., *Andy Warhol Prints: A Catalogue Raisonné* (New York: Ronald Feldman Fine Arts, Editions Schellmann, and Abbeville Press, 1985), pp. 15–21.
20. *See* Achille Bonito Oliva, *Warhol verso de Chirico* (Milan: Electa, 1982). (Reprinted in 1985 for Marisa del Re Gallery, New York.)
21. The New York exhibition of this work (1985) received little serious attention, with the important exception of Kim Levin's account, "The Counterfeiters: De Chirico vs. Warhol," *The Village Voice* (May 7, 1985). (Reprinted in *Beyond Modernism: Essays on Art from the '70s and '80s* [New York: Harper and Row, 1988], pp. 251–54.)
22. Carter Ratcliff also discusses these Oxidation paintings as possible spoofs of Jackson Pollock (*Andy Warhol* [New York: Abbeville Press, 1983], p. 94.)
23. Warhol replicated the Neapolitan newspaper's front page of November 28, 1980, with the headline FATE PRESTO, referring to the urgency of saving the thousands of victims of the local earthquake.
24. *See* William Rubin and Carolyn Lanchner, *The Paintings of Gerald Murphy* (New York: The Museum of Modern Art, 1974), pp. 24ff.; and Stich, *Made in U.S.A.*, pp. 114–15.
25. Stich (ibid.) was the first, to my knowledge, to publish this particular Davis, as opposed to his other versions of *Lucky Strike* and *Odol*, within a proto-Pop context.
26. I have already suggested this field of inquiry in my essay "Picasso and the Typography of Cubism," in Roland Penrose and John Golding, eds., *Picasso in Retrospect* (New York and Washington: Praeger, 1973), especially p. 75; and have amplified it in a lecture, "High Art vs. Low Art: Cubism as Pop," first given at the Hirshhorn Museum and Sculpture Garden, Washington, D.C., on May 11, 1975, in which I elaborated the many proto-Pop aspects of Cubism, ranging from the use of cartoon imagery to the replication of commercial logos.
27. Warhol's own collection included Picabia canvases of 1934 and 1946.
28. For varying interpretations of these works by Picabia, *see* William Camfield, *Francis Picabia: His Art, Life, and Times* (Princeton, N.J.: Princeton University Press, 1979), p. 83; and Maria Lluïsa Borràs, *Picabia* (New York, 1985), pp. 155–56.
29. As first suggested in "The Modernity of Late Sickert," *Studio International* 190 (July–August 1975), pp. 35–38; and then further elaborated in my essay on Warhol's portraiture (*see above*, note 15, pp. 9–10). For more on Sickert, *see* the exhibition catalogue *Late Sickert: Paintings 1927 to 1942* (London: Hayward Gallery, 1981–82).
30. *See above*, note 11, p. 28.
31. The most vivid, informative account of the Slavic religious background that permeated Warhol's life is by John Richardson: "The Secret Warhol," *Vanity Fair* 50 (May 1987), pp. 64ff.
32. Warhol's Skulls, in particular, and his death imagery, in general, were the subjects of a lecture by Trevor Fairbrother given at the Warhol symposium sponsored by the Dia Art Foundation, New York, on April 23, 1988. The proceedings are to be published.

# ANDY WARHOL'S ONE-DIMENSIONAL ART: 1956–1966

## BY BENJAMIN H. D. BUCHLOH

"If you want to know all about Andy Warhol, just look at the surface of my paintings and films and me, and there I am. There's nothing behind it."

"My work has no future at all. I know that. A few years. Of course my things will mean nothing."

—Andy Warhol[1]

A calling card designed by Andy Warhol on a long sheet of light green tissue paper, mailed to clients and patrons, advertising and design agencies about 1955, depicts a circus artiste holding a giant rose. Her tightly cropped costume reveals a body tattooed with over forty corporate logos and brand names (plate 25). The body displays such brands as Armstrong Tires and Wheaties; Dow chemicals and Pepsodent; Hunts Catsup, which would literally pop up as a three-dimensional can in *Andy Warhol's Index (Book)* in 1967; and Chanel No. 5 and Mobil, which would resurface thirty years later in his portfolio of silkscreen prints titled *Ads*.[2] The artiste's face carries a single tattoo, ennobling her doll-like features with a laurel wreath around the letter *L* for Lincoln (the car). The lower part of the costume carries an inscription in the *faux naif* script which had already endeared its author to his art-director clients, simply stating: "Andy Warhol Murry Hell 3-0555," the artist's telephone number.[3]

It would seem that even at the beginning of his various careers, Warhol "embodied" the paradox of modernist art: to be suspended between high art's isolation, transcendence, and critical negativity and the pervasive debris of corporate-dominated mass culture—or as Theodor W. Adorno has put it, "to have a history at all while under the spell of the eternal repetition of mass production"[4]—constitutes the fundamental dialectic within the modernist artist's role. Its origins in Romanticism and its imminent disappearance are invoked in War-

hol's ironic reference to the *saltimbanque* muse and her corporate tattooes. That this dialectic might originate in two types of collective consumption has been recently suggested: "With the aid of ideal types two distinct consumer styles may be seen emerging in the 1880's and the 1890's: an elitist type and a democratic one. For all their differences in detail, many, if not

1. Andy Warhol. Sketch for "Happy Butterfly Day" brochure. c. 1955. Ink and pencil on paper, 12⅝ × 9⅜" (32.1 × 23.8 cm). The Estate of Andy Warhol

most, of the experiments in consumer models of those decades fall into one or the other of these categories. Both the elitist and the democratic consumers rebelled against the shortcomings of mass and bourgeois styles of consumption, but in seeking an alternative they moved in opposite directions. Elitist consumers considered themselves a new type of aristocracy, one not of birth

but of spirit—superior individuals who would forge a personal mode of consumption far above the banalities of the everyday. Democratic consumers sought to make consumption more equal and participatory. They wanted to rescue everyday consumption from banality by raising it to the level of a political and social statement."[5]

It will remain a mystery whether Warhol attempted to reconcile these contradictions in his own life by changing his professional identity from commercial artist to fine artist in 1960.[6] By 1959 Warhol had become very successful in the field of advertising design, earning an average annual sum of $65,000 and numerous Art Directors Club medals and other tokens of professional recognition. Warhol's own later commentaries on commercial art and his motives for abandoning it are designed to construct a field of blague that seems to address the impertinence of the interviewers' inquisitiveness rather than the question itself.

Nevertheless, by 1954–55 Warhol had already shown his ambitions toward fine art: in order to distinguish himself within the mundane world of commercial design he (fraudulently) claimed success in the realm of fine art, which he would only attain ten years later. In a folder produced as a promotional gift for one of his clients, *Vanity Fair,* Warhol declared "Happy Butterfly Day" (figure 1), and in a gold-stamped text: "This Vanity Fair Butterfly Folder was designed for your desk by Andy Warhol, whose paintings are exhibited in many leading museums and contemporary galleries."[7]

This reference to the museum as the institution of ultimate validation is deployed again thirty years later by Warhol (or on his behalf), in rather different circumstances. Toward the end of his career it would seem that Warhol had successfully integrated the two poles of the modernist dialectic, the department store and the museum (what he once called "his favorite places to go to"). In the "1986 Christmas Book of the Neiman-Marcus Stores" a portrait session with Andy Warhol was offered for $35,000: "Become a legend with Andy Warhol.... You'll meet the Premier Pop artist in his studio for a private sitting. Mr. Warhol will create an acrylic on canvas portrait of you in the tradition of his museum quality pieces."[8] By contrast, on the occasion of his actual debut in the world of high art, his appearance in "New Talent U.S.A.," a special issue of *Art in America* in 1962, Warhol (equally fraudulently) described himself as "self-taught."[9]

Warhol's inverted bluffs (of the commercial world with fine-art legitimacy, the high-art world with brutish innocence) indicate more than a shrewd reading of the disposition of commercial artists to be in awe of museum culture, which they have failed to enter, or, for that matter, its complementary formation, the disposition of the high-art connoisseur to be shocked by anyone who has claimed to have broken the rules of high art's tightly controlled discursive "game." Such strategically brilliant blagues (earlier practiced by Charles Baudelaire, Oscar Wilde, and Marcel Duchamp and brought up to late twentieth-century standards by Warhol) indicate Warhol's awareness of the rapidly changing relationships between the two spheres of visual representation and of the drastic changes of the artist's role and the audience's expectations at the beginning of the fifties. He seemed to have understood early on that it would be the task of the new generation of artists to recognize and publicly acknowledge the extent to which the conditions that had permitted the formation of the Abstract Expressionist aesthetic, with its Romantic roots and notions of the transcendental critique, had actually been surpassed by the reorganization of society in the postwar period: "It was the Second World War... which cut off the vitality of modernism. After 1945, the old semi-aristocratic or agrarian order and its appurtenances were finished in every country. Bourgeois democracy was finally universalized. With that, certain critical links with a pre-capitalist past were snapped. At the same time, 'Fordism' arrived in force. Mass production and mass consumption transformed the West European economies along North American lines. There could no longer be the smallest doubt as to what kind of society this technology would consolidate:

an oppressively stable, monolithically industrial, capitalist civilization was now in place."[10]

This new civilization would create conditions in which mass culture and high art would be forced into an increasingly tight embrace, and these would eventually lead to the integration of the sphere of high art into that of the culture industry. But this fusion would not merely imply a transformation of the artist's role and changing cultural practices, or affect images and objects and their functions within society. The real triumph of mass culture over high culture would eventually take place—quite unexpectedly for most artists and critics—in the fetishization of high art in the larger apparatus of late twentieth-century ideology.

Allan Kaprow, one of the more articulate members of that new generation of artists, would grasp this transformation of the artistic role a few years later: "It is said that if a man hits bottom there is only one direction to go and that is up. In one way this has happened, for if the artist was in hell in 1946, now he is in business. ... There is a chance that the modern 'visionary' is even more of a cliché than his counterpart, the 'conformist,' and that neither is true."[11]

As his calling card suggested, Warhol was uniquely qualified to promote the shift from visionary to conformist and to participate in this transition from "hell" to business: after all, his education at the Carnegie Institute of Technology had not been a traditional fine-arts studio education and had provided him with a depoliticized and technocratically oriented American version of the Bauhaus curriculum, as it spread in the postwar years from László Moholy-Nagy's New Bauhaus in Chicago to other American art institutions.[12]

In fact, when reading early interviews with Andy Warhol one can still find traces of the populist, modernist credo that seems to have motivated Warhol (and Pop art in general), and both aspects—questions of production and reception—seem to have concerned him. For example, he remarked in a little-known interview of the mid-sixties: "Factory is as good a name as any. A factory is where you build things. This is where I make or *build* my work. In my art work, hand painting would take much too long and anyway that's not the age we live in. Mechanical means are *today*, and using them I can get more art to more people. Art should be for everyone."[13] Or, when addressing

the question of audiences for his work, in one of his most important interviews in 1967: "Pop art is for everyone. I don't think art should be only for the select few, I think it should be for the mass of American people and they usually accept art anyway."[14]

One of the first corporate art sponsors and one of the major supporters of Moholy-Nagy's work in Chicago, as well as a fervent advocate of the industrialization of modernist aesthetics in the United States, was Walter Paepcke, president of the Container Corporation of America. He had (prematurely) anticipated in 1946 that mass culture and high art would have to be reconciled in a radically commercialized Bauhaus venture but, in his view, purged of political implications concerning artistic intervention in social progress. The cognitive and perceptual devices of modernism would have to be deployed for the development of a new commodity aesthetic (product design, packaging, and advertisement) and would become a powerful and important industry in postwar America and Europe, without, however, resolving the contradictions of modernism. In the words of the "visionary" businessman: "During the last century in particular, the Machine Age with its mass production procedures has seemingly required specializations which have brought about an unfortunate divergence in work and philosophy of the individual producer and the artist. Yet artists and business men, today as formerly, fundamentally have much in common and can contribute the more to society as they come to complement their talents. Each has within him the undying desire to create, to contribute something to the world, to leave his mark upon society."[15]

Thirty years later this dogged entrepreneurial vision found its farcical echo in Warhol's triumphant proclamation of diffidence at a moment when he had replaced the last remnants of an aesthetic of transcendence or critical resistance with an aesthetic of ruthless affirmation: "Business art is the step that comes after Art. I started as a commercial artist, and I want to finish as a business artist. After I did the thing called 'art' or whatever it's called, I went into business art. I wanted to be an Art Businessman or a Business Artist. Being good in Business is the most fascinating kind of art."[16]

That triumph of mass culture over traditional aesthetic concepts produced two new types of "cultural" personalities. The first were the ad-men, who would become passionate collectors of avant-garde art (in order to embrace the "creativity" that would perpetually escape them and to possess privately what they would systematically destroy in their own "work" in the public sphere). The second type was represented by such artists as James Harvey, who, according to *Time* magazine, "draws his inspiration from religion and landscapes. . . . At nights he works hard on muscular abstract paintings that show in Manhattan's Graham Gallery. But eight hours a day, to make a living, he labors as a commercial artist."[17]

When Harvey, who had designed the Brillo box in the early sixties, encountered his design on 120 wood simulacra by Warhol (and/or his assistants) at the Stable Gallery in New York in 1964 (plate 182), he could only deflect his sense of profound crisis of artistic standards by threatening Warhol with a lawsuit.

Warhol, by contrast, was fairly well prepared to reconcile the contradictions emerging from the collapse of high culture into the culture industry and to participate in it with all the skills and techniques of the commercial artist. He had freed himself early on from outmoded concepts of originality and authorship and had developed a sense of the necessity for collaboration and a Brechtian understanding of the commonality of ideas.[18]

### COMMERCIAL FOLKLORE

Warhol's career, in fact, seems to exemplify each stage of the high-culture/mass-culture paradox, from its division through its eventual fusion, in his easy transition from one role to the other. In his early career as a commercial artist he featured all the debased and exhausted qualities of traditional concepts of the "artistic" that art directors and admen adored: the whimsical and the witty, the wicked and the *faux naif.* One of the resources for such an artistic realm of pleasure was the aristocratically refined preindustrial charm of rococo and neoclassical drawing, as had already been the case in twenties Art Deco advertisement, packaging, and book illustration. The other resource was a particularly charming variety of folk art with which dozens of artists in America—since Elie Nadelman—had identified, at least as collectors. After all, the folk-art object, with its peculiar form of an already extinct creativity,

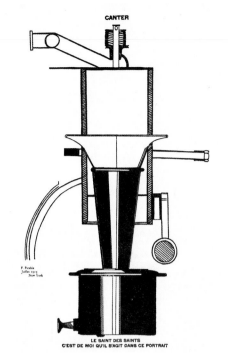

2. Francis Picabia. *Le Saint des Saints.* 1915. Ink on paper. Whereabouts unknown

3. Marcel Duchamp. *Bicycle Wheel.* 1951 (third version, after lost original of 1913). Assemblage: metal wheel mounted on painted stool; overall, 50½" (128.3 cm) high. The Museum of Modern Art, New York. The Sidney and Harriet Janis Collection

seemed to mirror the fate of traditional artistic creativity. Warhol's success as a commercial designer depended, in part, on his "artistic" performance, on his delivery of a certain notion of creativity that appeared all the more rarefied in a milieu whose every impulse was geared to increase commodification. Warhol introduced precisely those noncommercial elements (false naiveté, the charm of the uneducated and unskilled, his illiterate mother, preindustrial *bricolage*) into the most advanced and most sophisticated milieu of professional alienation: advertising design. Warhol was fully aware of this paradox and phrased it in his famous early interview with Gene Swenson in a language that reveals the extent to which its speaker had internalized the lessons of John Cage and transposed them into everyday experience: "It's hard to be creative and it's hard also not to think what you do is creative or hard not to be called creative because everybody is always talking about that and individuality. Everybody's always being creative. And it's so funny when you say things aren't, like the shoe I would draw for an advertisement was called a 'creation' but the drawing of it was not. But I guess I believe in both ways. I was getting paid for it, and I did anything they told me to do. I'd have to invent and now I don't; after all that 'correction' those commercial drawings would have feelings, they would have a style. The attitude of those who hired me had feeling or something to it; they knew what they wanted, they insisted, sometimes they got very emotional. The process of doing work in commercial art was machine-like, but the attitude had feeling to it."[19]

By contrast, his successful debut as an artist in the sphere of fine art—and here the paradox becomes fully apparent—would depend precisely on his capacity to erase from his paintings and drawings more completely than any of his peers (Jasper Johns and Robert Rauschenberg in particular) the traces of the handmade, of artistry and creativity, of expression and invention. What appeared to be cynical "copies" of commercial art early in 1960 scandalized the art world, whose expectations (and self-deceptions) at the moment of the climax of Abstract Expressionism were shaken even more since it had forgotten or conveniently disavowed the work of Francis Picabia (figure 2) or the implications of Marcel Duchamp's Readymades (figure 3).

The notorious anecdote in which Warhol showed two versions of a painting of a Coca-Cola bottle to Emile de Antonio in 1962, one gesturally dramatic, carrying the legacy of Abstract Expressionism, the other cold and diagrammatic, making the claim of the Ready-made, now in the domain of painting (plate 91), attests to Warhol's uncanny ability to produce according to the needs and demands of the moment (and to his technical skills to perform these tasks). It also seems to betray a brief instance of hesitation in Warhol's calculation of how far he could really go with the breakdown of local painterly conventions and the infusion of commercial design devices in order to make his entry into the New York art world. After all, at the time his status in this realm was tenuous at best. As late as July 1962, what was to have been Warhol's first New York exhibition—at the prestigious Martha Jackson Gallery—had been cancelled with the following argument: "As this gallery is devoted to artists of an earlier generation, I now feel I must take a stand to support their continuing efforts rather than confuse issues here by beginning to show contemporary Dada. The introduction of your paintings has already had very bad repercussions for us. This is a good sign, as far as your work and your statement as an artist are concerned. Furthermore, I like you and your work. But from a business and gallery standpoint, we want to take a stand elsewhere. Therefore, I suggest to you that we cancel the exhibition we had planned for December 1962."[20]

In fact, Warhol's early "art" work (between 1960 and 1962) was characterized by an apparent lack of painterly resolution, often misread as a parody of Abstract Expressionism. His pictures were painted in a loose, gesturally expressive manner, but their imagery was derived from close-up details of comic strips and advertisements.[21] De Antonio (in several recollections identified as a "Marxist") gave him the right advice (and so did the dealer Ivan Karp, who also saw both paintings): destroy the Abstract Expressionist Coca-Cola bottle and keep the "cold," diagrammatic one.[22]

What is most obvious in these early pairs of hand-painted depictions, such as *Storm Door*, 1960 and 1961 (plates 100, 101), or *Before and After 1, 2,* and *3* (plate 79), is that Warhol's technical expertise as a commercial artist qualified him for the diagrammatic nature of the new painting in the same way that his traditional artistic inclinations had once qualified him for success in the world of commercial design. It frequently has been argued that there is very little continuity between Warhol's commercial art and his fine art,[23] but a more extensive study of Warhol's advertisement design would, in fact, suggest that the key features of his work of the early sixties are prefigured: extreme close-up fragments and details, stark graphic contrasts

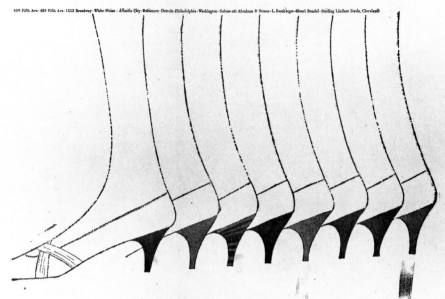

4. I. Miller advertisement by Warhol, *The New York Times*

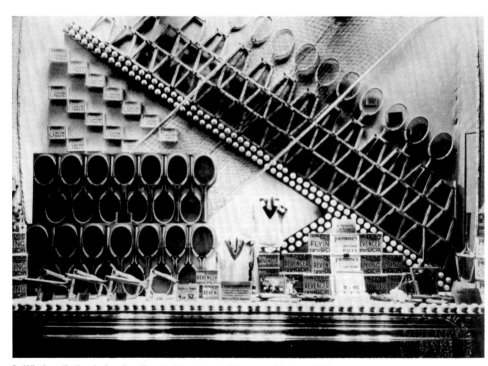

5. Window display design, Les Grands Magasins du Printemps, Paris. c. 1908

6. Ellsworth Kelly. *Colors for a Large Wall*. 1951. Oil on canvas, mounted on sixty-four wood panels; overall, 7′10¼″ × 7′10½″ (239.3 × 239.9 cm). The Museum of Modern Art, New York. Gift of the artist

7. Jasper Johns. *Gray Alphabets*. 1956. Encaustic on newspaper on canvas, 66 × 46″ (167.6 × 116.8 cm). Private collection

and silhouetting of forms, schematic simplification, and, most important, rigorous serial composition (figure 4).

The sense of composing depicted objects and arranging display surfaces in serially structured grids emerges after all from the seriality that constitutes the very nature of the commodity: its object status, its design, and its display. Such seriality had become the major structural formation of object-perception in the twentieth century, determining aesthetic projects as different as those of Siegfried Kracauer and Walter Benjamin, on the one hand, and Busby Berkeley, on the other. Amédée Ozenfant had rightfully included a serial commodity display in his 1931 book *Foundations of Modern Art* (figure 5). And by the mid-fifties the serial-grid composition had regained the prominence it had enjoyed in the twenties: Ellsworth Kelly's serial arrangement of monochrome display panels such as *Colors for a Large Wall*, 1951, and Johns's *Gray Alphabets*, 1956 (figures 6, 7), for example, prefigure the central strategy of Warhol's compositional principle as do, somewhat later, the serially structured arrangements of ready-made objects by Arman in Europe (figure 8).

And, of course, the opposite is also true: Warhol's real affinity for and unusual familiarity (for a commercial artist) with the avant-garde practices of the mid-fifties inspired his advertising design of that period and imbued it with a risqué stylishness that the average commercial artist would have been unable to conceive. Two outstanding examples from Warhol's campaigns for I. Miller shoes in *The New York Times* of 1956 confirm that Warhol had already grasped the full range of the painterly strategies of Johns and Rauschenberg, particularly those aspects that would soon determine his own pictorial production. The first one (figure 9) features the careful overall regularization of a nonrelational composition (as in the obvious example of Johns's Flag paintings after 1954), a strategy which would soon be mechanically debased in Warhol's hands and be depleted of all of Johns's culinary, painterly differentiation. And the second one (figure 10) shows the impact of Rauschenberg's direct imprinting techniques and persistent use of

8. Arman (Armand Fernandez). *Boom! Boom!* 1960. Assemblage of plastic water pistols in a plexiglass case, 8¼ × 23¼ × 4½″ (21 × 59 × 11.2 cm). The Museum of Modern Art, New York. Gift of Philip Johnson

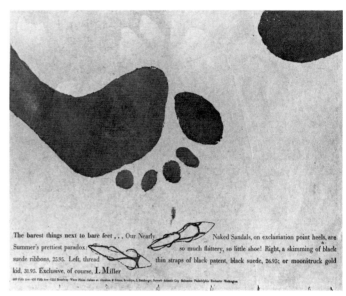

We cordially invite you to visit the Shoe Salon at Henri Bendel where slenderly elegant shoes by I. Miller, David Evins, and Ingenue, are now to be seen in addition to the beautiful Belgian imports for which Bendel has always been famous.

*I. Miller at Henri Bendel* 10 West 57th Street

9. I. Miller advertisement by Warhol, *The New York Times*

10. I. Miller advertisement by Warhol, *The New York Times*

indexical marking since his collaboration with John Cage on the *Automobile Tire Print* of 1951 (figure 11), a method soon to be emptied by Warhol of all the expressivity and decorative artistry the technique had regained in Rauschenberg's work of the late fifties.

### THE RITUALS OF PAINTING

It appears, then, that by the end of the fifties Warhol, both commercially competent and artistically canny, was singularly prepared to effect the transformation of the artist's role in postwar America. This transformation of an aesthetic practice of transcendental negation into one of tautological affirmation is perhaps best articulated by John Cage's famous dictum of 1961 in *Silence:* "Our poetry now is the realization that we possess nothing. Anything therefore is a delight (since we do not possess it . . . )."

The fact that this transformation would dismantle the traditional format of easel painting had already been stated in 1958 in a text by Allan Kaprow ("The Legacy of Jackson Pollock") that seems to have functioned as a manifesto for the new generation of American artists after Abstract Expressionism: "Pollock's near destruction of this tradition [of easel painting] may well be a return to the point where art was more actively involved in ritual, magic and life than we have known it in our recent past. If so, it is an exceedingly important step, and in its superior way, offers a solution to the complaints of those who would have us put a bit of life into art. But what do we do now? There are two alternatives. One is to continue in this vein. . . . The other is to give up the making of paintings entirely."[24]

In spite of Kaprow's acumen, the essay was marred by two fundamental misunderstandings. The first was the idea that the hegemony of Abstract Expressionism had come to an end because Pollock "had destroyed painting,"[25] and because of the vulgarization of the Abstract Expressionist style by its second-generation imitators. This assumption suggests—as historians and critics have argued ever since—that a mere stylistic rebellion against New York School painting and its academicization was the principal motivating force in the advent of Pop art.[26] This stylistic argument, descriptive at best, mistakes the effects for the cause, and can be most easily refuted by remembering two historical facts. First, that painters such as Barnett Newman and Ad Reinhardt were only recognized in the mid-sixties and that Willem de Kooning and Mark Rothko continued to work with ever-increasing visibility and success. If anything, by the mid-sixties, their work (and most certainly Pollock's) had achieved an almost mythic status, representing aesthetic and ethical standards that seemed, however, lost and unattainable for the future. Second, the

11. Robert Rauschenberg and John Cage. *Automobile Tire Print*. 1951. Monoprint on paper, mounted on canvas, 16½″ × 22′ (41.9 × 671.8 cm). Collection Robert Rauschenberg (on extended loan to the National Gallery of Art, Washington, D.C.)

younger generation of New York School artists, from Johns and Rauschenberg to Claes Oldenburg and Warhol, continually emphasized—both in their works and statements—their affiliation with, and veneration of, the legacy of Abstract Expressionism. Of course, they also emphasized the impossibility of achieving that generation's transcendental artistic aspirations and standards.

The second (and major) misconception in Kaprow's essay becomes evident in his contradictory remarks on the revitalization of artistic ritual and the simultaneous disappearance of easel painting. Kaprow conceives of the ritualistic dimension of aesthetic experience (what Walter Benjamin had called the "parasitical dependence of art upon the magic ritual") as a transhistorical, universally accessible condition that can be reconstituted at any time merely by altering obsolete stylistic means and artistic procedures. Kaprow's ideas of 1958 are in fact comparable to Benjamin's thought of the twenties, when the latter developed the notion of a participatory aesthetic in the context of his discussion of Dadaism. Kaprow speaks with astonishing naiveté of the possibility of a new

participatory aesthetic emerging out of Pollock's work: "But what I believe *is* clearly discernible is that the *entire* painting comes out at the participant (I shall call him that, rather than observer) right into the room. . . . In the present case the 'picture' has moved so far out that the canvas is no longer a reference point. Hence, although up on the wall, these marks surround us as they did the painter at work, so strict a correspondence has there been achieved between his impulse and the resultant art."[27]

In fact, what *did* occur in the formation of Pop art in general, and Warhol's work in particular, was just the opposite of Kaprow's prophecy: the demise of easel painting, as initiated by Pollock, was accelerated and extended to comprise as well the destruction of the last vestiges of the ritual in aesthetic experience itself. Warhol came closer than anybody since Duchamp (in the Western European and American avantgarde at least) "to [giving] up the making of paintings entirely." What is more, Warhol's paintings eventually would oppose those aspirations toward a new aesthetic of participation (as it had been preached and practiced by Cage, Rauschenberg, and Kaprow) by degrading pre-

cisely those notions to the level of absolute farce.

*Tango,* for example, had been the title of one of Johns's crucial monochromatic and participatory paintings in 1955, embodying Cage's concept of participation in its invitation to the viewer to wind up the painting's built-in music box (figure 12). Johns explicitly stated that such a participatory concept motivated his work at the time: "I wanted to suggest a physical relationship to the pictures that was active. In the Targets one could stand back or one might go very close and lift the lids and shut them. In *Tango* to wind the key and hear the sound, you had to stand relatively close to the painting, too close to see the outside shape of the picture."[28]

Seven years after Johns's *Tango* and four years after Kaprow's "prophetic" text, Warhol produced two groups of diagrammatic paintings, the Dance Diagrams of 1962 (plates 160–163) and the Do It Yourself paintings, begun the same year (plates 153–159). These works seem to have been conceived in response to the idea of renewing participatory aesthetics, if not in direct response to Johns's and Rauschenberg's paintings or even Kaprow's "manifesto."

Both the Dance Diagrams and the Do It Yourself paintings bring the viewer, almost literally, into the plane of visual representation in what one might call a "bodily synecdoche"—a twentieth-century avant-garde practice intended to instigate active identification of the viewer with the representation, replacing the contemplative mode of aesthetic experience with an active one. However, this tradition had, in the meantime, become one of the key strategies—if not the principal one—of advertisement design itself, soliciting the viewer's active participation as Consumption.

Accordingly, in Warhol's work, the diagrams that entice the viewer's feet onto the Dance Diagram paintings and engage the viewer's hands to fill in the Do It Yourself paintings are frivolously transferred onto the pictorial plane from the domain of popular entertainment (rituals that are slightly "camp" and defunct: fox trot, tango, etc.). What is more, they seem to suggest that if participatory aesthetics were at so infantile a level as to invite participants to wind up a music box, to clap their hands, or to hide an object (as suggested in some of Johns's and Rauschenberg's work; in fact he speaks admiringly of Pollock's "dance"), one might just

12. Jasper Johns. *Tango.* 1955. Encaustic on canvas with music box, 43 × 55″ (109.2 × 139.7 cm). Ludwig Museum, Cologne

as well shift from the strategic games of high art to those real rituals of participation within which mass culture contains and controls its audiences.

This dialogic relationship of the Dance Diagram paintings with Kaprow's essay and the status of participatory aesthetics was made even more explicit in Warhol's rather peculiar decision to present these paintings in their first public installation horizontally, on the floor, making the display an essential element of the painting's reading.[29] Simulating the function of actual diagrams for dance lessons, the installation on the floor not only emphasized the facetious invitation to the viewer to participate in a trivial ritual of mass culture, but literally parodied the position of the painting in Jackson Pollock's working procedure on the floor of the studio, as it had been described in Harold Rosenberg's famous essay "The American Action Painters" of 1952 (which reverberated through Kaprow's text as well): "At a certain moment the canvas began to appear to one American painter after another as an arena in which to act—rather than as a space in which to reproduce, re-design, analyze or 'express' an object, actual or imagined. What was to go on the canvas was not a picture but an event. . . . The image would be the result of this encounter."[30]

The destruction of Pollock's painterly legacy and the critique of aesthetic experience as participatory ritual would resurface in Warhol's work once again almost twenty years later. Precisely at the moment of the rise of Neo-Expressionism Warhol delivered one of his last coups to an increasingly voracious high-culture industry desperately trying to revitalize the expressionist paradigm and its failed promises. His series of Oxidation paintings of 1978 (plates 376–379), whose monochrome surfaces were coated with metallic paint striated and spotted with the expressively gestural oxidizing marks of urination onto the canvas, brought full circle the critique begun in the Dance Diagrams.

### THE MONOCHROME

The Dance Diagrams of 1962 contain two other important aspects of Warhol's art, which, along with serial-grid composition, became the central strategies of Warhol's entire painterly production: mechanically reproduced ready-made imagery and monochromatic color schemes.

13. Jackson Pollock. *White Light*. 1954. Oil, enamel, and aluminum paint on canvas, 48¼ × 38¼" (122.4 × 96.9 cm). The Museum of Modern Art, New York. The Sidney and Harriet Janis Collection

Warhol's adoption of the modernist tradition of monochrome painting, frequently concealed in metallic monochrome sections of paintings or blatant in separate panels (the "blanks," as he called them with typically derogatory understatement), aligns his painterly work of the early sixties in yet another way with some of the key issues emerging from New York School painting at that time.

Pollock had included industrial aluminum paint in key paintings such as *Lavender Mist (Number 1)*, 1950, or *White Light,* 1954 (figure 13). The material's industrial derivation had generated a scandal, while its light reflectivity concretized the viewer's optical relationship to the paint in an almost mechanical manner. Warhol deployed the same industrial enamel, and his use of aluminum paint was only the beginning of a long involvement with "immateriality," both of light reflectivity and of the "empty" monochrome surface. Evolving from the various stages of gold Marilyns in 1962, followed by the series of silver Elvises and numerous other images silkscreened on silver throughout 1963–64 (such as *Silver Marlon* and *Tunafish Disaster* [plates 233, 269, 270]), Warhol produced the first diptych paintings with large monochrome panels in 1963 (*Mustard Race Riot* [plate 277] and *Blue Electric Chair* [plate 284]), the first monochrome metallic diptychs in 1964 (*Round Jackie,* plates 245, 246), and the silver Liz diptych in 1965. As was the case with the Dance Diagrams and the Do It Yourself paintings, the monochrome diptychs completely devalued and inverted one of modernism's most sacred pictorial strategies, the empty space, originating in Symbolist sources. Upon its appearance in twentieth-century art it had been hailed by Wassily Kandinsky in the following terms: "I always find it advantageous in each work to leave an empty space; it has to do with not imposing. Don't you think that in this there rests an eternal law—but it's a law for tomorrow."[31]

That "empty space," as Kandinsky's statement clearly indicates, was yet another strategy negating aesthetic imposition, functioning as a spatial suture allowing the viewer a relationship of mutual interdependence with the "open" artistic construct. The empty space functioned equally as a space of hermetic resistance, rejecting ideological meaning assigned to painting as well as the false comforts of convenient readings. It was certainly with those aspirations that the monochrome strategy had been utilized by Newman and Reinhardt throughout the fifties

and early sixties. Their monochrome paintings were imbued with a notion of transcendentalism, reminiscent of the Symbolist origins of the monochrome strategy. On the other hand, like other modernist strategies of reduction, the monochrome inadvertently turned into triviality, either as the result of incompetent execution of such a device of apparently supreme simplicity, or of merely exhausting the strategy by endless repetition, or as an effect of artists' and viewers' growing doubts about a strategy whose promises had become increasingly incompatible with its material objects and their functions.[32]

The process of critical re-evaluation of the monochrome tradition had begun once again in the American context in Rauschenberg's early 1951 White Paintings and would find its climax (along with the official termination of Warhol's painterly production) in the Silver Clouds—identified by Warhol as "paintings"—silver "pillows" inflated with helium, floating through (and supposedly out of) the Leo Castelli Gallery in 1966 (plate 302). Shortly before, Warhol announced publicly that he had abandoned painting once and for all, which would

seem to have led him to Kaprow's envisioned "action," except that he, typically, refrained from it.[33] Warhol's more skeptical evaluation of the options available for cultural practice would prove Kaprow's prophecies once again to be falsely optimistic.

Thus the monochrome field and the light-reflective surface, seemingly emptied of all manufactured visual incident, had become one of the central concerns of the neo-avant-garde artists of the early to mid-fifties. This was evident not only in Rauschenberg's work but equally in the work of Kelly and Johns (and a few years later that of Frank Stella) as much as their European contemporaries Lucio Fontana and Yves Klein. Rauschenberg, for instance, had done a series of small square collages with gold and silver leaf in 1953, which he exhibited at the Stable Gallery that year; and he continued through 1956 to use the crumpled foil on roughly textured fabric, a combination that eliminated drawing and gesture and, instead, generated surface and textural incident exclusively from the material's inherent textural and procedural qualities. Frank Stella, before engaging in his series of large aluminum paintings in 1960 (the square paintings *Averroes* and *Avicenna,* for example), had already produced a group of smaller squarish paintings in 1959, such as *Jill* (figure 14), which were covered with geometrically ordered, highly reflective metallic tape (as opposed to Rauschenberg's randomly broken and erratically reflective foil surfaces).

Warhol has explicitly stated that the monochrome paintings of the early to mid-fifties influenced his own decision to paint monochrome panels in the early sixties: "I always liked Ellsworth's work, and that's why I always painted a blank canvas. I loved that blank canvas thing and I wished I had stuck with the idea of just painting the same painting like the soup can and never painting another painting. When someone wanted one, you would just do another one. Does anybody do that now? Anyway, you do the same painting whether it looks different or not."[34]

In spite of Warhol's typically diffident remarks about the historical references for his use of monochrome panels, his flippancy clearly also indicates his awareness of the distance that separated his conception of the monochrome from that of Kelly, for example.

14. Frank Stella. *Jill.* 1959. Burglar-alarm tape on Masonite, 9¾ × 8¾" (24.8 × 22.2 cm). Collection Lawrence Rubin, New York

Recognizing that no single strategy of modernist reduction, of radical negation and refusal, could escape its ultimate fate of enhancing the painting's status as object and commodity, the destruction of any and all metaphysical residue of the device (be it in neoplasticist, Abstract Expressionist, or, as it was identified, hard-edge and color-field painting of the fifties) seems in fact to have been the task that Warhol had set for himself in the deployment of monochromy in the early sixties. It seems possible, therefore, to argue that Warhol's earliest paintings explicitly refer to that venerable legacy, and that paintings such as *Yellow Close Cover Before Striking,* 1962 (plate 109), or *Red Close Cover Before Striking,* 1962, perform the same critical inversion with regard to the color-field legacy and the work of Newman, for example, as the Dance Diagrams and the Do It Yourself paintings do with regard to the legacy of Jackson Pollock.

Once again, what makes Warhol's uncompromising negation of that legacy work is the ingenious realization of an external condition, not the individual assault on a venerated pictorial tradition. It is the contamination of the elusive monochrome with the vulgarity of the most trivial of commonplaces (in this case, the diagrammatic detail of the sulphur strip of a matchbook cover), which makes his work execute the task of destruction so convincingly. As had been the case with his assault on the ritualistic legacy of Abstract Expressionism, Warhol knew early on that this process would eventually dismantle more than just the strategy of the monochrome itself. He realized that any implementation of the monochrome would at this point inevitably lead to a different spatial definition (not to say dissipation) of painting in general, removing it from the traditional conception of a painting as a substantial, unified, integrated planar object whose value and authenticity lie as much in its status as a uniquely crafted object as in its modes of display and the readings ensuing from them.[35] In a little-known 1965 interview Warhol commented on these aspects: "You see, for every large painting I do, I paint a blank canvas, the same background color. The two are designed to hang together however the owner wants. He can hang it right beside the painting or across the room or above or below it. . . . It just makes them bigger and mainly makes them cost more. *Liz Taylor,* for instance, three feet by three feet,

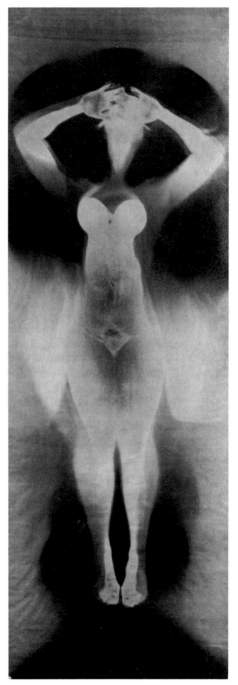

15. Robert Rauschenberg. *Female Figure (Blueprint).* c. 1949. Monoprint on blueprint paper, 8'¾" × 36" (266.7 × 91.4 cm). Private collection

in any color you like, with the blank costs $1600. Signed of course."[36]

## READY-MADE IMAGERY

Warhol's "found" representations and their diagrammatic nature departed from the paradox that the more spontaneous the pictorial mark had become in Pollock's work, the more it had acquired the depersonalized traits of mechanization.

Painterly execution since Pollock, therefore,

seemed to have shifted between the ritualistic performance of painting (to which Rosenberg's and Kaprow's readings had aspired) and the recognition that his painting had thrived on a profoundly antipainterly impulse. This promise of mechanistic anonymity within the process of pictorial mark-making, however, not only seemed to imply the eventual "destruction" of painting proper (as Kaprow had anticipated as well) but had also brought it (much less dramatically) into historical proximity with the post-Cubist devices of antipainterly strategies and ready-made imagery (a proximity which Pollock himself had reached in such works of 1949 as *Out of the Web [Number 7]* or *Cut Out*). If that anti-artistic and anti-authorial promise (and the rediscovery of that promise's historical antecedents) had perhaps not yet been fulfilled in Pollock's own work, then it had certainly become increasingly urgent in the responses that Pollock's work had provoked in Rauschenberg's and Johns's painting of the early to mid-fifties. Rauschenberg, for example, had made this evident as early as c. 1949 in *Female Figure (Blueprint)* (figure 15), where he rediscovered one of the conventions of ready-made imagery—the immediate (indexical) imprint of the photogram and rayogram—and introduced it into New York School painting.[37] Furthermore, he challenged traditional concepts of authorial authenticity and sublime expressivity in his collaboration with John Cage in 1951 on the *Automobile Tire Print,* in his *Erased de Kooning Drawing* in 1953 (figure 16), and most programmatically, of course, in his major assault on painterly presence in the seemingly devalidating and repetitious *Factum I* (figure 17) and *Factum II* (figure 18) in 1957. Johns, perhaps even more programmatically, had reestablished these parameters not only in his direct-casting methods, which he had derived from Duchamp, but equally in his stenciled, collage, and encaustic paintings since 1954.[38]

One should, therefore, realize that Warhol's apparently scandalous, radical mechanization of pictorial mark-making drew, in fact, on a fully developed tradition, a tradition which ranged from the key figures of New York Dada (Man Ray's Rayograms and Picabia's engineering diagrams) to Rauschenberg's and Johns's work of the early to mid-fifties, where ready-made imagery and indexical mark-making had been rediscovered, and had been inscribed into

16. Robert Rauschenberg. *Erased de Kooning Drawing*. 1953. Traces of ink and crayon on paper, 19 × 14½″ (48.3 × 36.8 cm). Collection the artist

17. Robert Rauschenberg. *Factum I*. 1957. Combine painting, 62 × 35½″ (157.5 × 90.2 cm). The Museum of Contemporary Art, Los Angeles. The Panza Collection

18. Robert Rauschenberg. *Factum II*. 1957. Combine painting, 62 × 35½″ (157.5 × 90.2 cm). Morton G. Neumann Family Collection, Chicago

the legacy of New York School painting. In light of this range of previously established techniques to apply and repeat mechanically factured pictorial marks, the frequently posed question of whether it was Rauschenberg or Warhol who first used the silkscreen process in painting is utterly futile.

Warhol's mechanization, at first timid and unresolved in his earliest paintings, which still adhered to the manual gesture, developed from 1960 to 1962 and led from the hand-painted diagrams through the rubber stamps and stencil paintings in 1961–62 to the first fully silk-screened canvases—*Baseball,* Troy Donahue, Marilyn Monroe, and Elvis Presley—which were shown, along with *Dance Diagram (Tango)* (plate 161), in his first New York exhibition.

The historical difficulty Rauschenberg and Johns had to overcome was that the preeminence of Abstract Expressionist painting—its definition of mark-making as expressive gestural abstraction—had not only completely obliterated the ready-made imagery and mechanical drawing procedures of Dadaism but had also required that, in order to be "seen" at all in 1954 they had to conform to the locally dominant painterly conventions. Hence, they engaged in pictorializing the radically antipictorial legacy of Dadaism. Clearly, Rauschenberg's development of his own pictorial *bricolage* technique—applied in the first dye-transfer drawings such as *Cage* or *Mona Lisa,* both 1958, and unfolded as a method subsequently in the monumental cycle *Thirty-four Illustrations for Dante's Inferno,* 1959–60 (figure 19)—had successfully fused both the increasingly dominant presence of mass-cultural imagery with high art and the inherited idiom of Dada collage with the conventions of expressive gestural abstraction. Clearly, therefore, Rauschenberg appeared to fifties audiences as the enigmatic genius of a new age.

What Warhol had to consider in 1962 was whether he too, like his peers, had to remain to some degree within the pictorial format in order to avoid the failed reception that some of Rauschenberg's own more radical nonpictorial works had encountered, or whether his efforts to depictorialize Johns and Rauschenberg could go as far as the more consequential work of artists such as Kaprow and Robert Watts or European *nouveaux réalistes* such as Arman. After 1958–59 all of these artists had abandoned all gestures of compromise with New York School pictorialism in order to reconstitute radical ready-made strategies; and like their Fluxus colleagues they would ultimately fail to generate interest among a New York audience avidly awaiting the next delivery of pictorial products that could be packaged in collections and exhibitions.[39] By contrast, Warhol seems at first to have felt reluctant about an outright commitment to mechanical representation and ready-made objects (as had already been evident in his earliest paintings), and as late as 1966 he considered it still necessary to defend his silkscreen technique against the commonly held suspicion that mechanical procedures and ready-made objects were ultimately unartistic and fraudulent: "In my art work, hand painting would take much too long and anyway that's not the age we're living in. Mechanical means are today.... Silkscreen work is as honest a method as any, including hand painting."[40]

But Warhol's solution, found in 1962, responded to all of these problems: in his painting he isolated, singularized, and centralized representation in the manner of a Duchampian Readymade (and in the manner of Johns's Flags and Targets), and extracted it, thereby, from the tiresome affiliation of collage aesthetics and the nagging accusation of neo-Dada, which had been leveled constantly against his older peers. Simultaneously, this strategy, with its increased emphasis on the mere photographic image and its crude and infinite reproducibility, furthered the erosion of the painterly legacy of the New York School and eliminated all traces of the compromises that Rauschenberg had had to make with that legacy. Warhol's photographic silkscreens of single images as well as the serial repetition of single images eliminated the ambiguity between expressive gesture and mechanical mark from which Rauschenberg's work had drawn its tension (and its relative conventionality). Also, the centralized ready-made image eliminated the relational composition, which had functioned as the spatial matrix of Rauschenberg's relatively traditional pictorial structure and temporal narrative. Yet, while seemingly a radical breakthrough, the photographic silkscreen procedure and the compositional strategies of singularization and serial repetition allowed Warhol at the same time to remain within the boundaries of the pictorial

19. Robert Rauschenberg. *Thirty-four Illustrations for Dante's Inferno. Canto XXVII: Circle Eight, Bolgia 8, The Evil Counselors.* 1959–60. Transfer drawing, watercolor, gouache, and pencil on paper, 14½ × 11½" (36.8 × 29.3 cm). The Museum of Modern Art, New York. Given anonymously

framework, a condition of compromise upon which he would always insist.

Warhol's adaptations of Rauschenberg's mechanical methods of image transfer (dye or silkscreen) subjected these techniques to numerous critical transformations. First of all, and most obviously, Warhol deprived his paintings of the infinite wealth of associative play and simultaneous multiple references, which Rauschenberg's traditional collage aesthetic had still offered to the viewer. By contrast, Warhol's image design (whether in its emblematic single-unit structure or in its repetition of a single unit) extinguishes all poetic resources and prohibits the viewer's free association of the pictorial elements, replacing the latter with the experience of a confrontational restriction. In a very literal manner Warhol's singularized images become hermetic: secluded from other images or stifled by their own repetition, they can no longer generate "meaning" and "narration" in the manner of Rauschenberg's larger syntactic assemblages. Paradoxically, the restriction and hermeticism of the semantically isolated image was at first generally experienced as the effect of absolute banality, or as an attitude of divine indifference, or, worse yet, as an affirmation of consumer culture. In fact it operated, first of all, as the rejection of conventional demands upon the artistic object to provide the plenitude of iconic representation. Warhol negates those demands for a pictorial

narrative with the same degree of asceticism with which Duchamp had negated them in his Readymades.

The restriction to the single iconic image/ repetition finds its procedural complement in Warhol's purging all remnants of painterliness from Rauschenberg's expressively compromised photographic images and in his confronting the viewer with a factual silkscreen reproduction of the photographic image (as in the Elvises, the Disasters, and the *Thirteen Most Wanted Men,* for example). In these paintings the silkscreened photographic imprint remains the only trace of the pictorial manufacturing process, and this technique assaults once again one of the central tenets of the modernist legacy—forcing those eager to rediscover medium-specific painterliness, individuality, and the uniqueness of the painterly mark to detect it in the accidental slippages and flaws of a casually executed silkscreen process. In the following statement, a fervent admirer of Clement Greenberg's painterly norms, confronted with Warhol's work, makes a grotesque attempt to regain discursive control and tries to accommodate the blows that the modernist painterly aesthetic had received from Warhol's propositions: "He [Warhol] can in fact now be seen as the sensitive master of a wide variety of surface incident, and a major effect of the experience of looking at his paintings is an unusually immediate awareness of the two-dimensional fact of their painted surfaces.... Both factors underline the reality of the paint itself as a deposit on the surface, quite apart from its interdependence with the image it supports."[41]

When paint is in fact added manually (as in many of the Marilyn and Liz portraits), it is applied in such a vapid manner, detached from gesture as expression as much as it is dislocated from contour as depiction (both features would become hallmarks of Warhol's later portrait work) that it increases rather than contradicts the laconic mechanical nature of the enterprise.

Extracting the photographic image from its painterly ambiguity not only brought the mechanical nature of the reproduction to the foreground but also emphasized the lapidary, factual (rather than "artistic" or "poetical") nature of the image, a quality which seems to have been much more surprising and scandalous to viewers in the early sixties than it is now. Even a critic who in the early sixties was unusually well acquainted with Duchamp and the Dada legacy seems to have been deceived by the apparent crudity of Pop art's factual imagery: "I find his images offensive; I am annoyed to have to see in a gallery what I'm forced to look at in the supermarket. I go to the gallery to get away from the supermarket, not to repeat the experience."[42]

### COMMON ICONOGRAPHY

Warhol's dialogue with Rauschenberg's work finds its parallel in his critical revisions of the legacy of Jasper Johns. If the emblematic centrality of the single image and the allover serial-grid composition were the key compositional devices that Warhol derived from Johns's Targets and Flags, Alphabets and Numbers, then he certainly insisted on counteracting the neutral and universal character of Johns's icons with explicit, mass-cultural images instantly recognizable as the real common denominators of collective perceptual experience. In spite of their commonality, Johns's Alphabets and Numbers, Targets and Flags, by comparison with Warhol's imagery suddenly looked arcane and hermetic, and appeared to represent objects remote from everyday experience. By responding to paintings such as Johns's *Flag on Orange Field, II*, 1958 (figure 20), with his emblematic *Gold Marilyn Monroe*, 1962 (plate 199), Warhol made Johns's work seem to be safely entrenched in a zone of unchallenged high-art hegemony. By contrast, his own new mass-cultural iconography of consumption and the portraits of collective scopic prostitution looked suddenly more specific, more concretely American than the American flag itself, perhaps in the way that Édouard Manet's *Olympia* had appeared more concretely Parisian to the French bourgeois in 1863 than Eugène Delacroix's *Liberté*.

Warhol's drastically different painterly execution (the chintzy monochrome canvas surface, brushed with cheap gold paint and enhanced with a crudely superimposed, silk-screened single photograph) drew the well-crafted quietism of Johns's paintings into an uncomfortable proximity to mass-cultural glamor and crass vulgarity where their high-art status seemed to disintegrate (if it were not for the irrepressible intimation that Warhol's paintings would soon be redeemed as the master-pieces which heralded an era of high art's own

final industrialization).

Several questions remain concerning the status and functions of the photographic imagery silkscreened by Warhol onto his canvases, questions that have been completely obliterated by the sensational effects of Warhol's iconography. In fact, one could say that most of the Warhol (and Pop) literature has merely reiterated the clichés of iconographic reading since the mid-sixties.

The first of these questions concerns the degree to which the sexualization of the commodity and the commodification of sexuality attracted artists, beginning in the early to

20. Jasper Johns. *Flag on Orange Field, II*. 1958. Encaustic on canvas, 54 × 36½″ (137.2 × 92.7 cm). Private collection

mid-fifties. British Pop, in particular, had thrived on juxtapositions of product imagery with (semipornographic) movie-star imagery, and had fused the language of vulgar gossip magazines with that of the idiocy of advertising copy (the most notable examples being Eduardo Paolozzi's *I Was a Rich Man's Plaything*, 1947, or Richard Hamilton's *Just What Is It That Makes Today's Homes So Different, So Appealing?*, 1956.[43] It is also in Rauschenberg's work of the mid- to late fifties that we can find the germination of that iconography and the methods for its display. Warhol's use of this iconography was prefigured not only in the numerous references to mass cultural consumption in Rauschenberg's work of the fifties (for example, *Coca-Cola Plan*, 1958 [figure 21]) but also in the frequent usage of pinup imagery, the serially repeated gossip-column image of Gloria Vanderbilt in *Gloria*, 1956 (figure 22), or the use of an FBI "wanted" poster in *Hymnal*, 1955.

Rather than search for the iconographic sources of Warhol's work, it seems more important to recognize the degree to which postwar consumer culture was a pervasive presence. It appears to have dawned on artists of the fifties that such imagery and objects had irreversibly taken total control of visual representation and public experience. The following exhibition review from 1960 not only indicates that awareness in the work of an artist other than Warhol working at the same time, but also delivers an astonishingly complete and detailed account of the images that Warhol himself subsequently chose as the key figures of his iconographic program: "The show, called 'Les Lions' (Boris Lurie, *Images of Life,* March Gallery, New York, May–June 1960), exciting disturbing nightmares of painting, montages cut out of magazines and newspapers, images of our life held together on canvases with paint …*atom bomb tests* [italics mine] and green Salem Cigarette ads…HomeMade Southern Style Instant Frozen Less Work For You *Tomato Juice.* Obsessively repeated throughout the paintings, girls…*Marilyn,* Brigitte, *Liz* and Jayne, the sweet and sticky narcotics that dull the pain….Life Magazine taken to its final ultimate absurd and frightening conclusion, pain and death given no more space and attention than pictures of Elsa Maxwell's latest party. And all of us spectators at our own death, hovering over it all in narcotized detachment, bored

21. Robert Rauschenberg. *Coca-Cola Plan.* 1958. Combine painting, 27 × 26 × 6″ (68.6 × 66 × 15.2 cm). The Museum of Contemporary Art, Los Angeles. The Panza Collection

22. Robert Rauschenberg. *Gloria.* 1956. Combine painting, 66½ × 63¼″ (168.9 × 168.3 cm). The Cleveland Museum of Art. Gift of the Cleveland Society for Contemporary Art

as gods with *The Bomb,* yawning over The Election, coming to a stop at last only to linger over the tender dream photos of *Marilyn.* (And they call it Life.)"[44]

How common the concern for these images actually was at the end of the fifties and how plausible and necessary Warhol's iconographic choices were becomes even more evident when looking once again at Kaprow's essay "The Legacy of Jackson Pollock." In the last two paragraphs, Kaprow predicts almost literally a number of Warhol's actual iconographic types (or, did Kaprow read these types from the same Rauschenberg paintings that Warhol had absorbed?): "Not only will these bold creators show us as if for the first time the world we have always had about us, but ignored, but they will disclose entirely unheard of happenings and events found in garbage cans, *police files,* hotel lobbies, seen in *store windows* and on the streets, and sensed in dreams and *horrible accidents* [italics mine]. . . . The young artist of today need no longer say 'I am a painter' or 'a poet' or 'a dancer.' All of life will be open to him. He will discover out of ordinary things the meaning of ordinariness. He will not try to make them extraordinary. Only their meaning will be stated. But out of nothing he will devise the extraordinary, and then maybe nothingness as well. People will be delighted, or horrified, critics will be confused or amused, but these, I am sure, will be the alchemies of the 1960's."[45]

In 1963 Warhol juxtaposed the most famous (and common) photographic images of glamorous stars with the most anonymous (and cruel) images of everyday life: photojournalists' images of automobile accidents and suicides (culled from an archive of photographs rejected even by the daily papers for their unbearable horror of detail). In the following year Warhol constructed another dialectic pair of photographic conventions: the police mug shot, from FBI "wanted" posters depicting the *Thirteen Most Wanted Men,* and the photo-booth picture, in his earliest series of self-portraits (plate 3).[46]

Warhol thus grouped together the photographic conventions that regulate social practices of looking: looking at the Other (in envy at fame and fortune, and in sadistic secrecy at catastrophe), and at the disappearing Self (in futile substitutes). And he articulated the dialectic of the photographic image as social representation with astonishing programmatic clar-

23. "The Personality of the Artist." Announcement for exhibition *Warhol*, Stable Gallery, New York, 1964

ity: "My death series was divided into two parts, the first one famous deaths and the second one people nobody ever heard of. . . . It's not that I feel sorry for them, it's just that people go by and it doesn't really matter to them that someone unknown was killed. . . . I still care about people but it would be much easier not to care, it's too hard to care."[47]

In a later interview, in 1972, Warhol described the dialectic of Self and Other in his images of death in terms that would seem to confirm, after all, that an early knowledge of Bertolt Brecht had left its mark on the self-declared indifferent cynic: "Actually you know it wasn't the idea of accidents and things like that, it's just something about, well it all started with buttons, I always wanted to know who invented buttons and then I thought of all the people who worked on the pyramids and then all those, I just always sort of wondered whatever happened to them why aren't they along, so I always thought, well it would be easier to do a painting of people who died in car crashes because sometimes you know, you never know who they are. . . . The people that you know they want to do things and they never do things and they disappear so quickly, and then they're killed or something like that you know, nobody knows about them so I thought well maybe I'll do a painting about a person which you don't know about or something like that. . . ."[48]

Early in 1964 Warhol used a photo-booth auto-portrait as the poster to announce his sec-

ond individual exhibition in New York (figure 23), and it seems that his simultaneous attraction to both the anonymous mug shot and the photo-booth portrait originated in the automatic photograph's achievement of destroying the last remnants of specialized artistic vision. Paradoxically, while denying the validity of manual skill and technical expertise, the photo-booth picture concretized (however grotesquely) the growing need for collective representation and made that instant representation universally accessible. In the automatic portraits of the photo booth the "author" of the picture had, in fact, finally become a machine (Warhol's frequently stated desire).

The systematic devaluation of the hierarchies of representational techniques corresponds to the abolition of the hierarchy of subjects worth while representing, as Warhol's most famous dictum makes clear: "In the future everybody will be famous for fifteen minutes." It was only logical that Warhol sent the first patrons to commission their own portraits to the photo booth, as the accounts of Ethel Scull (plate 325) and Holly Solomon (figure 24) testify.

While Warhol constructed images of Marilyn Monroe, Elizabeth Taylor, and Elvis Presley that refer to the tragicomical conditions of their existence in glamor, the lasting fascination of these paintings does not originate in the myth of these figures but in the fact that Warhol constructed their images from the perspective of the tragic condition of those who consume the stars' images: "I made my earliest films using for several hours just one actor on the screen doing the same thing: eating or sleeping or smoking: I did this because people usually just go to the movies to see only the star, to eat him up, so here at last is a chance to look only at the star for as long as you like no matter what he does and to eat him up all you want to. It was also easier to make."[49]

The dialectic of spectacle-culture and collective compulsion, revealing in every image that glamor is only the stunning reflex of collective scopic fixation, permeates Warhol's entire oeuvre. It culminates in his films, which operate in the movie theater as real-time experience during an expanded viewing time as a deconstruction of the audience's participation in that compulsion; at the same time they operate on the screen as instances of collective enablement, grotesque and deranged as the agents of 53

24. Andy Warhol. *Portrait of Holly Solomon*. 1966. Silkscreen ink on synthetic polymer paint on canvas; nine panels, overall 6′ 9″ × 6′ 9″ (205.7 × 205.7 cm). Collection Holly Solomon

a coat of silver-aluminum paint and letting them speak of having been silenced into abstract monochromy (plate 301).

## SERIAL BREAKDOWN AND DISPLAY

The endless discussions of Warhol's Pop iconography, and, even more, those of his work's subsequent definition in terms of traditional painting,[52] have oversimplified his intricate reflections on the status and substance of the painterly object and have virtually ignored his efforts to incorporate context and display strategies into the works themselves. Features that were aggressively antipictorial in their impulse and evidently among Warhol's primary concerns in the early exhibitions have been obliterated in the process of the acculturation of his art. This is true for his first exhibition at Irving Blum's Ferus Gallery in Los Angeles in 1962 and his second exhibition at that gallery a year later, and also for numerous proposals for some of the subsequent exhibitions, between 1963 and 1966. On the one hand, the installation of the thirty-two paintings at the Ferus Gallery was determined by the number of varieties of Campbell's soup available at that time (Warhol actually used a list of Campbell's products to mark off those flavors that had already been painted). Thus, the number of objects in an exhibition of high art was determined by the

that enablement might appear in the uncensored and unstructured, decentralized and rambling performances by individuals who have not been trained in the professional delivery of visual seduction. Warhol has declared the intentions of his real-time film projects with his usual clarity: "Well this way I can catch people being themselves instead of setting up a scene and shooting it and letting people act out parts that were written because it's better to act out naturally than act like someone else because you really get a better picture of people being themselves instead of trying to act like they're themselves."[50]

The subversive humor of Warhol's reversal of representational hierarchies culminated in his execution of a commission he had received with several other Pop artists from architect

Philip Johnson in 1964 to decorate the facade of the New York State Pavilion at the New York World's Fair. It was for this occasion that the collection of diptychs and single-panel portraits of the *Thirteen Most Wanted Men* (figure 25; plates 287–300) was originally produced, and it comes as no surprise that Warhol's realistic sabotage of a state government's desire to represent itself officially to the world was rejected under the pretext of legalistic difficulties.[51] When Warhol was notified of the decision that his paintings had to be removed he suggested that the pictures of the thieves be replaced by pictures of one of the chiefs, World's Fair director and park commissioner Robert Moses—a proposal that was also rejected. Warhol, with laconic detachment, settled for the most "obvious" solution, covering the paintings with

25. Andy Warhol. *Thirteen Most Wanted Men*. 1964. Installation view, New York State Pavilion, New York World's Fair, 1964

external factor of a product line. (What system, one should ask on this occasion, normally determines the number of objects in an exhibition?) On the other hand, the paintings' mode of display was as crucial as were the principle of serial repetition and their commercial, ready-made iconography. Standing on small white shelves running along the perimeter of the gallery in the way that display shelves for consumer

26. Installation view, *Campbell's Soup Cans*, Ferus Gallery, Los Angeles, 1962

objects would normally function in a store, the paintings were simultaneously attached to the wall in the way that pictures would be traditionally installed in a gallery (figure 26).[53] And finally, there is the inevitable dimension of Warhol's own biography explaining why he chose the Campbell's Soup Can image: "I used to drink it. I used to have the same lunch everyday, for twenty years, I guess, the same thing over and over again."[54]

All three factors affect the work itself, and take a reading of it beyond the mere "scandalous" Pop imagery for which it mostly became known. What has been misread as provocative banality is, in fact, the concrete realization of the paintings' reified existence, which denies the traditional expectation of an aesthetic object's legibility. Warhol's work abolishes the claim for aesthetic legibility with

the same rigor with which those systems of everyday determination deny the experience of subjectivity.

Yet, at the same time, these paintings are imbued with an eerie concreteness and corporeality, which in 1961 had distinguished Piero Manzoni's *Merda d'artista*. But Warhol differs here—as in his relationship to Johns's imagery—in that he transferred the universality of corporeal experience onto the paradoxical level of mass-cultural specificity (not bodily consumption but product consumption forms the material base of experience).

The absurdity of the individual, aesthetic decision-making process becomes all the more patent in the variations of details in the soup-can labels. It is precisely in the exact imitation of the minute variations and in the exact obedience to the available range of products that the series of Campbell's Soup Can paintings goes far beyond what has been perceived as a mere iconographic scandal.

Inevitably, the Campbell's Soup Cans of 1962 and their installation recall a crucial moment of neo-avant-garde history when seriality, monochromy, and mode of display broke down the reign of the easel painting: Yves Klein's installation of eleven identical

blue monochrome paintings in the Galleria Apollinaire in Milan in 1957 (repeated a few months later in Paris). Commenting on his exhibition Klein said: "All of these blue propositions, all alike in appearance, were recognized by the public as quite different from one another. The *amateur* passed from one to another as he liked and penetrated, in a state of instantaneous contemplation, into the worlds of the blue.... The most sensational observation was that of the 'buyers.' Each selected out of the...pictures that one that was his, and each paid the asking price. The prices were all different of course."[55]

Klein's installation (and his commentary on it) reveals both the degree of similarity between his attitude and that of Warhol's serial breakdown of modernist painting, and the radical difference between the two propositions, separated by five years. While Klein's high-culture conservatism clearly intended to create a paradox, paralleling that of painting's simultaneous existence as commodity and renewed metaphysical aspirations, Warhol's position of relentless affirmation cancelled any such aspirations and liquidated the metaphysical dimension of the modernist legacy by rigorously subjecting each painting to an identical product image and price.

That the serial breakdown of the painterly object and its repetition within the display were not just a topical idea for his first exhibition but, rather, a crucial aesthetic strategy, became evident in 1968, when Warhol was approached by Mario Amaya to install his first European retrospective exhibition at the Institute of Contemporary Art in London. Warhol suggested the installation of the series of thirty-two Campbell's Soup Can paintings throughout the entire space allocated for his show as the exclusive subject of the retrospective. Amaya refused this proposal just as the curators at the Whitney Museum of American Art in New York refused Warhol's 1970 proposal to install only Flower paintings or Cow Wallpaper (glued backwards onto the exhibition walls) as the contents of his retrospective exhibition at that institution.[56] For his second exhibition at the Ferus Gallery, in 1963 (the first one seems to have been at best a *succès de scandale,* judging by the fact only a few of the paintings, each offered at $300, were sold), Warhol suggested once again a "monographic" exhibition, the recently produced series of single and multiple Elvis images, silkscreened on large monochrome silver surfaces. In fact, he apparently suggested that the "paintings" should be installed as a "continuous surround," and he shipped a single continuous roll of canvas containing the silkscreened images to Los Angeles.[57]

As in his first installation in Los Angeles, this proposition threatened the boundaries of painting as an individual and complete pictorial unit. But now it not only subverted what remained of that status via serial repetition, but destroyed it altogether by the sheer spatial expansion of that repetition. What had been a real difficulty for Pollock, the final aesthetic decision of how and where to determine the size of painterly action, or, as Harold Rosenberg put it, how to avoid crossing over into the production of "apocalyptic wallpaper," had now become a promise fulfilled by Warhol's deliberate transgression of those sacred limits.

It was, therefore, utterly logical that Warhol conceived an installation of wallpaper for his supposedly final exhibition as a "painter" at the Leo Castelli Gallery in 1966, wallpaper imprinted with the by now notorious (then utterly bland) image of a cow, that animal whose reputation it is to have a particularly vapid and intent gaze. Juxtaposed with the Cow Wallpaper was Warhol's series of floating silver "pillows," the Silver Clouds, which moved through the gallery, animated by air and visitors' body movements (plates 302, 305). Rumor has it that Warhol said of the cows, "This is all of us." But the decor would not have needed that statement to make its point: all of modernism's most radical and utopian promises (to evolve from pictorial plane through sculptural object to architectural space, to shift the viewer from iconic representation to the self-reflexive, the indexical sign and the tactile mode of participation) are annihilated in this farcical sacking of the modernist legacy, the atopian *finale* of the first ten years of Warhol's art.

Warhol's art until 1966 (as opposed to his films) thus oscillates constantly between an extreme challenge to the status and credibility of painting and a continued deployment of strictly pictorial means operating within the narrowly defined framework of pictorial conventions. Inevitably, the question arises (and it has been asked again and again) whether or why Warhol never crossed the threshold into the actual conception (or, rather, reconstitution) of

the ready-made object. Except for the occasional joke campaign, such as signing actual Campbell's soup cans, Warhol would never use the three-dimensional ready-made object in its unaltered industrial existence, as a raw object of consumption. Yet at the same time he would go further than any of his peers in Pop art (not, however, as far as many of his peers in the Fluxus movement) to challenge the traditional assumptions about the uniqueness, authenticity, and authorship of the pictorial object, the very foundations upon which high modernist art had rested until Duchamp defined the Readymade in 1917, and upon which the reconstruction of modernism had rested in the New York School until the arrival of Warhol in 1962. Again and again, Warhol tantalized collectors, curators, and dealers by generating doubts about the authenticity and authorship of his work and actually succeeded in destabilizing his own market. For example: "I made multiple color silkscreen painting—like my comic strip technique. Why don't you ask my assistant Gerard Malanga some questions? He did a lot of my paintings."[58]

Two contradictory explanations seem to be necessary here. The first is that Warhol emerged from a local tradition of artists who had distinguished themselves by pictorializing the Dada legacy in their engagement with the heroic tradition of the New York School. In the early sixties Warhol aspired to the power and success of Johns and Rauschenberg, not to the increasing marginalization that awaited artistic practices that had abandoned picture making (Happenings and Fluxus, for example). The critical distance that Warhol wanted to insert between himself and his two major predecessors would thus still have to occur first of all within the means of painting. Warhol, therefore, had to work through the last phases of the pictorialization begun by Rauschenberg and Johns, and go to the threshold of painting's abolition, a consequence which would soon emerge, mediated to a considerable degree by Warhol's work, in the context of Minimal and Conceptual art.

The second explanation is more speculative and assumes that Warhol was so deeply involved with the pictorial medium, the autonomy of aesthetic conventions and the stability of artistic categories inherent in that medium, because he gradually had learned to accept the relative conventionality of his audience and of

the institutional control and validation of that medium. Therefore, he decided not to transgress these conservative limitations inherent in painterly practice and refrained from acquiring (or reconstituting) the status of the unaltered Readymade in any of his works until 1966. Perhaps it was Warhol's skeptical and opportunistic positivism (to anticipate that all radical gestures within the framework of high-art production would end up as mere "pictures" in a gallery) that allowed him to avoid the mistakes inherent in Duchamp's radical proposition of the Readymade. Duchamp had in fact been oblivious to both the false radicality of the Readymade and the problem of its inevitable aestheticization. One of the rare comments Duchamp actually made about Warhol's work seems to indicate that he himself understood that implication after all when looking at Warhol's work: "What interests us is the *concept* that wants to put fifty Campbell's Soup cans on a canvas."[59]

### RECEPTION

The recognition of Warhol's ingenuity and radicality obviously depended to a considerable degree on the historical limitations of his original audiences: in fact his strategies could appear to be scandalous only in the face of the New York School climate of the late fifties and that generation's general indifference, most often fused with aggressive contempt—as exemplified by Clement Greenberg—for the Dada and Duchamp legacy. By contrast, Warhol's interventions in the aesthetics of the early sixties would seem fully plausible and necessary to a viewer aware of the implications of the Dada legacy in terms of that movement's continual emphasis on and reflection of the symbiotic ties between the aesthetics of art production and those of commodity production.

Warhol's "scandalous" assaults on the status and the "substance" of pictorial representation were motivated by the rapidly dwindling options of credible artistic production (a fact that had become more and more apparent as the conventions of modernism and avant-garde practice had been finally rediscovered) and even more so by the increasing pressure now exerted by the culture industry on the traditionally exempt space of artistic marginality. Iconography and blague, production procedure and modes of display in Warhol's work mimetically internalize the violence of these changing conditions. His paintings vanish as artistic objects to the same degree as the option to sustain dissent disappears within an organized system of immediate commercial and ideological recuperation.

But of course, as had been the case with Duchamp and Dada before, these practices vehemently celebrated the destruction of the author and the aura, and of artistic skill, while at the same time they recognized in that destruction an irretrievable loss. And yet within this moment of absolute loss, Warhol uncovered the historical opportunity to redefine (aesthetic) experience. To understand the radicality of Warhol's gesture, both with regard to the legacies of Duchamp and Dada and with regard to the immediately preceding and contemporary artistic environment of the Cage legacy, does not minimize his achievements at all.

Quite the contrary: the ambition to make him an all-American Pop artist belittles Warhol's historical scope as much as it underrates the universality of those conditions of experience determining Warhol's work. As early as 1963 Henry Geldzahler described the reasons for this universality with the breathtaking frankness of the imperialist victor: "After the heroic years of Abstract Expressionism a younger generation of artists is working in a new American regionalism, but this time because of the mass media, the regionalism is nationwide, and even exportable to Europe, for we have carefully prepared and reconstructed Europe in our own image since 1945 so that two kinds of American imagery, Kline, Pollock, de Kooning on the one hand, and the Pop artists on the other, are becoming comprehensible abroad."[60]

In the advanced, capitalist European countries Warhol's work was adamantly embraced (at first in West Germany, but subsequently also in France and Italy) as a kind of high-culture version of the preceding and subsequent low-culture cults of all things American. It seems that these cult forms celebrated in masochistic folly the subjection to the massive destruction that the commodity production of late capitalism would hold in store for the postwar European countries. Inevitably, Warhol's work would acquire the suggestion of prophetic foresight.

Therefore, it cannot surprise us to find entrepreneurs, industrialists, and advertising tycoons among the key collectors of Warhol's work in Europe. It seems that they recognize their identity just as well in Warhol's work and perceive it as cultural legitimization. While they are instrumental in inflicting those conditions of enforced consumption that Warhol's work seems to condone passively as "our universal nature," it would still seem that they are mistaken in reading his postures and his artifacts as an affirmative celebration of theirs.

Warhol has unified within his constructs both the entrepreneurial world-view of the late twentieth century and the phlegmatic vision of the victims of that world view, that of the consumers. The ruthless diffidence and strategically calculated air of detachment of the first, allowed to continue without ever being challenged in terms of its responsibility, combines with that of its opposites, the consumers, who can celebrate in Warhol's work their proper status of having been erased as subjects. Regulated as they are by the eternally repetitive gestures of alienated production and consumption, they are barred—as are Warhol's paintings —from access to a dimension of critical resistance.

# NOTES

1. Quoted in Gretchen Berg, "Andy: My True Story," *Los Angeles Free Press* (March 17, 1967), p. 3 (reprinted from *East Village Other*); and Gregory McDonald, "Built-in Obsolescence: Art by Andy Warhol," *Boston Sunday Globe* (October 23, 1966), p. 17.

   For generously sharing research and detailed knowledge of Andy Warhol's work with me in the preparation of this essay, I would like to thank the Department of Painting and Sculpture of The Museum of Modern Art. Equally, I would like to thank The Andy Warhol Foundation for the Visual Arts, for giving me information and access to its archives.

2. *See* Frayda Feldman and Jörg Schellmann, eds., *Andy Warhol Prints: A Catalogue Raisonné* (New York: Ronald Feldman Fine Arts, Editions Schellmann, and Abbeville Press, 1985), pp. 106–07.

3. Patrick Smith has suggested that the script is actually the handwriting of Warhol's mother and that Warhol had a stamp made so he could replicate his mother's naive handwriting at any time. *See* Patrick S. Smith, *Andy Warhol's Art and Films* (Ann Arbor: UMI Research Press, 1986), p. 32.

   The pun on his telephone number, Murray Hill 3-0555, seems to have been a persistent joke; thus, in 1954 he had published an advertisement in *Ergo*, a cooperative brochure by a group of free-lance commercial artists, listing his phone as "Mury heel." *See* Andreas Brown, compiler, *Andy Warhol: His Early Works 1947–1959* (New York: Gotham Book Mart Gallery, 1971), p. 14.

4. Theodor W. Adorno, "Rückblickend auf den Surrealismus," in *Gesammelte Schriften* 11 (Frankfurt: Suhrkamp, 1974), p. 103.

5. Rosalind H. Williams, *Dream Worlds* (Berkeley: University of California Press, 1982), p. 67; quoted in Simon Frith and Howard Horne, *Art into Pop* (New York and London: Methuen, 1987), p. 12.

6. This change of professional identity was, of course, not that abrupt; it appears that Warhol continued to work as a commercial designer at least until 1962.

7. Andy Warhol, "Happy Butterfly Day," published by *Vanity Fair*, c. 1955. The Estate of Andy Warhol.

8. *See* Trevor Fairbrother, "Warhol Meets Sargent at Whitney," *Arts Magazine* 61 (February 1987), pp. 64–71.

9. "New Talent U.S.A.," *Art in America* 50 (1962), p. 42. A reproduction of Andy Warhol's painting *Storm Door*, 1960, was surprisingly included in the "prints and drawings" section of this issue, selected by Zachary Scott, an actor and print collector. The size is incorrectly indicated as 36 × 34″ (as opposed to the painting's actual size of 46 × 42⅛″), which causes one to wonder whether inclusion of the work in this section required some adjustment of medium and size.

10. Perry Anderson, "Modernity and Revolution," *New Left Review* (London) 144 (March–April 1984), p. 106.

11. Allan Kaprow, "Should the Artist Become a Man of the World?" *Artnews* 63 (October 1964), p. 34.

12. Nan Rosenthal has recently discussed the details of the curriculum at Carnegie Institute of Technology and its profound impact on Warhol's education, in a paper delivered at the Warhol symposium organized by the Dia Art Foundation in New York in April 1988.

    Patrick Smith has suggested a comparison between Warhol's mechanization of fine-art production procedures and the ideas taught by Moholy-Nagy at The Institute of Design in Chicago and in his writings, in particular *The New Vision* (1930). Apparently, this book was well known to Warhol and discussed by him and his friends in the late forties. *See* Smith, *Andy Warhol's Art*, pp. 110–12 and nn. 191–205.

13. Douglas Arango, "Underground Films: Art or Naughty Movies," *Movie TV Secrets* (June 1967), n.p.

14. Gretchen Berg, "Nothing to Lose: Interview with Andy Warhol," *Cahiers du Cinéma in English* 10 (May 1967), pp. 38–43.

    In 1971 Warhol said: "If I remember correctly, I felt that if everyone couldn't afford a painting the printed poster would be available...." (Gerard Malanga, "A Conversation with Andy Warhol," *Print Collector's Newsletter* 1 [January–February 1971], pp. 125–27.)

    The same argument for the egalitarian conceptions motivating Pop art was made by Claes Oldenburg, for example: "I think it would be great if you had an art that could appeal to everybody." (Bruce Glaser, "Oldenburg, Lichtenstein, Warhol: A Discussion," *Artforum* 4 [February 1966], pp. 20–24.)

    It is all the more astonishing that one of Pop art's early critical opponents (and subsequent converts) refused to acknowledge the egalitarian potential of Pop art from the beginning (and, in retrospect, it turns out that the skepticism was wholly justified). In her review of Lawrence Alloway's 1963 exhibition *Six Painters and the Object* at The Solomon R. Guggenheim Museum, Barbara Rose wrote: "In the past, when an artist like Courbet or van Gogh appropriated material from popular culture, it was with the intent of reaching a larger public—in fact of producing a kind of elevated popular art. *Pop art in America had no such intention; it was made for the same exclusive and limited public as abstract art*" [italics mine]. ("Pop Art at the Guggenheim," *Art International* 2 [1963], p. 20.)

15. Walter P. Paepcke, "Art in Industry," *Modern Art in Advertising* (Chicago: Paul Theobald, 1946), n.p.

16. *The Philosophy of Andy Warhol (From A to B and Back Again)* (New York: Harcourt Brace Jovanovich, 1975), p. 92.

17. "Boxing Match," *Time* (May 15, 1964), p. 86.

18. Warhol was notorious for consciously employing other people's ideas, and he was quite candid (and coy) about this supposed absence of originality: "I always get my ideas from people. Sometimes I change the idea to suit a certain project I'm working on at the time. Sometimes I don't change the idea. Or, sometimes I don't use the idea right away, but may remember it and use it for something later on. I love ideas." (Malanga, "A Conversation with Andy Warhol," pp. 125–27.)

19. G. R. Swenson, "What Is Pop Art?: Answers from 8 Painters, Part I," *Artnews* 62 (November 1963), pp. 24–27, 60–63.

20. Martha Jackson, letter to Andy Warhol, July 20, 1962. The Estate of Andy Warhol.

21. A similar hesitation with regard to style can be found in the early work of Roy Lichtenstein, who in the late fifties was making the transition from Abstract Expressionism to the deployment of ready-made imagery and ready-made (commercial) techniques of pictorial execution. This led to Warhol's surprise discovery that he had not been the only one to use the iconography of comic strips in his work. What was worse for Warhol was that Leo Castelli at that time believed that his gallery should show only one artist using this type of imagery. Lichtenstein has recorded his memory of his encounter with Warhol's work of this kind: "I saw Andy's work at Leo Castelli's about the same time I brought mine in, about the spring of 1961.... Of course, I was amazed to see Andy's work because he was doing cartoons of Nancy and Dick Tracy and they were very similar to mine." (Glaser, "Oldenburg, Lichtenstein, Warhol," p. 21.)

22. Emile de Antonio's commentary has been reported in two versions. In the first, he said, "One of these is crap. The other is remarkable—it's our society, it's who we are, it's absolutely beautiful and naked, and you ought to destroy the first and show the second." (Jesse Kornbluth, "Andy," *New York* [March 9, 1987], p. 42.)

    The other version confirms the assumption that there was a moment of real hesitation in Warhol's early work: "One day he put up two huge paintings of Coke bottles. Two different ones. One was, I could say, an early Pop Art piece of major importance. It was just a big black-and-white Coke bottle. The other was the same thing except it was surrounded by Abstract Expressionist hatches and crosses. And I said to Andy, 'Why did you do two of these? One of them is so clearly your own. And the second is just kind of ridiculous because it's not anything. It's part Abstract Expressionism and part whatever you're doing.' And the first one was [the only] one that was any good. The other thing—God only knows what it is. And, I think that helped Andy make up his mind as to—you know: that was almost the birth of Pop. Andy did it." (Smith, *Andy Warhol's Art*, p. 97.)

    Warhol followed this advice only partially: he exhibited the "cold" version at his first New York exhibition at the Stable Gallery in 1962 but did not destroy the other version.

23. *See* Carter Ratcliff, *Andy Warhol* (New York: Abbeville Press, 1983), p. 17: "Though Warhol has never changed his personal style, he did abandon commercial art as decisively as he possibly could. The line between his first and second

24. Allan Kaprow, "The Legacy of Jackson Pollock," *Artnews* 57 (October 1958), p. 56.
25. Ibid.
26. For an early example of this argument, *see* Robert Rosenblum, "Pop and Non-Pop: An Essay in Distinction," *Art and Literature* 5 (Summer 1965), pp. 80–93.

    *See also* Alan Solomon, *Andy Warhol* (Boston: Institute of Contemporary Art, 1966), n.p.: "In a broader sense, I suppose the prevalence of cool passivity can be explained as part of the reaction to abstract expressionism, since the present attitude is the polar opposite of the action painting idea of kinetic self-expression. (This has a great deal to do with Warhol's attitudes toward style and performance.)"

    For a more recent example, proving the persistence of this simplistic argument of stylistic innovation, *see* Ratcliff, *Andy Warhol*, p. 7.
27. Kaprow, "The Legacy of Jackson Pollock," p. 56.
28. *See* Michael Crichton, *Jasper Johns* (New York: Whitney Museum of American Art/Harry N. Abrams, 1978), p. 30. Andrew Forge described this new collaborative aesthetic in the context of Rauschenberg's work in terms that equally de-emphasize visuality: "The idea of collaboration with others has preoccupied him endlessly, both through the medium of his own work and in an open situation in which no single person dominates. In *Black Market* (a 1961 combine painting) he invited the onlooker to exchange small objects with the combine and to leave messages." (*Robert Rauschenberg* [New York: Harry N. Abrams, 1972], p. 15.)
29. According to Eleanor Ward, *Dance Diagram (Tango)* was included in Warhol's first individual New York exhibition at her Stable Gallery in 1962 and installed on the floor. *See* Ward's recollection of that exhibition in John Wilcock, ed., *The Autobiography & Sex Life of Andy Warhol* (New York: Other Scenes, 1971), n.p. Subsequently, a Dance Diagram was installed in a horizontal position in Sidney Janis's exhibition *The New Realists* in October 1962 and in Warhol's first "retrospective" exhibition, in 1965 at the Institute of Contemporary Art in Philadelphia. It was a particularly Warholian irony, even if unintended, that the attendance at the exhibition's opening was so great that all the paintings (not just those on the floor) had to be removed from the exhibition for the duration of the preview.
30. Harold Rosenberg, "The American Action Painters," *Artnews* 51 (December 1952), pp. 22–23, 48–50.
31. Quoted in Annabelle Melzer, *Dada and Surrealist Performance* (Ann Arbor: UMI Research Press, 1980), p. 17.

    Such a moment of the "breakdown" of the strategy of the monochrome is poignantly described by Michael Fried in a review of an exhibition of Newman's work in 1962, which he published (as historical chance would have it) side by side with his review of Warhol's first New York exhibition: "From the start—which I take to be the late forties—his art was conceived in terms of its absolute essentials, flat color and a rectilinearity derived from the shape of the canvas, and the earliest paintings on view have a simplicity which is pretty near irreducible....

    "When the equilibrium is not in itself so intrinsically compelling and the handling of the paint is kept adamant the result is that the painting tends not to hold the eye: the spectator's gaze keeps bouncing off, no matter how hard he tries to keep it fixed on the painting. (I'm thinking now most of all of the vertical painting divided into unequal halves of ochre yellow and white dated 1962 in the current show, in which the colours themselves, unlike the warm fields of blue that are perhaps Newman's most effective element—have no inherent depth to them and end up erecting *a kind of hand-ball court wall for the eye*)" [italics mine]. (Michael Fried, "New York Letter," *Art International* 6 [December 1962], p. 57.)

    That the monochrome aspects in the work of Newman were subject to a more general reflection in the early sixties was also indicated by Jim Dine's rather unsuccessful parody *Big Black Zipper*, 1962 (The Sonnabend Collection, Baltimore Museum of Art).
32. A typical example was Rothko's refusal to supply the meditative panels for the Seagram Building's corporate dining room. Kaprow in 1964 cited "the blank canvas" among these critical acts in which the elitist hermeticism and the metaphysical claims of monochromy had been revised: "Pursuit of the idea of 'best' becomes then (insidiously) avoidance of the idea of 'worst' and Value is defeated by paradox. Its most poignant expressions have been the blank canvas, the motionless dance, the silent music, the empty page of poetry. On the edge of such an abyss all that is left to do is *act*." (Kaprow, "Should the Artist Become a Man of the World?" p. 34.)
33. Allan Solomon made the connection between the monochrome paintings and the floating Silver Clouds in 1966, albeit in the rather evasive language of the enthusiastic critic: "When Warhol made the *Clouds* which are floating plastic sculpture, he called them paintings, because he thought of filling them with helium and sending them out of the window, never to return. 'That would be the end of painting,' he said, as serious as not. (He also likes the idea of plain surfaces as ultimate art. Many of his paintings have matching bare panels which he feels increase their beauty appreciably.)" (Solomon, *Andy Warhol*.)

    A year later Warhol described the project in more concise terms: "I didn't want to paint anymore so I thought that the way to finish off painting for me would be to have a painting that floats, so I invented the floating silver rectangles that you fill up with helium and let out of your windows." (Berg, "Nothing to Lose," p. 43.)

    Later, Warhol remembered that it was on the occasion of his exhibition at the Ileana Sonnabend Gallery in Paris, where he had installed the Flower paintings on the recently designed Cow Wallpaper, that he decided to publicly declare the end of painting (or at least his involvement with it): "I was having so much fun in Paris that I decided it was the place to make the announcement I'd been thinking about making for months: I was going to retire from painting. Art just wasn't fun for me anymore." (Andy Warhol and Pat Hackett, *POPism: The Warhol '60s* [New York: Harcourt Brace Jovanovich, 1980], p. 113.)

    It seems noteworthy, once again, that while Warhol considered it appropriate to emphasize ironically that "Paris was the place to make the announcement," some American critics have not been able to acknowledge that Warhol's declaration of silence placed him in a Rimbaud/Duchamp tradition of self-imposed refusal to produce art. *See* Ratcliff, *Andy Warhol*, p. 7, where Warhol's renunciation of painting is identified as a "Garboesque" decision.

    Ten years after his first declaration Warhol, after having taken up painting again, still struggled with the problem (or the pose): "I get so tired of painting. I've been trying to give it up all the time, if we could just make a living out of movies or the newspaper business, or something. It's so boring, painting the same picture over and over." (Quoted in Glenn O'Brien, *High Times* 24 [August 1977], p. 21.)
34. Barry Blinderman, "Modern 'Myths': An Interview with Andy Warhol," *Arts Magazine* 56 (October 1981), pp. 144–47. (Reprinted in Jeanne Siegel, *Artwords 2* [Ann Arbor: UMI Research Press, 1988], p. 16.)
35. One could refer to the complexity of Warhol's critical reflection on *all* of the implications of modernist pictorial conventions and his actual decision to feature these in rather unusual displays in order to point out—if it were not already obvious—how tame and conservative by comparison the so-called Neo-Geo and the neo-Conceptualist artists are in their simple-minded and opportunistic "painting and sculpture" mentality, disguised behind the facade of postmodernist pretense.
36. Roger Vaughan, "Superpop, or a Night at the Factory," *New York Herald Tribune* (August 8, 1965). Ironically, as a member of the staff of the Castelli gallery recalls, many collectors left the blank panel behind when acquiring a diptych by Warhol at that time.
37. One of Rauschenberg's Blueprints was shown in the exhibition *Abstraction in Photography* at The Museum of Modern Art, New York, in May–July 1951, and was listed in the catalogue as *Blueprint: Photogram for Mural Decoration*.

    An article on Rauschenberg's photograms/blueprints was published in "Speaking of Pictures," *Life* (April 19, 1951). *See also* Lawrence Alloway, "Rauschenberg's Development," *Robert Rauschenberg* (Washington, D.C.: National Collection of Fine Arts, Smithsonian Institution, 1976), pp. 16, 63.
38. The complex relationship between Warhol, his

slightly older peer Robert Rauschenberg, and his slightly younger, but considerably more established, peer Jasper Johns remains somewhat elusive. Apparently, Warhol's ambition to be recognized by these two artists was frustrated on several occasions, as Emile de Antonio has reported, for two reasons: first, because Warhol's background as a real commercial artist disqualified him in the eyes of these artists who, if they had to make money, would decorate Bonwit Teller windows under a pseudonym; and second, because, it seems, they sensed that Warhol's work was outflanking theirs. Warhol later reflected on their relationship in a conversation with Emile de Antonio, who remarks: "You're too swish, and that upsets them. . . . You are a commercial artist, which really bugs them because when they do commercial art—windows and other jobs I find them—they do it just 'to survive.' They won't even use their real names. Whereas you've won prizes! You're famous for it." (*POPism*, pp. 11–12.) Or: "Rauschenberg and Jasper Johns didn't want to meet Andy at the beginning. . . . Andy was too effeminate for Bob and Jap. . . . I think his openly commercial work made them nervous. . . . They also, I think, were suspicious of what Andy was doing—his serious work—because it had obvious debts to both of them in a funny way." (Smith, *Andy Warhol's Art*, pp. 294–95.)

Leo Castelli remembers Warhol visiting his gallery in 1958–59 as "a great admirer of Rauschenberg and Jasper Johns and he even bought a drawing, a good one, a light bulb drawing of Jasper Johns." (In David Bailey, *Andy Warhol: Transcript of David Bailey's ATV Documentary* [London: Bailey Litchfield/Mathews Miller Dunbar Ltd, 1972], n.p.) *See also* Ann Hindry, "Andy Warhol: Quelques grand témoins: Sidney Janis, Leo Castelli, Robert Rosenblum, Clement Greenberg," *Artstudio* (Paris, 1988), p. 115. Recognition by his peers seems to have occurred after all, since in the mid-sixties both Johns and Rauschenberg became owners of one or more paintings by Warhol.

39. For example, both Kaprow and Robert Watts were already omitted from Sidney Janis's crucial exhibition *The New Realists* in 1962, and their absence was explained in Sidney Janis's preface to the catalogue as due to "limitation of space." *See* Sidney Janis, "On the Theme of the Exhibition," *The New Realists* (New York: Sidney Janis Gallery, 1962), n.p.

40. Arango, "Underground Films."

41. Richard Morphet, "Andy Warhol," in *Warhol* (London: Tate Gallery, 1971), p. 6. Another, equally desperate attempt to detach Warhol's iconography from the reading of his work in order to force it back into the discursive strictures of (Greenbergian) modernism was made on the occasion of Warhol's exhibition at the Stable Gallery in 1962 by Donald Judd: "The subject matter is a cause for both blame and excessive praise. Actually it is not very interesting to think about the reasons, since it is easy to imagine Warhol's

paintings without such subject matter, simply as 'overall' paintings of repeated elements. The novelty and the absurdity of the repeated images of Marilyn Monroe, Troy Donahue and Coca-Cola bottles is not great. . . . The gist of this is that Warhol's work is able but general. It certainly has possibilities, but it is so far not exceptional. It should be considered as it is, as should anyone's, and not be harmed or aided by being part of a supposed movement, 'pop,' 'O.K.,' neo-Dada or New Realist or whatever it is." (Donald Judd, "Andy Warhol," *Arts Magazine* [January 1963], reprinted in Donald Judd, *Complete Writings 1959–1975* [Halifax and New York: Press of Nova Scotia College of Art and Design and New York University Press, 1975], p. 70.)

42. Barbara Rose, "Pop Art at the Guggenheim," pp. 20–22. (It is not quite clear from the text whether this statement relates to Warhol or Lichtenstein, but, in any case, it indicates the intense shock of factuality that the new mass-cultural iconography of Pop art provided even to well-prepared eyes.)

In 1962 Sidney Janis identified the artists in his exhibition *The New Realists* as "Factualists," and distinguished them from Rauschenberg and others who are "less factual than they are poetic or expressionist." (Janis, *New Realists*.) In his review of Warhol's movie *The Chelsea Girls*, Andrew Sarris recognized this "factualist" quality in Warhol's work and went as far as comparing Warhol's film to one of the key works in the history of documentary film: "*The Chelsea Girls* is actually closer to *Nanook of the North* than to *The Knack*. It is as *documentary* that *The Chelsea Girls* achieves its greatest distinction." (Andrew Sarris, "The Sub–New York Sensibility," *Cahiers du Cinéma* [May 1967], p. 43.)

43. For a recent discussion of the history of British Pop art, *see* Brian Wallis, *This Is Tomorrow Today* (New York: Institute for Art and Urban Resources, 1987).

44. Bill Manville, "Boris Lurie, March Gallery, Images of Life," *The Village Voice* (June 16, 1960).

45. Kaprow, "The Legacy of Jackson Pollock," p. 57.

46. It should be remembered that the identification of the artist with the criminal is one of the *topoi* of modernity since Baudelaire and that the identification of the two roles would have been familiar to Warhol from his readings of Jean Genet, to whom he referred on several occasions. Of course, as has been pointed out before, the conflation of the artist's portrait with the police mug shot goes back to Duchamp, who had superimposed the image of the artist over that of the "Most Wanted Man" in his rectified Readymade *Wanted $2,000 Reward*, 1923. Duchamp had included a replica of this Readymade in his *Boîte-en-valise* in 1941, and had also used the image quite appropriately for the poster of his first American retrospective at the Pasadena Art Museum in 1963. Warhol attended the opening of this exhibition and it is quite likely that the poster initiated Warhol's *Thirteen Most Wanted Men* in 1964. Furthermore, as Patrick Smith has pointed out, Rauschenberg had

used an FBI "wanted" poster in *Hymnal*, 1955.

The use of the photo-booth strip leads directly into the work of Jasper Johns, particularly in the image of an unidentified man in *Flag Above White with Collage* (1955), but also the self-portraits by Johns used in *Souvenir I* and *II*, 1964.

For the cover of *Time* magazine in 1965 Warhol used a whole series of photo-booth pictures, and there are still dozens of photo-booth strips of Warhol and his friends in the Warhol archives.

47. Warhol, as quoted by Peter Gidal, *Andy Warhol: Films and Paintings* (London and New York: Studio Vista, 1971), p. 38.

48. Bailey, *Andy Warhol: Transcript.*

The statement about the anonymous people who built the pyramids is of course an unconscious quotation from Bertolt Brecht's famous poem "Questions from a Worker Who Reads." An early argument for the profound influence of Brecht's work on Warhol had been made by Rainer Crone in his monograph (*Andy Warhol* [New York: Praeger, 1970]), partially on the evidence of one reference by Warhol to Brecht in his 1963 interview with Gene Swenson. More recently, Patrick Smith has anxiously attempted to detach Warhol from this political affiliation on the grounds of totally unconvincing "memories" by early acquaintances of Warhol, who were interviewed by Smith. *See* Patrick S. Smith, "Theatre 12 and Broadway," in *Warhol: Conversations About the Artist* (Ann Arbor: UMI Research Press, 1988), p. 41; and Smith, *Andy Warhol's Art*, pp. 78ff.

49. Berg, "Nothing to Lose," p. 40. In this regard, Michael Fried's brilliant review of Warhol's first New York exhibition has been proven wrong, since it is not the dependence of Warhol's images on mass-cultural myths but participation in mass-cultural experience that animates the work: "An art like Warhol's is necessarily parasitic upon the myths of its time, and indirectly therefore upon the machinery of fame and publicity that markets these myths; and it is not at all unlikely that these myths that move us will be unintelligible (or at best starkly dated) to generations that follow. This is said not to denigrate Warhol's work but to characterize it and the risks it runs—and, I admit, to register an advance protest against the advent of a generation that will not be as moved by Warhol's beautiful, vulgar, heart breaking icons of Marilyn Monroe as I am." (Fried, "New York Letter," p. 57.)

50. In *Andy Warhol's Index (Book)* (New York: Random House, 1967), n.p.

51. The argument was that some of the criminals depicted in the *Thirteen Most Wanted Men* had already received fair trial and that their images could therefore no longer be publicly displayed. Previously (see Crone, *Andy Warhol*), this decision was attributed to Governor Nelson A. Rockefeller; however, recent research has placed this in some doubt, suggesting that the decision was made by the fair's officials. Apparently the decision to censor the second proposal by Warhol as

well caused a considerable strain on Philip Johnson's relationship with Warhol: "'And then he proposed to show a portrait of Robert Moses instead of the *Thirteen Most Wanted Men*?' 'Yes, that's right . . . since he was the boss of the World's Fair, but I prohibited that. . . . Andy and I had a quarrel at that time, even though he is one of my favorite artists.'" (Crone, *Andy Warhol*, p. 30.)

52. The first step in this direction was, as usual, to convince Warhol that each work had to be signed individually by him (no longer by his mother, for example, as in the days of being a commercial artist), in spite of the fact that he had originally considered it to be crucial to *abstain* from signing his work: "People just won't buy things that are unsigned. . . . It's so silly. I really don't believe in signing my work. Anyone could do the things I am doing and I don't feel they should be signed." (Vaughan, "Superpop," p. 7.)

53. As early as 1961–62 Claes Oldenburg created a programmatic fiction of a store (*The Store*) as a framing institution for the production and reception of his work.

54. Swenson, "What Is Pop Art?" p. 26.

55. This is not to suggest that Warhol knew about Klein's exhibition; quite the opposite. The parallels indicate to what extent these gestures originated in a universal condition. However, one should note that Klein had an exhibition at the Leo Castelli Gallery in New York in April 1961 and in May–June of the same year at the Dwan Gallery in Los Angeles, both titled *Yves le monochrome*. Warhol was certainly interested in Klein's work at a later point in his life, when he acquired two paintings by Klein in the mid-seventies. For an extensive discussion of Klein's project and his own commentaries on this exhibition, *see* Nan Rosenthal, "Assisted Levitation: The Art of Yves Klein," in *Yves Klein* (Houston and New York: Institute for the Arts, Rice University, and Arts Publisher, 1982), pp. 91–135.

56. For an excellent, detailed discussion of Warhol's reflections on exhibition formats, *see* Charles F. Stuckey, "Andy Warhol's Painted Faces," *Art in America* (May 1980), pp. 102–11. My remarks are indebted to this essay in many ways, as well as to a presentation by Stuckey at the Warhol symposium at the Dia Art Foundation in New York in April 1988.

57. *See* John Coplans, "Andy Warhol and Elvis Presley," *Studio International* (February 1971), pp. 49–56. There are slightly conflicting opinions about who made the decision to stretch the canvas on stretchers: Coplans suggests that it was Warhol who sent the stretchers prefabricated to size from New York (which doesn't seem to make a lot of sense); Wolfgang Siano, in his essay "Die Kunst Andy Warhol's im Verhältnis zur Oeffentlichkeit" (in Erika Billeter, ed., *Andy Warhol* [Bern, 1971]), suggests (without giving his source) that it was originally Warhol's intention to install the canvas roll continuously along the perimeter of the gallery walls and that it was the decision of Irving Blum to divide the canvas roll into segments and stretch them as paintings. More recently, Gerard Malanga has voiced doubts that a roll of that size could have been screened continuously in the space available at the Factory at that time.

58. *See* Nat Finkelstein, "Inside Andy Warhol," *Cavalier Magazine* (September 1966), p. 88.

   As late as 1971 Warhol would still dispute the curator's and collector's insistence on the stability of artistic categories (and thereby weaken his work's institutional value): "I suppose you could call the paintings prints, but the material used for the paintings was canvas. . . . Anyone can do them." *See* Malanga, "Conversation with Andy Warhol," p. 127. Even after he resumed painting in 1968 Warhol disseminated rumors that the new paintings were in fact executed by his friend Brigid Polk. As she stated in *Time* magazine (October 17, 1969): "Andy? I've been doing it all for the last year and a half, two years. Andy doesn't do art anymore. He's bored with it. I did all his new soup cans."

   By contrast, since the mid-seventies, quite appropriately for both the general situation of a return to traditional forms of easel painting and his own complacent opportunism, Warhol recanted those rumors, not, however, without turning the screw once again. Answering the question of whether collectors had actually called him and tried to return their paintings after Polk's statement, Warhol said: "Yes, but I really do all the paintings. We were just being funny. If there are any fakes around I can tell. . . . The modern way would be to do it like that, but I do them all myself." *See* Blinderman, "Modern 'Myths': An Interview," pp. 144–47; and Siegel, *Artwords 2*, p. 21.

   A similar attitude is displayed by Warhol in a series of photographs that were used as endpapers for Carter Ratcliff's monograph, where Warhol, staring into the camera, displays the tools of painting.

59. Quoted in Gidal, *Andy Warhol*, p. 27.

   According to both Teeny Duchamp and John Cage, Marcel Duchamp was apparently quite fond of Warhol's work (which does not really come as a surprise); *see* David Bailey's interviews with Teeny Duchamp and John Cage in his *Andy Warhol: Transcript*.

60. Henry Geldzahler, in Peter Selz, ed., "A Symposium on Pop Art," *Arts Magazine* (April 1963) pp. 18ff. Ten years later Geldzahler would address the question of the European success of Pop art once again, slightly toned down, but no less imperialist in attitude, and certainly confusing the course of historical development: "And the question is why would Germany be particularly interested in this American phenomenon and the reason goes back, I think, to a remark that Gertrude Stein made quite early in the twentieth century which is that America is the oldest country in the world because it entered the twentieth century first and the point really is that the Germans in their postwar boom got into a mood that America was in in the twenties and Andy essentializes the American concentration on overabundance of commercial objects." The fact is that the "mood that America was in in the twenties" had been the mood that the Europeans had been in in the twenties, as well, and that mood had generated Dadaism, the very artistic legacy at the origin of Pop art.

# DO IT YOURSELF: NOTES ON WARHOL'S TECHNIQUES

*BY MARCO LIVINGSTONE*

The common perception of Andy Warhol as a man-machine—passive, indifferent, and reveling in mechanical anonymity and repetitiveness—has carried with it the assumption that his art relied very little on his personal intervention. He often led the public to believe that his art could thus be made by others using images and subjects that were not even invented by him. He employed assistants throughout his life and consistently presented himself merely as a mediator. The Do It Yourself paintings of 1962 (plates 153–159) are emblematic of this. Based on paint-by-number kits, these ironic statements about individual creativity were among the last canvases Warhol painted by hand before turning to the assembly-line production methods of silkscreen printing: "I tried doing them by hand," he later remarked, "but I find it easier to use a screen. This way, I don't have to work on my objects at all. One of my assistants or anyone else, for that matter, can reproduce the design as well as I could."[1]

This abnegation of personal responsibility and involvement has generally been taken at face value, while the numerous, bewildering interpretations that have been imposed on his work—from the political to the social—fail to square with his insistence that no such meanings were intended. It may be that his own advice has not been taken seriously enough: "If you want to know all about Andy Warhol, just look at the surface of my paintings and me, and there I am. There's nothing behind it."[2] Often taken as a provocative, ambiguous avowal of his own superficiality and emptiness, it may have been a plain statement of fact: that any search for meaning in his work need go no further than the surfaces on which he provided all the necessary evidence of the procedures and preprocessed imagery that make his art. It is to such technical matters, and to their implications for the themes of Warhol's work, that this essay is devoted.

Beginning with the blotted-line technique of his commercial art of the fifties (figure 1) and ending with his final works on canvas, screen printed from photographic enlargements of his own drawings, Warhol devised numerous ways—both obvious and devious—of creating surfaces that looked as though they had barely been touched by his hand. Thus, a deliberate ambiguity between what is printed and what is painted or drawn, between tasks and decisions executed by someone else and

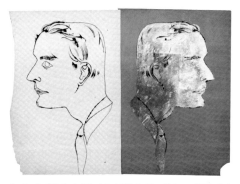

1. Andy Warhol. *Untitled (Male Profile).* c. 1957. Ink and gold leaf on paper, 18 × 25½″ (45.8 × 64.7 cm). The Estate of Andy Warhol

those that only he could undertake, between chance and control, becomes a crucial feature of Warhol's art, and lends support to the notion that what his art was about was, in large part, its methods and mediums—in other words, just what is on the surface.

Collaboration with others was an essential part of this enterprise. While working as a commercial artist in the fifties Warhol employed his first assistants, notably Nathan Gluck, from 1955 to 1964. In the early sixties he had casual help on the mechanical tasks necessary for making his paintings, and from June 1963 to August 1967, and again from September 1968 to November 1970, he employed Gerard Malanga as a full-time assistant, pri-

marily to assist him with screen printing. In 1972, after a period during which he was doing less painting, he hired another assistant, Ronnie Cutrone, many of whose tasks were taken over by Jay Shriver in 1980, and from February 1977 he employed Rupert Smith particularly for screen printing.[3]

Warhol's assistants and associates attest to the fact that he seemed to need collaboration not just to satisfy a high level of production, but as a means of seeking security and reassurance and of avoiding the solitude of the studio.[4] He was always open to suggestions, not only from them but from almost anyone he happened to meet: "I was never embarrassed about asking someone, literally, 'What should I paint?' because Pop comes from the outside, and how is asking someone for ideas any different from looking for them in a magazine?"[5] Although the people he worked with closely soon got to know what he wanted, and learned to work in his style, Warhol liked to allow them the latitude of "minor misunderstandings" by which they could "transmute" rather than merely "transmit" his ideas.[6]

The systems devised by Warhol allowed sufficient variation, either through the introduction of chance or through input from others, to create an unpredictable result: "My paintings never turn out the way I expect them to but I'm never surprised."[7] To this end he sometimes was intentionally vague about what he wanted from others, not out of indecision but to multiply the variables. As Malanga laconically recalls, "His vagueness was pretty precise."[8] However much Warhol may have benefited from his two-heads-are-better-than-one philosophy, he remained fully in control of decisions as to what and how to paint, taking ideas about subject matter only if they suited his needs; he controlled the work by setting the parameters during production and by surveying and approving the final result.[9]

Even before he left Pittsburgh for New York in 1949, Warhol had developed working methods that were arrived at less by deliberation than by intuition and a canny exploitation of chance and accident. The first such technique, which sustained him in his highly successful commercial work of the fifties, was an irregular, blotted line, which he discovered as a student when using blotting paper on one of his ink drawings; he immediately liked the effect of the transferred imprint, in part because it allowed him to imagine what his drawings would look like in reproduction.[10] The process was, indeed, a primitive kind of printmaking or monotype.[11] Warhol would generally begin by drawing in pencil on a nonabsorbent paper, sometimes copying or tracing the image from a photograph. This sheet was then hinged to a second sheet of more absorbent Strathmore paper so that the outline of the master drawing, retraced in India ink with an old fountain pen,[12] could be transferred by folding the sheet over and pressing the two together. The final drawing would develop in a succession of such operations, a section of line at a time, until the image was complete. The resulting outline, although hesitant and broken in appearance, looked unplanned while still being very much under his control. Once the transfer was completed, the master was often discarded. Although some pairs still survive hinged together, there is no evidence that Warhol intended them to be seen in that way.

Although Warhol continued through the fifties to produce continuous-line drawings with ball-point pen, for example in his essentially private drawings of boys, it was the blotted-line technique that offered him the greatest scope for his more public art. In the first of many reversals that came to characterize his methods, he exchanged the usual definitions of the terms *original* and *copy*, not only by asserting the pre-eminence of the transferred image, which presented his personal touch at one remove, but also by devising a system whereby a number of virtually identical images could be produced from a single sheet simply by retracing the pencil line in ink. The so-called copies, however, like Warhol's later screen-printed images, never came out exactly the same twice because of variations in the thickness and weight of the ink. The images, moreover, could be colored in with Dr. Martin's aniline

2. Christmas card for I. Miller, depicting Warhol's wood shoes

watercolor dyes or filled in with gold leaf or a cheaper substitute called Dutch metal, applied in blocks on a water-based glue, for a more glamorous, shimmering surface. In such cases the drawing might be reblotted over the gold in such a way that the contours would nearly coincide, a casual effect that prefigured the way in which Warhol would later screen print photographs over colored areas painted by hand.

The variations suggested by the blotted-line technique were explored in a number of different ways. The most elaborate were the gold-leaf drawings to which were attached silver and gold paper-lace doilies. Such methods were applied also to sculptures of shoes (figure 2), a development from drawings of the same subject, which Warhol made from wood shoe lasts attached to wood heels. These were then decorated with a hand-painted line made to look like the blotted-line technique, since that technique was unworkable in three dimensions, and this was then supplemented by gold leaf and trim. Warhol also used blotting on a much more ambitious scale in large drawings on walls,[13] and he may have experimented with a cruder variant of the technique by tracing an outline through carbon paper so as to register the uneven pressure of the hand in the inky deposit.[14]

The most useful application of the blotted-

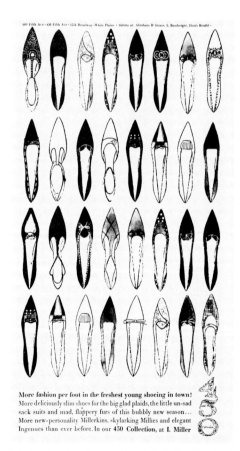

More fashion per foot in the freshest young shoeing in town! More deliciously slim shoes for the big glad plaids, the little un-sad sack suits and mad, flappery furs of this bubbly new season... More new-personality Millerkins, skylarking Millies and elegant Ingenues than ever before. In our **450 Collection**, at I. Miller

3. I. Miller advertisement by Warhol, *The New York Times*

line technique, however, was in Warhol's commercial work, such as I. Miller shoe advertisements and other commissions designed to be printed in newspapers (figure 3). The irregular and coarse quality of newsprint reproduction, rather than being regarded as a hindrance, was taken as a given that could enhance the already fragmented look of his line. It is not unreasonable to deduce from Warhol's later screen printing of images from press-agency photographs that the grainy character of newsprint reproduction, which he imitated in the unevenness of his own printing, held an innate appeal for him.

A further application of Warhol's blotted-line drawings lay in the promotional flyers and books that he sent to potential clients. These were commercially printed by offset lithography[15] by Seymour Berlin, a New York City printer with no experience in fine-art printing, usually to the dimensions of the original drawing supplied by Warhol as the artwork.[16] Some were sent out as single sheets, while others were inexpensively bound into books; to increase their appeal, Warhol signed and numbered them as limited editions, often giving them all low numbers, which he thought would be especially prized. Hand-coloring the images turned them from reproductions into originals, but he cleverly hit upon the energy-saving device of organizing "coloring parties" at which friends and acquaintances, such as Ted Carey, Tom Lacy, George Hartman, and Buddy Radish, were each given a single color with which to fill in the outlines, much as popular prints would have been farmed out for hand-tinting in the nineteenth century.[17] At this stage it was not so much a factory production as a cottage industry.

The desire for anonymity and depersonalization so evident in Warhol's work of the sixties can be seen in incipient form in his art of the fifties in his use of photographs, as well as other distancing devices.[18] His habit of drawing or tracing from photographs began when he was a student in Pittsburgh, long before he made his first Pop paintings.[19] Even when a subject was readily at hand, he often preferred to work from photographs, which had already translated the image into two dimensions.[20] One early associate has observed that Warhol's interpolation of such source material into his blotted-line technique "divorced him from the photograph twice," first by the act of copying

4. Title page from *Wild Raspberries* (New York, 1959), including Warhol's signature, written by Mrs. Warhola

5. Page from *Wild Raspberries*, written by Mrs. Warhola

and then by that of blotting.[21] In fact, this process of detachment can be taken one step further, in that by choosing a photograph in the first place Warhol had already placed himself

at one remove from the subject.

The florid handwriting used in Warhol's early drawings for written inscriptions and also for his trademark signature was not his own, but his mother's (figures 4, 5); furthermore, this was later imitated by Gluck. It provided the remoteness of another personality and introduced a further element of unpredictability, in that her limited English was often translated into misspellings and malapropisms, which Warhol made no attempt to correct. After Warhol adopted mechanical procedures in his Pop paintings, the appearance of personality represented by this script—even though it was clearly not his own—was dispensed with. In its place he created a signature worthy of *The Invisible Man:* a simple rubber stamp of the type used by, or on behalf of, officials too busy or remote from their work to be able to sign their own names to it.

In spite of Warhol's possible attraction to the effortless contours of Jean Cocteau's drawings and to the use of outline by other artists, such as Ben Shahn and Henri Matisse, he continued to experiment with impersonal techniques that implicitly rejected not only traditional draftsmanship but also the importance accorded by the Abstract Expressionists to gesture and personal touch as the authentic mark of an artist's personality. He learned from Gluck how to marbleize paper by dipping it in a mixture of oil and water, another means of creating a decorative surface design by a mixture of chance and control, and tried using it both as a background for blotted-line drawings and for a group of crumpled paper works displayed on the floor in his exhibition at the Loft Gallery in New York in 1954.[22] In the paintings that he continued to make in the fifties, and in large fashion drawings at the end of that decade, he superimposed a linear drawing on patches of pastel colors by means of an overlay. The procedure was comparable to that of some of his window displays for department stores, in which the mannequins were viewed through images painted in outline on the glass.[23] Such methods, which perhaps bear a superficial resemblance to certain works by Raoul Dufy, possibly by way of Larry Rivers, were abandoned by Warhol about 1960 and not taken up again by him until 1975 in works such as the collages and prints of Mick Jagger (plate 334).

The single technique from the fifties that

held the most possibilities for Warhol when he again turned seriously to painting in 1960 was that of the hand-stamped image, although he used it in only a few paintings in 1962 before turning to the even more mechanical procedure of screen printing after a period of uncertainty about the degree of precision that he wanted in his hand-painted canvases. In the late fifties it was not commercially made rubber stamps that Warhol used, as is sometimes assumed, but stamps carved by hand out of a soft gum eraser known as Artgum. This was generally available in small bars measuring two by one by one inch, although Warhol managed to find pieces that were about two inches thick and four or five inches square. Warhol or Gluck would draw simple shapes on the surface, such as stars, sunbursts, hearts, butterflies, flowers, and strawberries, and then carve them as one would a linoleum block. A single image was sometimes stamped repeatedly in a grid formation, the first instance of Warhol's use of serial imagery, and then hand-colored like the blotted-line ink drawings.[24]

By 1960 Warhol's commercial career gave him the means to begin collecting works by Jasper Johns and other contemporary artists; and collecting itself became one of the factors that redirected his attention to his original ambition to be a painter. For his art he turned to images of such banality that they appeared shocking: newspaper advertisements, comic strips, mass-produced items such as matchbooks, and consumer products such as canned soup and Coca-Cola. The Pop label was not to gain general currency until 1962, and when he embarked on this new direction he was unaware of the similar sources to which other painters—notably Roy Lichtenstein—were beginning to make reference, although he soon was made aware of the common purpose that led a number of artists to a shared fund of imagery.

Warhol's first Pop paintings of 1960–62 were for the most part hand-painted on primed, stretched canvas with synthetic polymer paint, a water-based plastic paint which had only just come into use as a fast-drying substitute for oil paint. He briefly explored the possibility of using his mass-media reference material intact, for example, in a group of collages that placed frames from Superman comic strips against a gesturally splattered watercolor back-

6. A Superman comic strip used by Warhol as a source for his painting *Superman,* 1960. The Estate of Andy Warhol

ground (plates 114–120), but he soon settled on the idea of enlarging his two-dimensional sources by means of an opaque projector so as to transfer their outlines in pencil onto the canvas.[25]

At this point, Warhol vacillated between two different techniques.[26] The first type, exemplified by *Wigs,* 1960 (plate 86), involved a loose and incomplete transcription of the source, with gestural handling and exaggerated drips as shorthand signs of expressiveness borrowed from Abstract Expressionism.[27] Examples of the second type, such as *Where Is Your Rup-*

*ture?,* 1960 (taken from an advertisement), were impassive in treatment, replicating the source material as closely as possible (plate 83): sharply defined, regular edges, achieved by means of masking tape as a kind of ad-hoc stencil, give the image a mechanical appearance in keeping with the stylized form of printed illustration to which it refers. Warhol painted contrasting versions of particular images such as *Storm Door,* 1960 and 1961 (plates 100, 101), which he then showed to others to gauge their reactions. He later recalled that he himself preferred "the cold 'no comment' paintings" to the "lyrical" versions, and finally decided to follow the former course when he was convinced that it was the one likely to meet the most approval in the right quarters of the art world.[28]

Warhol's equation of the canvas with an appropriated image can be viewed as an extension of Marcel Duchamp's concept of the Readymade by way of Jasper Johns's paintings of Flags and Targets, which had been the subjects of considerable acclaim and critical discussion when they were exhibited at the Leo Castelli Gallery in New York in 1958. In paintings such as *Superman,* 1960 (plate 113), which reproduced a single comic-strip frame (figure 6), or the Before and After works initiated in the same year (plates 79–81), based on a crudely drawn advertisement for plastic surgery of the nose, Warhol enlarged and transcribed his source material with as little intervention as possible. In *Superman,* for example, he simplified the linear treatment of the superhero's breath and removed some of the detail from the clouds of smoke; at the same time he smudged over the caption to render it less legible and activated the sky area with a rhythmic linear pattern. The composition, however, has been transposed just as he found it. By contrast, Lichtenstein's virtually contemporaneous comic-strip paintings, which Warhol saw at the Castelli gallery in 1961, took more liberties in making formal adjustments from the source material. Once Warhol had seen Lichtenstein's paintings he decided to abandon such subject matter and, likewise, pursued no further the use of the hand-painted halftone dot in one of the Before and After paintings (plate 81) as soon as it was apparent that the Benday dot was to be his colleague's trademark.[29]

Warhol's awareness of Lichtenstein's work may well have strengthened his resolve to impose himself even less on his material, to limit his role to that of the initial selection of the subject and then to submit himself as thoroughly as possible to the apparently mindless task of reproducing it. In 1962 Lichtenstein, in spite of having been sued by Erle Loran for appropriating diagrams from his book *Cézanne's Composition*[30] for his *Portrait of Madame Cézanne* (figure 7) and *Man with Folded Arms,* was in fact using textbook diagrams of famous paintings only as starting-points for compositional manipulations of

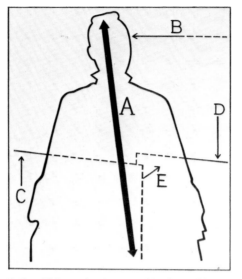

7. Roy Lichtenstein. *Portrait of Madame Cézanne.* 1962. Synthetic polymer paint on canvas, 68 × 56" (172.7 × 142.2 cm). Private collection

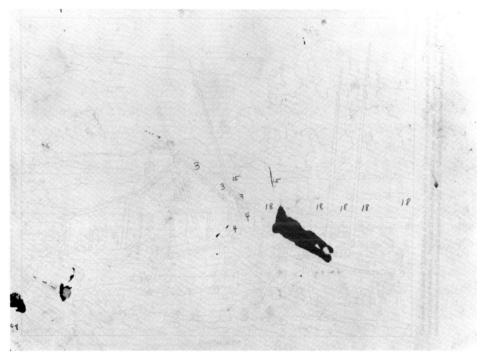

8. Source for *Do It Yourself (Seascape)*, 1963. The Estate of Andy Warhol

great subtlety. By contrast, Warhol in his Dance Diagram paintings of the same year (plates 160–163) was content to work his way through various pages of an instruction book printed in black-and-white, making no changes other than those of scale, medium, and installation.

The simple choice of subject provided, in a form as ready-made as convenience food, all the necessary decisions with regard to composition and to the otherwise arbitrary number of variations that could be produced within a

given series. Having come across an appealingly bland set of paint-by-number diagrams (figure 8), printed on thin paper rather than on the usual board, Warhol had an entire set of Do It Yourself paintings (plates 153–159) already mapped out for him, leaving him free to concentrate on the process of transposition and on the fragmentary filling-in of colored shapes for decorative effect. In order to simplify his task and to stress the impression that the pictures were produced by mechanical means, he transferred printed numbers onto the canvas rather than draw them by hand.[31]

In 1961, taking up a suggestion reputedly made to him by art dealer Muriel Latow, Warhol painted the first of his Campbell's Soup Cans, although supermarket items had been featured in his work as early as his *Peach Halves,* 1960 (plate 89).[32] The soup-can pictures exist in various formats, but the first groups of them were all hand-painted, using his standard procedures: enlargement by projection, tracing, and masking. *Campbell's Soup Cans,* 1962 (plate 164), a set of thirty-two canvases each measuring twenty by sixteen

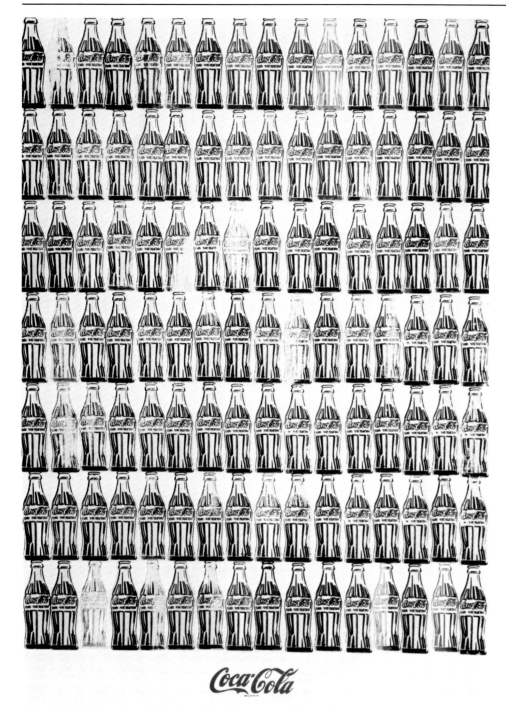

Coca-Cola

9. Andy Warhol. *Green Coca-Cola Bottles*. 1962. Oil on canvas, 6′10″ × 57″ (208.3 × 144.8 cm). Whitney Museum of American Art, New York. Purchase, with funds from the Friends of the Whitney Museum of American Art

10. Andy Warhol. *Two Coke Bottles*. 1962. Synthetic polymer paint on canvas, 10 × 8″ (25.4 × 20.3 cm). Collection Nathan Gluck

cans stacked in various configurations, all of which were traced from enlargements of black-and-white studio shots on the opaque projector. Comparison of the finished paintings with their photographic sources reveals that Warhol sacrificed a certain amount of detail in his tracing, eliminating for example the design printed on the central circle, but the lettering was conscientiously masked for a clean and uniform edge. The corroded metal effect in some of these works—those depicting peeling labels—appears to have been achieved by means of another chance discovery; by rubbing grease from his fingers into sections of the canvas surface he may have created a kind of resist over which he then brushed India ink.

The idea of serial repetition was pursued in single canvases in 1962 using various mechanical or pseudomechanical means that are at times difficult to distinguish from one another. The technique used on small pictures such as *Red Airmail Stamps* and *S & H Green Stamps,* both 1962 (plates 149, 150, 151), was an elaboration of the Artgum stamp, and perhaps was prompted by a play on the word *stamp,* which forms the subject.[33] The first of the Coca-Cola paintings using repeated images, such as *Green Coca-Cola Bottles,* 1962 (figure 9), may

inches, were shown together as Warhol's first individual show at the Ferus Gallery, Los Angeles, in 1962; the dealer Irving Blum sold a few of them but bought them back in order to keep them together as a set. Here, more clearly than in any previous works, the limits of the series were set by the subject itself, as the paintings correspond precisely to the number of varieties of Campbell's soup then available. To simplify his procedure and to treat each one

identically, as if it—like the product—were mass-produced by machine, he appears to have established the outlines by means of a single pencil tracing, which he transferred to the canvas by rubbing the other side of the paper: a variation of his blotted-line method, which he continued to use in commercial work.

Variations on the Campbell's Soup Cans proliferated from then on, and included images of cans crushed, cans with peeling labels, and

have been stamped by hand with a single balsa-wood carving, the varying amounts of color visible in each bottle having first been applied within penciled outlines established by a transfer drawing, as in *Two Coke Bottles,* 1962 (figure 10).[34]

Then it occurred to Warhol that a more regular printed effect, requiring far less handwork and more appropriate in reproducing the range of mass-media material to which he was referring, could be achieved by means of a hand-cut silkscreen (or serigraph) commercially produced from an outline drawing.[35] Acting on Latow's suggestion that he make paintings of money, Warhol had to take into account the legal regulations governing the way in which banknotes could be reproduced. Eliminating certain details, he made drawings of one- and two-dollar bills, the latter in front and back views, and sent them to the screen printers, Richard Miller and Floriano Ecchi at the Tiber Press, whom he knew as printers of Christmas cards, specifying the size to which he wanted them enlarged.[36] In effect, the procedure was an elaboration of a simple stenciling method: a design was hand-cut from glue or varnish and applied to a gauze fabric stretched tightly across a rectangular frame, so that only the pores not blocked out by the hand-cut stencil would allow ink to be pushed through with a rubber blade known as a squeegee.

The first of Warhol's 1962 silkscreened paintings, sometimes somewhat incorrectly listed as stenciled images, included Dollar Bill paintings consisting of one (figure 11; plates 137–140) or several banknotes (plates 144–146), *Handle with Care—Glass—Thank You, Martinson Coffee* (plates 147, 152), and Coca-Cola paintings such as *210 Coca-Cola Bottles* (plate 192), the latter using a repeat image of three bottles against different levels of background color to create the impression of endlessly varied single units. All these were printed with an oil-based enamel in a regular grid formation straight onto the white primed canvas in an appropriate color; the small seals applied in a separate color on some of the one- and two-dollar bills, always oriented in the same direction but varying slightly in their registration against the other colors, were most likely printed from a separate screen but may have been rubber-stamped. Among the paintings that followed were images of numerous

11. Andy Warhol. *Printed Dollar Bill.* 1962. Silkscreen ink on canvas, 6 × 10″ (15.2 × 25.4 cm). Collection Burton J. Tremaine, Meriden, Connecticut

dollar bills haphazardly scattered across the surface (plate 146). These were printed with the same screen of a single dollar bill, but the location of the banknotes was established by means of a projected photograph produced in the studio under Warhol's direction; the effect of overlapping was probably created by shielding the bills already printed with a cardboard mask of the same size as the image, since there are only a few instances of overprinting.

From the hand-cut screens it was only a small step to Warhol's use of photo-silkscreens, produced commercially from black-and-white photographs by exposing a screen coated with light-sensitive material. The only areas to harden are those exposed to light, thus selectively blocking the screen so as to let the ink through as a pattern of tiny dots. Much of Warhol's subsequent work was a variation on this technique, which he had begun to use in August 1962. Among the simplest and earliest of the photo-silkscreened paintings was *Baseball,* 1962 (plate 198), followed by the Disasters series, initiated with works both on paper and canvas such as *Suicide,* 1962 (plate 266). In these the screen was hand-printed directly onto the primed canvas or paper laid flat on the floor, or sometimes onto a coat of a single color generally painted by hand.

As with the hand-cut screens, synthetic polymer paint was used only as a background, as its quick-drying properties would have clogged up the mesh if used for the printing itself; for

this purpose oil-based enamel and occasionally vinyl ink was used instead, usually in black to reinforce the association with newsprint photographs. Very little retouching or "in-painting" was ever carried out for the simple reason that synthetic polymer paint cannot be applied over oil without the danger of its peeling. The screens could be ordered to any size either from images already printed or from original photographs; many of the Disasters, for instance, were taken not directly from newspapers but from glossy press-agency photographs, which Warhol was able to obtain complete with captions (figure 12).[37] In such cases, the "positive" on clear acetate from which the photo-screen was made was produced by an overlay on the photograph of a halftone screen of the desired fineness. Screens could be "blown out," in readiness for other photographs, but Warhol kept many of them intact for possible reuse in other paintings.

Warhol and Robert Rauschenberg both began using photo-silkscreens in 1962 (figure 13).[38] Apart from the fact that for both artists the medium was a logical development from their previous procedures—in Rauschenberg's case from the transfer drawings from newspapers that he had been making since the late fifties—it served them in different ways. For Rauschenberg it supplied another texture and painterly effect; for Warhol it was a bald and immediate method for appropriating an image, easy to use, capable of indefinite reproduction, 69 and all the more attractive for its mechanical nature.[39] The elimination of the personal touch—the "no-hands look," as Rupert Smith refers to Warhol's work of the sixties—was complete.

Warhol took up photo-screens at a time when any use of machinery in the production of art seemed technologically sophisticated by contrast with the handmade image. The primitive appearance which such works acquired with time was not courted by Warhol, but was the direct by-product of improvised methods that he accepted as "part of the art." Apparently Warhol had never had the patience, even in preparing artwork for color separations in the fifties, for assuring proper registration of his images, and in his paintings he was prepared to embrace whatever accidents occurred.[40] When, for example, Gluck tried to explain to Warhol how to achieve a more exact registration for a painting of Elizabeth Taylor, the advice was shrugged off with the comment: "I kind of like it that way." Many things could go wrong: irregularities would appear if the squeegee had softened with age, if too much or too little ink was poured onto the screen, if too much pressure was exerted, or if bad backing was used to hold the canvas in place. The more the screen was reused before cleaning, the more clogged with ink it became, leading to an ever more faint imprint or to a streaky black surface if the ink was forced through with a squeegee that had become hardened with dried ink.

The casual effects of Warhol's screen printing were not premeditated and should thus be interpreted with caution; if Warhol never contradicted the assumptions and elaborate theories promoted by others on his behalf, it was not only because it was part of his style to

12. Press-agency photograph used by Warhol as a source for his painting *Ambulance Disaster,* 1963. The Estate of Andy Warhol

remain enigmatic but because he saw it as one of his roles to give the critics a job to do. Malanga is adamant in his assertion that they never "faked" their mistakes, but that they were genuinely trying to produce the most precise result possible. Warhol would not, in his view, have considered eliminating his manual involvement altogether by sending the paintings out to be commercially printed, because he wanted to operate automatically, as if he himself were a machine. He never surrendered the human element, accepting the disjunction between the machinelike perfection toward which he was striving and the human fallibility to which the process inevitably gave rise.

Warhol's screened paintings were all made on unstretched canvas laid flat on the floor (figure 14). Very occasionally they were printed on uncut rolls, as with the paintings of Elvis Presley of 1962, which were shipped to Irving Blum for exhibition in Los Angeles accompanied by sets of stretcher bars and only the vaguest instructions as to how they were to be cropped and stretched.[41] Normally, however, he would work on canvas already cut to the appropriate size, calculating the few extra inches needed for stretching. The background for the single-color paintings was generally applied by hand with a large brush, sometimes before the roll was cut if a number of paintings were planned with the same hue; the paint

  13. Robert Rauschenberg. *Barge*. 1962. Combine painting, 6′ 7⅞″ × 32′ 3″ (202.9 × 980.4 cm). Courtesy Leo Castelli Gallery, New York

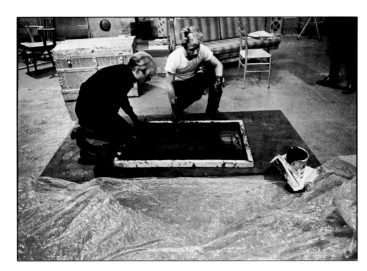

14. Warhol and Gerard Malanga screen printing Campbell's Soup Can paintings, c. 1964–65

seems to have generally been taken straight from the bottle, although Warhol is also known to have mixed a color himself if he was unable to find a satisfactory one.[42] Only on rare occasions does he appear to have used a house painter's roller, which when he tried it again in later years produced a texture that was not to his liking.[43] The silver background used in the Elvis paintings and in some images of Elizabeth Taylor was sprayed on from aerosol cans of automobile paint.

A penciled grid sometimes indicated the positioning of the screen, but the repeated images of news photographs were often printed sequentially on the colored background, lined up by eye through the screen, with only a rough idea of the number of times that they would be used. More complicated were the iconic images, beginning with the paintings of Troy Donahue which were among the first of his photo-screened pictures, in which he introduced hand-painted areas in various colors corresponding to the face, hair, and chest. The characteristic method that he evolved for the Marilyn pictures, the image of which was cropped by Warhol from a publicity still by Gene Kornman for the 1953 film *Niagara* (figure 15), was subsequently applied to other portraits such as those of Elizabeth Taylor and later still to commissioned portraits. A pencil tracing was taken from the full-sized acetate prepared for the photographic screen. Either by transferring the penciled line by pressing onto the front of the acetate or sheet of paper, or by placing a sheet of carbon paper beneath the tracing and then drawing the line one section at a time, a rough guide was established for each color area, for example, the lips and the eyelids. The colors were then brushed on by hand, often with the use of masking tape to create a clean junction between them, with the eventual imposition of the black screened image also serving to obscure any unevenness in the line. The acetates were examined by Warhol before they were made into screens, so that he could indicate, by means of instructions, written and drawn with a china-marking crayon, any changes to be made: for example, to increase the tonal contrast by removing areas of halftone, thereby further flattening the image. The position of the image would be established by taping the four corners of the acetate to the canvas and then tearing off the tape along the corner edges of the acetate; the fragments of tape remaining on the canvas would serve as a guide in locating the screen on top. The position of the screen would be confirmed by eye, and it would then be printed.

Warhol explored a number of variants of this procedure. Images displayed against single-color backgrounds were sometimes printed in colors other than black, as in variations of the Electric Chairs initiated in 1963 (plates 282–285). Color screenings were used also in

15. Publicity still of Marilyn Monroe, marked by Warhol for cropping. The Estate of Andy Warhol

the Self-Portraits of 1967 (plates 4–10), whose blotchy surfaces were possibly an adaptation of the marbleizing technique he had used in the fifties. As early as the paintings of bosoms of 1963, Warhol even produced a small number of virtually invisible soft-porn images that fully materialized as "blue pictures" only when viewed under black light (plate 321). A single screen could be overprinted—casually, to obliterate some of the images, as in *Natalie,* 1962 (plate 197); in a deliberate rhythmic pattern suggestive of stop-action photography, as in *Triple Elvis,* 1962 (plate 254); or as two slightly off-register printings in complementary colors, as in the red-and-green works *Statue of Liberty,* 1963, and *Optical Car Crash,* 1962 (plates 239, 240, 256), all of which were intended to be viewed through "3-D" glasses. *Mona Lisa,* 1963 (plate 238), combines overlappings of three separate screens printed in the four colors of commercial printing (black, yellow, cyan blue, and magenta), multiplying the familiarity of a much-reproduced image into a dizzying profusion.[44]

Serial images were printed not just on a single surface but on separate canvases of a standard size, painted in various colors and joined together as one work. Such is the case with *Ethel Scull 36 Times,* 1963 (plate 325), one of Warhol's first commissioned portraits and an early example of his use of photo-booth pictures, whose throw-away quality was a useful disguise for the artistic manipulation to which they were actually subjected.[45] In 1963 Warhol produced the first of a group of diptychs in which a screened panel was paired with another canvas of the same dimensions, consisting simply of a uniform surface painted in one color. As reductive and formally austere as any Minimalist artworks, they appeared without the support of lofty theories. Malanga's explanation, following Warhol's own remarks, is even more down-to-earth: "It made the painting twice as valuable."

The first works printed by superimposing two or more screens were not paintings but the Brillo Boxes and other sculptures made in 1964, which replicated cardboard packing cases. Warhol had wanted to make sculpture for some time, having produced nothing more substantial in that medium than the decorated wood shoe lasts of the late fifties. Probably inspired by two Johns sculptures of 1960, both titled *Painted Bronze,* trompe l'oeil replications of a pair of beer cans (figure 16) and a Savarin coffee can with paint brushes, Warhol thought of making a stack of Campbell's Soup Cans by printing the sides, tops, and bottoms on a wood box made to his specifications by a carpenter (plate 181). Warhol realized that it went counter to the logic of his art. Why not take actual boxes as a subject, so that each side represented nothing but itself? He sent Gluck to the supermarket to find suitable models, but in the end had to go himself in order to exchange Gluck's "arty" choices for a plainer set consisting of Heinz tomato ketchup, Kellogg's corn flakes, Mott's apple juice, and two versions of Brillo soap pads.[46] Plywood boxes were made to order in large numbers to the specified sizes, painted to match the color of the cardboard used for each, and then printed by hand from separate sets of screens on which were duplicates of the designs found on the various sides of the original boxes (figures 17, 18).

The Flower canvases of 1964 (plate 306), based on a doctored fragment of a photograph in a magazine, were produced in two versions. In the first set, the green background was painted by hand, and the color for some of the flowers may have been sprayed through heavy-duty paper stencils cut to the required shapes. The second set was printed from multiple screens as a practical solution to the great number of paintings Warhol wished to produce for his exhibition at the Leo Castelli Gallery, in which they were densely hung. The flowers were printed in different color combinations (as flat areas of color screened from a hand-cut red acetate sheet known as ruby lith) before the photograph was printed over it in black. Although they all seemed alike, each, in fact, was different. Like the Boxes that preceded them, they were good examples of Warhol's use of assembly-line production as the most efficient procedure for achieving the results that he envisaged.[47]

Beginning in 1963 Warhol became increasingly preoccupied with filmmaking. He announced his retirement from painting at his 1966 Castelli gallery exhibition by treating two rooms separately: one concentrated on the walls by covering them with wallpaper repeating a cow's head printed in Day-Glo colors (plate 305), the other on the empty space of the room itself, which he emphasized by floating in it silver-colored helium "clouds." In the same year Warhol produced several works in which he screened onto plexiglass enlargements from several of his early films—*Sleep, Eat,* and *Kiss* of 1963 (plates 319, 320); and *Empire, Henry Geldzahler,* and *Couch* of 1964—acknowledging the common ground of form and technique in his paintings and films. The idea may have been suggested by the visual parallels between celluloid and the photographic images screened on acetates for his paintings. So static were his early movies that a succession of frames, taken out of context and printed like an enlarged contact sheet, looked very much like the repeated images on his canvases.[48] Their transparency and almost sculptural presence were emphasized by War-

16. Jasper Johns. *Painted Bronze II*. 1964 (original cast 1960). Painted bronze, 5½ × 8 × 4½″ (14 × 20.3 × 11.4 cm). Collection the artist

17. Warhol and Campbell's Boxes, c. 1964

18. Warhol carrying a Brillo Box in his studio, c. 1964    73

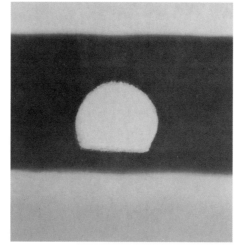

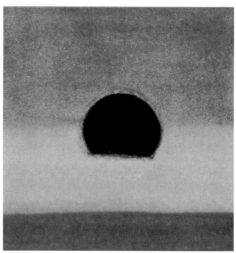

hol's decision to display them mounted on bases so that they were freestanding.

Warhol's gradual removal from direct involvement with painting and printing processes was apparent in his collaborations with printers on editions of silkscreen prints that made his earlier images available to a wide market. The *Marilyn* portfolio of 1967 (plate 212), in which the same image was subjected to a series of ten lurid color variations, is often viewed as one of Warhol's best-known works. Yet he left most of the decisions in this case to project director David Whitney, and was not even present when they were proofed. This stands in stark contrast to the unique proofs that he printed on canvas. His comparatively late entry into the booming print market of the sixties was fundamentally motivated by commercial considerations and was to a lesser degree a conceptual gesture against the importance accorded the unique work of art.

Only in the seventies, after his enthusiasm for painting returned, did Warhol become fully involved in technical procedures for his various editions of prints. Having refuted the definition of paintings as unique objects by printing them to look as much alike as possible, he now looked at ways of subverting the concept of prints as sets of identical images. In the 1972 series of *Sunset* prints (figure 19) commissioned by Philip Johnson to decorate the rooms of the Marquette Inn designed by him in Minneapolis, a simple and virtually abstract image was subjected to 632 color variations. In the following year, a line drawing of Mao Zedong underwent a process of mutation in a sequence of three hundred photocopy prints, drawing attention to the fallibility of machines as reproductive agents just as he had earlier remarked on his own shortcomings in this respect.

Warhol's renewed interest in painting was marked in 1972 by the first of his Mao images (plates 348–352), which were based on the ubiquitous photograph printed as the frontispiece to *Quotations from Chairman Mao Tse-tung*. These were among the first of his paintings to feature not only a gestural handling of the background, in ambivalent homage to the Abstract Expressionists, but also black scribbled lines that were screened on separately. Warhol later remarked, "I really would still rather do just a silkscreen of the

74

19. Andy Warhol. *Sunsets*. 1972. Serigraphs on paper; four prints, each 34 × 34″ (86.4 × 86.4 cm). Courtesy Ronald Feldman Fine Arts, Inc., New York

face without all the rest, but people expect just a little bit more. That's why I put in all the drawing."[49]

In two print portfolios of 1975, *Mick Jagger* and *Ladies and Gentlemen* (plates 333, 334), Warhol first systematically used two techniques which were to remain standard elements of his late style: torn paper and the superimposition of a stylized linear drawing as a kind of visual echo of the photographic image. In these he used Color-Aid paper—a cheap paper used by graphic designers which was available in more than two hundred shades, tints, and hues—torn into fragments and then glued onto the surface of full-scale collage maquettes as a decorative backdrop for a screened image (figure 20).[50] The effect recalls that of Warhol's fifties paintings and fashion drawings, particularly when used as a backdrop to outline drawings, as in the *Mick Jagger* series. An initial drawing would be traced from Warhol's Polaroid photograph pro-

jected to the desired size; this would sometimes give rise to further variations, drawn freehand rather than from the original Polaroid. One drawing would then be chosen to be photographed, printed as a positive on acetate, and made into a screen. The color areas, if they registered clearly enough through the layers of collage, were likewise photographed (in a vacuum frame),[51] or else were traced in order to be cut as Rubyliths for separate screens. The line took on a mottled, frosted quality when printed directly on the Arches paper, but was uniformly black and even in texture when printed over gloss enamel color areas. This was yet another instance of Warhol's ability to exploit accidental effects.

Paintings were not preceded by collages in the same way, but the increased technical complexity and sophistication of Warhol's later work is indebted in many specific ways to innovations first made in prints. Rupert Smith, who with assistants made the screens, encouraged Warhol to try diamond dust, line, wash, "rainbow rolls" (a process in which different colored inks appear on the paper in a rainbowlike progression—also called "split fountains"), and other complicated processes often developed in the proofing process. Dozens of trial proofs were sometimes pulled in preparation for the final selection, and in certain cases these were published as separate editions. Smith recalls that Warhol sensed that such complexity had come to be expected of him, but that he sometimes found Smith's proposals too "arty." To avoid the danger of self-parody in belaboring an idea, the best way was often, as before, the most direct way.

In the seventies the gradual move to a more slick "product" in Warhol's oeuvre is perhaps most evident in the development of his formula for commissioned "vanity portraits," which he regarded as essentially no different from the serialization of any of his other images. The notion of collaboration was particularly strong in these works, since Warhol wanted the clients to be happy with the results and was quite prepared to involve them in the choices of image and color.

This form of portraiture, which became Warhol's principal source of income, can be traced to the early seventies. The basic principles were adapted from the procedures first used on Marilyn Monroe's image in 1962, except that in place of found photographs Warhol began taking his own snapshots of sitters in a studio using various cameras—an "instamatic," later a Leica, but as a general rule Polaroid cameras (particularly the Big Shot model, the focal length of which he found most suitable for his needs), always with a flash. Persuading the sitter to adopt a particular pose just as a film director might behind the camera, he often took dozens of shots from which a small number were selected, rephotographed in 35mm and printed as eight-by-ten-inch acetates. One of these (or, later, sometimes a composite of two or more photographs by which he performed a kind of instant plastic surgery on his client) would then be further enlarged to forty by forty inches in preparation for the making of the screen. The square format, although it did not correspond exactly to the shape of the Polaroid print, appealed to him for its neutrality and for the simplicity it allowed in centralizing the composition. The photographs

were often cropped so that the head filled most of the surface, unless he felt it appropriate to show more skin or to exaggerate the length of a woman's neck.

The background painting in the portraits of the early to mid-seventies was generally done very quickly, perhaps in no more than half an

20. Cover for *Time* magazine by Warhol

hour. To exaggerate the painterly look, he would sometimes drag his finger quickly over the borders between two color areas while the paint was still wet. His remarks at the time revealed, with an almost lacerating honesty, the extent to which he saw such work not as expressive but simply as a surface embellishment: "Now I'm trying to put style back into them. I'm sort of hand painting. When I do the portraits, I sort of half paint them just to give it a style. It's more fun—and it's faster to do. It's faster to be sloppy than it is to be neat."[52] The sloppiness of the early seventies portraits extended also to the rather brutal way in which the screens were produced from the Polaroids, with sections of the white border often still intact.

Later in the decade, after he had produced the *Ladies and Gentlemen,* Warhol sometimes printed photographs onto purely abstract backgrounds, with no preparatory tracing. He would begin either by taping up the canvas to produce geometric shapes or simply by cover-

ing the surface with broad brushstrokes. Such methods were also applied to other subjects, such as the mammoth series of Shadows in 1978 (figure 21; plates 380, 381) or the Reversals (plates 382–385) inaugurated the following year as reflections on his own artistic past: skeins of color were broadly brushed (or mopped, in the case of the Shadows) on a continuous length of canvas as it was unrolled for him, with no account of the imagery to be printed over them. This apparently arbitrary relationship between printed and hand-painted elements was compounded by Warhol in his Reversals, in which he cannily increased his reputation for contrariness as well as his income by recycling many of his most familiar images in negative form, sometimes also printing them back to front.

By the end of the seventies Warhol and his production crew had the portrait system down to a fine art. A heavy white makeup would be applied to the sitter to hide wrinkles and also to exaggerate the flattening of the image effected by flash photography, so that when printed it would almost have the quality of a line drawing. As Smith prepared the screens, he would also make the changes requested by Warhol to the acetate, for example, by burning out unwanted areas of halftone with a mild bleach. Warhol's tracing corresponding to the acetate might, likewise, alter the shape of the sitter's neck or nose.

All the portraits of women would begin with the same background "flesh" color (aqua red mixed with cadmium light yellow, white, and a little medium) painted on a roll of canvas long enough for six portraits; the portraits of men also had standard backgrounds, a deeper bronze tint. A blow-dryer began to be used to speed up the process so that additional coats of color could be applied. In the portraits of women the lips were often printed separately in a bright red, and highlights applied to the eyes for a glossy, sexy look. The synthetic, airbrushed flattery of studio photography was mimicked and parodied in support of Warhol's professed belief that everyone should "look good." The irony was that in order to produce a mechanical-looking result which made both the sitter's beauty and his own painting look effortless, Warhol was forced to go to great lengths to disguise the conventional artistic processes, especially drawing, to which he had recourse. 75

As a relief, perhaps, from the dazzling technical complexity of Warhol's later work, especially in the editions of prints, he abandoned all his usual procedures in 1978 in a series of paintings that eliminated photography altogether. Among these, only the Oxidation paintings (plates 376–379), or "piss" paintings as they are more familiarly referred to by his associates, have been publicly exhibited. Like the series of large Shadow paintings screen printed in the same year, these were both abstract in appearance and representational in a literal sense. The procedure was simple: the canvas was painted with synthetic polymer medium mixed with metallic powder, and while still wet was urinated on, which turned the surface green in various configurations and "lyrical" linear designs. As part of the same impulse to abstraction, Warhol also made paintings at the time out of other unconventional substances, including melted and crushed chocolate, strawberry jam, and semen, perhaps following the example of Edward Ruscha.[53] In the Rorschach series (plates 422–424), named for the personality test used by psychiatrists, he explored the suggestive readings of casually blotted shapes in another return to his exploitation of chance and accident.

Photography and silkscreen printing, however, remained at the core of Warhol's work, even in his contributions to numerous collaborations with Francesco Clemente and Jean-Michel Basquiat in 1984 and in the Camouflage series on which he was engaged in 1986 (plates 442–445, 460).[54] In his second series of collaborative works with Basquiat in 1984 (plates 408, 409), however, he returned to the straightforward methods of hand-painting from enlarged headlines and advertisements which had served him so well in his first Pop paintings in the early sixties. In his last work is a double-take on his lifelong ambivalence between the artist's hand and the machine. Appearances continued to the end to be deceptive, yet the evidence of his methods remained in full view.

21. Andy Warhol. *Shadows*. 1979. Silkscreen ink on synthetic polymer paint (one of 102 canvases), 6′ 4″ × 52″ (193 × 132.1 cm). Dia Art Foundation, New York. Courtesy The Menil Collection, Houston

# NOTES

1. Quoted in Andy Warhol, Kasper König, Pontus Hultén, and Olle Granath eds, *Andy Warhol* (Stockholm: Moderna Museet, 1968), n.p.

   Silkscreen: a printing process by which inks are squeezed with a rubber blade known as a squeegee through a fine mesh of silk or similar fabric stretched over a wood frame; the image is formed by the selective stopping-out of the pores by means of stencils or with substances such as glue, varnish, or a gelatin or emulsion sensitive to light.

2. Ibid.

3. In this essay I have relied extensively on interviews conducted in New York in 1988 with four of Warhol's assistants: Nathan Gluck (July 15), Gerard Malanga (July 14), Rupert Smith (July 13), and Jay Shriver (July 14). I should like to thank them all for their candid discussions; and I also thank the English painter Mark Lancaster, who observed work at the Factory and helped perform basic tasks for a few weeks in July 1964 (telephone interview, July 20, 1988). Unless otherwise specified, all remarks attributed to these associates are from my interviews.

4. Shriver recalls that Warhol disliked being on his own in the studio, and sometimes asked him to come in simply to keep him company. He seems to have sought reassurance about his work before he started it; as Gluck remarked, "It was the reassurance first, and then 'Let's do it.' I think it was just his strange way of working."

5. *POPism: The Warhol '60s*, by Warhol and Pat Hackett (New York: Harcourt Brace Jovanovich, 1980), p. 16.

6. *The Philosophy of Andy Warhol (From A to B and Back Again)* (New York: Harcourt Brace Jovanovich, 1975), p. 99. According to Rupert Smith: "However much or however little Andy puts into his work, it always comes out him" (in Patrick S. Smith, *Andy Warhol's Art and Films* [Ann Arbor: UMI Research Press, 1986], p. 472). Nathan Gluck says that although differences are detectable between his work and Warhol's, not only in the drawn line but even in the stamps carved from Artgum, "the whole point" was that his work should look as much like Warhol's as possible: "I completely subordinated [myself] as much as I could to work in his style." Although some of Warhol's later associates may feel aggrieved that their role was not properly acknowledged, Gluck, as a commercial artist, found it perfectly acceptable that he should be paid by the hour and that Warhol should get all the credit, seeing the situation as no different from working in an advertising agency.

7. Quoted in Warhol, König, et al., *Andy Warhol* (Stockholm).

8. Gluck says that Warhol often had insufficient time to explain what he wanted in detail, but trusted his judgment and sense of layout. Warhol's last assistants testify to how open-ended his requests could be. Shriver would sometimes be told, "Oh, you know how to make a nice line, why don't you just go out and do it?" Both Shriver and Smith recount how Warhol might specify "nice, bright colors" or "funny colors" and then leave the choice to them. The process was like a game of Chinese whispers by which variants would be introduced not simply by will but as part of the retelling from one person to the next.

9. Mark Lancaster recalls, for example, that Warhol would ask for paintings to be restretched if he found the way they had been done "too 'arty.'" Moreover, in spite of the stance that he took about anyone theoretically being able to produce his work for him and in spite of his own collusion in the mid-sixties story that he left it to Brigid Polk to paint his pictures, he in fact "subcontracted" only those tasks that did not need his handwork. Although Polk remains tight-lipped about the story by saying, "Nobody will ever know, it will remain a mystery" (my interview, July 14, 1988), it is now generally accepted that the story was a joke that went too far. Warhol later maintained: "I really worked on all of them" (Phyllis Tuchman, "Pop!: Interviews with George Segal, Andy Warhol, Roy Lichtenstein, James Rosenquist, and Robert Indiana," *Artnews* 73 [May 1974], p. 26). *See also* Barry Blinderman, "Modern 'Myths': An Interview with Andy Warhol," *Arts Magazine* 56 (October 1981), p. 146.

10. *See* the interview with Ted Carey in Patrick S. Smith, *Warhol: Conversations About the Artist* (Ann Arbor: UMI Research Press, 1988), p. 84, and the remarks by Lisanby quoted in Smith, *Andy Warhol's Art*, p. 16, which also address the possibility that Warhol was emulating the effect of Ben Shahn's drawings, which he was known to admire.

11. Monotype: a print produced by transferring an image drawn or painted on a nonporous surface, such as metal or glass, onto paper; as its name suggests, generally it is possible to make only one impression.

12. Fritzie Wood, interviewed by Patrick S. Smith (*Warhol: Conversations*, p. 43), recalls that Warhol used "an old stubby fountain pen" for these drawings.

13. *See* Smith, *Andy Warhol's Art*, p. 17. None of these appears to have survived.

14. *See* Ralph Pomeroy, "The Importance of Being Andy Andy Andy Andy Andy," *Art & Artists* 5 (February 1971), p. 15. From summer 1962, in the Marilyns and other canvases combining screen printing and hand-painting, Warhol was to use carbon paper to transfer the outlines of the photograph on acetate to the surface of the canvas as a guide to filling in the color areas, so such a precedent in his work of the fifties would seem plausible.

15. Offset lithography: in this case the commercial form of printing in which an image is transferred first from a photomechanically made plate to an intermediate surface, such as a rubber blanket, and then to the surface to be printed; the resulting print thus appears the same way around as the original image.

16. Seymour Berlin, interviewed by Patrick S. Smith (*Warhol: Conversations*, p. 159), recalled that halftone values were sometimes added but that it was usually a question of a photo-offset line reproduction. He confirms that Warhol, as in all his work, was happy to accept the changes to his conception introduced by the process itself: "If a job didn't come out right, Andy maybe liked it even better coming out differently than he had made it. So, he wasn't the type of customer that you had to duplicate *exactly* what he gave you."

17. George Hartman and Buddy Radish, art directors and copy writers, who, as friends of Nathan Gluck, participated in many of Warhol's coloring parties, say that Warhol may have been alone among commercial artists in sending out personalized examples of his work to promote himself (Smith, *Warhol: Conversations*, p. 125). Gluck recalls that it was an aspect of Warhol's talent that he created "a spirit of fun," which enabled him to get others to help him with his coloring parties for free.

18. For a recent psychological interpretation see Bradford R. Collins, "The Metaphysical Nosejob: The Remaking of Warhola, 1960–1968," *Arts Magazine* (February 1988), pp. 47–55.

19. Patrick Smith (*Andy Warhol's Art*, p. 39) specifies photographs torn from magazines such as *Life* and *Vogue* as the reference material used by Warhol in Pittsburgh.

20. Gluck (Smith, *Warhol: Conversations*, p. 63) thinks that even Warhol's drawings of his own cats may have been from photos, adding that "Andy was notorious for having things around and just drawing from photographs."

21. George Klauber, in Smith, *Warhol: Conversations*, p. 22.

22. *See* Smith, *Warhol: Conversations*, p. 50, and idem, *Andy Warhol's Art*, pp. 16–17.

23. Gene Moore, who was head of display at Tiffany and Bonwit Teller from 1951 to 1961, thinks that it was Nathan Gluck who first used this technique; *see* Smith, *Warhol: Conversations*, p. 110. Vito Giallo states that the color areas of paintings from this period may have been made with an airbrush (ibid., p. 52).

24. *See* the Wrapping Paper, c. 1959, reproduced in Smith, *Andy Warhol's Art*, p. 28, and Stars [undated], reproduced in Christie, Manson and Woods sale catalogue, November 17, 1977, lot 1.

25. In his 1981 interview with Barry Blinderman ("Modern 'Myths': An Interview," p. 145), Warhol recalled that he used not only an opaque projector but also a slide projector and a light box as devices for copying images in the early sixties.

26. Even after he settled for the mechanical homogeneity of screen printing from photographs in August 1962, Warhol continued to think of style as an element that could be chosen at will rather than as a personal sign to which the artist had to remain committed. Interviewed by G. R. Swenson ("What Is Pop Art?: Answers from 8 Painters, Part I," *Artnews* 62 [November 1963], p. 26), he said, "How can you say one style is better than another? You ought to be able to be an Abstract Expressionist next week, or a Pop artist, or a realist, without feeling you've given up something."

27. Warhol may have known recent paintings by Larry

Rivers such as *Cedar Bar Menu*, 1959, which similarly transcribed ordinary objects into an Abstract Expressionist style.

28. He particularly valued the preferences expressed by Emile de Antonio and Ivan Karp, as he recalled in *POPism*, pp. 6–7.

29. *See POPism*, p. 18. Warhol's dots, irregular in both size and pattern, may have been produced by stamping the canvas with an inked pencil eraser.

30. Erle Loran, *Cézanne's Composition* (Berkeley and Los Angeles: University of California Press, 1946).

31. Gluck (Smith, *Warhol: Conversations*, p. 60) referred to the use of Prestype, but John Coplans ("Early Warhol: The Systematic Evolution of the Impersonal Style," *Artforum* 8 [March 1970], p. 53) stated: "The numerous numbers…are of mechanical origin, printed onto transfer paper and pasted to the surface by the application of heat."

32. *See* Smith, *Andy Warhol's Art*, p. 130.

33. Warhol's choice of S & H Green Stamps as a subject can be seen as an ironic statement about the art market, a caustic expression of the aesthetic worth of his own enterprise and of the commercial system that equates aesthetics with investment. In such a context, paintings, like trading stamps, are only of potential rather than intrinsic value as tokens that can be exchanged for other consumer items.

34. According to Gluck, who owns *Two Coke Bottles*, 1962, in which the left-hand bottle is identical to those in the Whitney museum painting.

35. According to Patrick Smith (*Andy Warhol's Art*, p. 14): "Contrary to what Warhol may claim, he was trained in the techniques of silkscreening and had used the medium in his Pittsburgh window displays." Malanga confirms that Warhol was clearly aware that silkscreens were used in window displays in New York.

    Serigraph: another term for a silkscreen print, generally applied to fine art prints drawn or cut by hand, in contrast to commercial work or to continuous-tone screens produced photographically.

36. In Glenn O'Brien, "Interview: Andy Warhol," *High Times* 24 (August 1977), pp. 20ff., Warhol confirmed that the money pictures were the first that he had screen printed.

37. *See* Malanga's comments on the treatment of press-agency photographs (Smith, *Warhol: Conversations*, p. 162); and Warhol's observations on his selection of images by a process of elimination in Gerard Malanga, "A Conversation with Andy Warhol," *Print Collector's Newsletter* 1 (January/February 1971), p. 126.

38. *See* Ellen H. Johnson, "Image Duplicators—Lichtenstein, Rauschenberg, and Warhol," *Canadian Art* 23 (January 1966), p. 16; and Coplans, "Early Warhol," p. 54.

39. Warhol (*POPism*, p. 22) recalled: "In August '62 I started doing silkscreens. The rubber-stamp method I'd been using to repeat images suddenly seemed too homemade; I wanted something stronger that gave more of an assembly-line effect.

    "With silkscreening, you pick a photograph, blow it up, transfer it in glue onto silk, and then roll ink across it so that the ink goes through the silk but not through the glue. That way you get the same image, slightly different each time. It was all so simple—quick and chancy. I was thrilled with it."

    By rubber stamps he evidently meant stamps hand-carved from Artgum. *See also* Warhol's remarks on silkscreen in Swenson, "What Is Pop Art?" p. 26.

40. *See* Robert Fleisher's comments in Smith, *Warhol: Conversations*, p. 118.

41. *See* John Coplans, "Andy Warhol and Elvis Presley," *Studio International* 181 (February 1971), pp. 49–56.

42. Mark Lancaster recalls watching Warhol fastidiously mixing the cream color for the 1964 paintings known variously as *The American Man—Watson Powell* and *Mr. Nobody*.

43. Malanga has no recollection of a roller ever being used, but Lancaster thinks it was possible; Ultra Violet (in "Ultra Violet on Andy," *New York Magazine* [March 9, 1987], p. 46) recounts Warhol's use of a roller on one of the Flower paintings of 1964.

44. Four-color printing: a photographically based process by which a full-color image is broken down with the aid of filters into four component images known as separations, and then reconstituted as superimposed printings in standard colors—yellow, cyan blue, magenta, and black.

45. Photo-booth images, which occurred also in Warhol's 1964 *Self-Portrait*, seem to have first been used by him in a spread for *Harper's Bazaar* in early 1963, according to Malanga (in Smith, *Warhol: Conversations*, p. 181). Such images were used in the same manner as found photographs, except that Warhol felt free to make a selection from them and to cut up and reassemble the strips in a different order; these then served as the basis for the photo-enlargements from which the screens were eventually made. Although such portraits suggested a casual readiness to accept the image just as it was found, Lancaster recalls Malanga telling him that he had to retouch Scull's image to eliminate signs of her double chin.

46. *See* Gluck in Smith, *Warhol: Conversations*, p. 66; and Warhol's own comments in O'Brien, "Interview," pp. 20ff. An unintended irony is that the Brillo box itself was designed by an Abstract Expressionist painter, James Harvey (*see* Irving Sandler, in Smith, *Andy Warhol's Art*, p. 467).

47. Warhol is quoted in 1965 as saying that many people helped to make the Flowers, both "filling in the colors and stretching the canvases" (Rainer Crone, *Andy Warhol* [New York: Praeger, 1970], p. 30).

48. Warhol may have known Rauschenberg's use of a similar technique in works such as the 1964 multiple *Shades*, which consisted of a lithograph printed on six sheets of plexiglass in an aluminum frame with an electric light fixture; for a reproduction *see Robert Rauschenberg* (Washington, D.C.: National Collection of Fine Arts, 1976), p. 155.

49. Quoted in Blinderman, "Modern 'Myths': An Interview," p. 145. A more gestural handling of paint can be found in some earlier commissioned portraits, for example in one of the four panels depicting Bruno Bischofberger, of 1970.

50. Warhol had used a similar technique as early as 1970 for a *Time* magazine cover: "Jane, Henry and Peter: The Flying Fondas."

51. Vacuum frame: a device for flattening out original artwork through suction in preparation for photography.

52. Quoted in Tuchman, "Pop!" p. 26.

53. Ruscha, who held his first individual exhibition at the Ferus Gallery in Los Angeles the year after Warhol had showed there, began exhibiting at the Leo Castelli Gallery in New York in 1973. He first introduced organic substances, including bodily fluids such as semen, along with numerous fruit and vegetable extracts, in his 1969 portfolio *Stains*.

54. In setting up inanimate subjects, such as the Skulls of 1976, the Hammer and Sickles of 1977, or the Space Fruits of 1978–79—in which the synthetically perfect and Kodachrome-colored products of modern chemical farming were presented as strange, alien objects—Warhol left the photography to Ronnie Cutrone and his 35mm camera. For the portraits and other human subjects such as the "sex parts" and Torsos of 1977, however, he continued to take his own Polaroids. For many of the commissioned print portfolios, such as *Endangered Species*, 1983, and *Details of Renaissance Paintings*, 1984, photographs were provided by the publisher or researched for Warhol by Rupert Smith.

    The Camouflage paintings were based on a swatch of army camouflage that was photographically enlarged and traced in order to be made into separate screens cut from Rubyliths, corresponding to three of the four colors (the lightest color was painted by hand as the background). Some of these were painted in fluorescent colors, which Warhol had begun using in 1982, sometimes mixed into other paints, in response to the work of a younger generation of New York artists such as Keith Haring and Kenny Scharf. The idea of camouflage itself was associated with youthful street culture, *machismo*, and militarism. It was attractive to Warhol because it was both specifically referential and abstract. According to Jay Shriver, Warhol was approached by Stephen Sprouse, who had seen the Camouflage paintings, with the idea of making fabric after the paintings; this resulted in a "collaboration" between Warhol and Sprouse in the design and manufacture of fabric and also clothing.

# PLATES

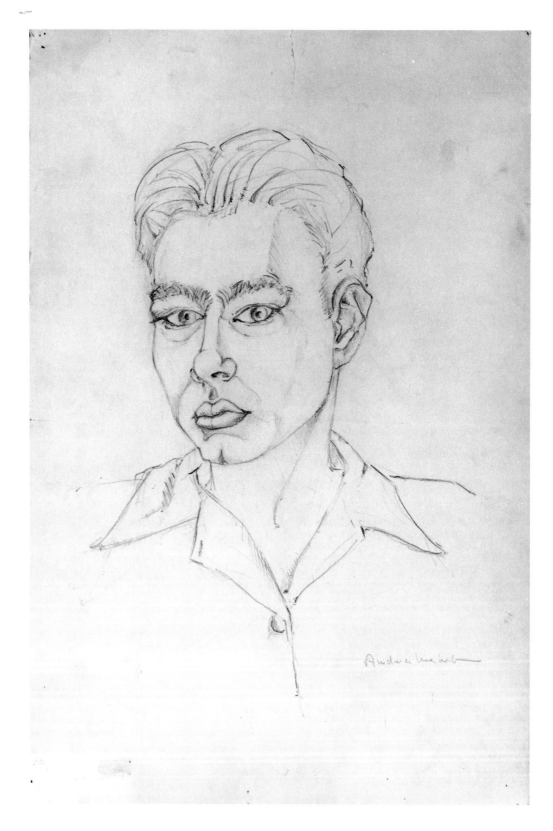

1. **Self-Portrait.** 1942
Pencil on paper,
19 × 13⅜″ (48.3 × 34 cm)
Private collection

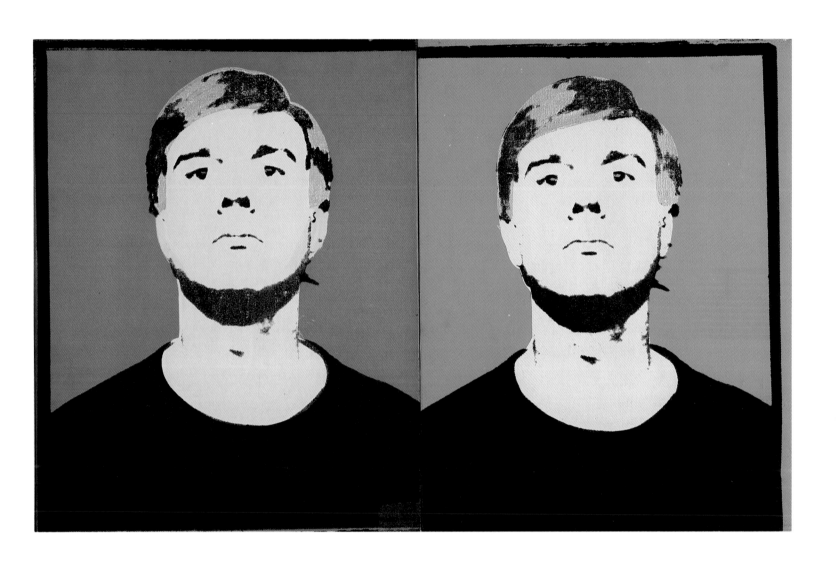

2. **Self-Portrait.** 1964
Silkscreen ink on synthetic polymer paint on canvas;
two panels, each 20 × 16″ (50.8 × 40.6 cm)
Collection Gerald S. Fineberg

3. **Self-Portrait.** 1964
Silkscreen ink on synthetic polymer paint on canvas;
four panels, each 20 × 16″ (50.8 × 40.6 cm)
Collection Mr. and Mrs. S. Brooks Barron

4. **Self-Portrait.** 1967
Silkscreen ink on synthetic polymer paint on canvas,
6 × 6′ (182.9 × 182.9 cm)
Courtesy Leo Castelli Gallery, New York

5. **Double Self-Portrait.** 1967
Silkscreen ink on synthetic polymer paint on canvas;
two panels, each 6 × 6′ (182.9 × 182.9 cm)
The Detroit Institute of Arts. Founders Society Purchase, Friends of Modern Art Fund

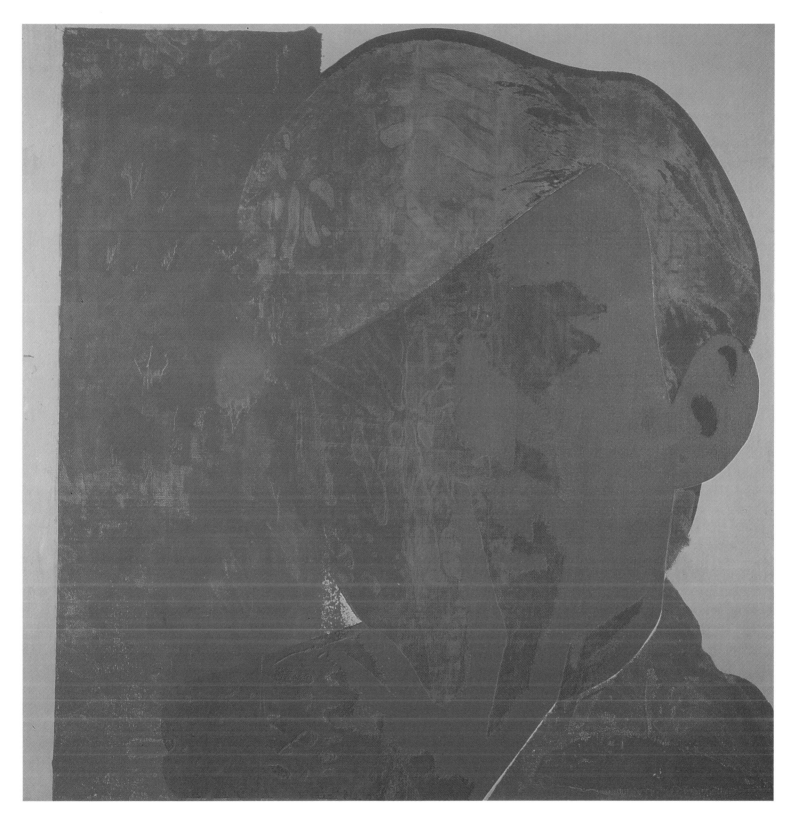

6. **Self-Portrait.** 1967
Silkscreen ink on synthetic polymer paint on canvas,
6′ ⅛″ × 6′ ⅛″ (183.2 × 183.2 cm)
The Trustees of the Tate Gallery

7. **Self-Portrait.** 1967
Silkscreen ink on synthetic polymer paint on canvas,
6 × 6′ (182.9 × 182.9 cm)
Bayerische Staatsgemäldesammlungen, Munich

8. **Self-Portrait.** 1967
Silkscreen ink on synthetic polymer paint on canvas,
6 × 6′ (182.9 × 182.9 cm)
Collection Mr. and Mrs. Harry W. Anderson

9. **Self-Portrait.** 1967
Silkscreen ink on synthetic polymer paint on canvas,
6 × 6′ (182.9 × 182.9 cm)
Collection Mr. and Mrs. Joseph Pulitzer, Jr.

10. **Self-Portrait.** 1967
Silkscreen ink on synthetic polymer paint on canvas,
6 × 6′ (182.9 × 182.9 cm)
Saatchi Collection, London

11. **Self-Portrait with Hands Around Neck.** 1978
Silkscreen ink on synthetic polymer paint on canvas,
16 × 13″ (40.6 × 33 cm)
The Estate of Andy Warhol

12. **Self-Portrait with Skull.** 1978
Silkscreen ink on synthetic polymer paint on canvas,
16 × 13″ (40.6 × 33 cm)
The Menil Collection, Houston

13. **Self-Portrait.** 1979
Instant color print (Polaroid),
24 × 20″ (61 × 50.8 cm)
The Estate of Andy Warhol

14. **The Shadow.** 1981
Serigraph on paper,
38 × 38″ (96.5 × 96.5 cm)
Courtesy Ronald Feldman Fine Arts, Inc., New York

15. **Self-Portrait.** 1978
Silkscreen ink on synthetic polymer paint on canvas;
two panels, each 40⅜ × 40⅜″ (102.6 × 102.6 cm)
Dia Art Foundation, New York. Courtesy The Menil Collection, Houston

16. **Camouflage Self-Portrait.** 1986
Silkscreen ink on synthetic polymer paint on canvas,
6′ 8″ × 6′ 8″ (203.2 × 203.2 cm)
Private collection

17. **Camouflage Self-Portrait.** 1986
Silkscreen ink on synthetic polymer paint on canvas,
6′ 8″ × 6′ 8″ (203.2 × 203.2 cm)
The Estate of Andy Warhol

18. **Self-Portrait II.** 1986
Six gelatin-silver prints stitched with thread,
21½ × 27½″ (54.6 × 69.9 cm)
Courtesy Robert Miller Gallery, New York

19. **Six Self-Portraits.** 1986
Silkscreen ink on synthetic polymer paint on canvas;
six portraits, each 22¾ × 22″ (58 × 56 cm)
Collection J. W. Froehlich, Stuttgart

  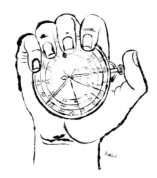

20. **Untitled (Huey Long).** 1948–49
Pen and ink on paper,
29 × 23″ (73.7 × 58.4 cm)
The Carnegie Museum of Art, Pittsburgh. Gift of Russell G. Twiggs

21. **Automat.** 1958
Ink and watercolor on paper,
28¾ × 22⅝″ (73 × 57.5 cm)
The Estate of Andy Warhol

22. **Untitled.** c. 1951
Ink on paper,
18 × 14⅛″ (45.7 × 35.9 cm) (irregular)
The Estate of Andy Warhol

23. **Untitled.** c. 1955
Ink on paper,
19⅛ × 23″ (48.6 × 58.4 cm)
The Estate of Andy Warhol

24. **Untitled.** c. 1955
Ink on paper,
22½ × 28½″ (57.2 × 72.4 cm)
The Estate of Andy Warhol

25. **Untitled.** c. 1955
Offset lithograph on tissue,
29 × 11″ (73.7 × 27.9 cm)
The Estate of Andy Warhol

26. **Untitled.** c. 1962
Pencil and synthetic polymer paint on paper,
29 × 23″ (73.7 × 58.4 cm)
The Estate of Andy Warhol

27. **Untitled.** c. 1962
Pencil, crayon, and synthetic polymer paint
with photographs pasted on paper,
28⅞ × 23″ (73.3 × 58.4 cm)
The Estate of Andy Warhol

28. **Untitled.** c. 1962
Pencil, crayon, and synthetic polymer paint
with photographs pasted on paper,
29 × 23″ (73.7 × 58.4 cm)
The Estate of Andy Warhol

29. **Untitled.** c. 1962
Pencil and synthetic polymer paint
with torn paper pasted on paper,
23 × 28⅞″ (73.3 × 58.4 cm)
The Estate of Andy Warhol

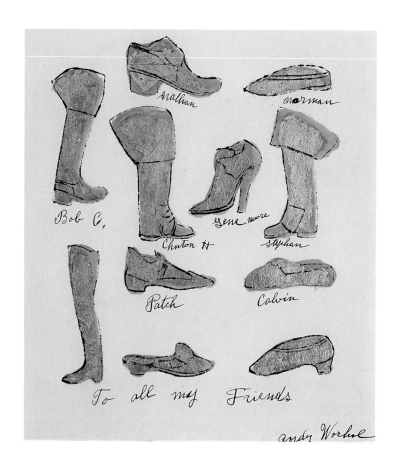

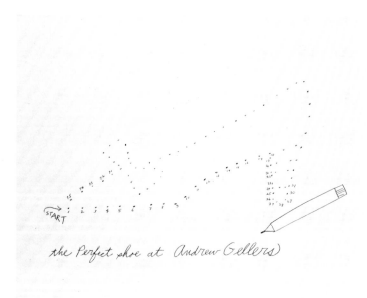

30. **Untitled.** c. 1956
Ink and gold leaf on paper,
9 × 8″ (22.9 × 20.3 cm)
The Estate of Andy Warhol

31. **Untitled.** c. 1955
Ball-point pen on paper,
14⅛ × 18⅛″ (35.9 × 46 cm)
The Estate of Andy Warhol

32. **A la Recherche du Shoe Perdu.** 1955
Offset lithography, watercolor, and pen on paper;
cover, 26⅛ × 20″ (66.4 × 50.8 cm);
sixteen sheets (of seventeen), each 9¾ × 13¾″ (24.8 × 34.9 cm)
The Estate of Andy Warhol

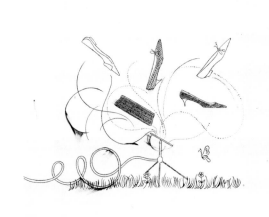

33. **Untitled.** c. 1954
Ball-point pen on paper,
16⅞ × 13¾″ (42.9 × 34.9 cm)
The Estate of Andy Warhol

35. **Untitled.** c. 1955
Ink on paper, 17⅞ × 23⅞″
(45.4 × 60.6 cm) (irregular)
The Estate of Andy Warhol

34. **Untitled.** c. 1955
Ink and wash on paper,
22½ × 16⅜″ (57.2 × 41.6 cm)
The Estate of Andy Warhol

36. **Untitled.** c. 1955
Ink on paper, 13¾ × 17⅞″
(34.9 × 45.4 cm) (irregular)
The Estate of Andy Warhol

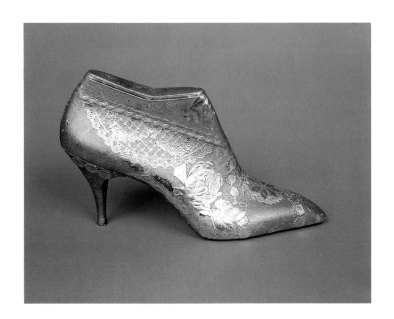

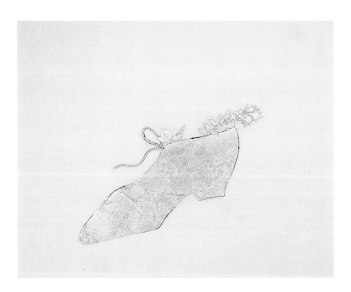

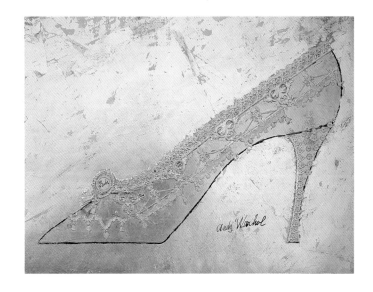

37. **Untitled.** c. 1956
Gold leaf and gold trim on wood,
5 × 9 × 3″ (12.7 × 22.9 × 7.6 cm)
Collection Goldie Heller

38. **Untitled.** c. 1956
Ink, gold leaf, and collage on paper,
23 × 29″ (58.4 × 73.7 cm)
The Estate of Andy Warhol

39. **Babs.** c. 1956
Ink, collage, and gold and silver leaf on paper,
12 × 16″ (30.5 × 40.6 cm)
The Estate of Andy Warhol

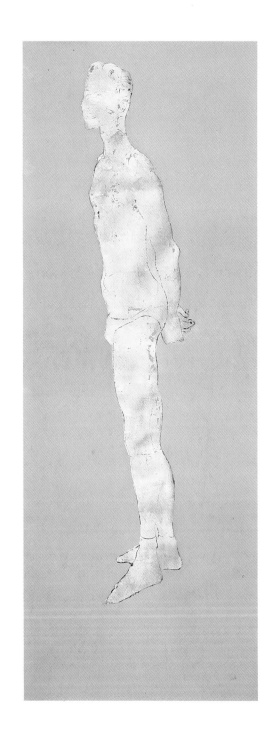

40. **Untitled.** 1957
Ink and gold leaf on paper,
8′ 1″ × 35⅝″ (246.5 × 90.5 cm)
Collection Dr. Marx, Berlin

41. **Untitled.** 1957
Ball-point pen on paper,
7′ 3″ × 36″ (221 × 91.4 cm)
The Estate of Andy Warhol

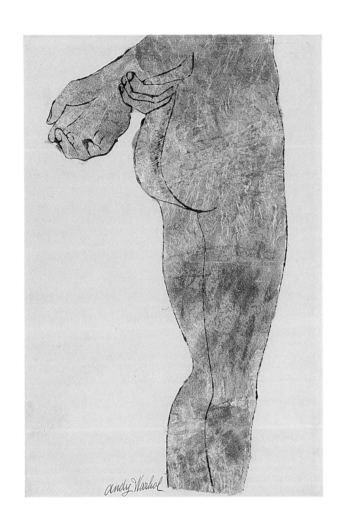

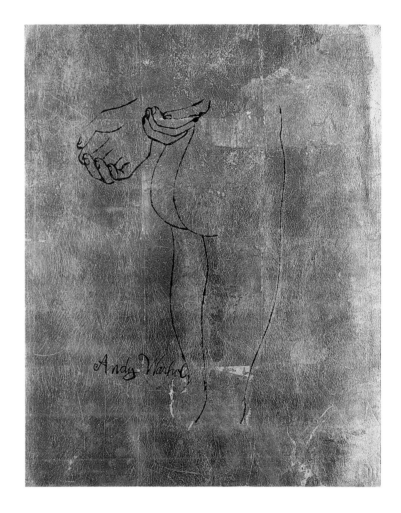

42. **Untitled.** 1957
Ink and gold leaf on paper,
17½ × 11½″ (44.4 × 29.2 cm)
Collection J. W. Froelich, Stuttgart

43. **Untitled.** 1957
Ink and gold leaf on paper,
20 × 16″ (51 × 41 cm)
Courtesy Thomas Ammann, Zürich

44. **Untitled.** c. 1957
Ink and gold leaf on paper,
23 × 14⅝″ (58.4 × 37.1 cm)
The Estate of Andy Warhol

45. **Untitled.** 1957
Ink and gold leaf on paper,
22 × 14⅝″ (55.9 × 37.1 cm)
The Estate of Andy Warhol

46. **Untitled.** 1957
Ink, gold leaf, and collage on paper,
22⅞ × 16″ (58.1 × 40.6 cm)
The Estate of Andy Warhol

47. **Untitled.** c. 1957
Ink and gold leaf on paper,
24⅛ × 18″ (61.3 × 45.7 cm)
The Estate of Andy Warhol

48. **Untitled.** c. 1957
Pen and ink, gold leaf, and collage on paper,
23 × 15″ (58.4 × 38 cm) (irregular)
The Estate of Andy Warhol

49. **Untitled.** c. 1957
Ink and gold leaf on paper,
20 × 14½″ (50.8 × 36.8 cm)
The Estate of Andy Warhol

50. **Untitled.** 1957
Ink and gold leaf on paper,
20 × 18″ (50.8 × 45.7 cm)
Courtesy Anthony D'Offay Gallery, London

51. **Untitled.** c. 1957
Ink, watercolor, and gold leaf on paper,
16½ × 13¼″ (41.9 × 33.7 cm)
Courtesy Anthony D'Offay Gallery, London

52. **Untitled.** 1957
Ink, gold leaf, and collage on paper,
18 × 14″ (45.7 × 35.6 cm)
The Estate of Andy Warhol

53. **Untitled.** c. 1957
Ink and gold leaf on paper,
20 × 16″ (50.8 × 40.6 cm)
The Estate of Andy Warhol

54. **Untitled.** c. 1957
Ink and gold leaf on paper,
22⅞ × 19⅛″ (58.1 × 48.6 cm)
The Estate of Andy Warhol

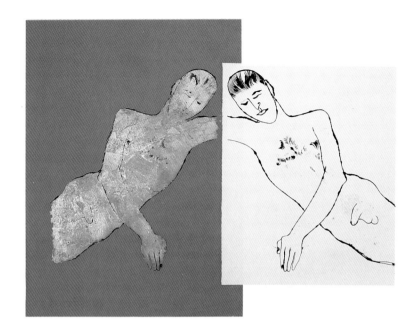

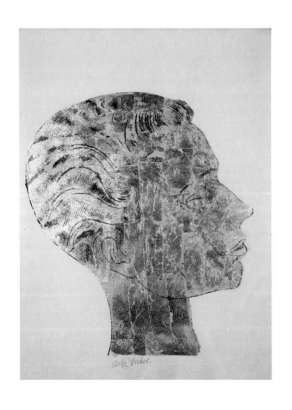

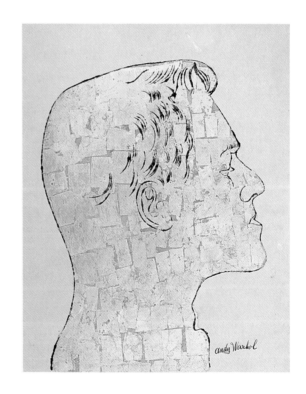

<table>
</table>

*Top*
58. **Untitled.** c. 1957
Two sheets: ink and gold leaf on paper, pen and ink on paper;
20 × 23″ (50.8 × 58.4 cm), 16⅛ × 17⅞″ (41 × 45.4 cm)
The Estate of Andy Warhol

*Bottom left*
59. **Untitled.** c. 1957
Ink and gold leaf on paper,
20 × 14½″ (50.8 × 36.8 cm)
Courtesy Kent Fine Arts, New York

*Bottom right*
60. **Untitled.** c. 1957
Ink and gold leaf on paper,
20 × 16″ (50.8 × 40.6 cm)
The Estate of Andy Warhol

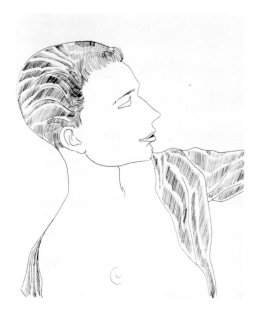

61. **Untitled.** c. 1955
Ball-point pen on paper,
16⅞ × 13¾″ (42.9 × 34.9 cm)
The Estate of Andy Warhol

62. **Untitled.** c. 1957
Ball-point pen on paper,
16½ × 14″ (41.9 × 35.6 cm)
The Estate of Andy Warhol

63. **Untitled.** c. 1956
Ball-point pen on paper,
16⅞ × 14″ (42.9 × 35.6 cm)
The Estate of Andy Warhol

64. **Untitled.** c. 1957
Ball-point pen on paper,
16⅞ × 13⅞″ (42.9 × 35.2 cm)
The Estate of Andy Warhol

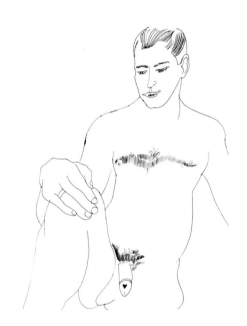 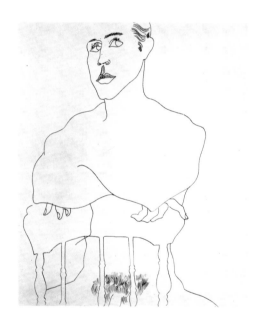

**65. Untitled.** c. 1957
Ball-point pen on paper,
16¾ × 13⅞″ (42.5 × 35.2 cm)
The Estate of Andy Warhol

**66. Untitled.** c. 1957
Ball-point pen on paper,
16¾ × 14″ (42.5 × 35.6 cm)
The Estate of Andy Warhol

**67. Untitled.** c. 1957
Ball-point pen on paper,
17 × 13½″ (43.2 × 34.3 cm)
The Estate of Andy Warhol

**68. Untitled.** c. 1957
Ball-point pen on paper,
16¾ × 13⅞″ (42.5 × 35.2 cm)
The Estate of Andy Warhol

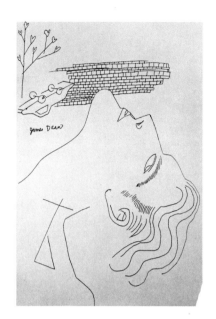

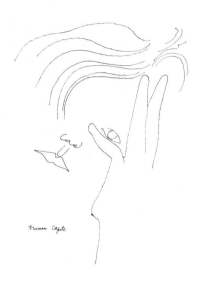

69. **Untitled.** c. 1957
Ball-point pen on paper,
16¾ × 13⅞″ (42.5 × 35.2 cm)
The Estate of Andy Warhol

70. **James Dean.** c. 1955
Ball-point pen on paper,
17¾ × 11⅞″ (45 × 30.2 cm)
The Estate of Andy Warhol

71. **Truman Capote.** c. 1955
Ball-point pen on paper,
16¾ × 13¾″ (42.5 × 34.9 cm)
The Estate of Andy Warhol

72. **Untitled.** c. 1957
Ball-point pen on paper,
16⅝ × 14″ (42.2 × 35.6 cm)
The Estate of Andy Warhol

73. **Untitled.** c. 1957
Ball-point pen on paper,
17 × 13⅞″ (43.2 × 35.2 cm)
The Estate of Andy Warhol

74. **Untitled.** c. 1957
Ball-point pen on paper,
17 × 13⅛″ (43.2 × 35.6 cm)
The Estate of Andy Warhol

75. **Untitled.** c. 1957
Ball-point pen on paper,
17 × 14″ (43.2 × 35.6 cm)
The Estate of Andy Warhol

76. **Untitled.** c. 1957
Ball-point pen on paper,
16¾ × 13⅞″ (42.5 × 35.2 cm)
The Estate of Andy Warhol

77. Window display, Bonwit Teller, New York, April 1961

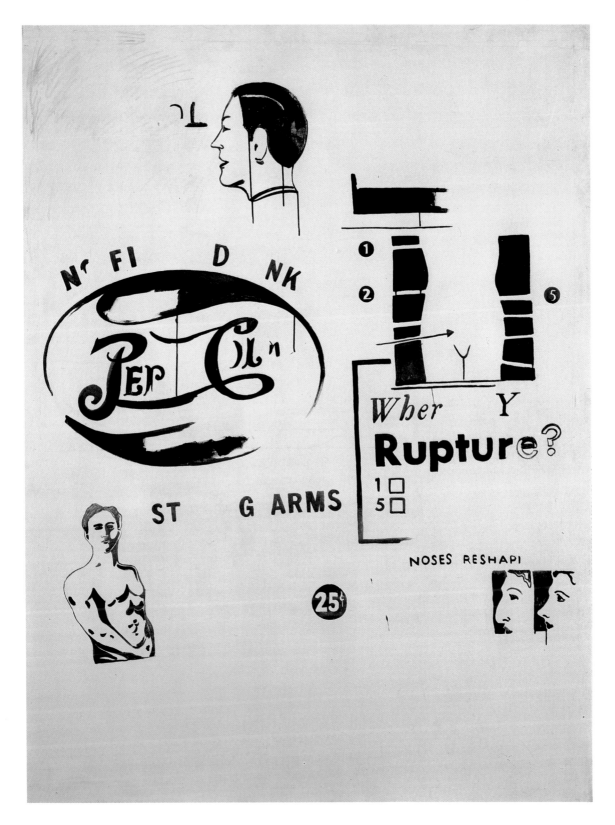

78. **Advertisement.** 1960
Synthetic polymer paint on canvas,
6′ × 54″ (182.9 × 137 cm)
Collection Dr. Marx, Berlin, on extended loan to
the Städtisches Museum Abteiberg, Mönchengladbach

79. **Before and After 3.** 1962
Synthetic polymer paint on canvas.
6′ × 8′ 3⅝″ (182.9 × 255.9 cm)
Whitney Museum of American Art, New York
Purchase, with funds from Charles Simon

80. **Before & After—May, 25¢.** 1962
Pencil on paper,
23¾″ × 18 (60.3 × 45.7 cm)
Collection Miriam and Erwin Kelen, Minneapolis

81. **Before and After.** 1960
Synthetic polymer paint on canvas,
54 × 70″ (137.2 × 177.8 cm)
The Estate of Andy Warhol

82. **Untitled.** 1960
Pencil and cut newspaper pasted on paper,
14 × 11½″ (35.6 × 29.2 cm) (irregular)
The Estate of Andy Warhol

83. **Where Is Your Rupture?** 1960
Synthetic polymer paint on canvas,
69¾ × 54″ (177.2 × 137.2 cm)
Private collection

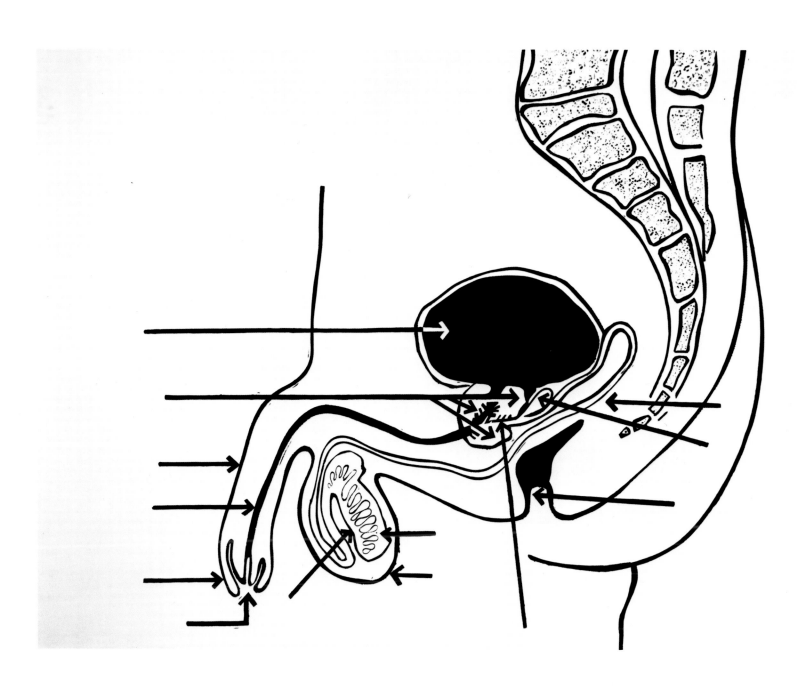

84. **Untitled.** c. 1960–62
Synthetic polymer paint on canvas,
54″ × 6′ (137.2 × 182.9 cm)
The Estate of Andy Warhol

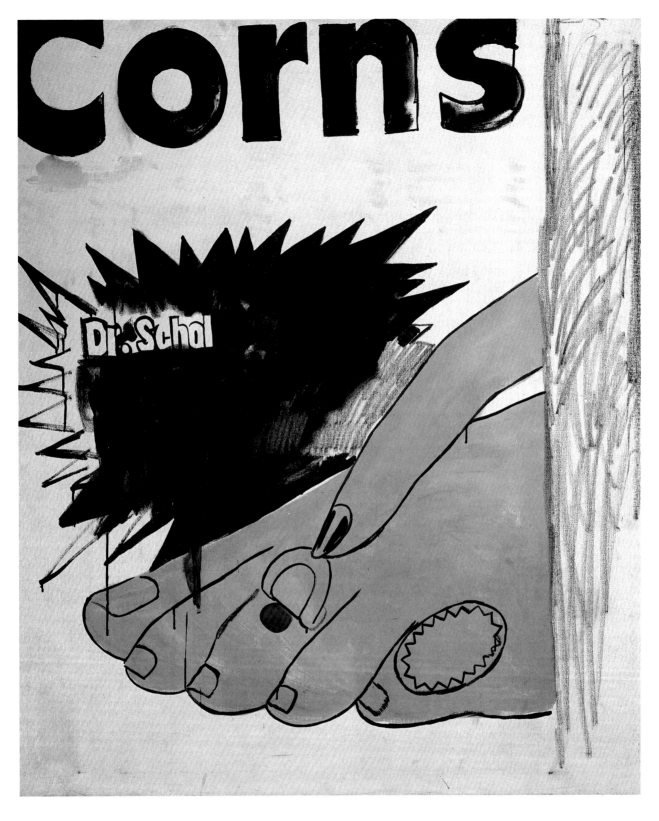

85. **Dr. Scholl.** 1960
Synthetic polymer paint on canvas,
48 × 40″ (121.9 × 101.6 cm)
The Metropolitan Museum of Art, New York. Gift of Halston

86. **Wigs.** 1960
Oil and wax crayon on canvas,
70⅛ × 40″ (178.1 × 101.5 cm)
Dia Art Foundation, New York
Courtesy The Menil Collection, Houston

87. **Untitled.** 1960
Pencil and cut newspaper pasted on paper,
13⅞ × 11½″ (35.2 × 29.2 cm) (irregular)
The Estate of Andy Warhol

88. **Icebox.** 1960
Oil, ink, and pencil on canvas,
67 × 53⅛″ (170.2 × 134.9 cm)
The Menil Collection, Houston

89. **Peach Halves.** 1960
Synthetic polymer paint on canvas,
70 × 54″ (177.5 × 137.5 cm)
Staatsgalerie Stuttgart

90. **Coca-Cola.** 1960
Oil and wax crayon on canvas,
6′ × 54″ (182.9 × 137.2 cm)
Dia Art Foundation, New York. Courtesy The Menil Collection, Houston

91. **Large Coca-Cola.** 1962
Synthetic polymer paint on canvas,
6′ 10″ × 57″ (208.3 × 144.8 cm)
Collection Elizabeth and Michael Rea

92. **TV $199.** 1960
Oil on canvas,
62¼ × 49½″ (158.1 × 125.7 cm)
Collection John and Kimiko Powers

*Top left*
93. **Campbell's Soup Can (Tomato Rice).** 1960
Ink, tempera, crayon, and oil on oil-primed canvas,
36¼ × 34¾″ (92.1 × 88.3 cm)
Dia Art Foundation, New York
Courtesy The Menil Collection, Houston

*Bottom left*
94. **199 Television.** 1960
Ink and pencil on paper,
29 × 33″ (73.7 × 83.8 cm)
Dia Art Foundation, New York
Courtesy The Menil Collection, Houston

*Right*
95. **Cooking Pot.** 1962
Photo-engraving on paper,
11¾ × 9½″ (29.8 × 24.1 cm)
The Museum of Modern Art, New York
Gift of Peter Deitsch Gallery

96. **Water Heater.** 1960
Synthetic polymer paint on canvas,
44¾ × 40" (113.7 × 101.5 cm)
The Museum of Modern Art, New York
Gift of Roy Lichtenstein

97. **Drills 7.88.** 1960
Synthetic polymer paint on canvas,
$42\frac{5}{8} \times 39\frac{3}{4}''$ (108.3 × 101 cm)
The Estate of Andy Warhol

98. **3-D Vacuum.** 1960
Synthetic polymer paint on canvas,
26⅝ × 39⅞″ (67.6 × 101.3 cm)
The Estate of Andy Warhol

99. **Icers' Shoes.** 1960
Synthetic polymer paint on canvas,
42¾ × 40⅜″ (108.6 × 102.6 cm)
The Estate of Andy Warhol

100. **Storm Door.** 1960
Synthetic polymer paint on canvas,
46 × 42⅛″ (117 × 107 cm)
Courtesy Thomas Ammann, Zürich

101. **Storm Door.** 1961
Synthetic polymer paint on canvas,
6′ × 60″ (182.9 × 152.4 cm)
Collection Robert and Meryl Meltzer

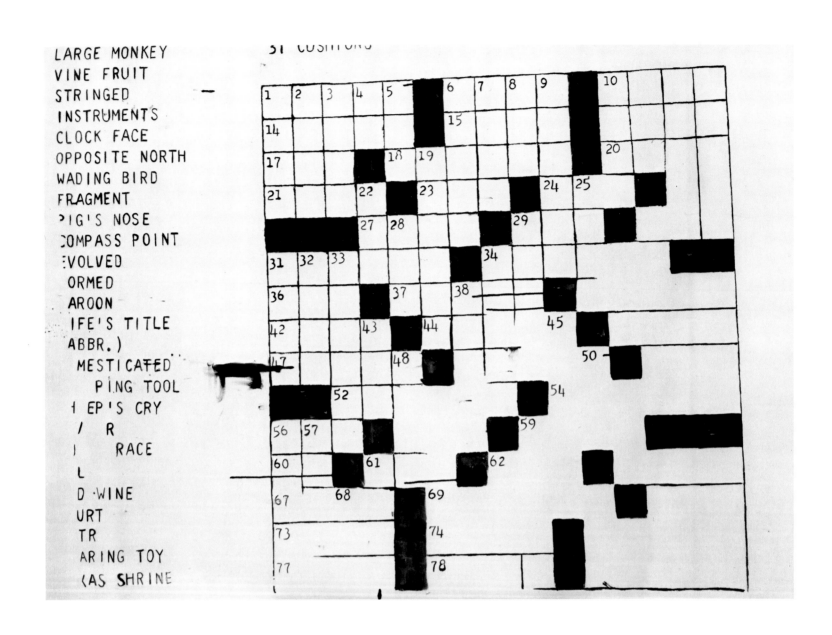

LARGE MONKEY
VINE FRUIT
STRINGED
INSTRUMENTS
CLOCK FACE
OPPOSITE NORTH
WADING BIRD
FRAGMENT
PIG'S NOSE
COMPASS POINT
EVOLVED
FORMED
MAROON
WIFE'S TITLE
(ABBR.)
DOMESTICATED
PING TOOL
SHEEP'S CRY
/ R
RACE
L
D WINE
URT
TR
ARING TOY
KAS SHRINE

51 CUSHIONS

102. **Crossword.** 1960
Synthetic polymer paint on canvas,
44⅓ × 63″ (112.6 × 160 cm)
The Estate of Andy Warhol

138

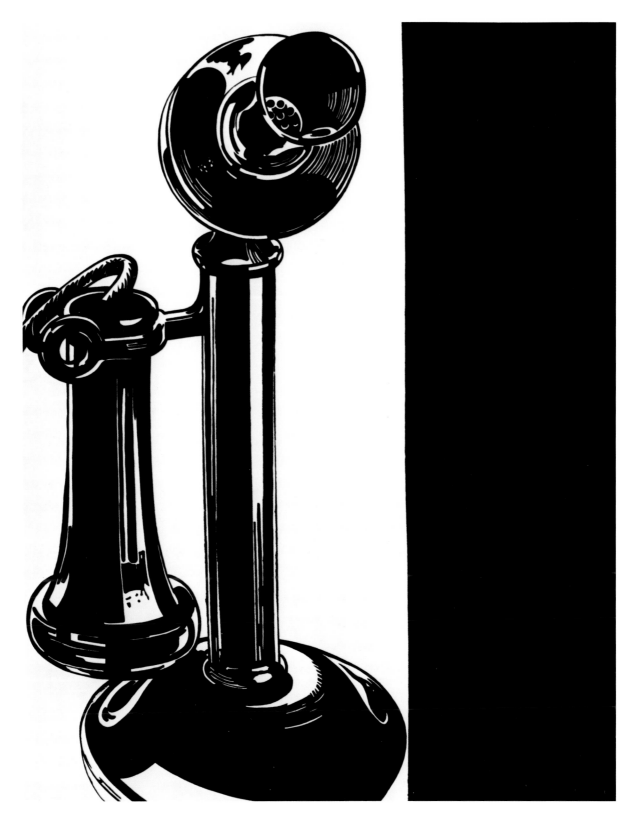

103. **Telephone.** 1961
Oil on canvas,
69¾ × 54″ (177.2 × 137.2 cm)
The Estate of Andy Warhol

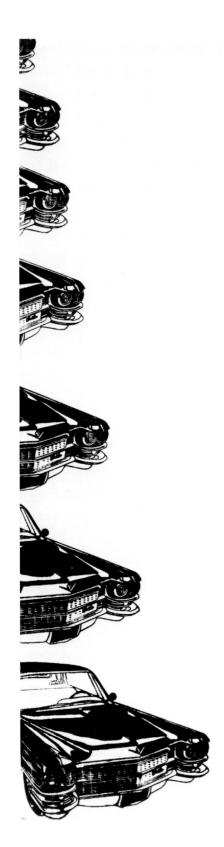
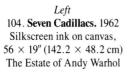

| *Left* | *Top right* | *Bottom right* |
|---|---|---|
| 104. **Seven Cadillacs.** 1962 | 105. **Untitled.** c. 1962 | 106. **Untitled.** c. 1962 |
| Silkscreen ink on canvas, | Pencil on paper, | Silkscreen ink on paper, |
| 56 × 19″ (142.2 × 48.2 cm) | 24 × 18″ (61 × 45.7 cm) | 23 × 18″ (58.4 × 45.7 cm) |
| The Estate of Andy Warhol | The Estate of Andy Warhol | The Estate of Andy Warhol |

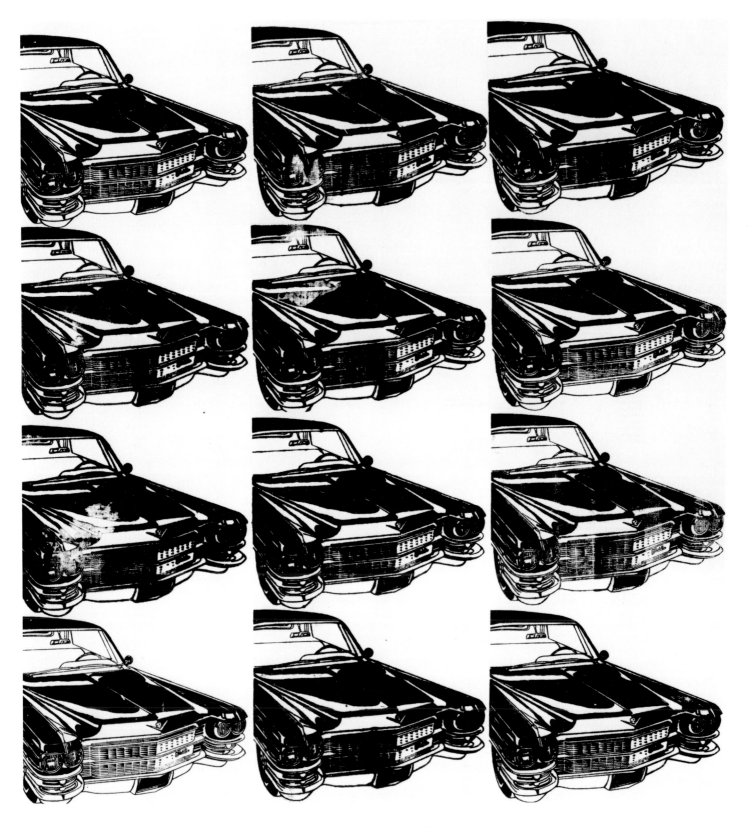

107. **Twelve Cadillacs.** 1962
Silkscreen ink on canvas,
46 × 42″ (116.8 × 106.7 cm)
The Estate of Andy Warhol

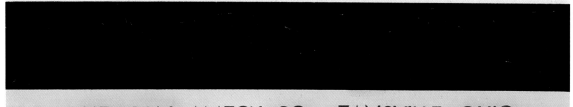

108. **Close Cover Before Striking (Pepsi-Cola).** 1962
Synthetic polymer paint and sandpaper on canvas,
6′ × 54″ (182.9 × 137 cm)
Museum Ludwig, Cologne

109. **Yellow Close Cover Before Striking.** 1962
Synthetic polymer paint and sandpaper on canvas,
16 × 20″ (40.6 × 50.8 cm)
Private collection

110. **Dick Tracy.** 1960
Casein and crayon on canvas,
48 × 33⅞″ (122 × 86 cm)
Private collection

111. **Dick Tracy.** 1960
Synthetic polymer paint on canvas,
6′ 7″ × 45″ (201 × 114 cm)
Collection Mr. and Mrs. S. I. Newhouse, Jr.

112. **Batman.** 1960
Synthetic polymer paint and crayon on canvas,
30 × 40″ (76 × 101.5 cm)
Private collection

113. **Superman.** 1960
Synthetic polymer paint and crayon on canvas,
67 × 52″ (170 × 133 cm)
Collection Gunter Sachs

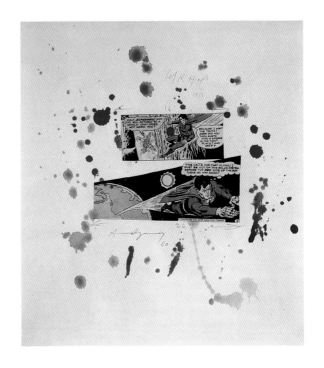

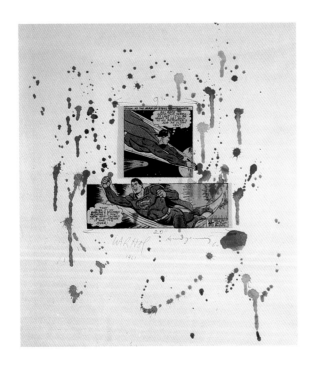

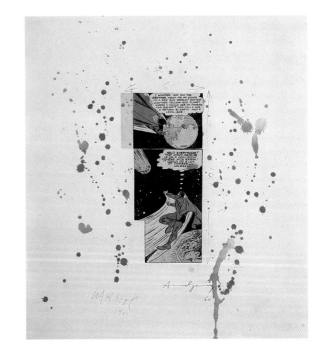

**114. Untitled.** 1960–61
Watercolor, pencil, and cut newspaper pasted on paper,
13¼ × 11⅝″ (33.7 × 29.5 cm)
Courtesy Robert Miller Gallery, New York

**115. Untitled.** 1960–61
Watercolor, pencil, and cut newspaper pasted on paper,
13¾ × 11¾″ (34.9 × 29.8 cm)
Courtesy Robert Miller Gallery, New York

**116. Untitled.** 1960–61
Watercolor, pencil, and cut newspaper pasted on paper,
14¾ × 10¾″ (37.5 × 27.3 cm)
Courtesy Robert Miller Gallery, New York

**117. Untitled.** 1960–61
Watercolor, pencil, and cut newspaper pasted on paper,
13 × 11¾″ (33 × 29.8 cm)
Courtesy Robert Miller Gallery, New York

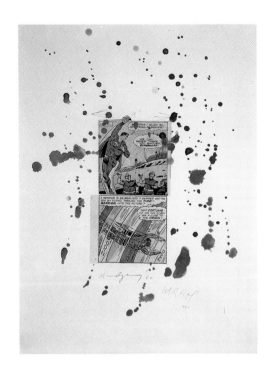

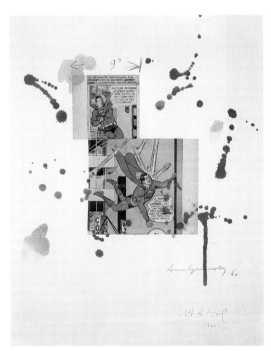

118. **Untitled.** 1960–61
Watercolor, pencil, and cut newspaper pasted on paper,
15 × 11″ (38.1 × 27.9 cm)
Courtesy Robert Miller Gallery, New York

119. **Untitled.** 1960–61
Watercolor, pencil, and cut newspaper pasted on paper,
13¼ × 11⅝″ (33.7 × 29.5 cm)
Courtesy Robert Miller Gallery, New York

120. **Untitled.** 1960
Watercolor, pencil, and cut newspaper pasted on paper,
14 × 11″ (35.6 × 27.9 cm)
Private collection

121. **Untitled.** 1960
Watercolor, pencil, and cut newspaper pasted on paper,
16¾ × 8½″ (42.5 × 21.6 cm)
The Estate of Andy Warhol

122. **Saturday's Popeye.** 1960
Synthetic polymer paint on canvas,
43 × 39″ (108.5 × 98.7 cm)
Landesmuseum, Mainz

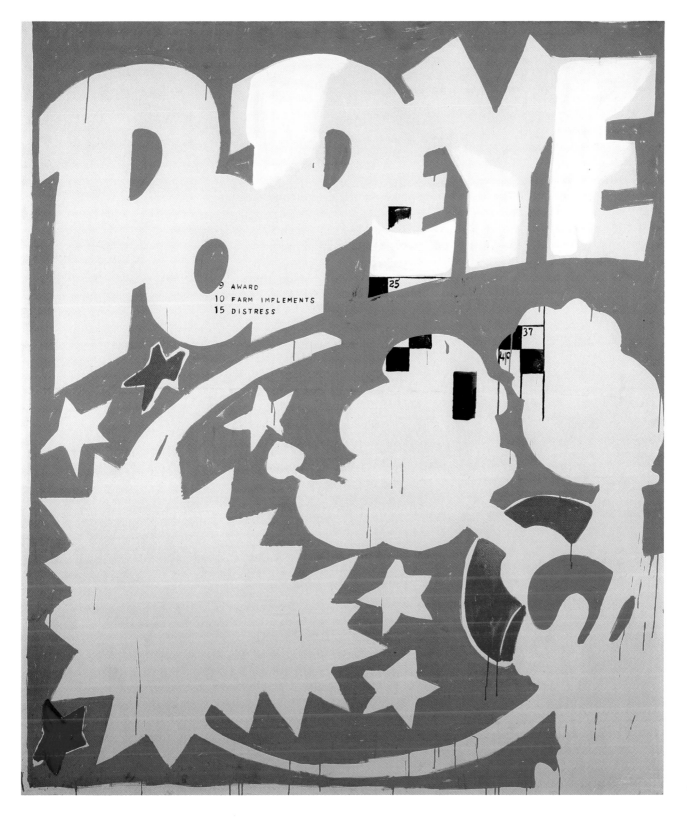

123. **Popeye.** 1961
Synthetic polymer paint on canvas,
68¼ × 58½" (173 × 150 cm)
Collection Mr. and Mrs. S. I. Newhouse, Jr.

124. **Little King.** 1961
Synthetic polymer paint on canvas,
54 × 40″ (137.1 × 101.5 cm)
Whereabouts unknown

125. Comic strip, The Little King, April 4, 1961. The Estate of Andy Warhol

126. **Nancy.** 1960
Synthetic polymer paint on canvas,
40 × 54″ (101.5 × 137.1 cm)
Collection Mr. and Mrs. S. I. Newhouse, Jr.

127. **Journal American.** 1960
Ink on paper,
23¾ × 17⅛″ (60.3 × 45.4 cm)
Dia Art Foundation, New York
Courtesy The Menil Collection, Houston

128. **Untitled.** c. 1956
Ball-point pen on paper,
16¾ × 13⅞″ (42.5 × 35.2 cm)
The Estate of Andy Warhol

129. **Untitled.** c. 1958
Ball-point pen on paper,
22¼ × 17⅝″ (56.5 × 44.8 cm)
The Estate of Andy Warhol

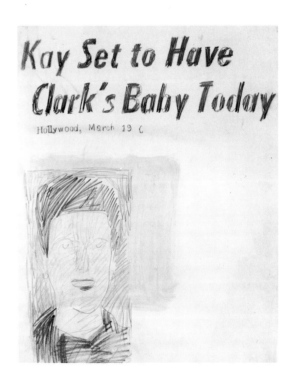

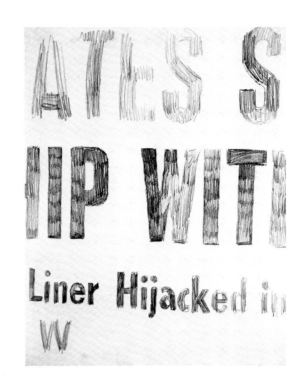

130. **Untitled.** 1961
Pencil on paper,
29 × 23″ (73.7 × 58.4 cm)
The Estate of Andy Warhol

131. **Untitled.** 1961
Pencil on paper,
29 × 23″ (73.7 × 58.4 cm)
The Estate of Andy Warhol

132. **Untitled.** 1961
Pencil on paper,
29 × 23″ (73.7 × 58.4 cm)
The Estate of Andy Warhol

133. **Untitled.** 1962
Pencil and gouache on paper,
28⅝ × 22″ (72.7 × 55.9 cm)
Private collection

134. **A Boy for Meg.** 1961
Synthetic polymer paint on canvas,
6' × 52" (182.9 × 132.1 cm)
National Gallery of Art, Washington, D.C.
Gift of Mr. and Mrs. Burton Tremaine

# DAILY NEWS
#### NEW YORK'S PICTURE NEWSPAPER®

# DAILY NEWS
#### NEW YORK'S PICTURE NEWSPAPER®

5¢

## MET RALLY EDGES LA, 4-3
## YANKS CURB CARDS, 4-1

Stories on Page 78

# EDDIE FISHER
# BREAKS DOWN
## In Hospital Here; Liz in Rome

135. **Daily News.** 1962
Synthetic polymer paint on canvas,
6′ ¼″ × 8′ 4″ (183.5 × 254 cm)
Museum für Moderne Kunst, Frankfurt

136. **129 Die in Jet (Plane Crash).** 1962
Synthetic polymer paint on canvas,
8′ 4″ × 6′ (254 × 183 cm)
Museum Ludwig, Cologne

137. **One-Dollar Bill with Lincoln's Portrait.** 1962
Pencil and gouache on paper,
17¾ × 23⅝″ (45 × 60 cm)
Private collection

138. **#1 Printed Two Dollar.** 1962
Silkscreen ink on canvas,
9 × 10⅛″ (22.9 × 25.7 cm)
Dayton Art Institute
Gift of Mr. and Mrs. Thomas C. Colt, Jr.

139. **Two-Dollar Bill with Jefferson.** 1962
Pencil on paper,
18 × 24″ (45.7 × 61 cm)
Collection Louise Ferrari, Houston

140. **Ten-Dollar Bill.** 1962
Pencil and watercolor on paper,
10 × 23″ (25.4 × 58.4 cm)
Private collection, New York

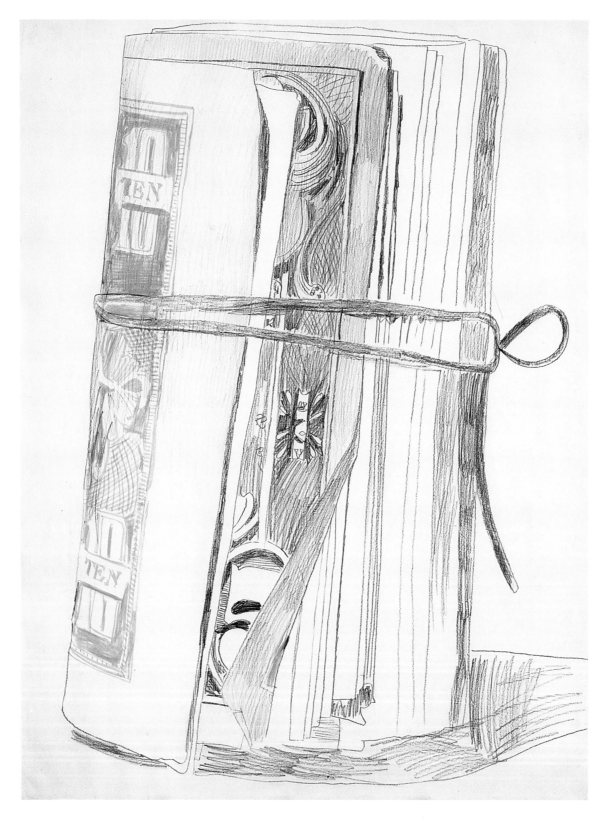

141. **Roll of Bills.** 1962
Pencil, crayon, and felt-tip pen on paper,
40 × 30⅛″ (101.6 × 76.5 cm)
The Museum of Modern Art, New York. Purchase

142. **One-Dollar Bill.** 1962
Synthetic polymer paint and pencil on canvas,
52″ × 6′ (132.1 × 182.9 cm)
Private collection

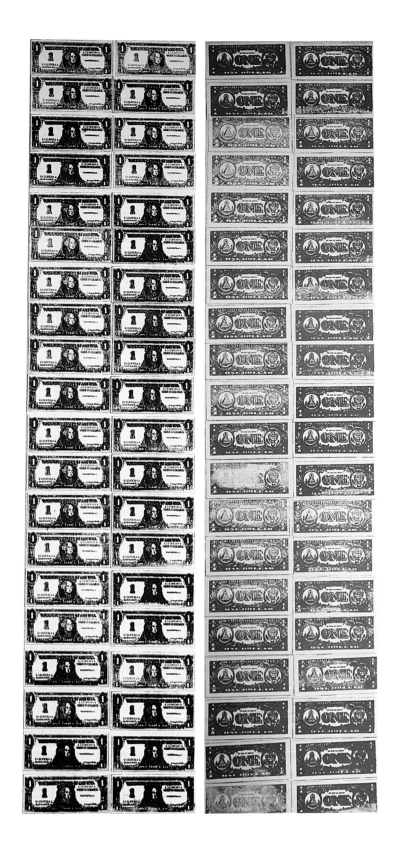

143. **Front and Back Dollar Bills.** 1962
Silkscreen ink on canvas;
two panels, each 6′ 11″ × 19″ (210.8 × 48.2 cm)
Collection Jed Johnson

144. **Eighty Two-Dollar Bills, Front and Rear.** 1962
Silkscreen ink on canvas,
6′ 11″ × 38″ (210 × 96 cm)
Museum Ludwig, Cologne

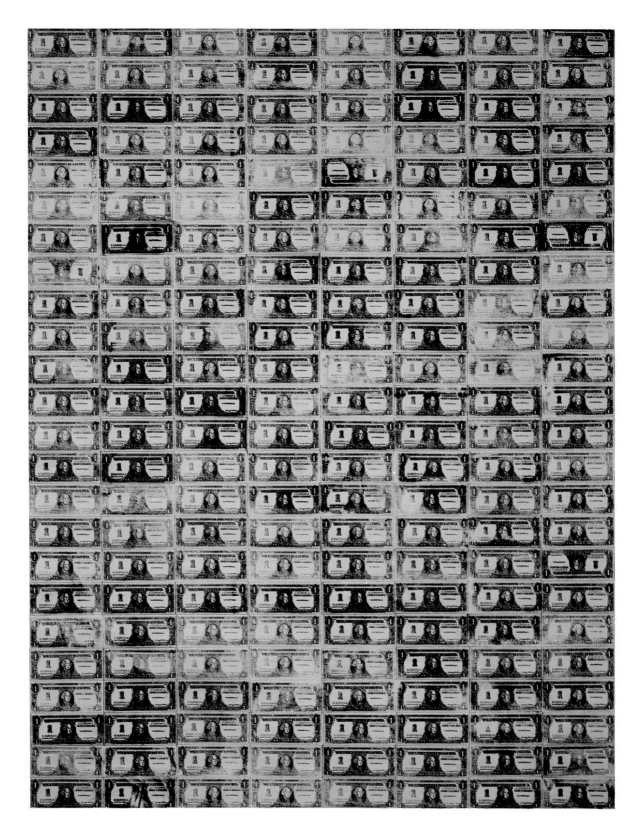

145. **192 One-Dollar Bills.** 1962
Silkscreen ink on canvas,
8' 1¼" × 6' 2⅜" (242 × 189 cm)
Collection Dr. Marx, Berlin, on extended loan to
the Städtisches Museum Abteiberg, Mönchengladbach

146. **Many One-Dollar Bills.** 1962
Silkscreen ink on canvas,
6′ × 54″ (182.9 × 137.2 cm)
The Estate of Myron Orlofsky

147. **Handle with Care—Glass—Thank You.** 1962
Silkscreen ink on canvas,
6′ 10⅛″ × 66⅛″ (208.5 × 168 cm)
Collection Dr. Marx, Berlin, on extended loan to the
Städtisches Museum Abteiberg, Mönchengladbach

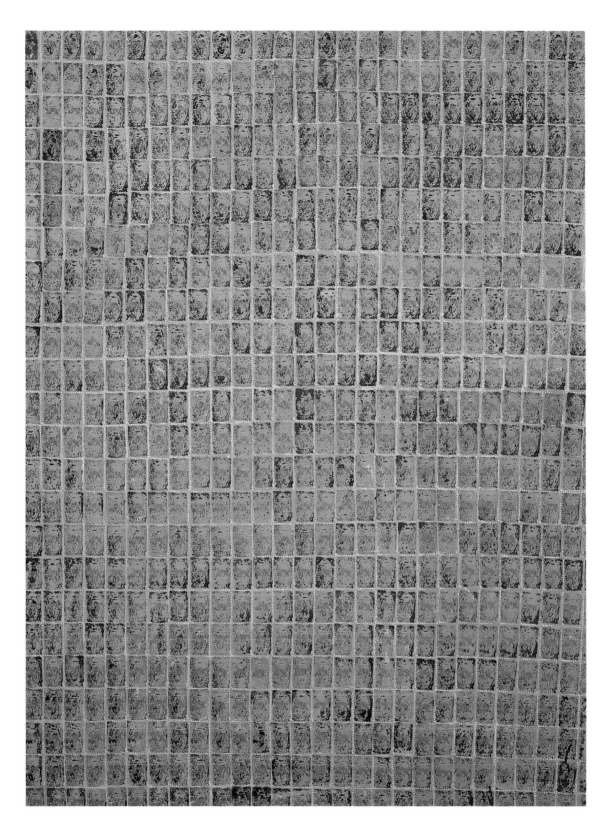

148. **S & H Green Stamps.** 1962
Silkscreen ink on canvas,
71¾ × 53¾″ (182.2 × 136.5 cm)
Collection Philip Johnson

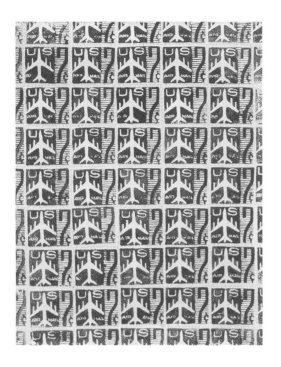

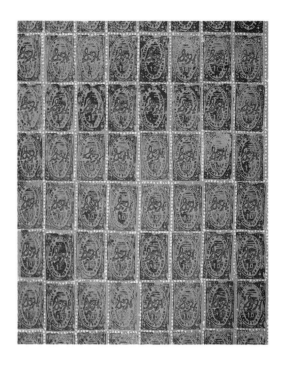

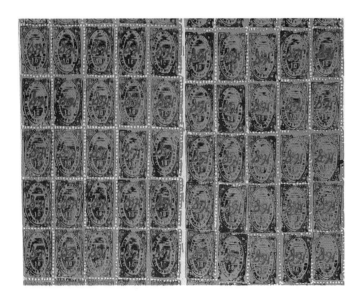

149. **Red Airmail Stamps.** 1962
Silkscreen ink on canvas,
20 × 16″ (50.8 × 40.6 cm)
Private collection, Scarsdale, New York

150. **S & H Green Stamps.** 1962
Silkscreen ink on canvas,
20 × 16″ (50.8 × 40.6 cm)
Collection Betty Asher

151. **Seventy S & H Green Stamps.** 1962
Silkscreen ink on canvas with metal staples,
16⅛ × 20¼″ (41 × 51.4 cm)
Collection Martin and Janet Blinder. Courtesy
Martin Lawrence Limited Editions, Los Angeles

152. **Martinson Coffee.** 1962
Silkscreen ink on canvas,
20 × 16″ (51 × 40.5 cm)
Private collection

153. **Do It Yourself (Violin).** 1962
Synthetic polymer paint and Prestype on canvas,
54″ × 6′ (137 × 182.9 cm)
Private collection

**154. Do It Yourself (Sailboats).** 1962
Synthetic polymer paint and Prestype on canvas,
6′ × 8′ 4″ (182.9 × 254 cm)
Private collection, Berlin

155. **Do It Yourself (Narcissus).** 1962
Pencil and colored pencil on paper,
23 × 18″ (60.3 × 45.7 cm)
Oeffentliche Kunstsammlung Basel, Kupferstichkabinett
Karl August Burckhardt-Koechlin Fonds

156. **Do It Yourself (Flowers).** 1962
Colored crayon on paper,
25 × 18″ (63.5 × 45.7 cm)
The Sonnabend Collection

157. **Do It Yourself (Flowers).** 1962
Synthetic polymer paint and Prestype on canvas,
69 × 59″ (175 × 150 cm)
Courtesy Thomas Ammann, Zürich

158. **Do It Yourself (Seascape).** 1963
Synthetic polymer paint and Prestype on canvas,
54⅓″ × 6′ (138 × 182.9 cm)
Collection Dr. Marx, Berlin

159. **Do It Yourself (Landscape).** 1962
Synthetic polymer paint and Prestype on canvas,
70 × 54″ (178 × 137 cm)
Museum Ludwig, Cologne

160. **Dance Diagram.** 1962
Synthetic polymer paint on canvas,
6′ × 51¾″ (182.9 × 131.5 cm)
The Estate of Andy Warhol

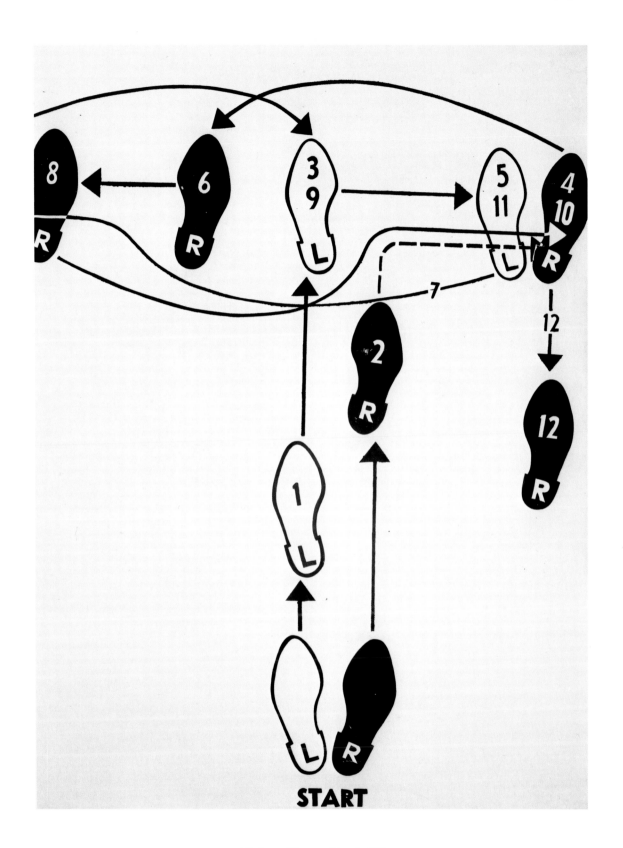

START

161. **Dance Diagram (Tango).** 1962
Synthetic polymer paint on canvas,
71¼ × 52″ (181.1 × 132.1 cm)
The Estate of Andy Warhol

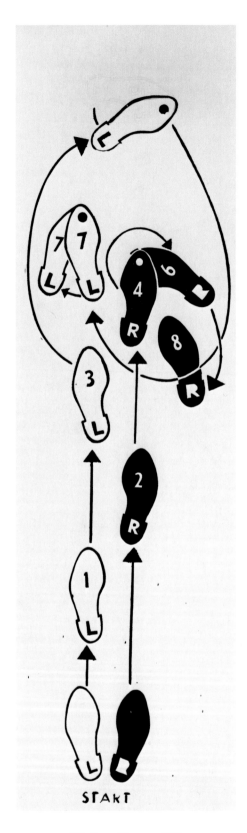

162. **Dance Diagram.** 1962
Synthetic polymer paint on canvas,
6′ 11″ × 24″ (210.8 × 60.9 cm)
The Estate of Andy Warhol

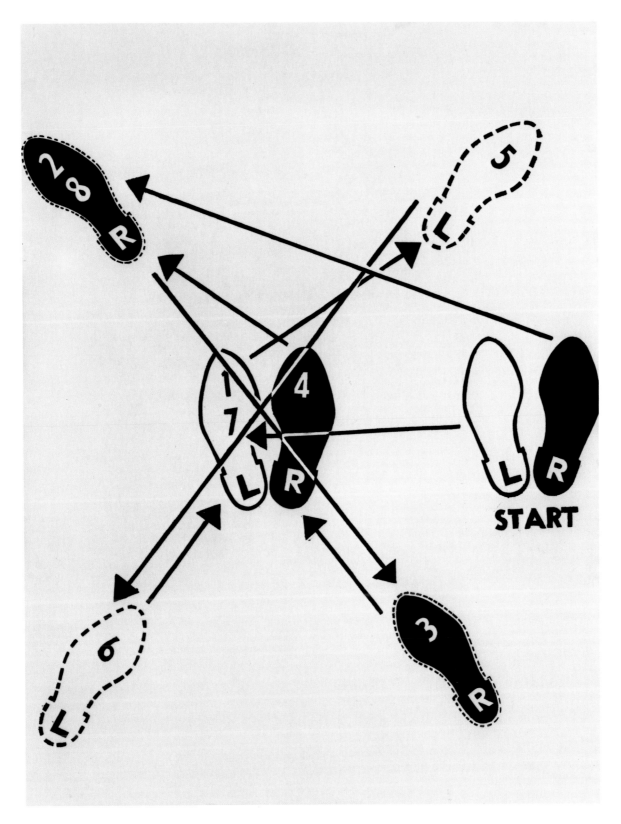

163. **Dance Diagram.** 1962
Synthetic polymer paint on canvas,
6′ × 54″ (182.9 × 137 cm)
The Estate of Andy Warhol

164. **Campbell's Soup Cans.** 1962
Synthetic polymer paint on canvas;
thirty-two works, each 20 × 16″ (50.8 × 40.6 cm)
Collection Irving Blum, New York

165. **Campbell's Soup Cans**
**(Chicken with Rice, Bean with Bacon).** 1962
Synthetic polymer paint on canvas;
two panels, each 20 × 16″ (51 × 40.5 cm)
Städtisches Museum Abteiberg, Mönchengladbach

**166. Big Torn Campbell's Soup Can (Vegetable Beef).** 1962
Synthetic polymer paint on canvas,
6′ × 53½″ (182.9 × 136 cm)
Kunsthaus Zürich

167. **Big Torn Campbell's Soup Can (Black Bean).** 1962
Synthetic polymer paint on canvas,
6′ × 54″ (182.9 × 137 cm)
Kunstsammlung Nordrhein-Westfalen, Düsseldorf

168. **Big Torn Campbell's Soup Can (Pepper Pot).** 1962
Oil, synthetic polymer paint, and Prestype on canvas,
71¾ × 51¾" (182.2 × 131.4 cm)
The Estate of Andy Warhol

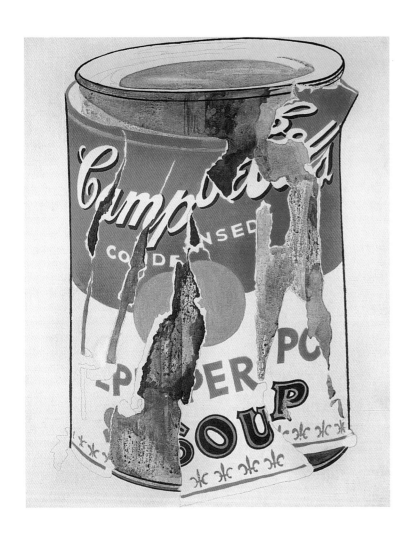

169. **Small Torn Campbell's Soup Can (Pepper Pot).** 1962
Synthetic polymer paint on canvas,
20 × 16″ (50.8 × 40.6 cm)
Collection Irving Blum, New York

170. **Crushed Campbell's Soup Can (Beef Noodle).** 1962
Synthetic polymer paint and pencil on canvas,
6′ × 52″ (182.9 × 132.1 cm)
The Estate of Andy Warhol

171. **Can.** 1961
Pencil and wash on paper,
39¾ × 29⅞″ (100.9 × 75.9 cm)
Collection J. Y. Mock, London

172. **Big Campbell's Soup Can, 19¢.** 1962
Synthetic polymer paint and pencil on canvas,
6′ × 54½″ (182.9 × 138.4 cm)
The Menil Collection, Houston

173. **Campbell's Soup Can with Can Opener.** 1962
Silkscreen ink on synthetic polymer paint on canvas,
6′ × 52″ (182.9 × 132 cm)
Collection Windsor, Inc.

174. **Campbell's Soup Can with Ketchup Bottle.** 1962
Pencil on paper,
24 × 18″ (60 × 45 cm)
Collection Robert and Meryl Meltzer

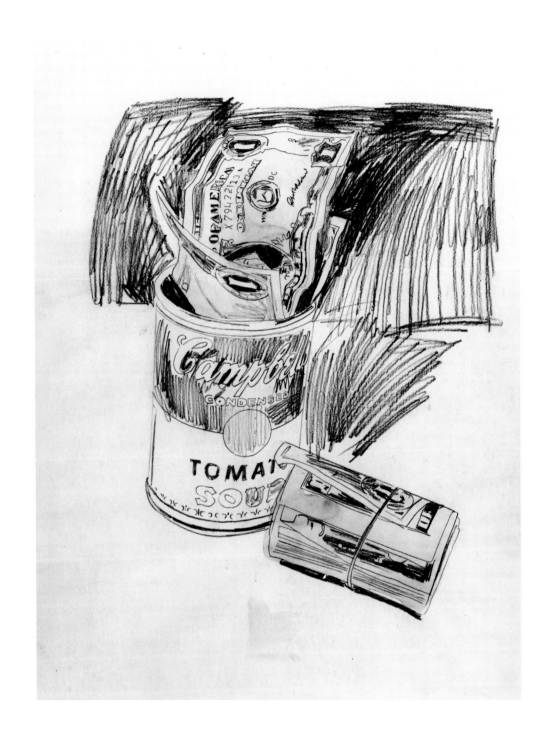

175. **Campbell's Soup Can and Dollar Bills.** 1962
Pencil and watercolor on paper,
24 × 18″ (60 × 45 cm)
Collection Roy and Dorothy Lichtenstein

176. **Two Hundred Campbell's Soup Cans.** 1962
Synthetic polymer paint on canvas,
6′ × 8′ 4″ (182.9 × 254 cm)
Collection John and Kimiko Powers

177. **One Hundred Cans.** 1962
Oil on canvas,
6′ × 52″ (182.9 × 132.1 cm)
Albright-Knox Art Gallery, Buffalo
Gift of Seymour H. Knox

178. **Campbell's Soup Can on a Shopping Bag.** 1964
Serigraph printed on shopping bag,
19¼ × 17″ (48.8 × 43.2 cm)
Private collection

179. **Campbell's Soup Can.** 1965
Silkscreen ink on synthetic polymer paint on canvas,
36⅛ × 24″ (91.7 × 60.9 cm)
The Museum of Modern Art, New York. Philip Johnson Fund

180. **Campbell's Soup Can.** 1965
Silkscreen ink on synthetic polymer paint on canvas,
36⅛ × 24⅛″ (91.7 × 61 cm)
The Museum of Modern Art, New York. Elizabeth Bliss Parkinson Fund

181. **Untitled (Unique Campbell's Soup Box).** 1964
Synthetic polymer paint and pencil on wood,
22 × 15½ × 15¾″ (55.9 × 39.4 × 40 cm)
The Estate of Andy Warhol

*Left*
182. Installation view, *Warhol,* Stable Gallery,
New York, 1964

*Top right*
183. Installation view, *Andy Warhol,*
Institute of Contemporary Art of the University of Pennsylvania,
Philadelphia, 1965

*Bottom right*
184. Installation view, *Andy Warhol,*
Institute of Contemporary Art, Boston, 1966

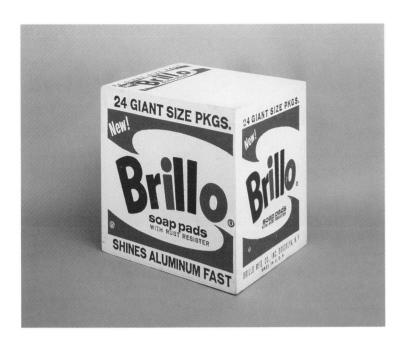

185. **Brillo Box (Soap Pads).** 1964
Silkscreen ink on wood,
17⅛ × 17⅛ × 14″ (43.5 × 43.5 × 35.6 cm)
The Estate of Andy Warhol

186. **Campbell's Box (Tomato Juice).** 1964
Silkscreen ink on wood,
10 × 19 × 9½″ (25.4 × 48.3 × 24.1 cm)
The Estate of Andy Warhol

187. **Del Monte Box (Peach Halves).** 1964
Silkscreen ink on wood,
9½ × 15 × 12″ (24.1 × 38.1 × 30.5 cm)
The Estate of Andy Warhol

188. **Heinz Box (Tomato Ketchup).** 1964
Silkscreen ink on wood,
8½ × 15½ × 10½″ (21.6 × 39.4 × 26.7 cm)
The Estate of Andy Warhol

189. **Kellogg's Boxes (Corn Flakes).** 1971
Silkscreen ink on wood,
each 27 × 24 × 19″ (68.6 × 61 × 48.3 cm)
Los Angeles County Museum of Art
Gift of Andy Warhol through the Contemporary Art Council Fund

190. **Various Boxes.** 1964
Silkscreen ink on wood,
dimensions variable
The Estate of Andy Warhol

191. **Five Coke Bottles.** 1962
Silkscreen ink on synthetic polymer paint on canvas,
16 × 20″ (40.5 × 51 cm)
Private collection

192. **210 Coca-Cola Bottles.** 1962
Silkscreen ink on synthetic polymer paint on canvas,
6′ 10½″ × 8′ 9″ (208 × 267 cm)
Collection Martin and Janet Blinder
Courtesy Martin Lawrence Limited Editions, Los Angeles

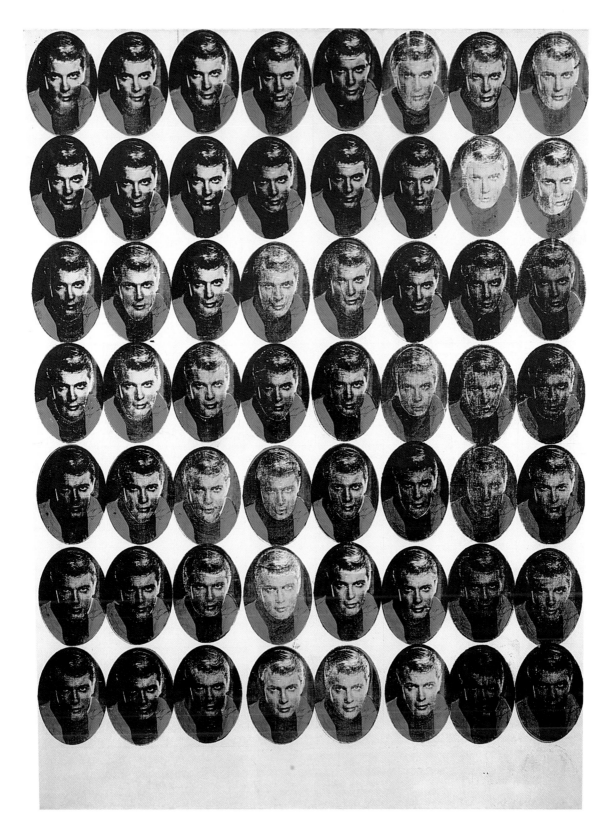

193. **Troy Donahue.** 1962
Silkscreen ink on synthetic polymer paint on canvas,
6′ 8¾″ × 60″ (205.1 × 152.4 cm)
Courtesy Sperone Westwater, New York

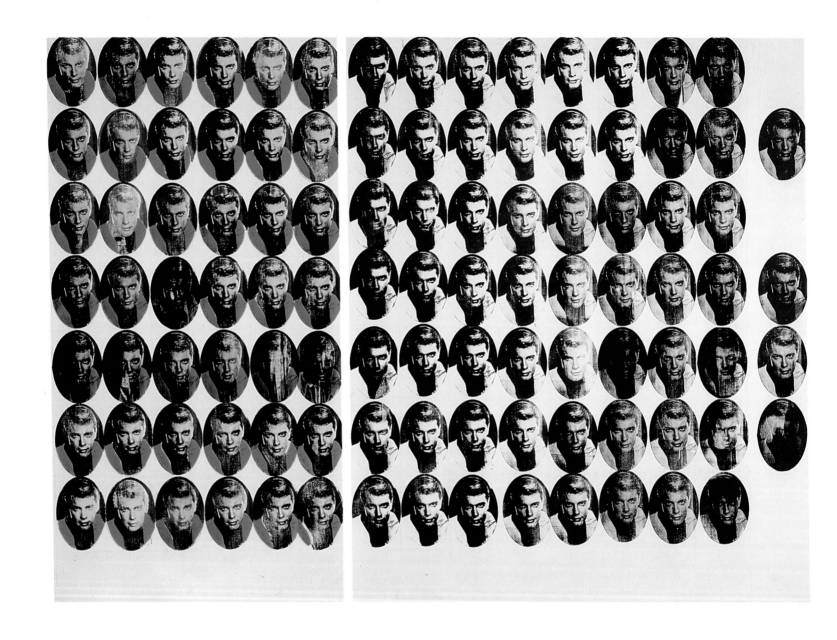

194. **Troy Diptych.** 1962
Silkscreen ink on synthetic polymer paint on canvas;
two panels, 6′ 10″ × 43″ (208 × 109 cm), 6′ 10″ × 68″ (208 × 173 cm)
Museum of Contemporary Art, Chicago
Gift of Mrs. Robert B. Mayer

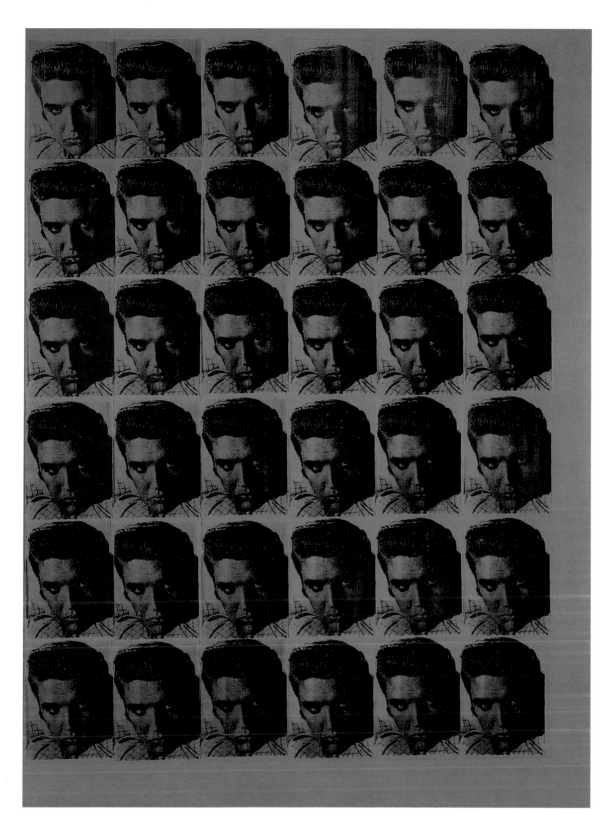

195. **Red Elvis.** 1962
Silkscreen ink on synthetic polymer paint on canvas,
69 × 52″ (175 × 132 cm)
Private collection. Courtesy Anders Malmberg, Sweden

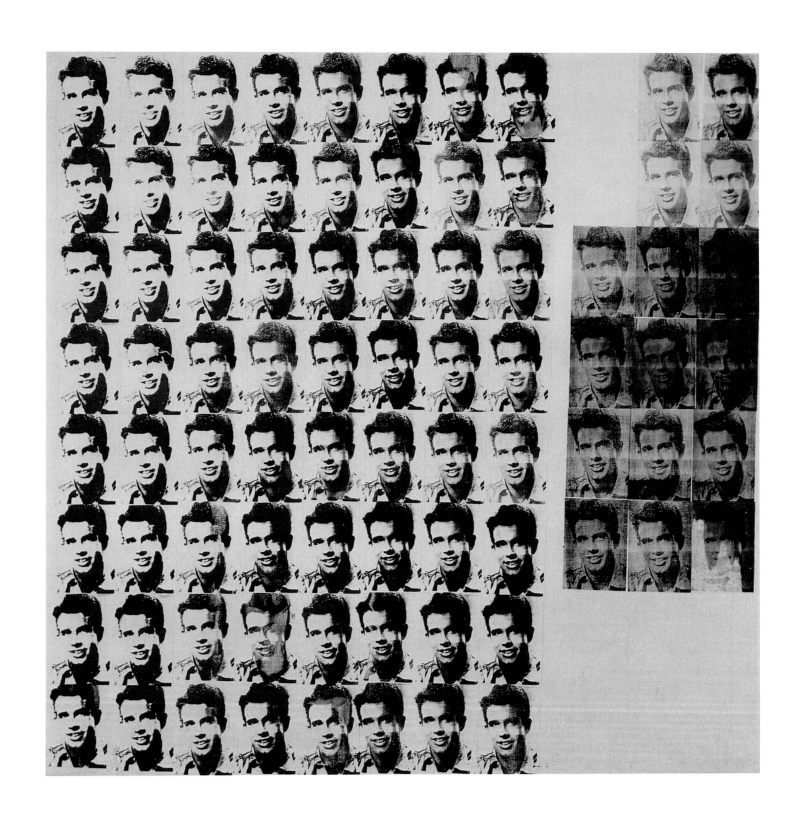

196. **Warren.** 1962
Silkscreen ink on canvas,
6′ 9½″ × 6′ 11″ (207 × 210.8 cm)
Private collection

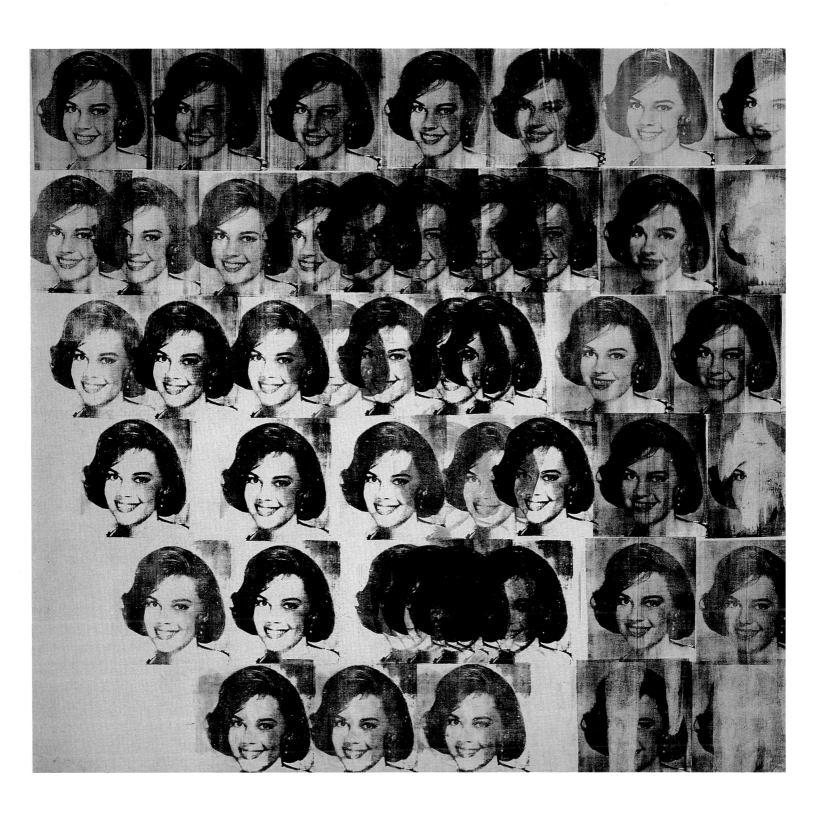

197. **Natalie.** 1962
Silkscreen ink on canvas,
6′ 11½″ × 7′ 7″ (212.1 × 231.1 cm)
The Estate of Andy Warhol

198. **Baseball.** 1962
Silkscreen ink and oil on canvas,
7′ 7½″ × 6′ 10″ (232.4 × 208.3 cm)
The Nelson-Atkins Museum of Art, Kansas City, Missouri
Gift of the Guild of the Friends of Art and a group of friends of the gallery

199. **Gold Marilyn Monroe.** 1962
Silkscreen ink on synthetic polymer paint and oil on canvas,
6′ 11¼″ × 57″ (211.4 × 144.7 cm)
The Museum of Modern Art, New York. Gift of Philip Johnson

**200. Gold Marilyn.** 1962
Silkscreen ink on synthetic polymer paint on canvas;
two tondi, each 17¾″ (45.1 cm) diameter
Private collection

**201. Head of Marilyn Monroe.** 1962
Silkscreen ink on synthetic polymer paint on canvas,
17¾″ (45.1 cm) diameter
Private collection

202. **The Six Marilyns (Marilyn Six-Pack).** 1962
Silkscreen ink on synthetic polymer paint on canvas,
43 × 22¼″ (109 × 56 cm)
Collection Emily and Jerry Spiegel

203. **Marilyn Monroe's Lips.** 1962
Silkscreen ink on synthetic polymer paint and pencil on canvas;
two panels, 6′ 10¾″ × 6′ 8¾″ (210.2 × 205.1 cm),
6′ 11⅜″ × 6′ 11″ (211.8 × 210.8 cm)
Hirshhorn Museum and Sculpture Garden, Smithsonian Institution, Washington, D.C.
Gift of Joseph H. Hirshhorn

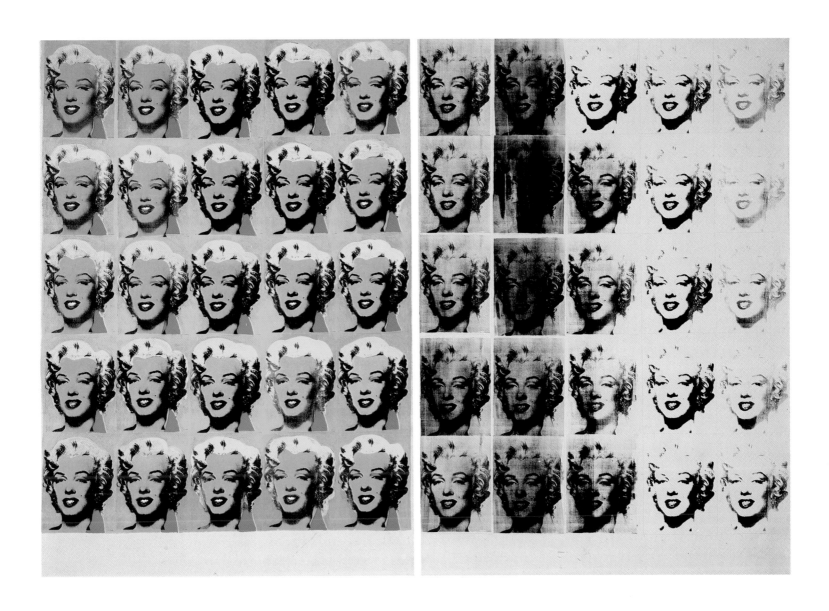

204. **Marilyn Diptych.** 1962
Silkscreen ink on synthetic polymer paint on canvas;
two panels, each 6′ 10″ × 57″ (208.3 × 144.8 cm)
The Trustees of the Tate Gallery

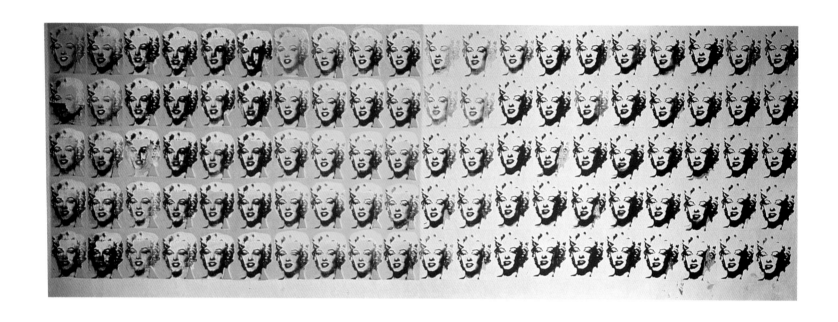

205. **Marilyn** × **100.** 1962
Silkscreen ink on synthetic polymer paint on canvas,
6′ 9″ × 18′ 7½″ (205.7 × 567.7 cm)
Saatchi Collection, London

206. **Turquoise Marilyn.** 1962
Silkscreen ink on synthetic polymer paint on canvas,
40 × 40″ (101.6 × 101.6 cm)
Collection Stefan T. Edlis

207. **Green Marilyn.** 1964
Silkscreen ink on synthetic polymer paint on canvas,
20 × 16″ (50.8 × 40.6 cm)
Collection Mrs. Irma S. Seitz

208. **Blue Marilyn.** 1964
Silkscreen ink on synthetic polymer paint on canvas,
20 × 16″ (50.8 × 40.6 cm)
The Art Museum, Princeton University, Princeton, New Jersey
Gift of Mr. and Mrs. Alfred H. Barr, Jr.

209. **Black and White Marilyn.** 1964
Silkscreen ink on synthetic polymer paint on canvas,
20 × 16″ (50.8 × 40.6 cm)
Collection Douglas S. Cramer

210. **Mint Marilyn.** 1964
Silkscreen ink on synthetic polymer paint on canvas,
20 × 16″ (50.8 × 40.6 cm)
Collection Jasper Johns

211. **Lemon Marilyn.** 1964
Silkscreen ink on synthetic polymer paint on canvas,
20 × 16″ (50.8 × 40.6 cm)
Private collection

212. **Marilyn.** 1967
Nine serigraphs on paper from a portfolio of ten,
each 36 × 36″ (91.5 × 91.5 cm)
Private collection

213. **Ginger Rogers.** 1962
Pencil on paper,
23¾ × 18″ (60.3 × 45.7 cm)
Oeffentliche Kunstsammlung Basel, Kupferstichkabinett
Karl August Burckhardt-Koechlin Fonds

214. **Ginger Rogers.** 1962
Pencil on paper,
23¾ × 18″ (60.3 × 45.7 cm)
Whitney Museum of American Art, New York
Purchase, with funds from the Lauder Foundation–Drawing Fund

215. **Hedy Lamarr.** 1962
Pencil on paper,
24 × 18″ (61 × 45.7 cm)
Dia Art Foundation, New York
Courtesy The Menil Collection, Houston

216. **Joan Crawford.** 1962
Pencil on paper,
24 × 18″ (61 × 45.7 cm)
Dia Art Foundation, New York
Courtesy The Menil Collection, Houston

217. **Untitled.** c. 1962
Pencil on paper,
29 × 23″ (73.7 × 58.4 cm)
The Estate of Andy Warhol

218. **Untitled.** c. 1962
Pencil on paper,
29 × 23″ (73.7 × 58.4 cm)
The Estate of Andy Warhol

219. **Untitled.** 1962
Silkscreen ink on paper,
24 × 18″ (61 × 45.6 cm)
The Estate of Andy Warhol

220. **Untitled.** c. 1962
Pencil and synthetic polymer paint on paper,
29 × 22⅛″ (73.7 × 58.2 cm)
The Estate of Andy Warhol

221. **Untitled.** 1960
Pencil and collage on paper,
29 × 23″ (73.7 × 58.4 cm)
Private collection

222. **Untitled (Tuesday Weld).** 1962
Silkscreen ink on paper,
29 × 23″ (73.7 × 58.4 cm)
The Estate of Andy Warhol

223. **Cagney.** 1962
Silkscreen ink on paper,
30 × 40″ (76 × 101.5 cm)
Collection PaineWebber Group, Inc.

224. **The Kiss (Bela Lugosi).** 1963
Silkscreen ink on paper,
30 × 40″ (76 × 101.5 cm)
The Sonnabend Collection

225. **Young Rauschenberg #1.** 1962
Silkscreen ink on canvas,
35 × 22″ (88.9 × 55.9 cm)
Collection Emily and Jerry Spiegel

226. **Let Us Now Praise Famous Men.** 1963
Silkscreen ink on canvas,
6′ 10″ × 6′ 10″ (208.3 × 208.3 cm)
Collection Michael D. Abrams

227. **The Men in Her Life**
**(Mike Todd and Eddie Fisher).** 1962
Silkscreen ink on synthetic polymer paint on canvas,
6′ 10″ × 6′ 10″ (208.3 × 208.3 cm)
Morton G. Neumann Family Collection, Chicago

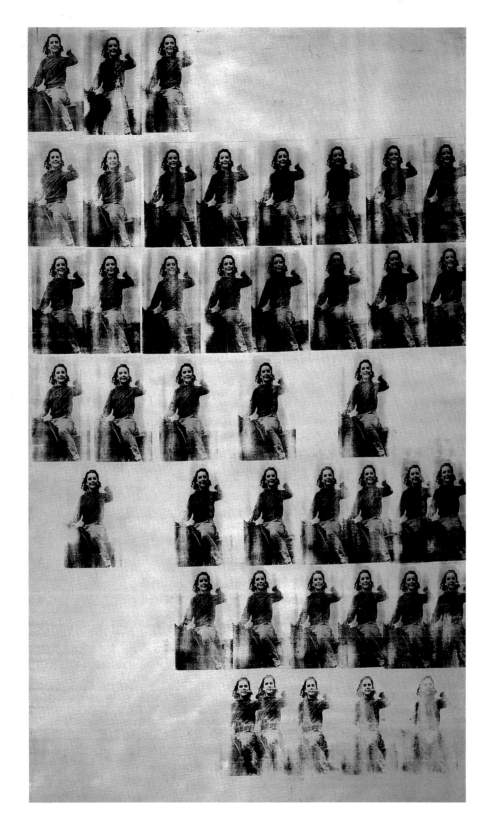

228. **National Velvet.** 1963
Silkscreen ink on synthetic polymer paint on canvas,
11′ 4⅜″ × 6′ 11½″ (346.4 × 212.1 cm)
The Estate of Andy Warhol

229. **Double Liz.** 1963
Silkscreen ink on synthetic polymer paint on canvas,
6′ 7¾″ × 6′ 11″ (202.6 × 210.8 cm)
The Estate of Andy Warhol

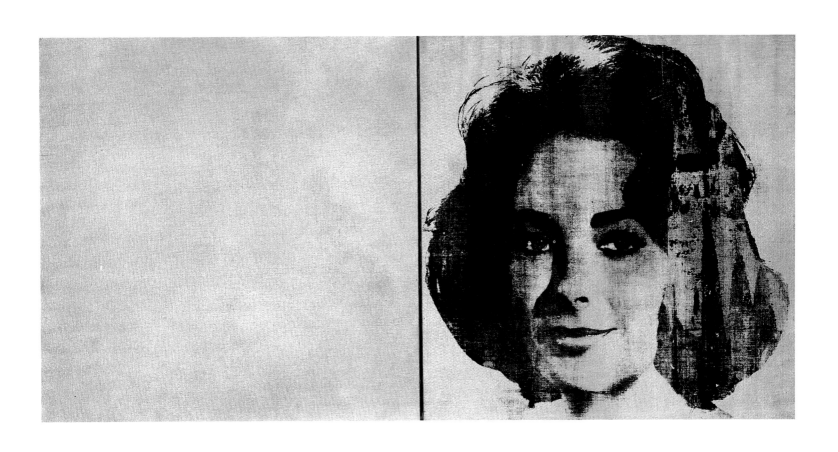

230. **'65 Liz.** 1965
Silkscreen ink on synthetic polymer paint on canvas;
two panels, each 40 × 40″ (101.6 × 101.6 cm)
Collection Irving Blum, New York

231. **Ten Lizes.** 1963
Silkscreen ink on synthetic polymer paint on canvas,
6′ 7⅛″ × 18′ 6″ (201 × 564 cm)
Musée National d'Art Moderne, Centre Georges Pompidou, Paris

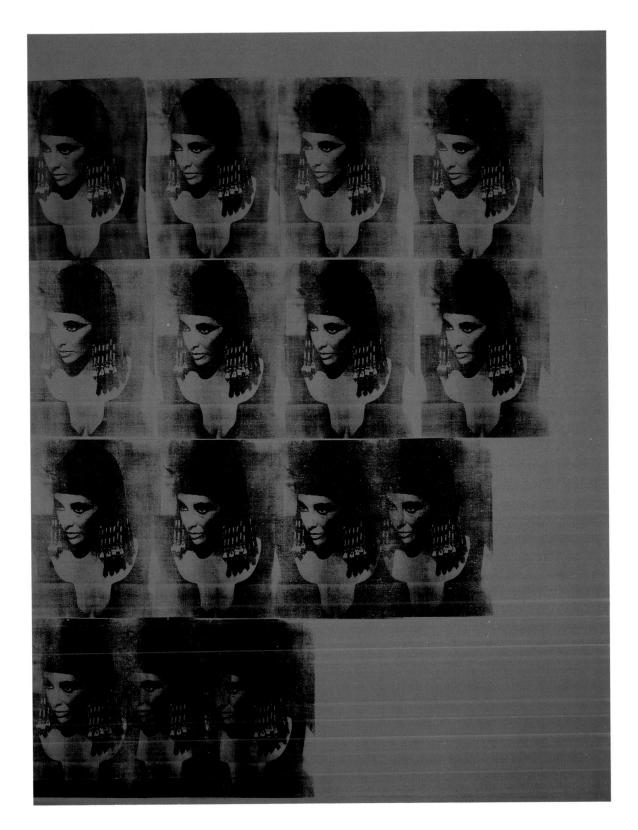

232. **Blue Liz as Cleopatra.** 1963
Silkscreen ink on synthetic polymer paint on canvas,
6′ 10″ × 65″ (208.3 × 165.1 cm)
Collection Adrian and Robert Mnuchin

233. **Silver Marlon.** 1963
Silkscreen ink on synthetic polymer paint on canvas,
70″ × 6′ 8″ (177.8 × 203.2 cm)
Collection A. Alfred Taubman, Bloomfield Hills, Michigan

234. **Double Marlon.** 1966
Silkscreen ink on canvas,
7′ × 7′ 11¾″ (213.4 × 243.2 cm)
Saatchi Collection, London

235. **Double Mona Lisa.** 1963
Silkscreen ink on canvas,
28½ × 37⅛″ (72.4 × 94.3 cm)
The Menil Collection, Houston

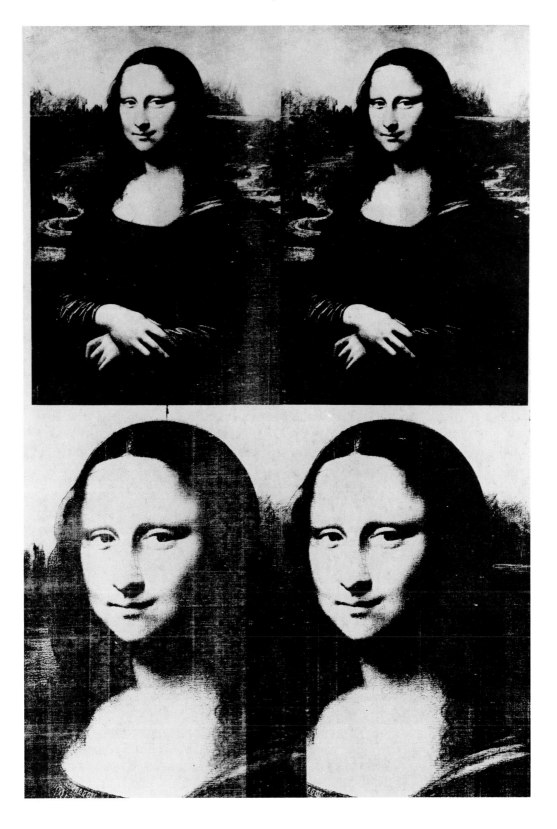

236. **Four Mona Lisas.** 1963
Silkscreen ink on synthetic polymer paint on canvas,
44 × 29″ (112 × 74 cm)
The Metropolitan Museum of Art, New York
Gift of Henry Geldzahler

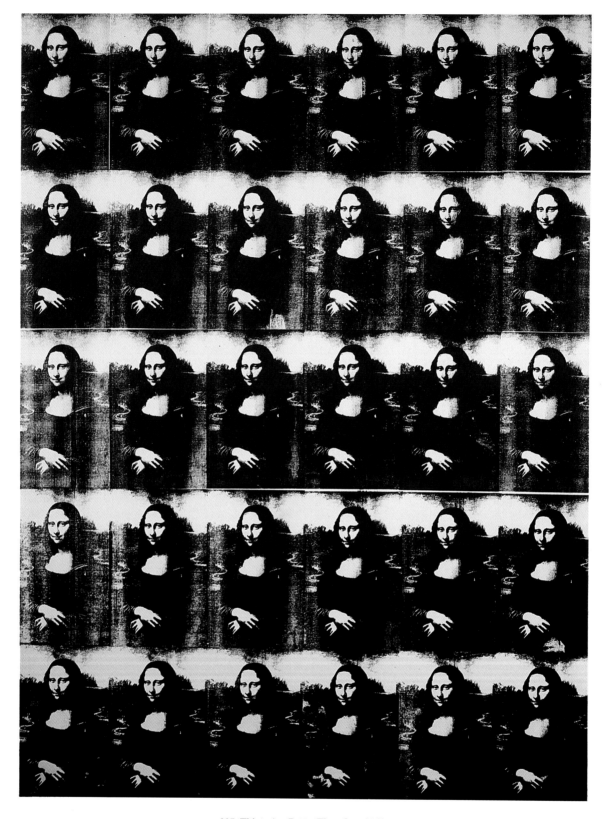

237. **Thirty Are Better Than One.** 1963
Silkscreen ink on synthetic polymer paint on canvas,
9′ 2″ × 7′ 10½″ (279.4 × 240 cm)
Private collection

238. **Mona Lisa.** 1963
Silkscreen ink on synthetic polymer paint on canvas,
10′ 5¾″ × 6′ 10⅛″ (319.4 × 208.6 cm)
Courtesy Blum Helman Gallery, New York

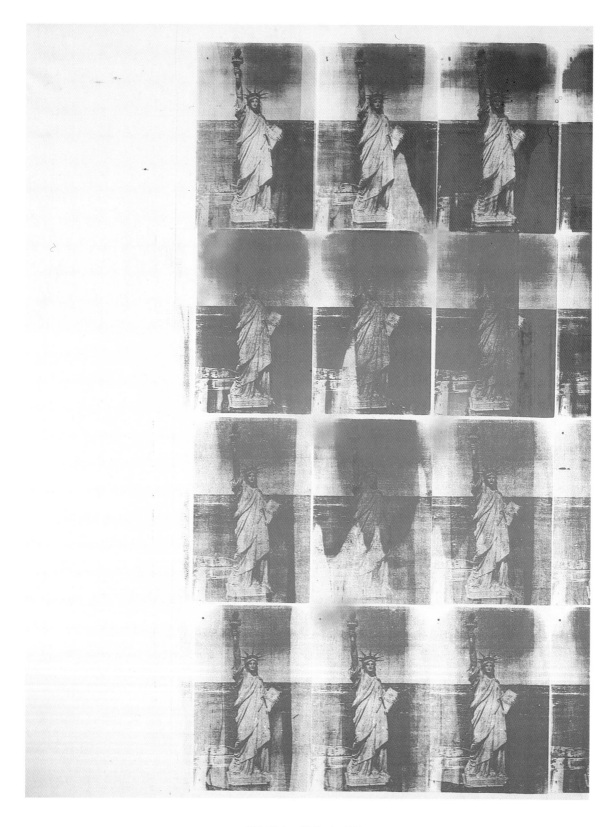

239. **Statue of Liberty.** 1963
Silkscreen ink on synthetic polymer paint on canvas,
6′ 7⅞″ × 61″ (202.8 × 154.9 cm)
The Estate of Andy Warhol

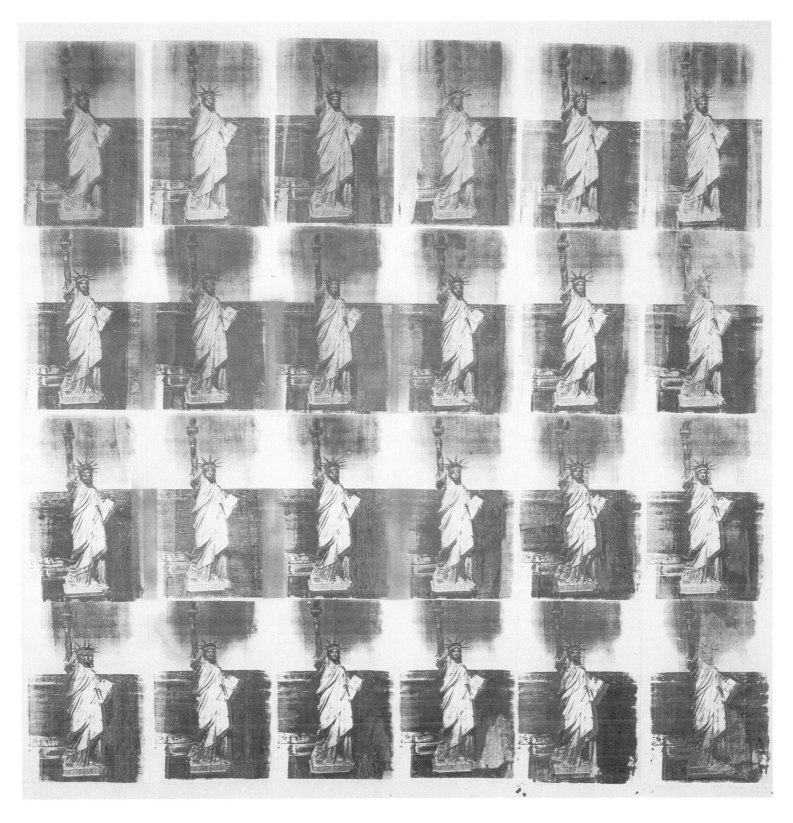

240. **Statue of Liberty.** 1963
Silkscreen ink on synthetic polymer paint on canvas,
6′ 6″ × 6′ 8⅔″ (198 × 205 cm)
Collection Dr. Marx, Berlin

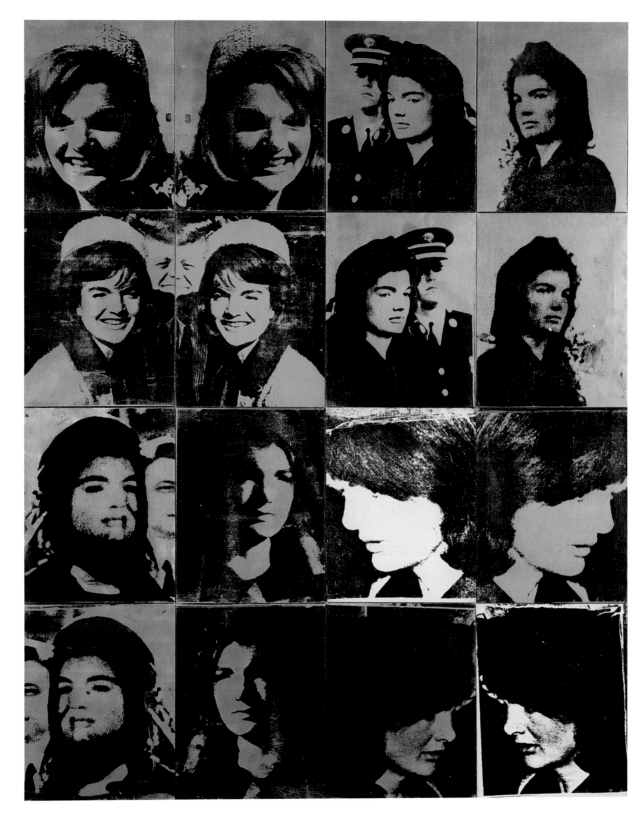

241. **Jackie (The Week That Was).** 1963
Silkscreen ink on synthetic polymer paint on canvas;
sixteen panels, each 20 × 16″ (50.8 × 40.6 cm),
overall 6′ 8″ × 64″ (203.2 × 162.6 cm)
Collection Mrs. Raymond Goetz

242. **Sixteen Jackies.** 1964
Silkscreen ink on synthetic polymer paint on canvas;
sixteen panels, each 20 × 16″ (50.8 × 40.6 cm),
overall 6′ 8″ × 64″ (203.2 × 162.6 cm)
Walker Art Center, Minneapolis
Art Center Acquisition Fund

243. **Three Jackies.** 1964
Silkscreen ink on synthetic polymer paint on canvas;
three panels, each 20 × 16″ (50.8 × 40.6 cm)
The Estate of Andy Warhol

244. **Gold Jackie.** 1964
Silkscreen ink on synthetic polymer paint on canvas,
18″ (45.7 cm) diameter
Courtesy Holly Solomon Gallery, New York

245. **Round Jackie.** 1964
Silkscreen ink on synthetic polymer paint on canvas,
17¾″ (45.1 cm) diameter
Collection Mr. and Mrs. John N. Rosekrans, Jr.

246. **Round Jackie.** 1964
Silkscreen ink on synthetic polymer paint on canvas,
17¾″ (45.1 cm) diameter
Collection Mr. and Mrs. John N. Rosekrans, Jr.

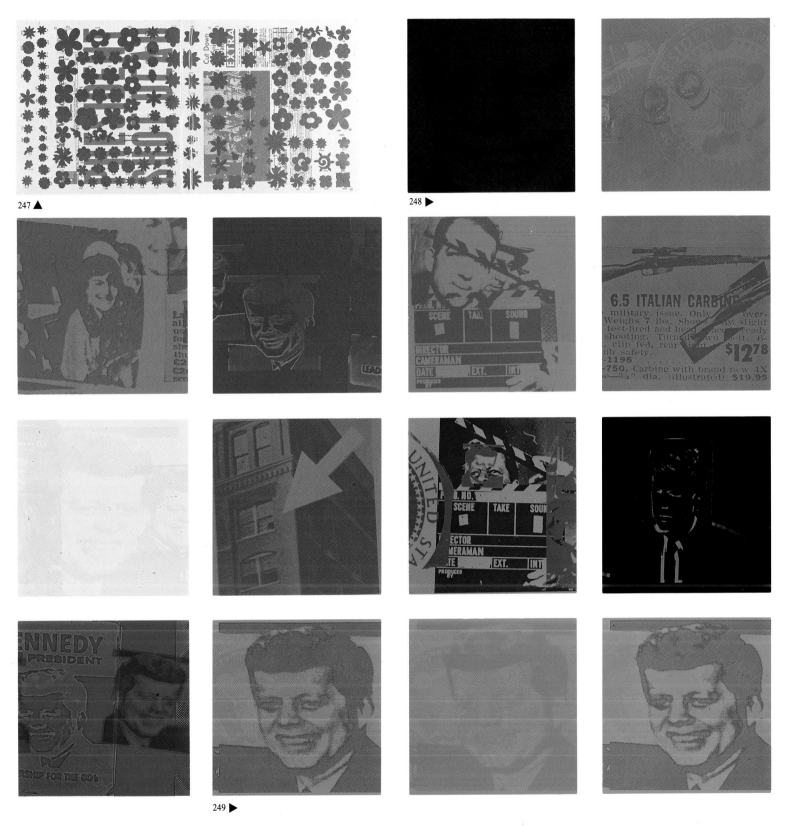

247. **Cover of "Flash—November 22, 1963."** 1968
Serigraph printed on fabric mounted on cardboard,
22½ × 44¾″ (57.2 × 113.7 cm)
Private collection

248. **Flash—November 22, 1963.** 1968
Portfolio of eleven serigraphs on paper,
each 21 × 21″ (53.3 × 53.3 cm)
Private collection

*Edition of two hundred*

249. **Flash—November 22, 1963.** 1968
Suite of three additional serigraphs on paper,
each 21 × 21″ (53.3 × 53.3 cm)
Private collection

*Included in portfolios lettered A through J*

250. **Red Jackie.** 1964
Silkscreen ink on synthetic polymer paint on canvas,
40 × 40″ (101.5 × 101.5 cm)
Private collection

251. **Early Colored Liz.** 1963
Silkscreen ink on synthetic polymer paint on canvas,
40 × 40″ (101.5 × 101.5 cm)
Collection Peder Bonnier

252. **Shot Orange Marilyn.** 1964
Silkscreen ink on synthetic polymer paint on canvas,
40 × 40″ (101.5 × 101.5 cm)
Private collection

253. **Single Elvis.** 1963
Silkscreen ink on synthetic polymer paint on canvas,
6′ 10⅝″ × 42″ (210 × 107 cm)
Hungarian National Gallery, Budapest, on loan from the Ludwig Collection, Aachen

254. **Triple Elvis.** 1962
Silkscreen ink on aluminum paint on canvas,
6′ 10″ × 60″ (208.3 × 152.4 cm)
Virginia Museum of Fine Arts, Richmond. Gift of Sydney and Frances Lewis

255. **Elvis I and II.** 1964
Two panels: silkscreen ink on synthetic polymer paint
on canvas, silkscreen ink on aluminum paint on canvas;
each panel 6′ 10″ × 6′ 10″ (208.3 × 208.3 cm)
Art Gallery of Ontario, Toronto. Gift from the Women's Committee Fund

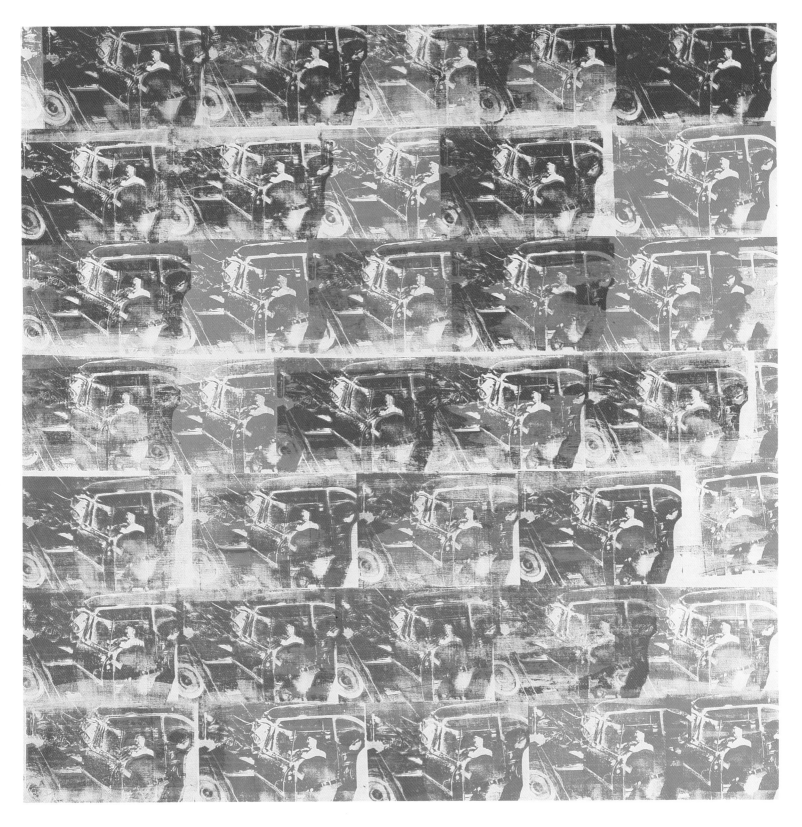

256. **Optical Car Crash.** 1962
Silkscreen ink on synthetic polymer paint on canvas,
6′ 9⅞″ × 6′ 10″ (208 × 208.3 cm)
Oeffentliche Kunstsammlung Basel, Kunstmuseum

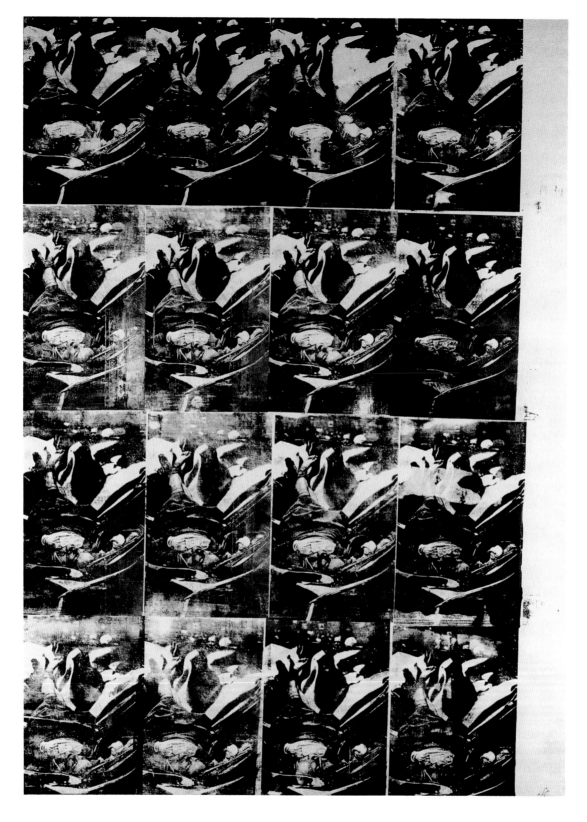

257. **Suicide (Fallen Body).** 1963
Silkscreen ink on synthetic polymer paint on canvas,
9′ 5″ × 6′ 8″ (283 × 204 cm)
Courtesy Thomas Ammann, Zürich

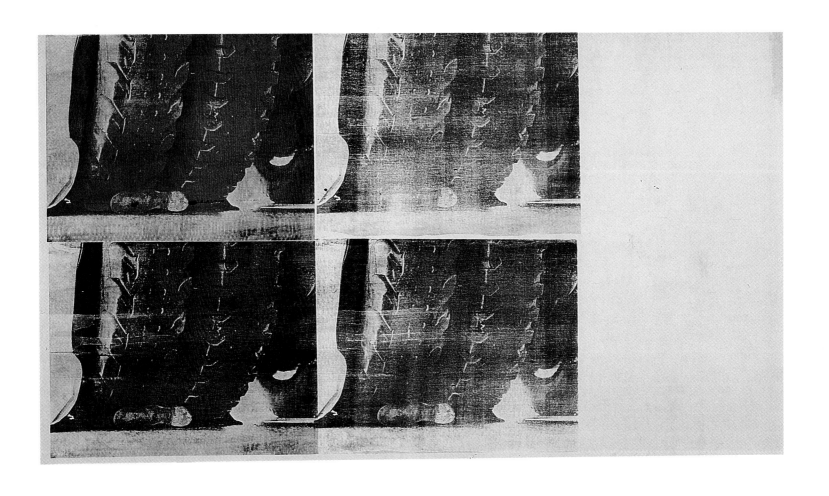

258. **Foot and Tire.** 1963
Oil and silkscreen ink on canvas,
6′ 8¼″ × 12′ ¾″ (203.8 × 367.7 cm)
Dia Art Foundation, New York
Courtesy The Menil Collection, Houston

**259. White Car Crash Nineteen Times.** 1963
Silkscreen ink on synthetic polymer paint on canvas,
12′ × 6′ 11″ (368.3 × 211.5 cm)
Courtesy Thomas Ammann, Zürich

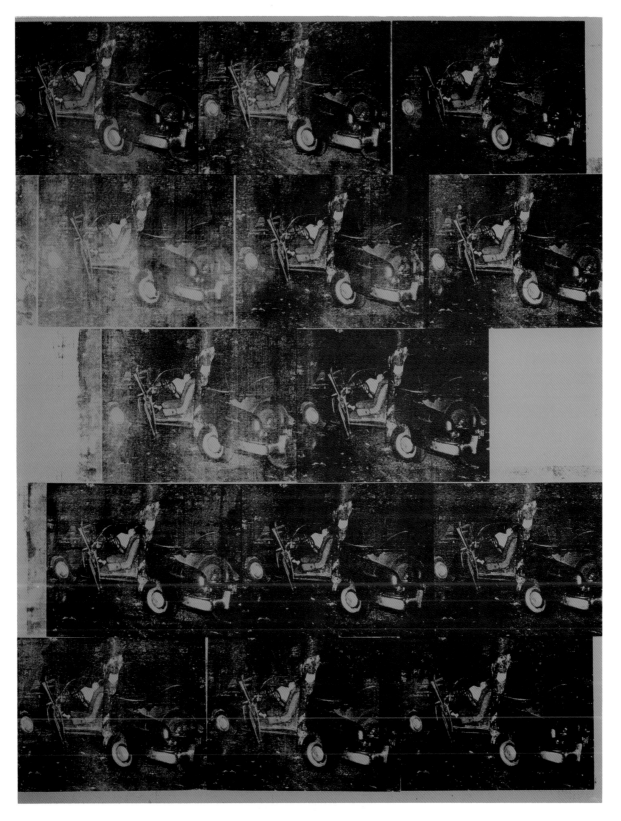

260. **Orange Car Crash Fourteen Times.** 1963
Silkscreen ink on synthetic polymer paint on canvas,
8′ 9″ × 6′ 10⅛″ (266.7 × 208.6 cm)
Collection Philip Johnson

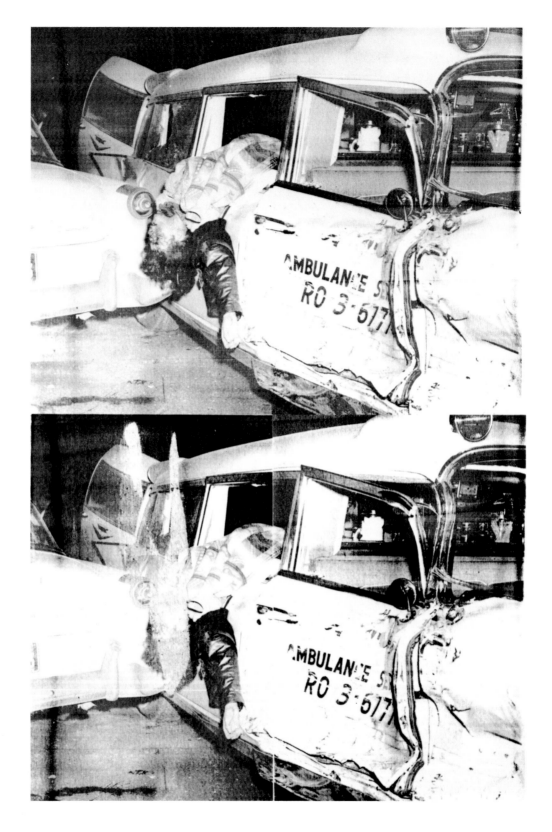

261. **Ambulance Disaster.** 1963
Silkscreen ink on canvas,
9′ 11¼″ × 6′ 8″ (302.9 × 203.2 cm)
Dia Art Foundation, New York
Courtesy The Menil Collection, Houston

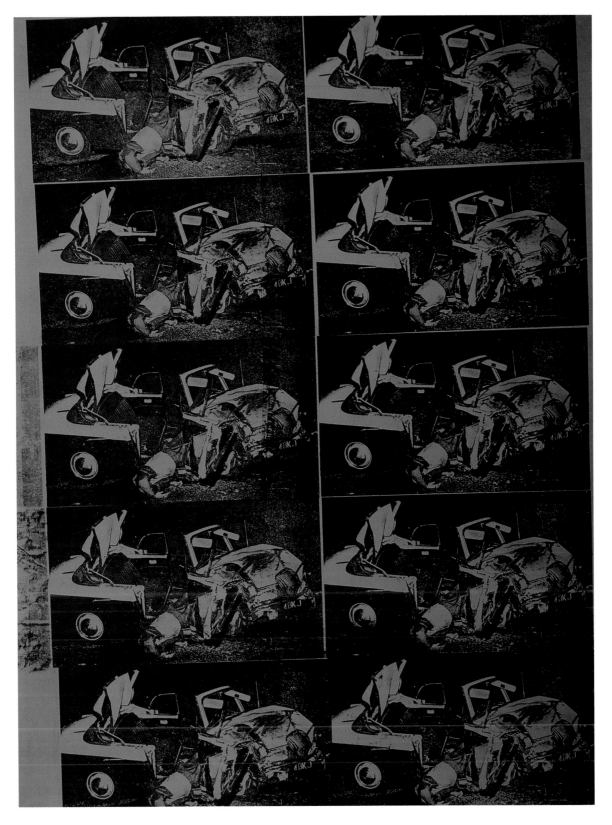

262. **Green Disaster Ten Times.** 1963
Silkscreen ink on synthetic polymer paint on canvas,
8′ 11⅓″ × 6′ 7⅛″ (267.5 × 201 cm)
Museum für Moderne Kunst, Frankfurt

263. **Five Deaths on Red.** 1962
Silkscreen ink on synthetic polymer paint on canvas,
30 × 30″ (76.2 × 76.2 cm)
Collection Stellan Holm, New York

264. **Five Deaths on Orange.** 1963
Silkscreen ink on synthetic polymer paint on canvas,
44 × 33″ (111.8 × 83.8 cm)
Private collection

265. **Five Deaths Seventeen Times**
**in Black and White.** 1963
Silkscreen ink on synthetic polymer paint on canvas;
two panels, each 8′ 7⅛″ × 6′ 10¼″ (262 × 209 cm)
Oeffentliche Kunstsammlung Basel, Kunstmuseum

266. **Suicide.** 1962
Silkscreen ink on paper,
40 × 30″ (101.5 × 76 cm)
Collection Adelaide de Menil, New York

267. **Bellevue II.** 1963
Silkscreen ink on synthetic polymer paint on canvas,
6′ 10″ × 6′ 10″ (208.5 × 208.5 cm)
Stedelijk Museum, Amsterdam
Purchase, with support of the Vereniging "Rembrandt"

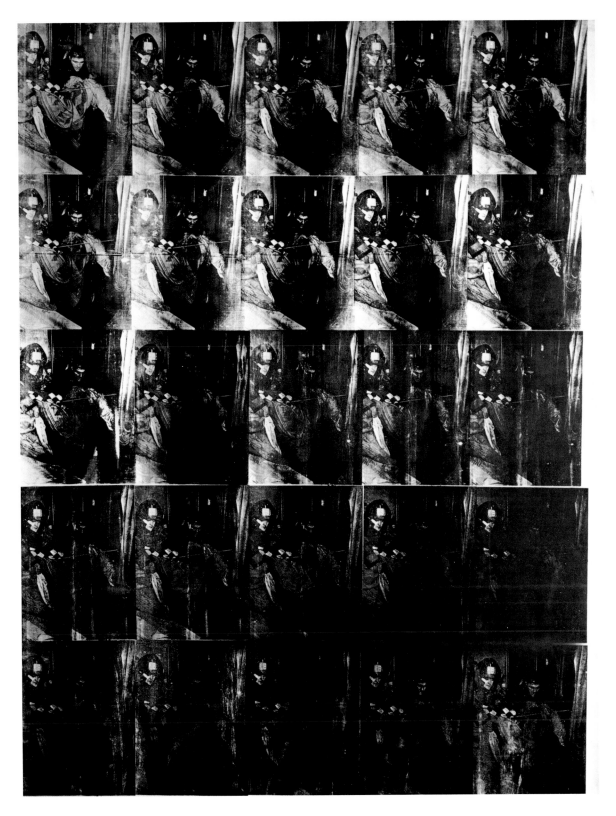

268. **Black and White Disaster.** 1962
Silkscreen ink on synthetic polymer paint on canvas,
8′ × 6′ (243.8 × 182.9 cm)
Los Angeles County Museum of Art
Gift of Leo Castelli Gallery and Ferus
Gallery through the Contemporary Art Council

269. **Tunafish Disaster.** 1963
Silkscreen ink on synthetic polymer paint on canvas,
10′ 4⅜″ × 6′ 11″ (316 × 211 cm)
Saatchi Collection, London

270. **Tunafish Disaster.** 1963
Silkscreen ink on synthetic polymer paint on canvas,
9′ 4″ × 6′ 10″ (284.5 × 208.3 cm)
Collection Mr. and Mrs. S. I. Newhouse, Jr.

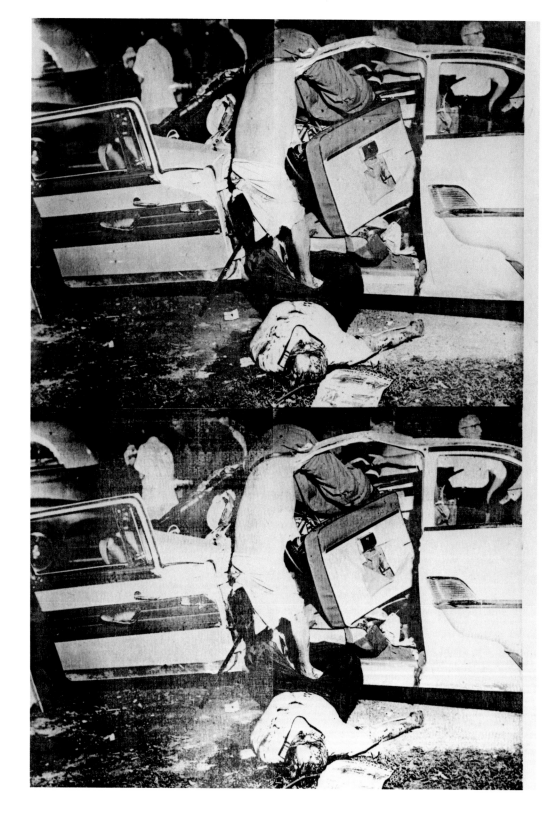

271. **Saturday Disaster.** 1964
Silkscreen ink on synthetic polymer paint on canvas,
9' 10⅞" × 6' 9⅞" (301.9 × 208 cm)
Rose Art Museum, Brandeis University,
Waltham, Massachusetts. Gervitz-Mnuchin Purchase Fund, by exchange

272. **White Burning Car III.** 1963
Silkscreen ink on canvas,
8′ 4½″ × 6′ 6¾″ (255.3 × 200 cm)
Dia Art Foundation, New York
Courtesy The Menil Collection, Houston

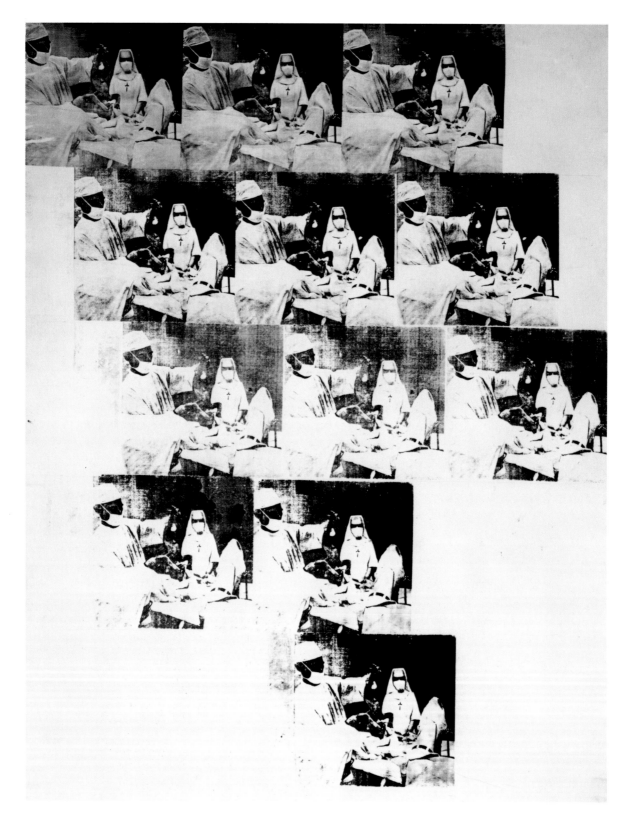

273. **Hospital.** 1963
Silkscreen ink on canvas,
8′ 11½″ × 6′ 10⅞″ (273.1 × 210.5 cm)
Dia Art Foundation, New York
Courtesy The Menil Collection, Houston

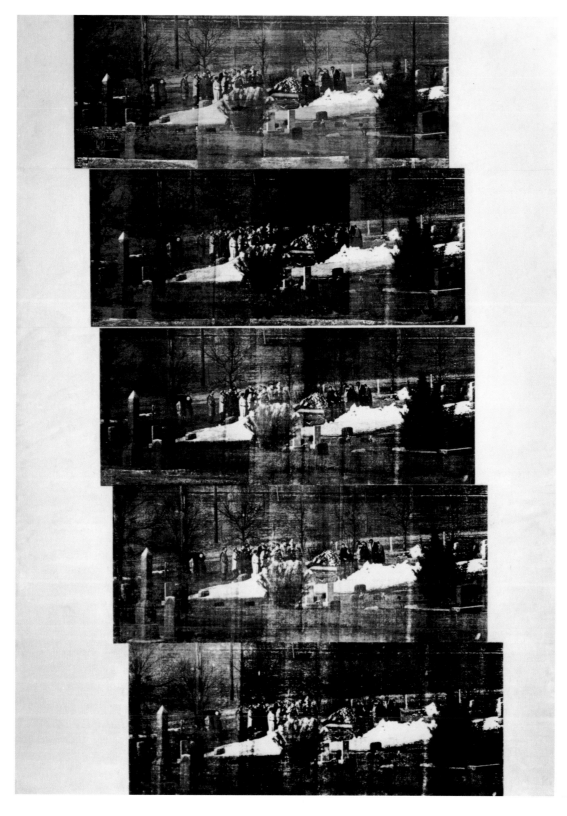

274. **Gangster Funeral.** 1963
Silkscreen ink on synthetic polymer paint on canvas,
8′ 9″ × 6′ 3⅝″ (266.7 × 192.1 cm)
Dia Art Foundation, New York
Courtesy The Menil Collection, Houston

275. **Little Race Riot.** 1964
Silkscreen ink on synthetic polymer paint on canvas;
four panels, each 30 × 33″ (76.2 × 83.8 cm)
Collection Robert Mapplethorpe

276. **Red Race Riot.** 1963
Silkscreen ink on synthetic polymer paint on canvas,
11′ 5″ × 6′ 10½″ (350 × 210 cm)
Museum Ludwig, Cologne

277. **Mustard Race Riot.** 1963
Silkscreen ink on synthetic polymer paint on canvas;
two panels, each 9′ 6″ × 6′ 10″ (289.6 × 208.3 cm)
Collection Mr. and Mrs. Richard S. Lane

278. **Red Disaster.** 1963
Silkscreen ink on synthetic polymer paint on canvas,
6′ 8¼″ × 7′ 9″ (203.9 × 236.2 cm)
Museum of Fine Arts, Boston. Charles H. Bayley Picture and Painting Fund

279. **Orange Disaster.** 1963
Silkscreen ink on synthetic polymer paint on canvas,
8′ 10″ × 6′ 10″ (269.2 × 208.3 cm)
The Solomon R. Guggenheim Museum, New York

280. **Silver Disaster.** 1963
Silkscreen ink on synthetic polymer paint on canvas,
42 × 60″ (106.7 × 152.4 cm)
The Sonnabend Collection, on extended loan to The Baltimore Museum of Art

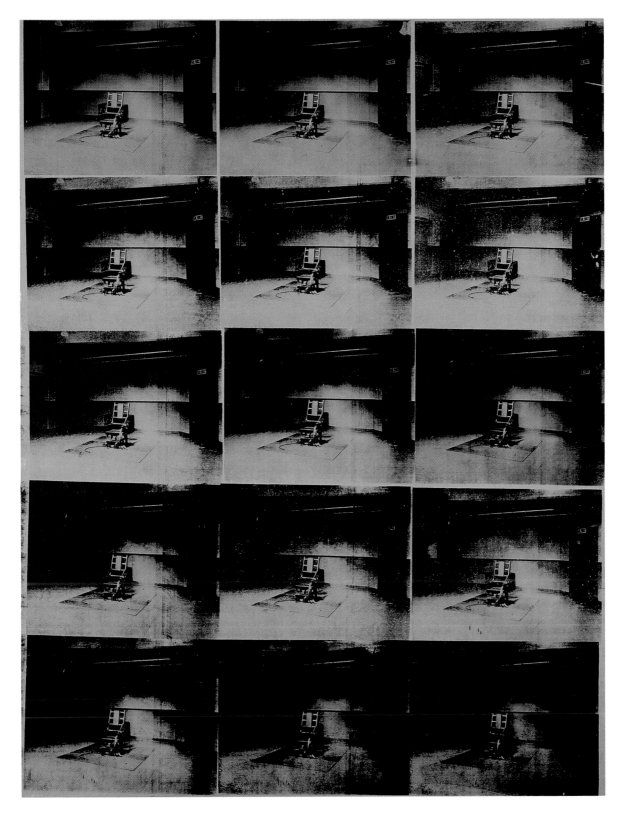

281. **Lavender Disaster.** 1963
Silkscreen ink on synthetic polymer paint on canvas,
8′ 10″ × 6′ 9⅞″ (269.2 × 208 cm)
The Menil Collection, Houston

282. **Big Electric Chair.** 1967
Silkscreen ink on synthetic polymer paint on canvas,
54″ × 6′ 1″ (137 × 185.4 cm)
Musée National d'Art Moderne, Centre Georges Pompidou, Paris
Gift of The Menil Foundation

283. **Big Electric Chair.** 1967
Silkscreen ink on synthetic polymer paint on canvas,
54″ × 6′ 1″ (137 × 185.4 cm)
Moderna Museet, Stockholm

284. **Blue Electric Chair.** 1963
Silkscreen ink on synthetic polymer paint on canvas;
two panels, each 8′ 9″ × 6′ 8¼″ (266.7 × 203.8 cm)
Saatchi Collection, London

285. **Little Electric Chair.** 1965
Silkscreen ink on synthetic polymer paint on canvas,
22 × 28″ (55.9 × 71.1 cm)
The Menil Collection, Houston

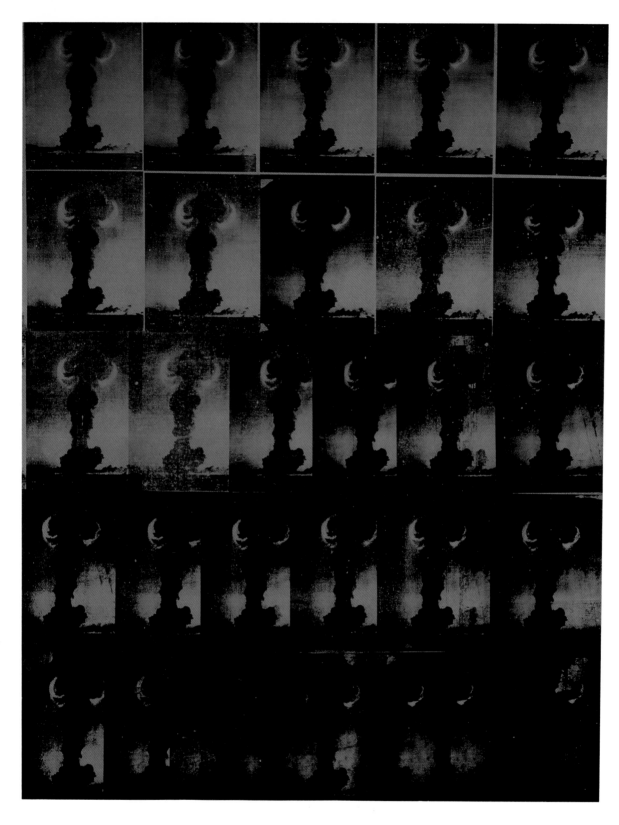

286. **Atomic Bomb.** 1965
Silkscreen ink on synthetic polymer paint on canvas,
8′ 8″ × 6′ 8½″ (264.1 × 204.5 cm)
Saatchi Collection, London

287. **Thirteen Most Wanted Men.** 1964
Installed at the New York State Pavilion, New York World's Fair, 1964
Silkscreen ink on masonite;
twenty-five panels, each 48 × 48″ (122 × 122 cm),
overall 20 × 20′ (610 × 610 cm)

288. **Most Wanted Men No. 1, John M.** 1964
Silkscreen ink on canvas;
two panels, each 48 × 40″ (122 × 101.5 cm)
The Herbert F. Johnson Museum of Art, Cornell University
Purchase funds from the National Endowment for the Arts and individual donors

289. **Most Wanted Men No. 2, John Victor G.** 1964
Silkscreen ink on canvas;
two panels, 48½ × 37″ (123.2 × 94 cm),
48½ × 38⅝″ (123.2 × 98.1 cm)
Dia Art Foundation, New York. Courtesy The Menil Collection, Houston

290. **Most Wanted Men No. 3, Ellis Ruez B.** 1964
Silkscreen ink on canvas,
48 × 40″ (122 × 101.5 cm)
Courtesy Thomas Ammann, Zürich

291. **Most Wanted Men No. 4, Redmond C.** 1964
Silkscreen ink on canvas,
48 × 40″ (122 × 101.5 cm)
Courtesy Gagosian Gallery, New York

292. **Most Wanted Men No. 5, Arthur Alvin M.** 1964
Silkscreen ink on canvas;
two panels, each 48 × 40″ (122 × 101.5 cm)
Collection Mr. and Mrs. S. I. Newhouse, Jr.

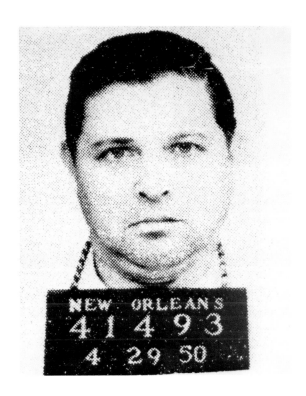

293. **Most Wanted Men No. 6, Thomas Francis C.** 1964
Silkscreen ink on canvas;
two panels, each 48 × 40″ (122 × 101.5 cm)
Courtesy Gagosian Gallery, New York

294. **Most Wanted Men No. 7, Salvatore V.** 1964
Silkscreen ink on canvas;
two panels, each 39⅛ × 39″ (99.5 × 99 cm)
Museum Ludwig, Cologne

295. **Most Wanted Men No. 8, Andrew F.** 1964
Silkscreen ink on canvas,
48 × 40″ (122 × 101.5 cm)
Courtesy Thomas Ammann, Zürich

296. **Most Wanted Men No. 9, John S.** 1964
Silkscreen ink on canvas,
48 × 40″ (122 × 101.5 cm)
Courtesy Thomas Ammann, Zürich

297. **Most Wanted Men No. 10, Louis Joseph M.** 1964
Silkscreen ink on canvas;
two panels, each 48 × 40″ (122 × 101.5 cm)
Städtisches Museum Abteiberg, Mönchengladbach

298. **Most Wanted Men No. 11, John Joseph H.** 1964
Silkscreen ink on canvas;
two panels, each 48 × 40″ (122 × 101.5 cm)
Saatchi Collection, London

299. **Most Wanted Men No. 12, Frank B.** 1964
Silkscreen ink on canvas;
two panels, each 48 × 40″ (122 × 101.5 cm)
Private collection

300. **Most Wanted Men No. 13, Joseph F.** 1964
Silkscreen ink on canvas;
two panels, each 48 × 40″ (122 × 101.5 cm)
The Sonnabend Collection

301. Aluminum paint covering *Thirteen Most Wanted Men*, New York State Pavilion, New York World's Fair, 1964

302. **Silver Clouds.** 1966
Installed at Leo Castelli Gallery, New York, 1966
Metalized polyester film with helium,
each 39 × 59 × c. 15" (99 × 150 × c. 38 cm)

303. **Cow Wallpaper.** 1966
Serigraph printed on wallpaper,
45½ × 29¾″ (115.5 × 75.5 cm)
The Estate of Andy Warhol

304. **Cow Wallpaper.** 1971
Serigraph printed on wallpaper,
45½ × 29¾″ (115.5 × 75.5 cm)
The Estate of Andy Warhol

305. Installation view, *Andy Warhol*, Leo Castelli Gallery, New York, 1966

306. Installation view, *Andy Warhol*, Galerie Ileana Sonnabend, Paris, 1965

307. **Flowers.** 1966
Silkscreen ink on synthetic polymer paint on canvas,
9′ 7½″ × 9′ 7½″ (293.4 × 293.4 cm)
The Menil Collection, Houston

308. **Flowers.** 1967
Silkscreen ink on synthetic polymer paint on canvas,
9′ 7½″ × 9′ 7½″ (293.4 × 293.4 cm)
La Jolla Museum of Contemporary Art
Purchased with the aid of funds from the Museum Art Council

309. **Flowers.** 1967
Silkscreen ink on synthetic polymer paint on canvas,
9′ 8″ × 9′ 8″ (294.6 × 294.6 cm)
Private collection, Berlin

310. **Flowers.** 1967
Silkscreen ink on synthetic polymer paint on canvas,
7′ × 12′ 1⅜″ (213.4 × 369.3 cm)
Private collection

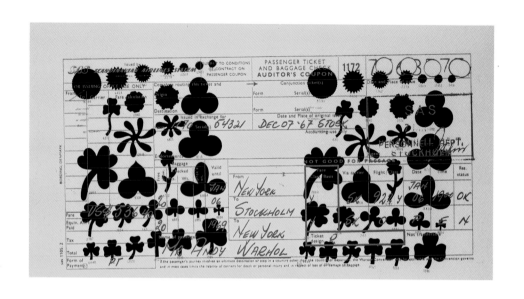

311. **SAS Passenger Ticket.** 1968
Serigraph on paper,
26¾ × 48¾″ (68 × 124 cm)
Private collection

312. **"Untitled 12" from the Portfolio "For Meyer Schapiro."** 1974
Serigraph on paper,
29⅞ × 22¹⁄₁₆″ (75.9 × 56 cm)
The Museum of Modern Art, New York
Gift of Mr. and Mrs. Bagley Wright

313. **Banana.** 1966
Serigraph printed on "peel-off" laminated plastic
on serigraph printed on white styrene;
peel image, 17⅞ × 36¼" (45.5 × 92 cm),
sheet, 24 × 53¼" (61 × 135.2 cm)
Private collection

314. **Space Fruit Oranges.** 1978
Serigraph on paper,
30 × 40" (76.2 × 101.6 cm)
Private collection

301

*Top*
315. **Vote McGovern.** 1972
Serigraph on paper,
42 × 42″ (106.7 × 106.7 cm)
Private collection

*Bottom*
316. **"Mao" (Two Variants) from the Portfolio**
**"Works by Artists in the New York**
**Collection for Stockholm."** 1973
Sequential Xerox prints on paper,
each 11 × 8½″ (27.9 × 21.6 cm)
*Left:* The Museum of Modern Art, New York
Gift of Steven M. Feinstein
*Right:* Private collection

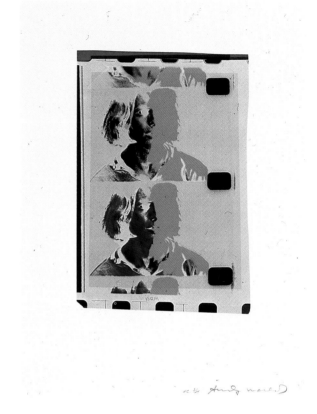

317. **"Portraits of the Artists"** from
the Portfolio **"Ten from Leo Castelli."** 1967
Serigraph printed on one hundred styrene boxes;
each box 2 × 2 × ¾″ (5.1 × 5.1 × 2 cm),
overall 20 × 20 × ¾″ (50.8 × 50.8 × 2 cm)
The Museum of Modern Art, New York. Gift of Mrs. Rosa Esman

318. **Eric Emerson (Chelsea Girls).** 1982
Serigraph on paper,
30 × 22″ (76.2 × 55.9 cm)
Courtesy Ronald Feldman Fine Arts, Inc., New York

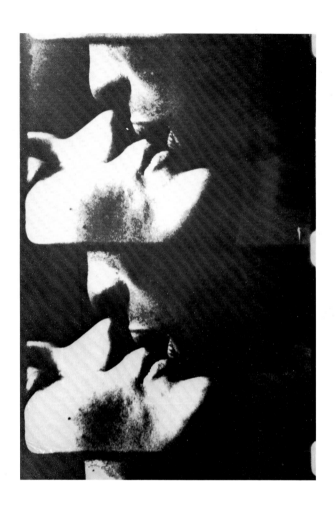

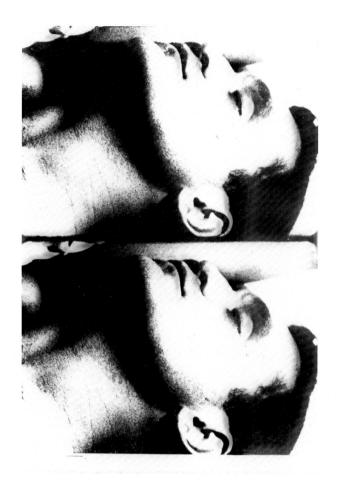

319. **Large Kiss.** 1966
Silkscreen ink on plexiglass
with metal stand (not shown);
plexiglass, 60¼ × 40½″ (153 × 102.9 cm)
The Estate of Andy Warhol

320. **Large Sleep.** 1965
Silkscreen ink on plexiglass
with metal stand (not shown);
plexiglass, 60¼ × 48⅜″ (153 × 122.9 cm)
The Estate of Andy Warhol

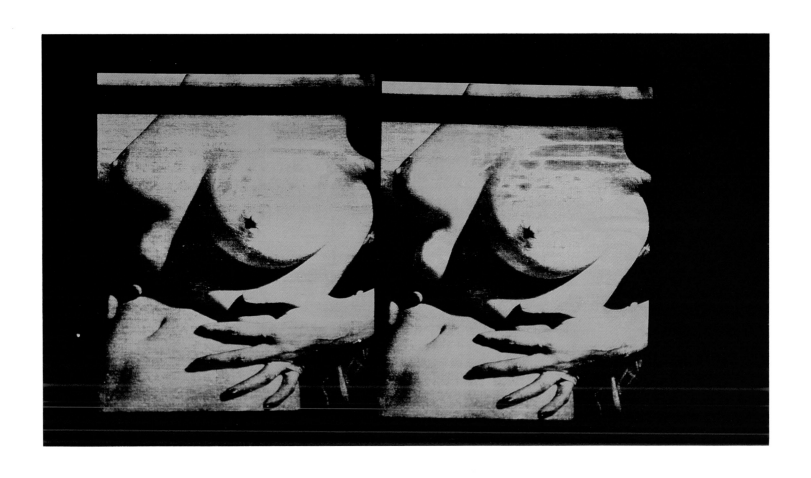

321. **Double Torso.** 1967
Viewed under ultraviolet light
Silkscreen ink on synthetic polymer paint on canvas,
43¾″ × 6′ 8″ (111.1 × 203.2 cm)
Collection Playboy Enterprises, Inc.

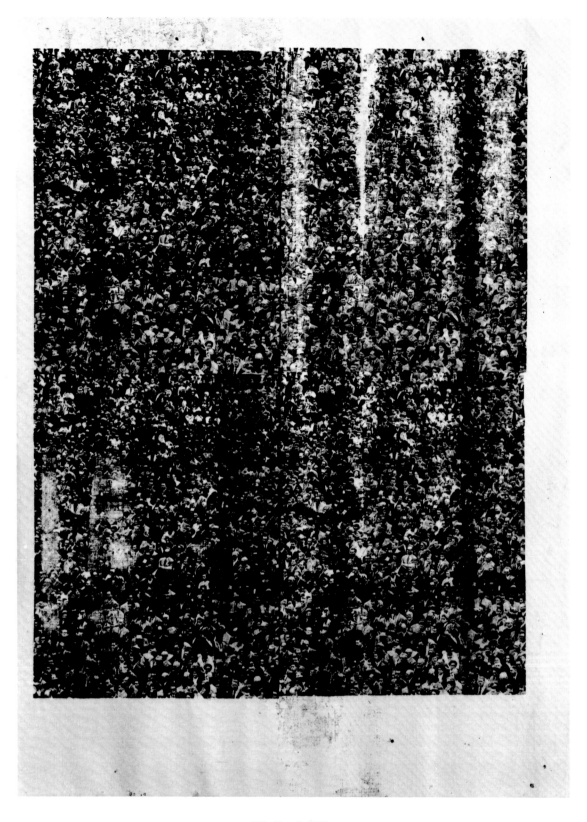

322. **Crowd.** 1963
Silkscreen ink on canvas,
50 × 36⅛″ (127 × 91.8 cm)
The Estate of Andy Warhol

323. **Merce.** 1963
Silkscreen ink on synthetic polymer paint on canvas,
6' 10" × 6' 10" (208.3 × 208.3 cm)
Private collection

**324. The American Man—Watson Powell. 1964**
Silkscreen ink on synthetic polymer paint on canvas;
thirty-two panels, each 16 × 16″ (40.6 × 40.6 cm),
overall 10′ 8½″ × 5′ 4½″ (326.4 × 163.8 cm)
Collection American Republic Insurance Company, Des Moines

325. **Ethel Scull Thirty-six Times.** 1963
Silkscreen ink on synthetic polymer paint on canvas;
thirty-six panels, each 19⅞ × 15⅞″ (50.5 × 40.3 cm),
overall 6′ 7¾″ × 11′ 11″ (202.6 × 363.2 cm)
Whitney Museum of American Art, New York. Gift of Ethel Redner Scull

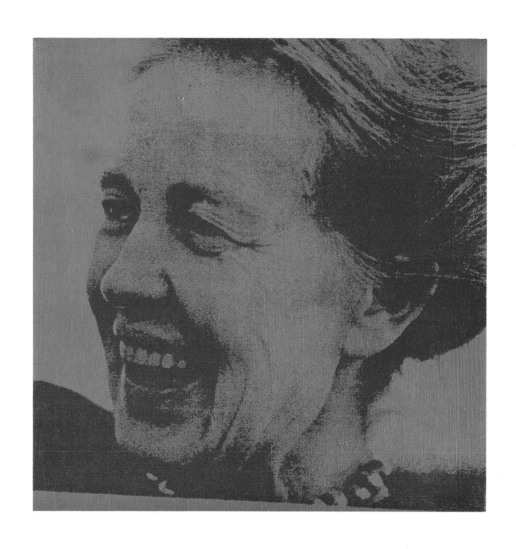

326. **Portrait of Dominique.** 1969
Silkscreen ink on synthetic polymer paint on canvas,
8 × 8″ (20.3 × 20.3 cm)
Private collection

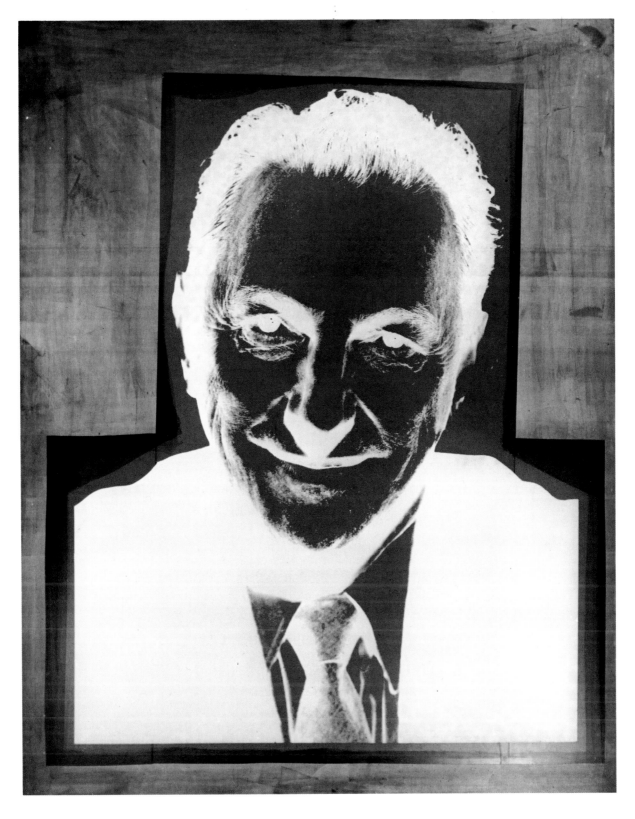

327. **Sidney Janis.** 1967
Photosensitive gelatin and tinted lacquer on silkscreen ink on wood frame,
7′ 8½″ × 6′ 4⅛″ (235 × 193.4 cm)
The Museum of Modern Art, New York. The Sidney and Harriet Janis Collection (fractional gift)

328. **Dennis Hopper.** 1971
Silkscreen ink on synthetic polymer paint on canvas,
40½ × 40½″ (102.9 × 102.9 cm)
Courtesy Nigel Greenwood Gallery, London

329. **Philip Johnson.** 1972
Silkscreen ink on synthetic polymer paint on canvas;
nine panels, each 32 × 32″ (81.3 × 81.3 cm),
overall 8 × 8′ (243.8 × 243.8 cm)
Collection David Whitney

330. **Julia Warhola.** 1974
Silkscreen ink and synthetic polymer paint on canvas,
40 × 40″ (101.5 × 101.5 cm)
The Estate of Andy Warhol

331. **Julia Warhola.** 1974
Silkscreen ink on synthetic polymer paint on canvas,
40 × 40″ (101.5 × 101.5 cm)
The Estate of Andy Warhol

332. **David Hockney.** 1974
Silkscreen ink and synthetic polymer paint on canvas,
40 × 40″ (101.5 × 101.5 cm)
Collection Shirley and Miles Fiterman

333. **Ladies and Gentlemen.** 1975
Silkscreen ink on synthetic polymer paint on canvas;
nine canvases, each 14 × 11″ (35.6 × 27.9 cm)
The Estate of Andy Warhol

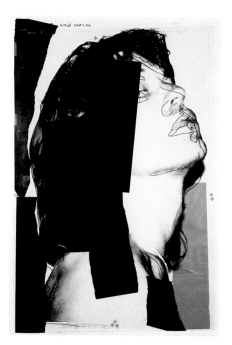

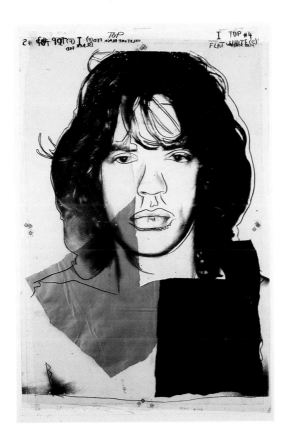

334. **Maquettes for the Portfolio "Mick Jagger."** 1975
Silkscreen ink on paper and acetate collaged on paper;
ten works, each 50 × 38⅛" (127 × 94 cm)
Museum moderner Kunst, Vienna, on loan from the Ludwig Foundation, Austria

335. **Leo Castelli.** 1975
Silkscreen ink on synthetic polymer paint on canvas,
40 × 40″ (101.5 × 101.5 cm)
Collection Leo Castelli, New York

336. **Portrait of an American Lady.** 1977
Silkscreen ink on synthetic polymer paint on canvas,
40 × 40″ (101.5 × 101.5 cm)
The Estate of Andy Warhol

337. **Henry Geldzahler.** 1979
Silkscreen ink on synthetic polymer paint on canvas,
40 × 40″ (101.5 × 101.5 cm)
Collection Henry Geldzahler

338. **Truman Capote.** 1979
Silkscreen ink on synthetic polymer paint on canvas;
two panels, each 40 × 40″ (101.5 × 101.5 cm)
Dia Art Foundation, New York. Courtesy The Menil Collection, Houston

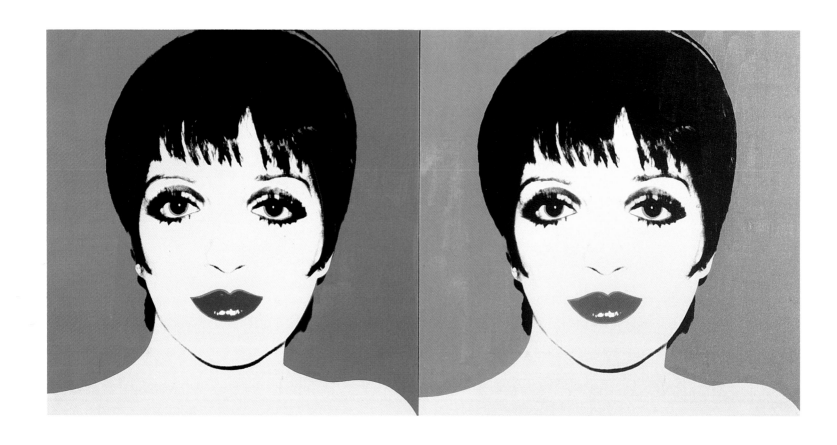

339. **Liza Minnelli.** 1978
Silkscreen ink on synthetic polymer paint on canvas;
two panels, each 40 × 40″ (101.5 × 101.5 cm)
Dia Art Foundation, New York. Courtesy The Menil Collection, Houston

340. **Lana.** 1985
Silkscreen ink on synthetic polymer paint on canvas,
40 × 40″ (101.5 × 101.5 cm)
Collection Mr. and Mrs. S. I. Newhouse, Jr.

341. **The American Indian (Russell Means).** 1976
Silkscreen ink on synthetic polymer paint on canvas,
50 × 42″ (127 × 106.7 cm)
The Estate of Andy Warhol

342. **Man Ray.** 1978
Silkscreen ink on synthetic polymer paint on canvas,
16 × 16″ (40.6 × 40.6 cm)
Collection Shirley and Miles Fiterman

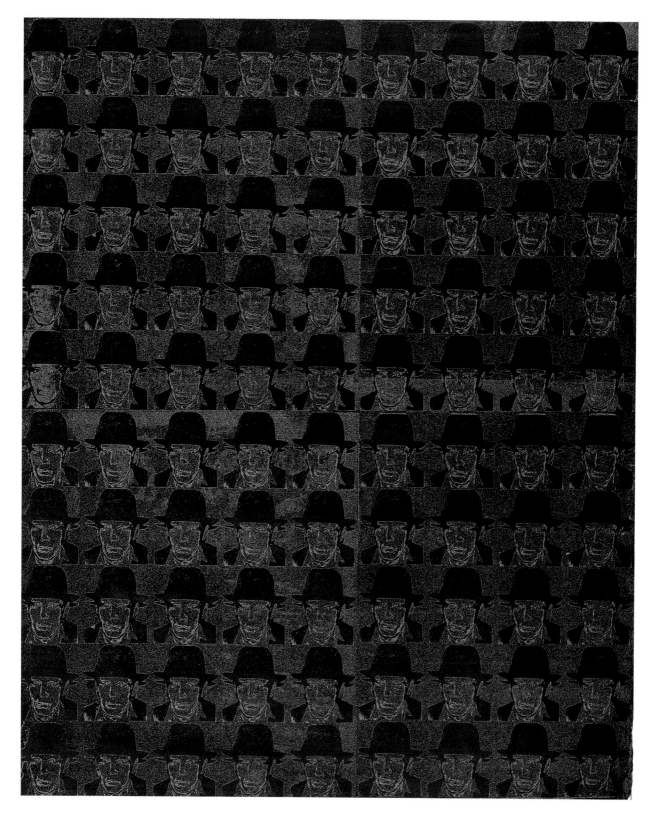

343. **Diamond Dust Joseph Beuys.** 1980
Silkscreen ink and diamond dust on synthetic polymer paint on canvas,
8′ 4″ × 6′ 8″ (254 × 203.2 cm)
The Estate of Andy Warhol

344. **Diamond Dust Joseph Beuys.** 1980
Silkscreen ink and diamond dust on synthetic polymer paint on canvas,
40 × 40″ (101.5 × 101.5 cm)
Collection Francesco Pellizzi

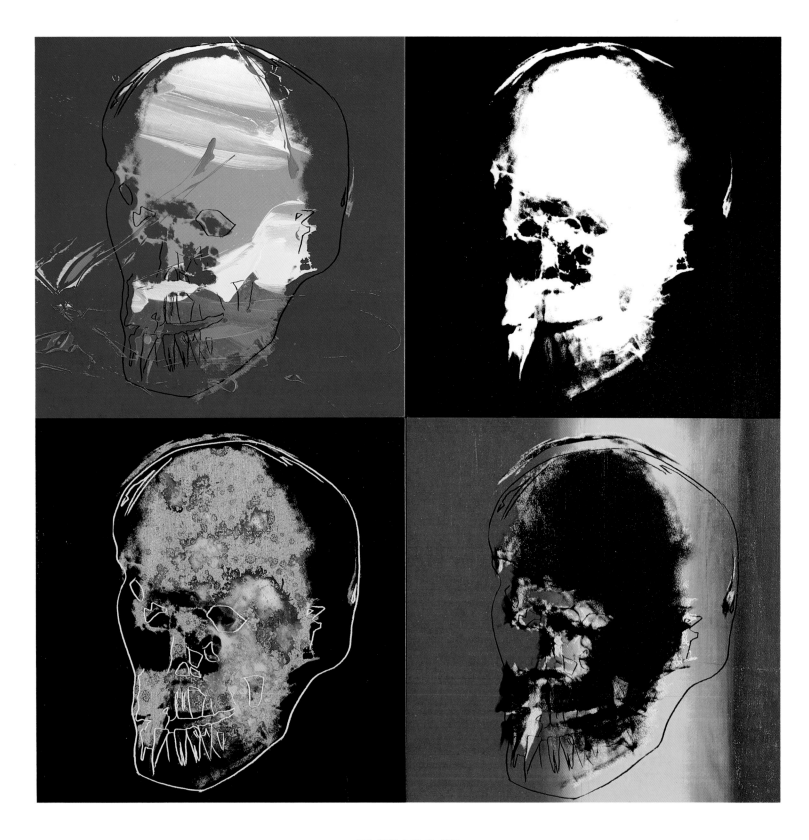

345. **Philip's Skull.** 1985
Silkscreen ink on synthetic polymer paint on canvas;
four panels, each 40 × 40″ (101.5 × 101.5 cm)
Private collection

346. **Mao Wallpaper.** 1974
Serigraph printed on wallpaper,
40 × 30″ (101.5 × 76.2 cm)
The Estate of Andy Warhol

347. Installation view, *Andy Warhol,* Musée Galliera, Paris, 1974

348. **Mao.** 1972
Silkscreen ink on synthetic polymer paint on canvas,
6′ 10″ × 61″ (208.3 × 155 cm)
Courtesy Thomas Ammann, Zürich

349. **Mao.** 1972
Silkscreen ink on canvas,
6′ 10″ × 61″ (208.3 × 155 cm)
The Estate of Andy Warhol

350. **Mao.** 1972
Silkscreen ink on synthetic polymer paint on canvas,
6′ 10″ × 61″ (208.3 × 155 cm)
Dia Art Foundation, New York. Courtesy The Menil Collection, Houston

351. **Mao.** 1972
Silkscreen ink on synthetic polymer paint on canvas,
6′ 10″ × 68″ (208.3 × 172.7 cm)
Dia Art Foundation, New York. Courtesy The Menil Collection, Houston

352. **Mao.** 1972
Silkscreen ink on synthetic polymer paint on canvas,
6′ 10″ × 58″ (208.3 × 145 cm)
Collection J. W. Froehlich, Stuttgart

353. **Mao.** 1973
Silkscreen ink and synthetic polymer paint on canvas,
12 × 10¼″ (30.5 × 26 cm)
Collection Joni and Monte Gordon, Los Angeles
Courtesy Newspace, Los Angeles

354. **Mao.** 1973
Silkscreen ink and synthetic polymer paint on canvas,
12 × 10″ (30.5 × 25.4 cm)
Dia Art Foundation, New York. Courtesy The Menil Collection, Houston

355. **Mao.** 1973
Silkscreen ink and synthetic polymer paint on canvas,
12 × 10″ (30.5 × 25.4 cm)
Dia Art Foundation, New York. Courtesy The Menil Collection, Houston

356. **Mao.** 1973
Silkscreen ink and synthetic polymer paint on canvas,
12 × 10″ (30.5 × 25.4 cm)
Collection Mr. and Mrs. Harold Siegel

357. **Mao.** 1973
Silkscreen ink and synthetic polymer paint on canvas,
12 × 10″ (30.5 × 25.4 cm)
Collection Roy and Dorothy Lichtenstein

358. **Mao.** 1974
Silkscreen ink and synthetic polymer paint on canvas,
12 × 10″ (30.5 × 25.4 cm)
Collection Douglas S. Cramer

359. **Mao.** 1973
Silkscreen ink and synthetic polymer paint on canvas,
12 × 10″ (30.5 × 25.4 cm)
Private collection

360. **Mao.** 1973
Silkscreen ink and synthetic polymer paint on canvas,
12 × 10″ (30.5 × 25.4 cm)
Private collection

361. **Mao.** 1973
Silkscreen ink on synthetic polymer paint on canvas,
14′ 6⅞″ × 11′ 4½″ (444.3 × 346.7 cm)
The Art Institute of Chicago
Mr. and Mrs. Frank G. Logan Purchase Prize and Wilson L. Mead Fund

362. **Mao.** 1973
Pencil on paper,
6′ 9¼″ × 42¼″ (206.4 cm × 107.3)
Collection Roger I. Davidson, Toronto

363. **Mao II.** 1973
Pencil on paper,
36½ × 32½″ (92.7 × 82.6 cm)
Collection Leo Castelli, New York

364. **Skull.** 1976
Silkscreen ink on synthetic polymer paint on canvas,
11′ × 12′ 6″ (335.3 × 381 cm)
Dia Art Foundation, New York. Courtesy The Menil Collection, Houston

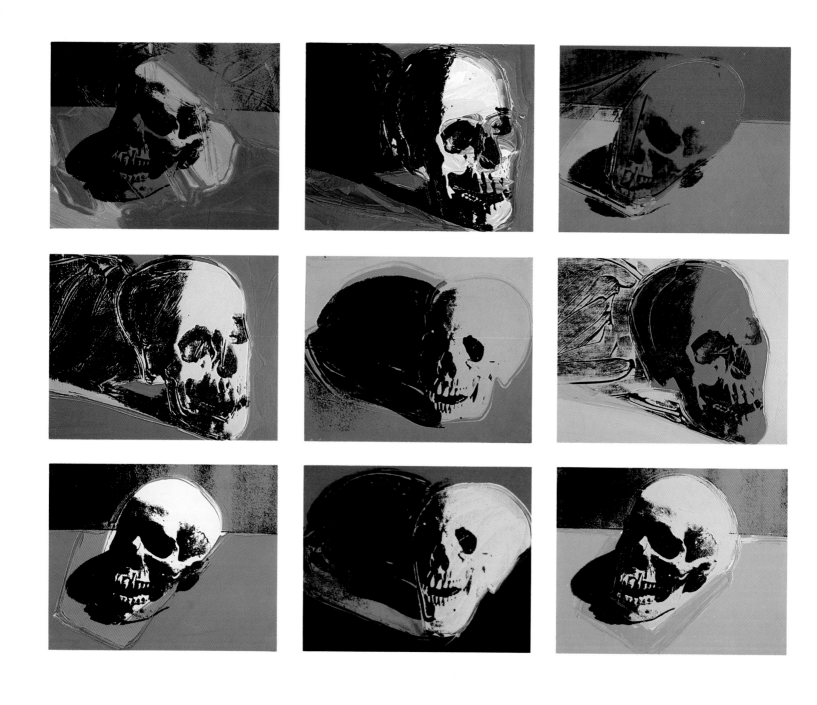

365. **Skulls.** 1976
Silkscreen ink on synthetic polymer paint on canvas;
nine canvases, each 15 × 19″ (38.1 × 48.3 cm)
The Estate of Andy Warhol

366. **Skull.** 1976
Silkscreen ink on synthetic polymer paint on canvas,
11′ × 12′ 6″ (335.3 × 381 cm)
Dia Art Foundation, New York. Courtesy The Menil Collection, Houston

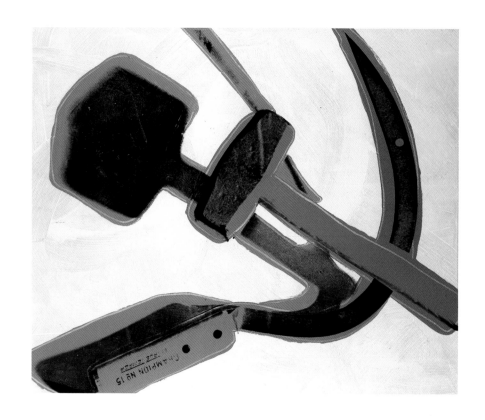

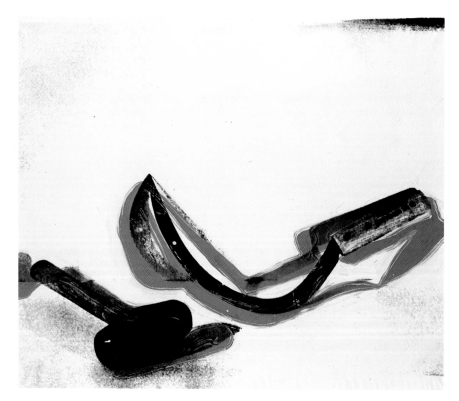

**367. Hammer and Sickle.** 1977
Silkscreen ink on synthetic polymer paint on canvas,
6′ × 7′ 2″ (182.9 × 218.4 cm)
The Estate of Andy Warhol

**368. Hammer and Sickle.** 1977
Silkscreen ink on synthetic polymer paint on canvas,
6′ × 7′ 2″ (182.9 × 218.4 cm)
The Estate of Andy Warhol

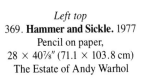

| *Left top* | *Left center* | *Left bottom* | *Right* |
| 369. **Hammer and Sickle.** 1977 | 370. **Hammer and Sickle.** 1977 | 371. **Hammer and Sickle.** 1977 | 372. **Hammer and Sickle.** 1977 |
| Pencil on paper, | Pencil and watercolor on paper, | Pencil and watercolor on paper, | Pencil and watercolor on paper, |
| 28 × 40⅞″ (71.1 × 103.8 cm) | 28 × 40½″ (71.1 × 102.9 cm) | 28 × 40½″ (71.1 × 102.9 cm) | 40⅞ × 28″ (103.8 × 71.1 cm) |
| The Estate of Andy Warhol | The Estate of Andy Warhol | The Estate of Andy Warhol | The Estate of Andy Warhol |

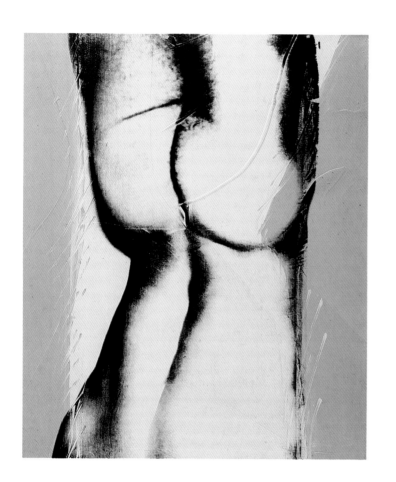

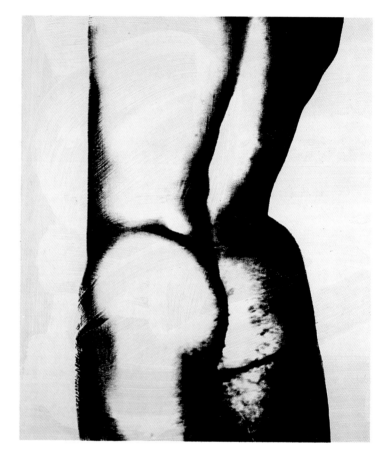

373. **Torso.** 1977
Silkscreen ink on synthetic polymer paint on canvas,
50 × 38″ (127 × 96.5 cm)
The Estate of Andy Warhol

374. **Torso.** 1977
Silkscreen ink on synthetic polymer paint on canvas,
50 × 42⅛″ (127 × 107 cm)
Collection Gian Enzo Sperone

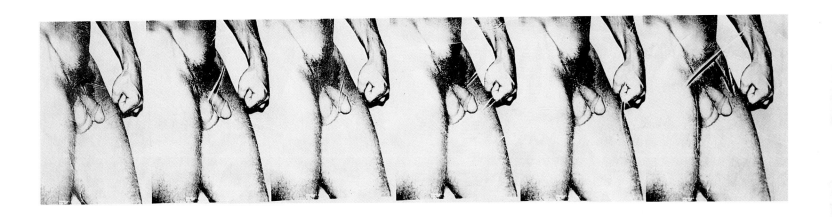

375. **Torsos.** 1977
Silkscreen ink on synthetic polymer paint on canvas,
50″ × 16′ 8″ (127 × 508 cm)
The Estate of Andy Warhol

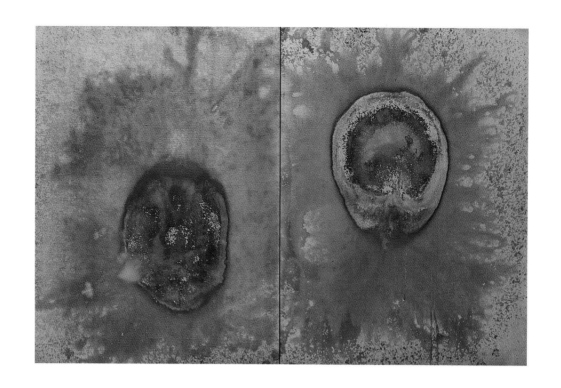

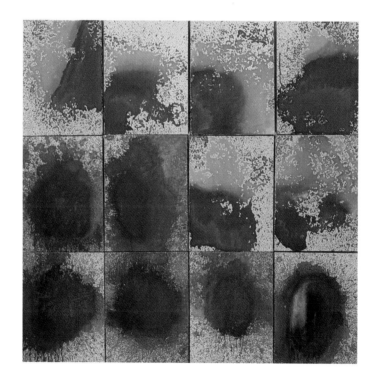

376. **Oxidation Painting.** 1978
Mixed mediums on copper metallic paint on canvas;
two panels, each 40 × 30″ (101.5 × 76.2 cm)
The Estate of Andy Warhol

377. **Oxidation Painting.** 1978
Mixed mediums on copper metallic paint on canvas;
twelve panels, each 16 × 12″ (40.6 × 30.5 cm),
overall 48 × 48″ (121.9 × 121.9 cm)
The Estate of Andy Warhol

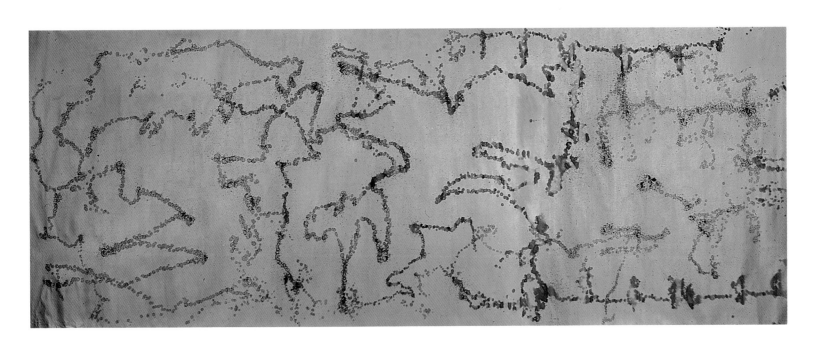

378. **Oxidation Painting.** 1978
Mixed mediums on bronze metallic paint on canvas,
9′ 6″ × 27′ (289.6 × 823 cm) (unstretched)
Courtesy Gagosian Gallery, New York

379. **Oxidation Painting.** 1978
Mixed mediums on copper metallic paint on canvas,
6′ 6″ × 17′ ½″ (198 × 519.5 cm)
Courtesy Thomas Ammann, Zürich

380. **Shadows.** 1978
Installed at 393 West Broadway, New York, 1979
Silkscreen ink on synthetic polymer paint on canvas;
102 canvases, each 6′ 4″ × 52″ (193 × 132.1 cm)
Dia Art Foundation, New York. Courtesy The Menil Collection, Houston

381. Installation view, *Warhol Shadows*,
Richmond Hall, The Menil Collection, Houston, 1987–88

382. **Black on Black Reversal.** 1979
Silkscreen ink on synthetic polymer paint on canvas,
6′ 5″ × 7′ 11″ (195.5 × 241.3 cm)
Collection Bruno and Christina Bischofberger, Küsnacht, Switzerland

383. **Big Retrospective Painting (Reversal Series).** 1979
Silkscreen ink on synthetic polymer paint on canvas,
6′ 9½″ × 35′ 5¼″ (207 × 1080 cm)
Courtesy Galerie Bruno Bischofberger, Zürich

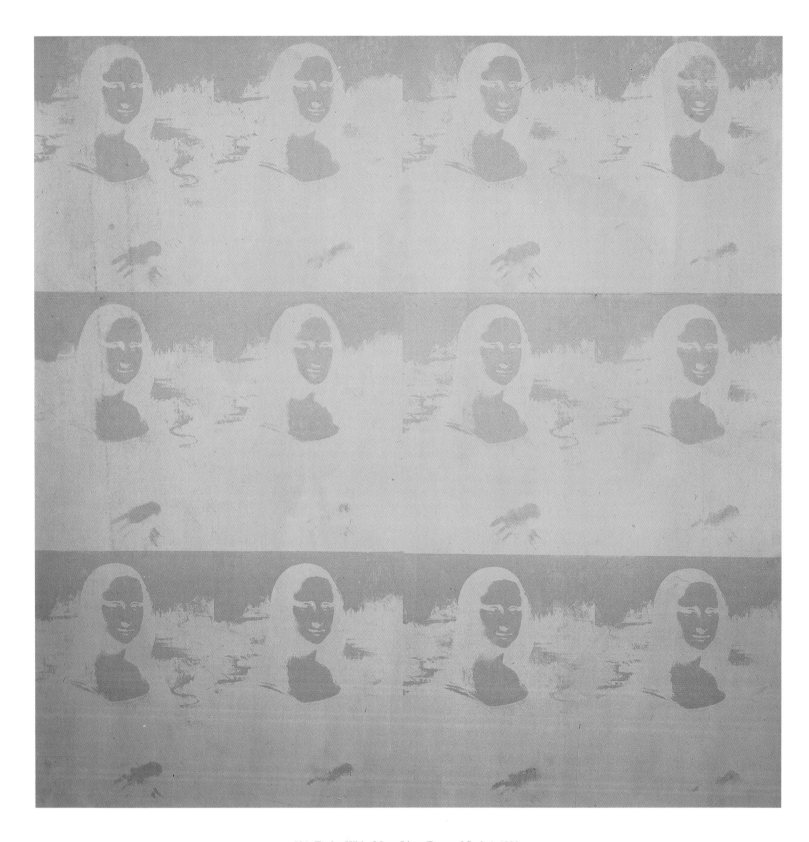

384. **Twelve White Mona Lisas (Reversal Series).** 1980
Silkscreen ink on synthetic polymer paint on canvas,
6′ 7⅞″ × 6′ 7⅞″ (202.9 × 202.9 cm)
Collection Georges Marciano, Beverly Hills, California

385. **Eighteen Multi-Colored Marilyns (Reversal Series).** 1979–86
Silkscreen ink on synthetic polymer paint on canvas,
53″ × 6′ 9⅞″ (137 × 208 cm)
Courtesy Galerie Bruno Bischofberger, Zürich

386. **Fate Presto.** 1981
Silkscreen ink on synthetic polymer paint on canvas;
three panels, each 8′ 10¼″ × 6′ 6¾″ (270 × 200 cm)
Collection Fondazione Lucio Amelio—Istituto per l'Arte Contemporanea, Naples

387. **Myths.** 1981
Silkscreen ink on synthetic polymer paint on canvas,
8′ 4″ × 8′ 4″ (254 × 254 cm)
Collection Noreen and Jack A. Rounick

388. **Superman (Myths Series).** 1981
Silkscreen ink on synthetic polymer paint on canvas,
60 × 60″ (152.4 × 152.4 cm)
Courtesy Ronald Feldman Fine Arts, Inc., New York

389. **Mickey Mouse (Myths Series).** 1981
Silkscreen ink on synthetic polymer paint on canvas,
60 × 60″ (152.4 × 152.4 cm)
Collection Lars and Maria Knutsson

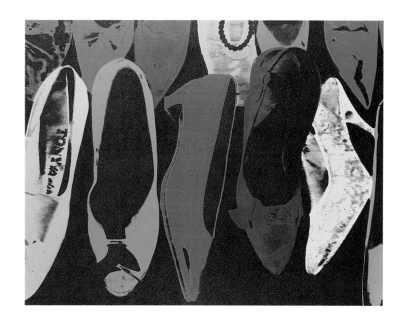

390. **Diamond Dust Shoes.** 1980
Silkscreen ink and diamond dust
on synthetic polymer paint on canvas,
70″ × 7′ 6″ (177.8 × 228.6 cm)
The Estate of Andy Warhol

391. **Diamond Dust Shoes.** 1980
Silkscreen ink and diamond dust
on synthetic polymer paint on canvas,
7′ 6″ × 70″ (228.6 × 177.8 cm)
Private collection

392. **Diamond Dust Shoes.** 1980
Silkscreen ink and diamond dust
on synthetic polymer paint on canvas,
7′ 6″ × 70″ (228.6 × 177.8 cm)
The Estate of Andy Warhol

393. **Dollar Signs.** 1981
Silkscreen ink on synthetic polymer paint on canvas,
7′ 6″ × 70″ (228.6 × 177.8 cm)
Courtesy Waddington Gallery, London,
and James Goodman Gallery, New York

394. Installation view, *Andy Warhol "Dollar Signs,"*
Leo Castelli Gallery, New York, 1982

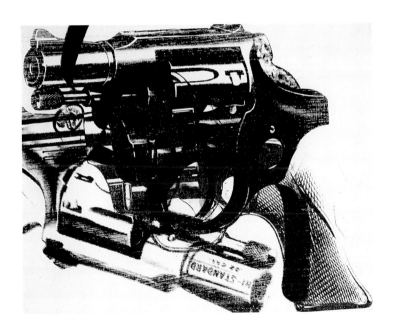

395. **Knives.** 1981
Silkscreen ink on synthetic polymer paint on canvas,
20 × 16″ (50.8 × 40.6 cm)
The Estate of Andy Warhol

396. **Guns.** 1981
Silkscreen ink on synthetic polymer paint on canvas,
16 × 20″ (40.6 × 50.8 cm)
The Estate of Andy Warhol

397. **Gun.** 1981
Silkscreen ink on synthetic polymer paint on canvas,
16 × 20″ (40.6 × 50.8 cm)
The Estate of Andy Warhol

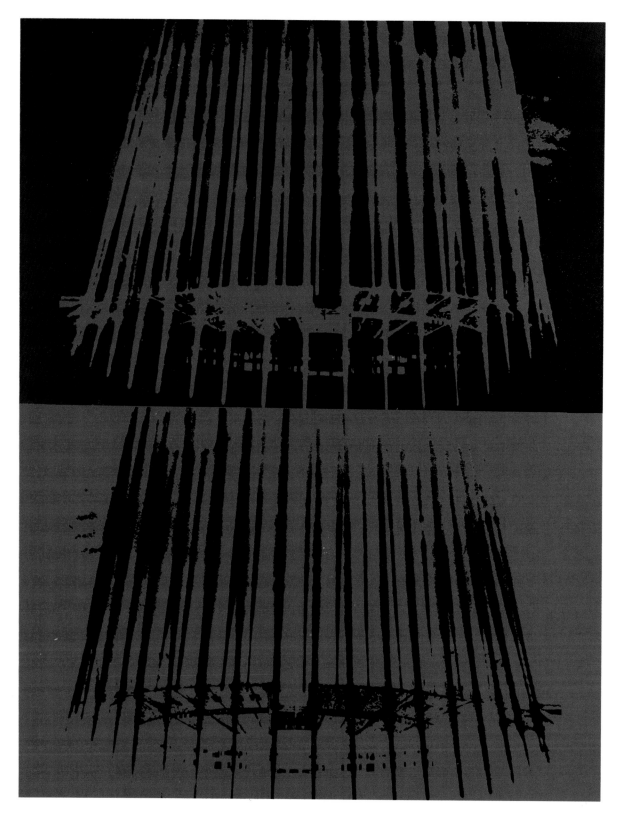

398. **Stadium (Zeitgeist Series).** 1982
Silkscreen ink on synthetic polymer paint on canvas,
7′ 5¾″ × 70⅛″ (228 × 178 cm)
Courtesy Galerie Bruno Bischofberger, Zürich

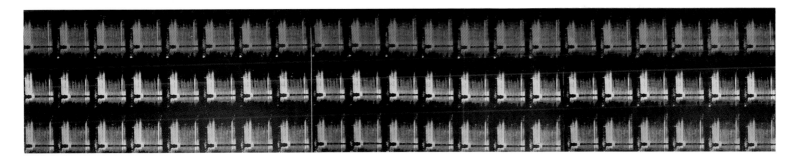

399. **The Berlin Friedrich Monument I**
**(Zeitgeist Series).** 1982
Silkscreen ink on synthetic polymer paint on canvas,
15' × 70" (457.2 × 177.8 cm)
Courtesy Galerie Bruno Bischofberger, Zürich

400. **Reflected (Zeitgeist Series).** 1982
Silkscreen ink on synthetic polymer paint on canvas,
7' × 39' 9" (213.4 × 1211.6 cm)
The Estate of Andy Warhol

367

401. **Goethe.** 1982
Serigraph on paper from a portfolio of four,
38 × 38″ (96.5 × 96.5 cm)
Private collection

402. **Details of Renaissance Paintings**
**(Sandro Botticelli, "Birth of Venus," 1482).** 1984
Serigraph on paper from a portfolio of four,
32 × 44″ (81.2 × 111.8 cm)
Courtesy Ronald Feldman Fine Arts, Inc., New York

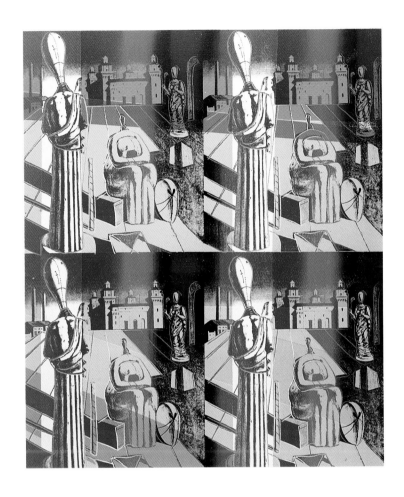

403. **The Disquieting Muses (After de Chirico).** 1982
Silkscreen ink on synthetic polymer paint on canvas,
50 × 42″ (127 × 106.7 cm)
The Estate of Andy Warhol

404. **The Two Sisters (After de Chirico).** 1982
Silkscreen ink on synthetic polymer paint on canvas,
50 × 42″ (127 × 106.7 cm)
The Estate of Andy Warhol

405. **Eva Mudocci (After Munch).** 1983
Pencil on paper,
31½ × 23½″ (80 × 59.7 cm)
The Estate of Andy Warhol

406. **The Scream (After Munch).** 1983
Pencil on paper,
31½ × 23½″ (80 × 59.7 cm)
The Estate of Andy Warhol

407. **Madonna and Self-Portrait with Skeleton's Arm (After Munch).** 1983
Silkscreen ink on synthetic polymer paint on canvas,
51 × 71″ (129.5 × 180.3 cm)
Collection Mr. and Mrs. Asher B. Edelman, New York

408. Jean-Michel Basquiat, Francesco Clemente, and Andy Warhol
**Alba's Breakfast.** 1984
Mixed mediums on paper, mounted on canvas,
46½ × 59⅞″ (118 × 152 cm)
Collection Bruno and Christina Bischofberger, Küsnacht, Switzerland

409. Jean-Michel Basquiat and Andy Warhol
**Untitled.** 1984
Synthetic polymer paint on canvas,
6' 4½" × 9' 7" (194.3 × 292.1 cm)
Private collection

410. **Vesuvius.** 1985
Synthetic polymer paint on paper,
31⅜ × 23¾″ (79.7 × 60.3 cm)
The Estate of Andy Warhol

411. **Vesuvius.** 1985
Synthetic polymer paint on paper,
23½ × 31½″ (59.7 × 80 cm)
The Estate of Andy Warhol

412. **Vesuvius.** 1985
Synthetic polymer paint on canvas,
28½ × 32″ (72.4 × 81.3 cm)
The Estate of Andy Warhol

413. **"Blackglama (Judy Garland)" from the Portfolio "Ads."** 1985
Serigraph on board from a portfolio of ten,
38 × 38″ (96.5 × 96.5 cm)
Courtesy Ronald Feldman Fine Arts, Inc., New York

414. **"Rebel Without a Cause (James Dean)" from the Portfolio "Ads."** 1985
Serigraph on board from a portfolio of ten,
38 × 38″ (96.5 × 96.5 cm)
Courtesy Ronald Feldman Fine Arts, Inc., New York

415. **"Van Heusen (Ronald Reagan)" from the Portfolio "Ads."** 1985
Serigraph on board from a portfolio of ten,
38 × 38″ (96.5 × 96.5 cm)
Courtesy Ronald Feldman Fine Arts, Inc., New York

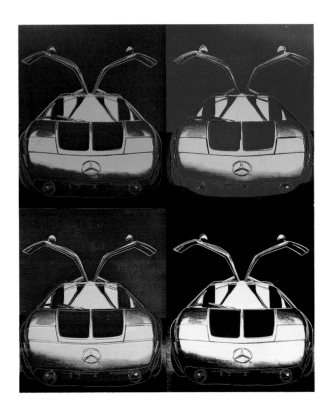

416. **Campbell's Soup Box.** 1986
Silkscreen ink on synthetic polymer paint on canvas,
44 × 44″ (111.8 × 111.8 cm)
Collection Martin and Janet Blinder
Courtesy Martin Lawrence Limited Editions, Los Angeles

417. **Mercedes-Benz Model C 111 Experimental Vehicle, 1970.** 1986
Silkscreen ink on synthetic polymer paint on canvas,
60 × 50⅜″ (152.5 × 128 cm)
Collection Daimler-Benz AG

418. **James Dean.** 1976–86
Four gelatin-silver prints stitched with thread,
27½ × 21½" (69.9 × 54.6 cm)
Courtesy Robert Miller Gallery, New York

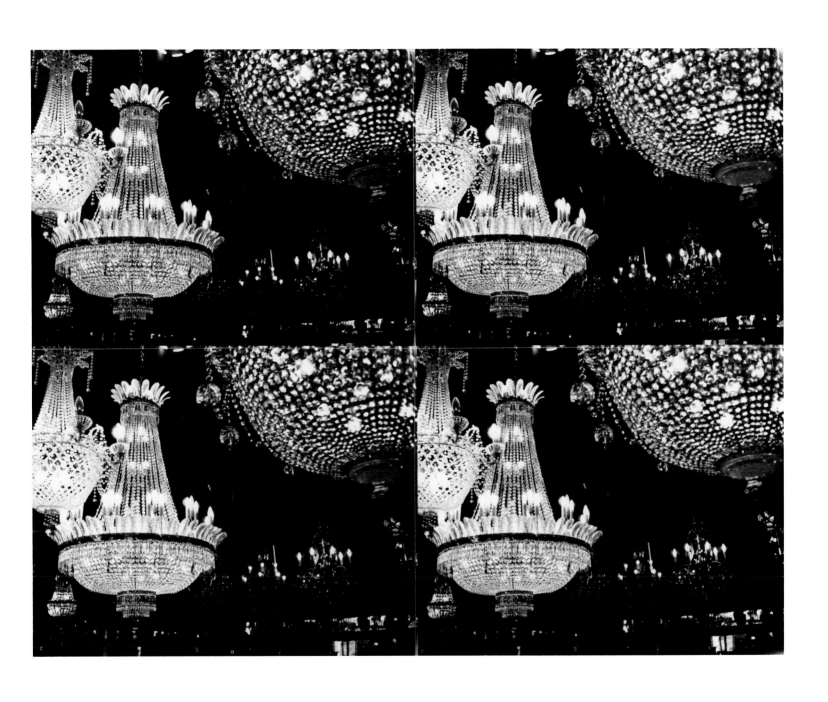

419. **Untitled.** 1976–86
Four gelatin-silver prints stitched with thread,
21½ × 27½″ (54.6 × 69.9 cm)
Courtesy Robert Miller Gallery, New York

420. **Untitled.** 1976–86
Four gelatin-silver prints stitched with thread,
27½ × 21½″ (69.9 × 54.6 cm)
The Estate of Andy Warhol

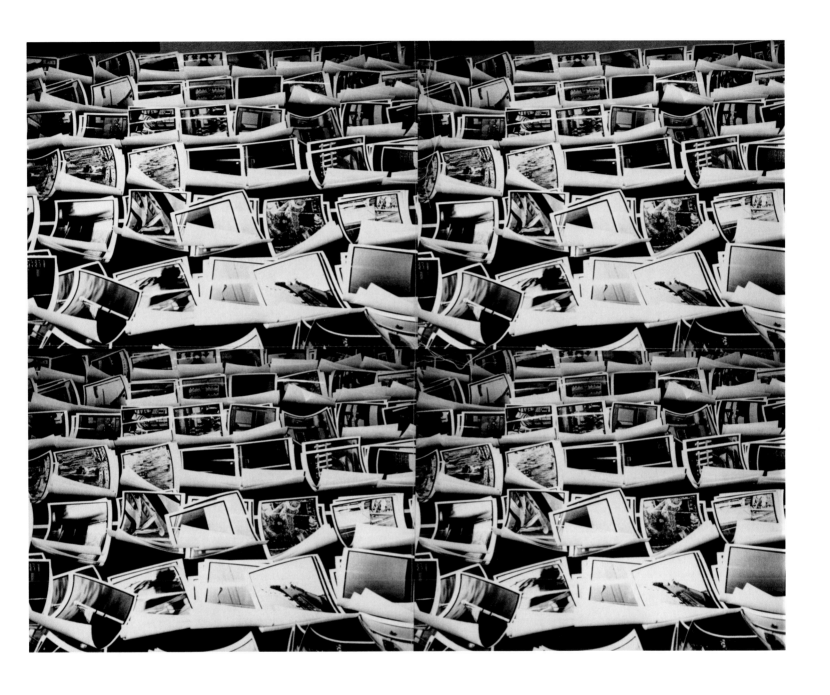

421. **Untitled.** 1976–86
Four gelatin-silver prints stitched with thread,
21½ × 27½″ (54.6 × 69.9 cm)
Courtesy Robert Miller Gallery, New York

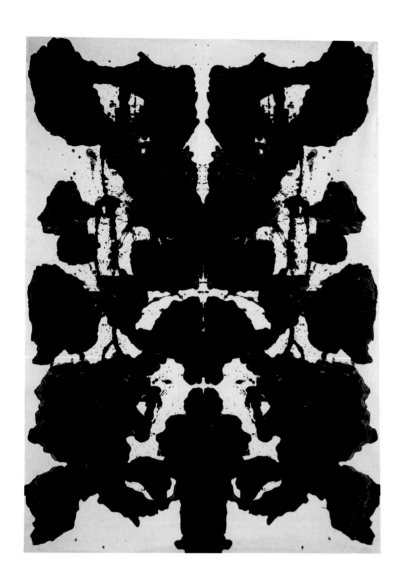

422. **Untitled (Rorschach Series).** 1984
Synthetic polymer paint on canvas,
13′ 10″ × 9′ 10″ (421.6 × 299.7 cm)
The Estate of Andy Warhol

423. **Untitled (Rorschach Series).** 1984
Synthetic polymer paint on canvas,
7′ 10″ × 6′ 8″ (238.8 × 203.2 cm)
The Estate of Andy Warhol

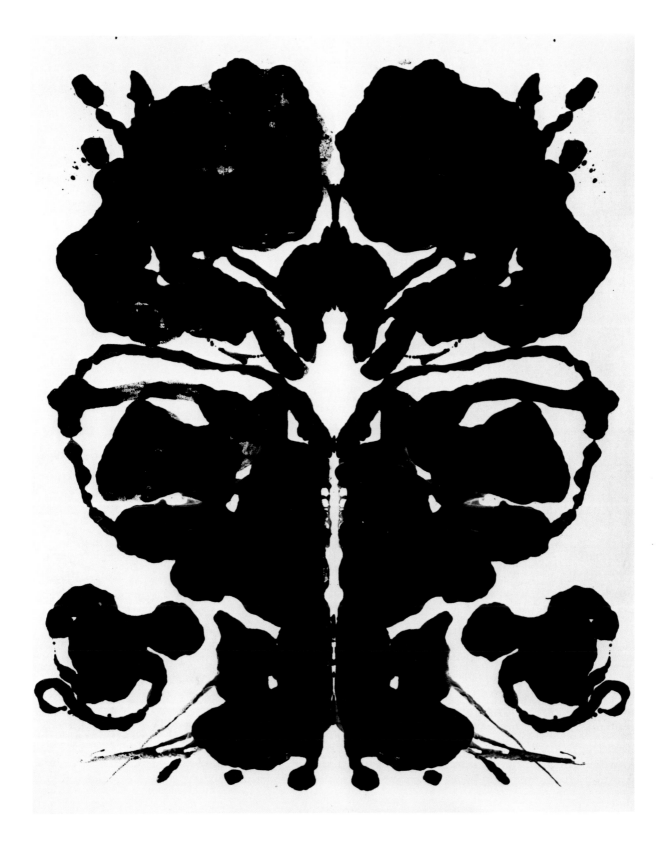

424. **Untitled (Rorschach Series).** 1984
Synthetic polymer paint on canvas,
10 × 8′ (304.8 × 243.8 cm)
The Estate of Andy Warhol

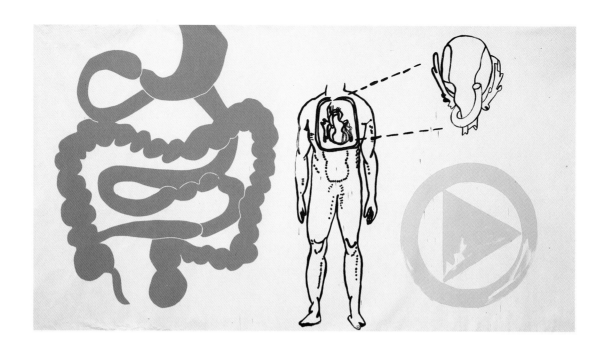

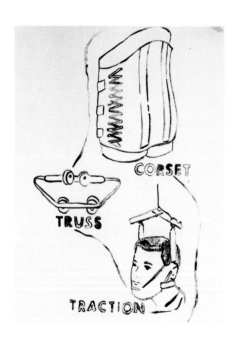

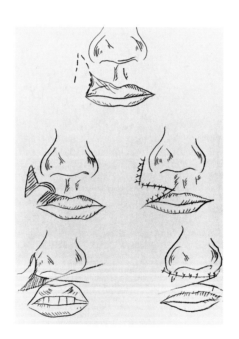

425. **Entrails.** 1985
Synthetic polymer paint on canvas,
9′ 8″ × 17′ 8″ (294.6 × 538.5 cm)
The Estate of Andy Warhol

426. **Untitled.** c. 1985
Synthetic polymer paint on paper,
31¾ × 23⅝″ (80.6 × 60 cm)
The Estate of Andy Warhol

427. **Untitled.** c. 1985
Pencil and crayon on paper,
31¾ × 23⅞″ (80.6 × 60.6 cm)
The Estate of Andy Warhol

428. **Untitled.** c. 1985
Synthetic polymer paint on paper,
31½ × 23⅝″ (80 × 60 cm)
The Estate of Andy Warhol

429. **Untitled.** c. 1985
Synthetic polymer paint on paper,
31⅝ × 24⅛″ (80.3 × 61.3 cm)
The Estate of Andy Warhol

430. **Untitled.** c. 1985
Synthetic polymer paint on paper,
31½ × 23″ (80.2 × 58.4 cm)
The Estate of Andy Warhol

431. **Untitled.** 1986
Synthetic polymer paint on paper,
31½ × 23½″ (80 × 59.7 cm)
Courtesy Anthony D'Offay Gallery, London

432. **Untitled.** 1985
Synthetic polymer paint on paper,
23½ × 31⅝″ (59.7 × 80.3 cm)
The Estate of Andy Warhol

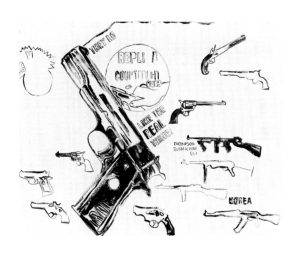

*Left top*
433. **Untitled.** c. 1985
Synthetic polymer paint on paper,
31⅝ × 23⅝″ (80.3 × 60 cm)
The Estate of Andy Warhol

*Left bottom*
434. **Untitled.** 1986
Synthetic polymer paint on paper,
31½ × 23½″ (80 × 59.7 cm)
The Estate of Andy Warhol

*Right top*
435. **Untitled.** c. 1985
Synthetic polymer paint on paper,
30⅛ × 39¾″ (76.5 × 101 cm)
The Estate of Andy Warhol

*Right center*
436. **Untitled.** c. 1985
Synthetic polymer paint on paper,
30 × 39¾″ (76.2 × 101 cm)
The Estate of Andy Warhol

*Right bottom*
437. **Untitled.** c. 1985
Synthetic polymer paint on paper,
30⅜ × 39¾″ (77.2 × 101 cm)
The Estate of Andy Warhol

438. **Untitled.** 1986
Synthetic polymer paint on paper,
32 × 24″ (81.3 × 61 cm)
The Estate of Andy Warhol

439. **Untitled.** 1986
Synthetic polymer paint on paper,
31½ × 23¾″ (80 × 60.3 cm)
The Estate of Andy Warhol

440. **Untitled.** 1986
Synthetic polymer paint on paper,
31¾ × 23¾″ (80.6 × 60.3 cm)
The Estate of Andy Warhol

441. **Untitled.** 1986
Synthetic polymer paint on paper,
31½ × 23½″ (80 × 59.7 cm)
Courtesy Anthony D'Offay Gallery, London

442. **Camouflage Statue of Liberty.** 1986
Silkscreen ink on synthetic polymer paint on canvas,
6 × 6′ (182.9 × 182.9 cm)
The Estate of Andy Warhol

443. **Camouflage Joseph Beuys.** 1986
Silkscreen ink on synthetic polymer paint on canvas,
9′ 11″ × 7′ 3″ (302.3 × 221 cm)
The Estate of Andy Warhol

444. **Camouflage.** 1986
Silkscreen ink on synthetic polymer paint on canvas,
9' 8" × 35' (294.7 × 1066.8 cm)
The Estate of Andy Warhol

445. **Camouflage Last Supper.** 1986
Silkscreen ink on synthetic polymer paint on canvas,
7′ × 37′ 6″ (213.4 × 1143 cm)
The Estate of Andy Warhol

446. **Sixty Last Suppers.** 1986
Silkscreen ink on canvas,
9′ 8″ × 32′ 9″ (294.6 × 998.2 cm)
Courtesy Leo Castelli Gallery, New York

*Left*
447. **Untitled.** 1985
Silkscreen ink and colored paper pasted on paper,
31⅝ × 23⅞″ (80.3 × 60.6 cm)
The Estate of Andy Warhol

*Top right*
448. **Untitled.** 1986
Silkscreen ink and colored paper pasted on paper,
23½ × 31⅝″ (59.7 × 80.3 cm)
The Estate of Andy Warhol

*Bottom right*
449. **Untitled.** 1986
Silkscreen ink and colored paper pasted on paper,
23½ × 31½″ (59.7 × 80 cm)
The Estate of Andy Warhol

*Top left*
450. **Untitled.** 1986
Synthetic polymer paint on paper,
31½ × 23½″ (80 × 59.7 cm)
Private collection

*Top right*
451. **Untitled.** 1986
Synthetic polymer paint on paper,
31½ × 23½″ (80 × 59.7 cm)
The Estate of Andy Warhol

*Bottom*
452. **Untitled.** 1986
Synthetic polymer paint on paper,
23½ × 31½″ (59.7 × 80 cm)
The Estate of Andy Warhol

453. **Raphael I—$6.99.** 1985
Synthetic polymer paint on canvas,
13′ ¼″ × 9′ 8″ (396.9 × 294.6 cm)
The Estate of Andy Warhol

454. **The Last Supper.** 1986
Synthetic polymer paint on canvas,
9′ 11″ × 21′ 11″ (302.3 × 668 cm)
The Estate of Andy Warhol

455. **Lenin.** 1986
Serigraph on paper,
39 × 29½″ (100 × 75 cm)
The Estate of Andy Warhol

456. **Lenin.** 1986
Silkscreen ink on synthetic polymer paint on canvas,
7′ × 70″ (213 × 178 cm)
The Estate of Andy Warhol

457. **Frederick the Great.** 1986
Silkscreen ink on synthetic polymer paint on canvas,
7′ × 6′ (213.4 × 182.9 cm)
The Estate of Andy Warhol

458. **Beethoven.** 1987
Silkscreen ink on synthetic polymer paint on canvas,
40 × 40″ (101.6 × 101.6 cm)
Courtesy Galerie Wünsche, Bonn

459. **Moonwalk (History of TV Series).** 1987
Serigraph on paper,
38 × 38″ (96.5 × 96.5 cm)
Courtesy Ronald Feldman Fine Arts, Inc., New York

460. **Camouflage Self-Portrait.** 1986
Silkscreen ink on synthetic polymer paint on canvas,
6′ 10″ × 6′ 10″ (208.3 × 208.3 cm)
The Metropolitan Museum of Art, New York
Purchase, Mrs. Vera List Gift

# *CHRONOLOGY*

*PREPARED BY MARJORIE FRANKEL NATHANSON*

Andy Warhol was a true collector, a saver not only of costly objects but also of ordinary invoices, receipts, letters, and original source material for his art. Noting each appointment and taxi fare in his date books (figure 1) or preserving odd papers and miscellaneous items in his "time capsules" (figure 2), Warhol obsessively documented his own existence. These documents have been important in the effort to establish the facts of Warhol's life, and I wish to thank The Estate of Andy Warhol and The Andy Warhol Foundation for the Visual Arts for granting me access to the papers in their collections.

The works of art named here were chosen for their importance or to give an overview of Warhol's oeuvre, and represent only a selective listing. Within each year the art and films that Warhol created are listed first, in alphabetical order, followed by significant events in his life and notable exhibitions of his art.

## *1928*

August 6, born Andrew Warhola, in Pittsburgh, to Andrej (born 1886) and Julia (née Zavacky, 1892) Warhola (figure 3). His parents had married in 1909 in Mikova in the Medzilaborce region of Czechoslovakia, and about 1913 his father had moved to the United States. Partly because of World War I, however, Julia was unable to immigrate until 1921. In the intervening years, Andrej Warhola worked as a coal miner. Prior to Warhol's birth, the Warholas had two other children, Paul (born 1922) and John (born 1925) (figure 4).

Warhol's family first lives at 73 Orr Street in Pittsburgh, then moves to 3252 Dawson Street in a section of Pittsburgh called Oakland. Father works in heavy construction; mother makes paper flowers, Easter eggs, and other handcrafts. During the Depression she sells the flowers, placed in tin cans covered with crepe paper, door to door.

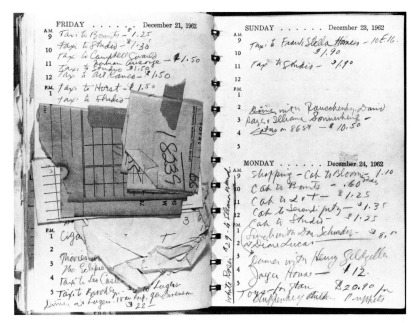

1. Pages from Warhol's diary, December 1962

2. One of Warhol's many "time capsules," boxes into which he placed miscellaneous papers and objects

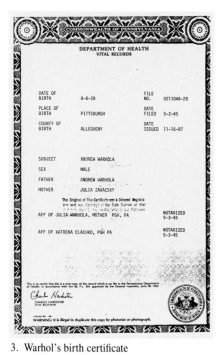

3. Warhol's birth certificate

4. Warhol with his mother and older brother John, c. 1931

5. Warhol's high-school graduation picture, 1945

## 1934–35

From about the age of six, Warhol collects autographed photographs of movie stars. His first is Shirley Temple, but his collection will also include Mickey Rooney, Freddie Bartholomew, and others.

About this time, he enters Holmes Elementary School, which he will attend through the eighth grade, skipping grades one and five.

## 1936–37

At the age of eight or nine, has a "nervous breakdown" (Saint Vitus's dance) during summer vacation. He spends approximately one month in bed, coloring, cutting designs from paper, and playing with paper dolls. A Charlie McCarthy doll, modeled after the dummy that ventriloquist Edgar Bergen uses in his popular performances, is another diversion. His family reads to him, sometimes from the comic strip Dick Tracy. Although Warhol has scarlet fever as a child, he is otherwise generally healthy.

## 1939

Family purchases a radio; throughout his childhood Warhol enjoys listening to it. He also enjoys drawing, painting, and reading comic books and magazines.

## 1941

Warhol has his picture taken in a photo booth.

## 1942

While he is working at a construction site in West Virginia, Andrej Warhola's health fails. He returns to Pittsburgh, is ill for several months, and dies on May 15 from tuberculous peritonitis.

At about the age of fourteen, Warhol attends a free program in art appreciation and art training at Carnegie Institute of Technology (now Carnegie-Mellon University), Pittsburgh.

## 1945

Spring, graduates from Schenley High School, Pittsburgh (figure 5).

Fall, enters Carnegie Institute of Technology, where he majors in pictorial design. During college years he meets Philip Pearlstein, also a student there, and studies under Balcomb Greene and Robert Lepper, among others.

During college he teaches art part-time at the Irene Kaufman Settlement in the Herron Hill section of Pittsburgh and, on three of his summer vacations, works as a window dresser at Joseph Horne department store.

Sometime in his college career he begins to experiment with the blotted-line technique that will become his commercial-art trademark.

## 1947–48

Junior year, wins the Mrs. John L. Porter Prize for Progress. Works as art editor of student magazine.

## 1948–49

Senior year, submits his painting The Broad Gave Me My Face, But I Can Pick My Own Nose (figure 6) to annual exhibition of Associated Artists of Pittsburgh. Jurors, including George Grosz, cannot agree on exhibition selection, and an alternative exhibition is organized that includes Warhol's submission.

June 16, 1949, graduates from Carnegie Institute of Technology (figure 7).

Summer 1949, moves to New York, where he shares an apartment on St. Mark's Place for two months with Philip Pearlstein. In September they move in with Francesca Boas, a dance therapist, who lives on West Twenty-first Street.

Seeks work as a commercial artist, carrying samples of his drawings to New York art directors. He meets the art editor of Glamour magazine and is hired to create drawings for the

6. Andy Warhol. *The Broad Gave Me My Face, But I Can Pick My Own Nose.* c. 1948. Oil on masonite, 24½ × 30″ (62.2 × 76.2 cm). Collection Paul Warhola family

CARNEGIE·INSTITUTE·OF·TECHNOLOGY

UPON·RECOMMENDATION·OF·THE·FACULTY·OF·THE
COLLEGE·OF·FINE·ARTS
HEREBY·CONFERS·ON
*Andrew Warhola*
THE·DEGREE·OF
BACHELOR·OF·FINE·ARTS·IN·PICTORIAL·DESIGN
IN·RECOGNITION·OF·THE·COMPLETION·OF·THE
COURSE·OF·STUDY·PRESCRIBED·FOR·THIS·DEGREE

GIVEN·UNDER·THE·SEAL·OF·THE·CORPORATION·AT·PITTSBURGH
IN·THE·COMMONWEALTH·OF·PENNSYLVANIA·ON·THE·SIXTEENTH
DAY·OF·JUNE·NINETEEN·HUNDRED·AND·FORTY·NINE

7. Warhol's college diploma

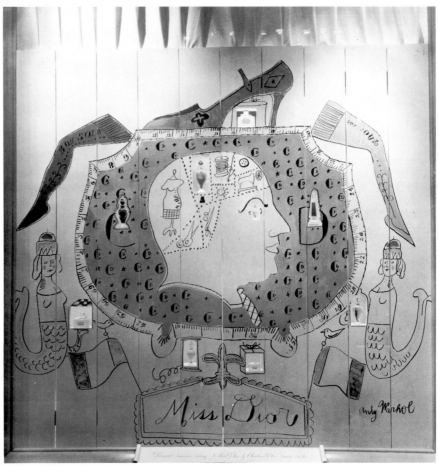

9. Bonwit Teller window display, 1955. Bottles of perfume are presented in illuminated display boxes set into the hand-painted scene

8. Illustration for "Success Is a Job in New York," *Glamour* magazine, 1949

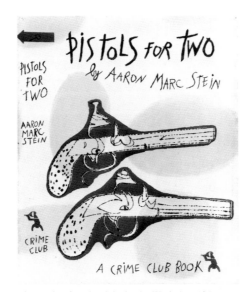

10. Design for a book jacket by Warhol, c. 1951

article "Success Is a Job in New York" (figure 8), published in September 1949. During his commercial career Warhol will work for *Vogue, Seventeen, The New Yorker, Harper's Bazaar,* Tiffany & Co., Bergdorf Goodman, Bonwit Teller (figure 9), I. Miller, and other concerns, creating advertisements, window displays, stationery, book jackets (figure 10), record covers, and other commercial works.

Begins to use the name "Warhol" instead of "Warhola."

Becomes infatuated with Truman Capote after seeing the author's photograph on the book jacket of Capote's novel *Other Voices, Other Rooms,* published 1948 (figures 11, 12). Some time after moving to New York, Warhol sends a series of letters and makes a number of phone calls to the writer, ceasing only when Capote's mother asks him to stop.

11. Photograph of Truman Capote on the book jacket of his novel *Other Voices, Other Rooms*, 1948

12. Warhol in pose echoing Truman Capote's, c. 1949

13. Warhol at home with his mother, 1966

### 1950

March, moves to 103rd Street and Manhattan Avenue, where he shares an apartment with young dancers, writers, and artists. Later moves to East Twenty-fifth Street between First and Second avenues.

Moves again, to an apartment at 216 East Seventy-fifth Street. His mother moves in with him, beginning a period of shared residence that will last some twenty years (figure 13), until her return to Pittsburgh about 1971 for health reasons.

Buys first television set.

Fritzie Miller becomes his commercial-art agent.

### 1951

Warhol is photographed by his friend George Klauber in a pose reminiscent of Greta Garbo's in a famous photograph by Edward Steichen (figures 14, 15).

### 1952

The Art Directors Club awards Warhol The Art Directors Club Medal for newspaper advertising art.

Warhol is one of three people hired to illustrate

*Amy Vanderbilt's Complete Book of Etiquette.*

First individual exhibition: *Andy Warhol: Fifteen Drawings Based on the Writings of Truman Capote,* Hugo Gallery, New York, June 16–July 3.

14. Edward Steichen. *Greta Garbo*. 1928. The Museum of Modern Art, New York. Gift of the photographer

### 1953

Moves to 242 Lexington Avenue.

With "Corkie" (Ralph Thomas Ward), publishes *A Is an Alphabet* (figure 16), the first of Warhol's promotional books sent as gifts to art directors. Uses images from *Life* magazine as the source of some of the illustrations. Also

15. Warhol in pose echoing Greta Garbo's, 1951

O was an otter
Who slept in the same bed with this young man,
And there never was an odder otter.

16. Illustration for Warhol's *A Is an Alphabet*, 1953

........................................................

collaborates with Ward in this year on the promotional books *There Was Snow on the Street and Rain in the Sky* and *Love Is a Pink Cake*.

Joins the theatrical group Theatre 12. Designs several backdrops but leaves the group after a few months.

Begins to make paintings incorporating lines that look similar to those in his blotted-line drawings.

## 1954

Receives a Certificate of Excellence from the American Institute of Graphic Arts in recognition of fine craftsmanship in an outstanding example of commercial printing.

Makes the promotional book *25 Cats Name Sam and One Blue Pussy*, with text by Charles Lisanby, a friend and scenic designer who was Cecil Beaton's assistant. Friends hand-color the illustrated cats. Serendipity, a New York restaurant and boutique, sells his drawings and books.

Individual exhibition: *Warhol*, Loft Gallery, New York, October (crumpled, marbleized paper pieces on the floor).

## 1955

With Ralph Pomeroy, who writes the text, pub-

lishes *A la Recherche du Shoe Perdu,* illustrated with drawings of fanciful shoes. The text is in Warhol's mother's handwriting. Warhol also publishes *In the Bottom of My Garden,* inspired by children's books, in this year.

Hires Vito Giallo and Nathan Gluck to work on commercial assignments. Gluck will be Warhol's assistant through 1964.

## 1956

The Art Directors Club presents Warhol with its Award for Distinctive Merit.

Receives a second Certificate of Excellence from the American Institute of Graphic Arts for an outstanding example of commercial printing.

Makes "personality" shoes: gold-leaf collages of shoes decorated to capture the personalities of famous people.

June 16–August 12, travels around the world with Lisanby, making sketchbooks during the journey. Itinerary: June 16, depart from New York; June 16–17, San Francisco; June 17–19, Honolulu; June 21–July 3, Tokyo (figure 17); July 3–5, Hong Kong; July 5–6, Manila; July 6–7, Djakarta; July 7–11, Bali; July 11–12, Singapore; July 12–14, Bangkok; July 14–17, Siem Reap, Cambodia; July 17–21, Bangkok; July 21–25, Colombo, Ceylon; July 25–26, Calcutta; July 26–29, Katmandu, Nepal; July 29–30, Benares, India; July 30–August 2, New Delhi; August 2–3, Agra, India; August 3–4, Aurangabad, India; August 5–9, Cairo and Luxor; August 9–11, Rome; August 11,

17. Andy Warhol. *Untitled (Kyoto, Japan).* 1956. Hand-painted lithograph on paper, 17¼ × 14¾" (44.3 × 37.8 cm). The Estate of Andy Warhol

........................................................

change flights in Amsterdam; August 12, arrive in New York.

Individual exhibitions: *Drawings for a Boy-Book by Andy Warhol*, Bodley Gallery, New York, February 14–March 3; and *Andy Warhol: The Golden Slipper Show or Shoes Shoe in America*, Bodley Gallery, New York, December 3–22 (figure 18).

First group exhibition: *Recent Drawings U.S.A.*, The Museum of Modern Art, New York, April 25–August 5 (shoe drawing).

18. An article on "personality" shoe drawings on view at Bodley Gallery, New York, in *Life* magazine, January 21, 1957

19. A photograph altered by Warhol to show him with a smaller nose and fuller hair

20. Warhol with profile painted over to make his nose appear smaller

## 1957

Receives The Art Directors Club Award for Distinctive Merit and The Art Directors Club Medal—both for newspaper advertising art.

Publishes *A Gold Book,* consisting of blotted-line drawings on gold paper.

Sells "personality" shoe collages at Serendipity.

Is unhappy with the shape of his nose (figures 19, 20), and has it altered.

Forms Andy Warhol Enterprises, Inc., for his commercial work.

Anna Mae Wallowitch represents Warhol's commercial work in Philadelphia and Chicago (through 1959). One project, a book cover for *Madhouse on Washington Square,* published by J. B. Lippincott, becomes a billboard in Times Square.

Individual exhibition: *A Show of Golden Pictures by Andy Warhol,* Bodley Gallery, New York, December 2–25.

## 1958

Buys Jasper Johns's drawing *Light Bulb,* 1958.

## 1959

Purchases a townhouse on Lexington Avenue near Eighty-ninth Street and moves there with his mother.

Receives a Certificate of Excellence from the American Institute of Graphic Arts (for work done in 1958).

With Suzie Frankfurt, publishes *Wild Raspberries,* a humorous cookbook.

Warhol and Nathan Gluck design wrapping paper using hand-carved stamps (figure 21).

Meets the filmmaker Emile de Antonio.

Individual exhibition: *Wild Raspberries,* Bodley Gallery, New York, December 1–24.

21. Wrapping paper by Warhol and Nathan Gluck, 1959

## 1960

First canvases depicting comic-strip characters: *Batman, Dick Tracy, Nancy, Saturday's Popeye,* and *Superman.* Also first advertisement works and Coca-Cola pictures.

De Antonio introduces him to Frank Stella.

About this time, meets Billy Linich (later known as Billy Name), who will be in Warhol's circle throughout the sixties.

A setting for a child's birthday party designed by Warhol is reproduced in the book *Tiffany Table Settings* (figure 22).

## 1961

Newspaper Front Pages.

Is hired to do all the illustrations for *Amy Vanderbilt's Complete Cookbook* but actually pays his friend Ted Carey to do them.

At Leo Castelli Gallery, sees Roy Lichtenstein's paintings based on comic strips and is surprised to learn that someone else is using this theme. Invites Ivan Karp, who works at the gallery, to his studio to see his own comic-strip paintings.

Meets Henry Geldzahler, who is on the curatorial staff of The Metropolitan Museum of Art.

April, displays the paintings *Advertisement, Before and After, Little King, Saturday's Popeye,* and *Superman* as background for mannequins in the window of Bonwit Teller, Fifty-seventh Street.

22. Setting for a child's birthday party, designed by Warhol, in *Tiffany Table Settings,* 1960

## 1962

Campbell's Soup Cans, Disasters, Do It Yourselfs, Elvises, and Marilyns. First silkscreens on canvas: *Baseball,* a small Dollar Bill, *Troy Donahue,* and *Warren.* Uses rubber stamps for *S & H Green Stamps* and *Red Airmail Stamps.* Makes a Coca-Cola print from a balsa-wood block. About this time, experiments with Oxidation paintings (which he will take up again in 1978) and with placing canvases on the sidewalk to pick up footprints of passersby.

De Antonio introduces Warhol to Eleanor Ward of the Stable Gallery, New York. Geldzahler brings Robert Rauschenberg to Warhol's studio.

Buys six small paintings by Frank Stella.

About this time, buys Marcel Duchamp's *Box in a Valise.*

Individual exhibitions: *Campbell's Soup Cans,* Ferus Gallery, Los Angeles, July 9–August 4; and *Andy Warhol,* Stable Gallery, New York, November 6–24 (Coca-Colas, Dance Diagrams, Disasters, Do It Yourselfs, *Handle with Care—Glass—Thank You,* Marilyns, a work based on a matchbook cover, and *Red Elvis*).

Group exhibition: *The New Realists,* Sidney Janis Gallery, New York, October 31–December 1 (Dance Diagrams) (figure 23).

## 1963

Electric Chairs, Race Riots (these reproduce a photograph of a clash between police and civil-rights demonstrators in Birmingham, Alabama, published in the May 17, 1963, issue of *Life* magazine). Begins Jackies after John F. Kennedy is assassinated on November 22.

Buys 16mm movie camera and shoots his first film, *Sleep.* Also films *Andy Warhol Films Jack Smith Filming "Normal Love," Blow Job, Dance Movie, Eat, Haircut, Kiss, Salome and Delilah,* and *Tarzan and Jane Regained . . . Sort Of.*

Moves studio to a firehouse on East Eighty-seventh Street. Later in year moves studio to 231 East Forty-seventh Street, which becomes known as the Factory. Billy Name moves in and covers the entire Factory in aluminum foil and silver paint (figure 24).

Creates a layout for *Harper's Bazaar* in which, for the first time, he uses photographs taken in a photo booth.

Devises costume concept for the Broadway musical *The Beast in Me* by James Thurber.

Uses a Polaroid camera for the first time, to make a cover for *C* magazine.

Gerard Malanga, a young poet, becomes Warhol's principal studio assistant (until 1967 and again from 1968 through 1970). "Baby" Jane Holzer, Brigid Polk (Brigid Berlin) (figure 25), and Ondine (Robert Olivio) also begin to frequent the Factory about this time. All appear in Warhol's films.

Meets Jonas Mekas, director of the Film-Makers' Co-operative, under whose auspices

23. Installation view, *The New Realists,* Sidney Janis Gallery, New York, 1962. One of Warhol's Dance Diagrams can be seen at left

24. Warhol at the East Forty-seventh Street Factory, which had been covered with silver paint and foil by Billy Name

25. Brigid Polk in *The Chelsea Girls* (1966)

........................................................

many of Warhol's films will receive their first public screenings.

Replaces the gray hairpiece he has worn since the early fifties with a silver-sprayed wig.

With Malanga, painter Wynn Chamberlain, and actor Taylor Mead, Warhol drives to Los Angeles for the opening of the exhibition *Andy Warhol* at the Ferus Gallery. Attends the opening of a Duchamp retrospective at the Pasadena Art Museum and meets Duchamp, whom he would later film (figure 26).

Individual exhibition: *Andy Warhol*, Ferus Gallery, Los Angeles, September 30–October (Lizes and Elvises).

## 1964

Boxes, Flowers, Most Wanted Men (figure 27), Self-Portraits.

Makes films *Mario Banana, Batman Dracula, Couch, Empire* (figure 28), *Fifty Fantastics and Fifty Personalities, Harlot, Henry Geldzahler, Shoulder, Soap Opera, Taylor Mead's Ass, The Thirteen Most Beautiful Boys,* and *The Thirteen Most Beautiful Women.*

Is commissioned to make a work for the New York State Pavilion, designed by Philip Johnson, at the New York World's Fair. Makes *Thirteen Most Wanted Men,* which is hung on the facade of the building. Fair officials feel it is politically charged and ask Warhol's permission to paint over it. Warhol grants permission and offers to exhibit a portrait of Robert Moses instead, but this also is refused by the officials.

Receives the Independent Film Award from *Film Culture* magazine.

The photographer of the image that Warhol uses for his Flower paintings sues Warhol. The suit is eventually settled out of court.

Acquires a tape recorder.

A woman with a gun enters the Factory and fires it at a stack of four Marilyns.

Individual exhibitions: *Warhol,* Galerie Ileana Sonnabend, Paris, January–February (Disasters) (figure 29); *Warhol,* Stable Gallery, New York, April 21–May 9 (Boxes) (figure 30); and *Andy Warhol,* Leo Castelli Gallery, New York, November 21–December 17 (Flowers).

## 1965

Colored Campbell's Soup Cans, Electric Chairs.

Films *Afternoon, Beauty #2, Bitch, Camp, The Closet, Drunk, Face, Hedy, Horse, Ivy and John, Kitchen, The Life of Juanita Castro,*

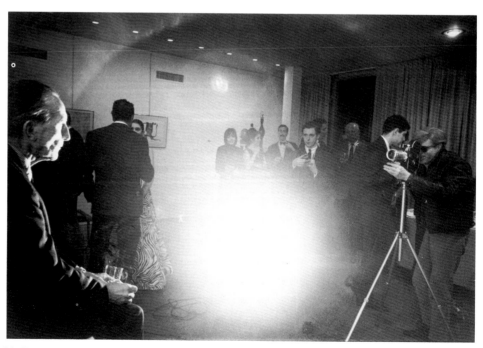

26. Warhol filming Marcel Duchamp, 1966

27. Claes Oldenburg, Tom Wesselmann, Roy Lichtenstein, Jean Shrimpton, James Rosenquist, and Warhol at the Factory in front of a painting from Warhol's Most Wanted Men series, 1966

28. *Empire* (1964)

29. Installation view, *Warhol,* Galerie Ileana Sonnabend, Paris, 1964

*Lupe, More Milk Yvette, My Hustler* (figure 31), *Outer and Inner Space, Poor Little Rich Girl, Prison, Restaurant, Screen Test #1, Screen Test #2, Space, Suicide, Paul Swan,* and *Vinyl* (figure 32).

Designs a cover for *Time* magazine using photographs taken in a photo booth (figure 33).

Malanga introduces Warhol to filmmaker Paul Morrissey (figure 34), who will be vital to film production at the Factory. Edie Sedgwick, Ultra Violet (Isabelle Collin-Dufresne), and Ingrid Superstar (Ingrid von Schefflin) all begin to frequent the Factory, as do Lou Reed, Maureen

Tucker, John Cale, and Sterling Morrison of the Velvet Underground, a rock-and-roll band (figure 35). All appear in Warhol's films.

Meets Ronnie Cutrone, who will be his studio assistant from 1972 to 1982.

Lester Persky, a film producer, gives "The Fifty Most Beautiful People" party at the Factory. Judy Garland, Rudolf Nureyev, Tennessee Williams, Brian Jones, Juliet Prowse, Allen Ginsberg, William Burroughs, and Montgomery Clift are among the guests.

With Sedgwick, Malanga, and Chuck Wein, another Factory regular, Warhol travels to Paris to attend an exhibition of his work at Galerie Ileana Sonnabend. While there he announces his intention to "retire" from painting and to focus on filmmaking instead.

Is present, again with Sedgwick, at the opening of a retrospective of his work at the Institute of Contemporary Art of the University of Pennsylvania, Philadelphia (figure 36). Some four thousand people attend the opening, but Warhol's paintings had been removed from the gallery walls and floors the previous day for security reasons, in anticipation of the crowd.

Individual exhibitions: *Andy Warhol,* Galerie Ileana Sonnabend, Paris, May (Flowers); *Andy Warhol,* Galeria Rubbers, Buenos Aires,

July 29–August 14; *Andy Warhol,* Jerrold Morris International Gallery, Toronto, September; *Andy Warhol,* Institute of Contemporary Art of the University of Pennsylvania, Philadelphia, October 8–November 21 (figures 37, 38); and *Warhol,* Gian Enzo Sperone, Turin.

30. Installation view, *Warhol,* Stable Gallery, New York, 1964

31. Paul America in *My Hustler* (1965)

32. Gerard Malanga and Edie Sedgwick in *Vinyl* (1965)

33. *Time* magazine cover, January 29, 1965

34. Warhol and Paul Morrissey, filming *My Hustler*

35. Clockwise from top: Warhol holding Nico's son Ari, Lou Reed, Nico, John Cale, Maureen Tucker, Mary Woronov, Sterling Morrison, and Gerard Malanga

## 1966

Cow Wallpaper, Self-Portraits, Silver Clouds.

Films *Bufferin* (also known as *Gerard Malanga Reads Poetry*), *The Chelsea Girls, Eating Too Fast,* \*\*\*\* (also known as *Four Stars;* it includes segments that were sometimes shown under different titles) (figure 39), and *The Velvet Underground and Nico*. Also makes a film about John F. Kennedy's assassination but never releases it.

The German actress and singer Nico (Christa Paffgen), International Velvet (Susan Bottomly) (figure 40), and Eric Emerson begin to participate in Factory activities. All appear in Warhol's films.

Begins to produce multimedia presentations, called the Erupting (later changed to Explod-

36. Edie Sedgwick (on steps) at the opening of *Andy Warhol,* Institute of Contemporary Art, Philadelphia, 1965

37. Mrs. H. Gates Lloyd, wearing an S & H Green Stamps blouse, and Sam Green, organizer of the exhibition, wearing an S & H Green Stamps tie, at *Andy Warhol,* Institute of Contemporary Art, Philadelphia, 1965
·················································

ing) Plastic Inevitable, featuring Nico and the Velvet Underground. These events include live music, dance, and monologues by the band and other Factory performers against a backdrop of Warhol's films (figure 41).

March, accompanies the Velvet Underground to performances at Rutgers University, New Brunswick, New Jersey, and the University of Michigan, Ann Arbor.

April, rents The Dom (Polsky Dom Narodny), a former Polish community center on St.

Mark's Place, for the month. Transforms it into a discotheque for Exploding Plastic Inevitable concerts.

April, at Leo Castelli Gallery, Warhol has the walls of one room papered with his Cow Wallpaper and floats his Silver Clouds throughout the space of another. (The Silver Clouds, helium-filled silver pillows, evolved from Warhol's unsuccessful attempts to create floating silver light bulbs in homage to Jasper Johns.)

Spring, travels with the Velvet Underground to Los Angeles for a month-long engagement at the Trip, a discotheque, but the club closes after one week. Performances at the Fillmore in San Francisco and in Chicago follow.

Summer, accompanies the Velvet Underground to Provincetown, Massachusetts, for performances at the Chrysler museum (now Provincetown Heritage Museum).

Fall, the film *The Chelsea Girls,* depicting people who might have lived at the Chelsea Hotel on West Twenty-third Street, is released. It is the first film by Warhol to be widely distributed and the first to receive attention from the national press, with *Newsweek* and *The New York Times* publishing reviews. In the screenings, two reels of the film are projected simultaneously, side by side, each with a different sound volume.

Warhol and his Factory entourage begin to frequent Max's Kansas City, a bar/restaurant on Park Avenue South owned by Mickey Ruskin, where artists, poets, and musicians gather (figure 42).

Late September, Warhol and the Velvet Underground travel to Boston for a performance at the opening of an exhibition of Warhol's art at the Institute of Contemporary Art.

November, accompanies the Velvet Underground to Detroit for concerts. At Detroit State Fairground Coliseum, Warhol gives away the bride at a "mod wedding" sponsored by a supermarket. The couple is given a three-day honeymoon in New York, including a screen test at the Factory.

Warhol places an advertisement in *The Village Voice:* "I'll endorse with my name any of the following: clothing, AC-DC, cigarettes, small tapes, sound equipment, Rock 'N Roll records, anything, film, and film equipment, Food, Helium, WHIPS, Money; love and kisses Andy Warhol. EL 5-9941."

Individual exhibitions: *Warhol,* Gian Enzo

38. Installation view, *Andy Warhol,* Institute of Contemporary Art, Philadelphia, 1965

39. On the set of ****, 1966

40. International Velvet
·················································

Sperone, Turin, March–April; *Andy Warhol,* Leo Castelli Gallery, New York, April 2–27 (Cow Wallpaper and Silver Clouds); *Andy Warhol Holy Cow! Silver Clouds!! Holy Cow!,* Contemporary Arts Center, Cincinnati, May; *Andy Warhol,* Institute of Contemporary Art, Boston, October 1–November 6; and Ferus Gallery, Los Angeles.

41. The Exploding Plastic Inevitable

42. Viva, Warhol, and Brigid Polk at Max's Kansas City

43. *I, a Man* (1967)

44. Taylor Mead and Viva in a publicity photograph for *Lonesome Cowboys* (1967)

45. Album cover designed by Warhol for *The Velvet Underground and Nico*, 1967

## 1967

Electric Chairs.

Continues to film **** and begins filming *Bike Boy; I, a Man* (figure 43); *Lonesome Cowboys* (on location in Arizona) (figure 44); *The Loves of Ondine;* and *Nude Restaurant.*

Produces the Velvet Underground's first album. Designs album cover with banana-peel sticker that peels off to reveal flesh-colored banana underneath (figure 45).

Makes poster for the Fifth New York Film Festival at Lincoln Center's Philharmonic Hall.

Random House publishes *Andy Warhol's Index (Book)* and Kulchur Press publishes *Screen Tests: A Diary* by Warhol and Gerard Malanga.

With Paul Morrissey, Malanga, Lester Persky, and others, Warhol goes to the Cannes Film Festival. He hopes to show *The Chelsea Girls* but does not receive an official invitation to exhibit it.

April, travels to Los Angeles and San Francisco with Morrissey, Persky, Ultra Violet, International Velvet, and friend Rod La Rod for the opening of *The Chelsea Girls.*

Early summer, Warhol goes to Philip Johnson's Glass House in New Canaan, Connecticut, where the Velvet Underground plays for a

Merce Cunningham Dance Company benefit. There Warhol becomes acquainted with Frederick Hughes from Texas (figure 46), who begins to come to the Factory regularly.

Meets Joe Dallesandro and Candy Darling, a transvestite. Becomes reacquainted with Viva (Susan Hoffmann), whom he had met a few years earlier. All three act in his films.

October, Warhol is hired for a lecture tour to colleges but because he is uncomfortable speaking before an audience he brings some Factory performers with him to answer questions. After several of these events, Warhol does not wish to continue and agrees to have Allen Midgette, a dancer who appears in several of Warhol's films, impersonate him. The ruse is successful for several engagements.

A man with a gun enters the Factory and threatens Morrissey, Hughes, Billy Name, Taylor Mead, Warhol, and others, placing the barrel at Morrissey's head and pulling the trigger. The gun does not fire. The stranger then points the gun toward the wall and pulls the trigger a second time, firing a shot. Mead jumps the gunman, then runs to the window to call for help. The stranger runs away.

Individual exhibitions: *Kühe und Schwebende Kissen von Andy Warhol,* Galerie Rudolf Zwirner, Cologne, January 24–February; *Andy*

46. Frederick Hughes and Warhol at The Museum of Modern Art, New York, 1975

47. Installation view, Expo '67, Montreal, with works by Warhol, Helen Frankenthaler, Jasper Johns, Tom Wesselmann, and others

48. Jed Johnson

*Warhol Most Wanted,* Galerie Rudolf Zwirner, Cologne, September 12–October 30; *Andy Warhol—The Thirteen Most Wanted Men,* Galerie Ileana Sonnabend, Paris; and Kunstkabinett Hans Neuendorf, Hamburg.

Group exhibition: Expo '67, Montreal, United States Pavilion (Self-Portraits) (figure 47).

## 1968

Films *Blue Movie* (also known as *Fuck*) and *Flesh.*

February, the Factory moves to 33 Union Square West.

Meets Jed Johnson (figure 48).

Winter, travels with Viva and Paul Morrissey to Stockholm for the opening of a retrospective of his work at Moderna Museet, the facade of which is covered with Cow Wallpaper for the event (figure 49).

Grove Press publishes *A: A Novel,* the transcription of Warhol's tapes of twenty-four hours of Ondine's life.

May, goes with Viva and Morrissey to California to speak at colleges. While there he begins to make a surfing film that is never completed.

Helium-filled Silver Clouds are used as the set

for *RainForest* (figure 50), a dance choreographed by Merce Cunningham.

June 3, Valerie Solanis, founder and sole member of S.C.U.M. (Society for Cutting Up Men), shoots Warhol at the Factory. Mario Amaya, a critic, is also wounded in the assault, but

Hughes, Johnson, and Morrissey, also present at the Factory, escape unscathed. Solanis turns herself in later the same day. Warhol undergoes several hours of surgery and nearly dies. He is hospitalized until July 28.

Paints small portraits of Mrs. Nelson A. Rockefeller while recuperating at home.

49. Facade of Moderna Museet, Stockholm, during the exhibition *Andy Warhol,* 1968

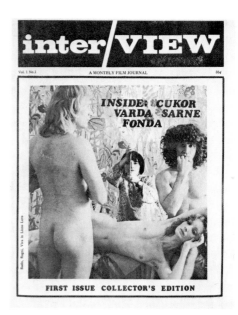

50. Merce Cunningham and a company dancer in *RainForest,* 1968

51. Joe Dallesandro in a publicity photograph for *Trash* (1969)

52. The first issue of *Interview* magazine, 1969

July, beginning with *Flesh,* Morrissey takes a more active directing role in Factory films.

September, Warhol returns to the Factory.

Individual exhibitions: *Andy Warhol,* Moderna Museet, Stockholm, February 10–March 17 (travels to Stedelijk Museum, Amsterdam; Kunsthalle, Bern; and Kunstnernes Hus, Oslo); and *Andy Warhol,* Rowan Gallery, London, March 8–28 (Most Wanted Men and Marilyn prints).

Group exhibition: Documenta 4, Kassel, June 27–October 6.

## 1969

Makes the film *Trash* (figure 51).

March, is hospitalized for further surgery in connection with his gunshot wounds.

Warhol and Morrissey fly to Los Angeles twice to discuss making a film for a major studio, but their proposal is rejected "for moral reasons."

Meets Vincent Fremont, who will later join Warhol's staff.

Fall, the first issue of *Interview,* a Warhol Enterprises, Inc., magazine, is published (figure 52). Editors are Malanga, Morrissey, Warhol, and John Wilcock.

53. Installation view, *Raid the Icebox I with Andy Warhol,* Rhode Island School of Design, Providence, 1970

Individual exhibitions: *Andy Warhol,* Nationalgalerie and Deutsche Gesellschaft für Bildende Kunst, Berlin, March 1–April 14; and *Andy Warhol,* Castelli/Whitney Graphics, New York, March 8–April 1 (Campbell's Soup Can prints).

## 1970

Throughout the seventies Warhol makes endorsements for various companies, including Air France, Braniff Airlines, Pioneer Electronics Corporation, Puerto Rican Rum, and *U.S. News and World Report.*

54. Installation view, *Andy Warhol,* Pasadena Art Museum, 1970

The script of *Blue Movie* is published by Grove Press.

At the suggestion of John and Dominique de Menil, Warhol directs the exhibition *Raid the Icebox I with Andy Warhol* at the Rhode Island School of Design, Providence (figure 53). Objects in the school's collection make up the show.

Individual exhibition: *Andy Warhol,* Pasadena Art Museum, May 12–June 21 (figure 54) (travels to Museum of Contemporary Art, Chicago; Stedelijk Van Abbe Museum, Eindhoven, The Netherlands; Musée d'Art Moderne de la Ville de Paris; Tate Gallery, London; and Whitney Museum of American Art, New York [figure 55]).

Group exhibition: Expo '70, Osaka, United States Pavilion (an untitled work composed of a Xograph print and a rain machine) (figure 56).

55. Installation view, *Andy Warhol,* Whitney Museum of American Art, New York, 1971

56. Andy Warhol. *Untitled.* 1970. Xograph print and rain machine. Installation view, Expo '70, Osaka

## 1971

Warhol's play, *Pork,* is performed at LaMama Experimental Theater Club, New York, and at the Round House Theater, London.

Individual exhibitions: *Andy Warhol,* Cenobio-Visualita, Milan, February–March; *Andy Warhol: His Early Works, 1947–1959,* Gotham Book Mart Gallery, New York, May 26–June 26 (figure 57); *Andy Warhol Graphik, 1964 bis 1970,* Museum Haus Lange, Krefeld, July; and *Andy Warhol,* Musée d'Art Moderne de la Ville de Paris.

## 1972

Maos.

Films *Heat* (figure 58), *Women in Revolt.*

Renews his focus on painting, from this time until his death executing approximately fifty to one hundred commissioned portraits a year. Truman Capote, Mick Jagger, Princess Caroline, Michael Jackson, the Shah of Iran, Chris Evert, and Sylvester Stallone will be among his subjects.

His mother dies in Pittsburgh at the age of eighty.

Individual exhibitions: *Warhol Maos,* Kunstmuseum, Basel, October 21–November 19; Modern Art Agency, Naples; Walker Art Center, Minneapolis (films).

## 1973

Films *L'Amour.*

Acts in the film *The Driver's Seat* with Elizabeth Taylor.

Individual exhibitions: John Berggruen Gallery, San Francisco; New Gallery, Cleveland; and Irving Blum Gallery, Los Angeles.

## 1974

Films *Andy Warhol's Frankenstein* and *Andy Warhol's Dracula* (figure 59).

About this time, experiments with creating an "invisible sculpture" consisting of motion detectors that set off alarms when the space demarcated by those detectors is violated.

Purchases a townhouse on East Sixty-sixth Street and moves there.

The Factory moves to 860 Broadway.

Individual exhibitions: *Andy Warhol,* Musée

57. Installation view, *Andy Warhol: His Early Works, 1947–1959,* Gotham Book Mart Gallery, New York, 1971

58. Still from the film *Heat* (1972)

59. Publicity photograph for *Andy Warhol's Dracula* (1974)

Galliera, Paris, February 23–March 18 (Maos); *Warhol,* Milwaukee Art Museum, July 17–August 24; *Andy Warhol: Old Paintings, New Prints,* Max Protetch Gallery, Washington, D.C., November 25–December; *Andy Warhol,* Museo de Arte Moderno, Bogotá; Galerie Ileana Sonnabend, Paris; Jared Sable Gallery, Toronto; and Mayor Gallery, London.

## 1975

Harcourt Brace Jovanovich publishes *The Philosophy of Andy Warhol (from A to B and Back Again).*

Individual exhibitions: *Andy Warhol: Paintings,* Margo Leavin Gallery, Los Angeles, April 3–May 3; *Andy Warhol: Paintings 1962–1975,* The Baltimore Museum of Art, July 22–September 14; Locksley Shea Gallery, Minneapolis, September 17–October 22; *Andy Warhol's Ladies and Gentlemen (Serigrafie),* Romani Adami, Rome, October 27–November; and *Andy Warhol,* Max Protetch Gallery, Washington, D.C., December 6–31.

## 1976

Skulls.

Individual exhibitions: *Andy Warhol: Das zeichnerische Werk 1942–1975,* Württembergischer Kunstverein, Stuttgart, February

12–March 28 (travels to Städtische Kunsthalle, Düsseldorf; Kunsthalle, Bremen; Städtische Galerie im Lenbachhaus, Munich; Haus am Waldsee, Berlin; Museum moderner Kunst, Museum des 20. Jahrhunderts, Vienna; and Kunstmuseum, Lucerne); *Andy Warhol Animals,* Arno Schefler, New York, May 25–June 11; *Andy Warhol & Jamie Wyeth: Portraits of Each Other,* Coe Kerr Gallery, New York, June; *Cats and Dogs by Andy Warhol,* Mayor Gallery, London, June 29–August 13; and *Andy Warhol: 1974–1976,* Centro Internazionale di Sperimentazioni Artistiche Marie-Louise Jeanneret, Boissano, Italy, July 29–September 12.

## 1977

Athletes, Hammer and Sickles, Torsos.

Films *Andy Warhol's Bad.*

The Museum of American Folk Art, New York, shows his folk-art collection in the exhibition *Andy Warhol's "Folk and Funk."*

Individual exhibitions: *Retrospective Exhibition of Paintings by Andy Warhol from 1962–1976,* Pyramid Galleries, Washington, D.C., January 17–February 19; *Andy Warhol Hammer and Sickle,* Galerie Daniel Templon,

Paris, May 31–July 9; *Andy Warhol Flash, Electric Chair, Campbell's Soup Serigraphien,* Museum Folkwang, Essen, October 14–November 13; *Andy Warhol: The American Indian,* Musée d'Art et d'Histoire, Geneva, October 28–January 22; *Athletes by Andy Warhol,* Coe Kerr Gallery, New York, December 9–January 7; Sable-Castelli Gallery, Toronto; Heiner Friedrich Gallery, Cologne; and Leo Castelli Gallery, New York.

## 1978

Oxidations, Shadows.

Individual exhibitions: *Athletes by Andy Warhol,* Virginia Museum of Fine Arts, Richmond, January 23–February 26; *Andy Warhol: Portraits,* University Gallery, Meadows School of the Arts, Southern Methodist University, Dallas, February 19–March 19; *Andy Warhol,* Kunsthaus, Zürich, May 26–July 30; *Andy Warhol Athletes,* Institute of Contemporary Art, London, July; *Andy Warhol: "Torsos,"* Ace Gallery, Venice, California, September 24–October 21; *Andy Warhol,* Lousiana Museum, Humlebaek, Denmark, October 6–November 26; and *Andy Warhol: Early Paintings,* Blum Helman Gallery, New York, December 1978–January 13, 1979.

## 1979

Retrospectives, Reversals.

Andy Warhol Books/Grosset & Dunlap publishes *Andy Warhol's Exposures,* a book of photographs.

Individual exhibitions: *Andy Warhol "Shadows,"* Heiner Friedrich Gallery, New York, January 27–March 10; Massimo Valsecchi, Milan, March; *Andy Warhol "Torsos,"* Ace Gallery, Vancouver, April; *Andy Warhol,* Wadsworth Atheneum, Hartford, June–August (travels to University Art Museum, University of California, Berkeley); *Andy Warhol, Multiple Images: Landscapes, City Spaces, Country Places,* Arts Gallery, Baltimore, November 15–December 13; and *Andy Warhol: Portraits of the 70s,* Whitney Museum of American Art, New York, November 20, 1979–January 27, 1980 (figure 60).

## 1980

Joseph Beuyses, Diamond Dust Shoes, Portraits of Jews of the Twentieth Century.

Jay Shriver becomes Warhol's painting assistant.

Travels to Düsseldorf, Paris, and Stuttgart.

60. Installation view, *Andy Warhol: Portraits of the 70s,* Whitney Museum of American Art, New York, 1979

POPism: The Warhol '60s by Warhol and Pat Hackett is published by Harcourt Brace Jovanovich.

Individual exhibitions: *Andy Warhol: American Indian Drawings,* Boehm Gallery, Palomar College, San Marcos, California, February 11–March 6; *Joseph Beuys by Andy Warhol,* Lucio Amelio Gallery, Naples, April; *Andy Warhol Reversals,* Bruno Bischofberger Gallery, Zürich, May 14–June 11; *Joseph Beuys by Andy Warhol,* Centre d'Art Contemporain, Geneva, June 7–30; *Andy Warhol: Fotografien,* Museum Ludwig, Cologne, August 20–September 28; *Andy Warhol: "Exposures,"* Stedelijk Museum, Amsterdam, August 28–October 26; *Andy Warhol: Ten Portraits of Jews of the Twentieth Century,* Lowe Art Museum, University of Miami, Coral Gables, Florida, September 6–28; *Andy Warhol: Photographs,* Lisson Gallery, London, September 16–October 18; *Portraits of Jews of the Twentieth Century,* The Jewish Museum, New York, September 17, 1980–January 4, 1981 (travels to Akron Art Museum); *Andy Warhol: Oeuvres récentes, "Reversal,"* Galerie Daniel Templon, Paris, September 20–October 23; *Andy Warhol: Paintings and Prints,* Portland Center for the Visual Arts, Portland, Oregon, September 26–November 7; *Andy Warhol's Portraits of Georgia O'Keefe* [sic], Gray Gaultney, New York, November 19, 1980–January 1981; and Schellmann & Klüser, Munich.

## 1981

Crosses, Dollar Signs, Guns, Knives, Myths.

Travels to Bonn, Munich, Paris, and Vienna.

Individual exhibitions: *The Shoe Portfolio,* Galerie Watari, Tokyo, February 25–April 4; *Warhol '80: Serie Reversal,* Museum moderner Kunst, Museum des 20. Jahrhunderts, Vienna, April 9–May 10; *Andy Warhol at Colorado State University,* Colorado State University, Fort Collins, September 1–25; *Andy Warhol Myths,* Ronald Feldman Fine Arts, Inc., New York, September 15–October 10; *Andy Warhol: Bilder 1961 bis 1981,* Kestner-Gesellschaft, Hannover, October 23–December 13 (travels to Städtische Galerie im Lenbachhaus, Munich); *Andy Warhol: A Print Retrospective,* Castelli Graphics, New York, November 21–December 22; *Andy Warhol: Myths 1981,* Thomas Segal Gallery, Boston, December 5, 1981–January 13, 1982; and *LeRoy Neiman, Andy Warhol: An Exhibition of Sports Paintings,* Los Angeles Institute of Contemporary Art.

Group exhibition: *Westkunst,* Museen der Stadt Köln, May 30–August 16 (Disasters).

## 1982

Goethes, Stadiums.

*Andy Warhol Television,* a series featuring numerous guests in short segments, is shown on cable television. Guests include David Hockney, Diana Vreeland, and others (figure 61).

Travels to Aspen, Beijing (figure 62), Bonn, East Berlin, Palm Beach, Paris, West Berlin, and Zürich.

Makes poster for the film *Querelle* by Rainer Fassbinder (figure 63).

Individual exhibitions: *Andy Warhol "Reversals,"* Leo Castelli Gallery (West Broadway), New York, January 9–30; *Andy Warhol "Dollar Signs,"* Leo Castelli Gallery (Greene Street), New York, January 9–30; *Andy Warhol: Myths,* Marianne Deson Gallery, Chicago, February 12–March 17; *Andy Warhol: Dollar Signs,* Galerie Daniel Templon, Paris, March 6–April 30; *Andy Warhol, Myths,* Modernism, San Francisco, May–June; *Warhol au plus juste,* Galerie des Ponchettes, Nice, May 8–June 20; *Andy Warhol: Dollar Signs/Knives/Guns,* Castelli/Goodman/Solomon, Easthampton, New York; *Andy Warhol: Schweizer Portraits,* Kunstsammlung der Stadt Thun, Switzerland, June 17–August 22; *Andy Warhol: Portrait*

61. Stills from *Andy Warhol Television,* 1982

*Screenprints 1965–80,* Dover Museum, Dover, England, September 1–October 9 (travels to Wansbeck Square Gallery, Ashington, England; Usher Gallery, Lincoln, England; and Aberystwyth Arts Center, Aberystwyth, Wales); and *Warhol verso de Chirico,* Campidoglio, Rome, November 20, 1982–January 31, 1983; *Andy Warhol: Guns, Knives & Crosses,*

62. Warhol in Beijing, 1982

63. Warhol on the set of Rainer Fassbinder's *Querelle*, 1982

Galeria Fernando Vijande, Madrid, December 16, 1982–January 21, 1983.

Group exhibitions: *Zeitgeist: Internationale Kunstausstellung,* Martin-Gropius-Bau, Berlin, October 15–December 19 (Stadium paintings); and Documenta 7, Kassel (Self-Portraits).

## 1983

Makes poster of the Brooklyn Bridge, the official poster for the bridge's centennial celebrations.

Travels to Denver, Paris, St. Maarten, and Spain.

Individual exhibitions: *Warhol's Animals: Species at Risk,* American Museum of Natural History, New York, April 12–May 8; *Andy Warhol's Electric Chairs,* Fraenkel Gallery, San Francisco, July 20–August 27; *Andy Warhol in the 1980's,* Aldrich Museum of Contemporary Art, Ridgefield, Connecticut, September 24–December 31 (travels to the Aspen Center for the Visual Arts, Aspen, Colorado); and *Paintings for Children,* Bruno Bischofberger Gallery, Zürich, December 3, 1983–January 14, 1984.

## 1984

Details of Renaissance Paintings, Munchs, Rorschachs.

Collaborates on paintings with Jean-Michel Basquiat and Francesco Clemente.

Individual exhibitions: *Three Portraits of Ingrid Bergman,* Galerie Börjeson, Malmö, Sweden, March; *Andy Warhol: Paintings & Prints,* Delahunty, Dallas, May 26–July 4; *Andy Warhol: Renaissance Paintings,* Waddington Graphics, London, September 5–29; *Collaborations: Jean-Michel Basquiat, Francesco Clemente, Andy Warhol,* Bruno Bi-

schofberger Gallery, Zürich, September 15–October 3; and *Andy Warhol: Details of Renaissance Paintings,* Editions Schellmann & Klüser, New York, October–November.

## 1985

Ads.

Harper & Row publishes *America,* by Andy Warhol.

At Area, a New York nightclub, Warhol creates an "invisible sculpture" (noted with a wall label) by standing on a pedestal (figure 64), and then leaving.

Individual exhibitions: *Ads,* Amelie A. Wallace Gallery, State University of New York at Old Westbury, February 4–March 2; *Warhol verso De Chirico,* Marisa del Re Gallery, New York, April; *Warhol, Basquiat Paintings,* Tony Shafrazi Gallery, New York, September 14–October 9; *Andy Warhol: Reigning Queens 1985,* Leo Castelli Gallery, New York, September 21–October 12; *The Silkscreens of Andy Warhol: 1962–1985,* Lehman College Art Gallery, Lehman College (CUNY), Bronx, November 14–December 20; and *Andy Warhol: Paintings 1962–1985 & Early Prints,* Galerie Paul Maenz, Cologne, December 6, 1985–January 31, 1986.

64. Warhol's "invisible sculpture" at Area, New York, 1985

**ANDY WARHOL**

**A Memorial Mass**

Wednesday, April 1, 1987 – St. Patrick's Cathedral

| | |
|---|---|
| Prelude | *March of the Priest – The Magic Flute –* Mozart<br>Piano – Christopher O'Riley |
| | *Louange a l'Immortalite de Jesu –* Oliver Messiaen<br>Cello – Carter Brey<br>Piano – Christopher O'Riley |
| Scriptures | The Book of Wisdom 3: 1 – 9<br>Brigid Berlin |
| Speakers | John Richardson • Yoko Ono • Nicholas Love |
| Communion | |
| | *Amazing Grace*<br>Soloist – Latasha Spencer |
| Postlude | *Recessional –* Ravel<br>Piano – Christopher O'Riley • Barbara Weintraub |
| Celebrant | Father Anthony Dalla Villa, St. Patrick's Cathedral |
| | John Grady, Director of Music, St. Patrick's Cathedral |

**A LESSER-KNOWN ELEMENT IN THE PORTRAIT OF ANDY WARHOL**

Five hundred homeless and hungry New Yorkers will assemble on Easter Day at the Church of the Heavenly Rest, on Fifth Avenue at 90th Street. They will be served a delicious meal, and they will be treated as honored guests by some eighty volunteers. They will also be saddened by the absence of one who, with dedicated regularity, greeted them on Thanksgiving, Christmas and Easter. Andy poured coffee, served food and helped clean up. More than that he was a true friend to these friendless. He loved these nameless New Yorkers and they loved him back. We will pause to remember Andy this Easter, confident that he will be feasting with us at a Heavenly Banquet, because he had heard another Homeless Person who said: "I was hungry and you gave me food...Truly, I say to you, as you did it to one of the least of these, my brothers and sisters, you did it to me."
The Reverend C. Hugh Hildesley, *Church of the Heavenly Rest*

*Raphael I –* $6.99 Andy Warhol 1985

Flowers to be donated to Mother Teresa – Missionaries of Charity, The Department of Parks – Forestry, and children's wards at various hospitals.

65. Program for memorial service for Warhol, 1987

## SELECTED POSTHUMOUS EXHIBITIONS

1987: *Lenin by Warhol,* Galerie Bernd Klüser, Munich, February 24–April 30; *Andy Warhol,* Robert Miller Gallery, New York, March 27–April 27; *Andy Warhol: Children's Paintings and Guns and Knives,* Librairie Beaubourg, Paris, May 30–July 10; *Warhol Shadows,* Richmond Hall, The Menil Collection, Houston, June 7, 1987–January 31, 1988; *Andy Warhol: Photographie inedités,* Galerie Gabrielle Maubrie, Paris, June 10–July 11; *Andy Warhol: Recent Work,* Leo Castelli Gallery (Greene Street), New York, June 20–July 31; *Andy Warhol: Arbeiten/Works,* 1962–1986, Galerie Thaddaeus Ropac, Salzburg, July–August; *Andy Warhol: A Memorial,* Dia Art Foundation, Bridgehampton, July 4–August 16; Akira Ikeda Gallery, Tokyo, September 8–30; Galerie Georges Lavrov, Festival International Art Contemporain (FIAC), Paris, October 10–18; and *Andy Warhol Skulls 1976,* Dia Art Foundation, New York, October 14, 1987–June 18, 1988.

1988: *Andy Warhol: Silkscreens of the '80s,* Dorsky Gallery, New York, February 9–March 5; *Andy Warhol: Photographs,* Texas Gallery, Houston, March 5–April 9; *Andy Warhol,* Vrej Baghoomian Inc., New York, April 2–23; *Andy Warhol: Prints,* Galerie Bernd Klüser, Munich, March 28–April 12; *The Films of Andy Warhol,* Whitney Museum of American Art, New York, April 26–June 5; *Warhol Drawings,* Robert Miller Gallery, New York, April 27–May 27; *Andy Warhol: Most Wanted Men: 1963,* Larry Gagosian Gallery, New York, April 30–June 30; *Andy Warhol Cars: Die letzten Bilder,* Kunsthalle, Tübingen (travels to The Solomon R. Guggenheim Museum, New York); *Andy Warhol: Drawings,* Anthony d'Offay Gallery, London, June 9–July 8; and *Andy Warhol Death and Disasters,* The Menil Collection, Houston, October 21, 1988–January 8, 1989.

## POSTSCRIPT

Spring 1988, more than ten thousand objects from Warhol's collections of contemporary art, Art Nouveau, Art Deco, American Indian art, jewelry, furniture, and Americana are sold at auction in support of The Andy Warhol Foundation for the Visual Arts.

December 1988, a second auction of other objects from Warhol's collection, primarily jewelry and watches, is held to benefit the work of the Foundation.

## 1986

Camouflages, Campbell's Soup Boxes, Cars, Flowers, Frederick the Greats, Self-Portraits.

*Andy Warhol Fifteen Minutes,* a second series in which guests appear in very short segments, is shown on MTV cable television.

Travels to Paris.

Individual exhibitions: *Andy Warhol: Major Prints,* Galerie Daniel Templon, Paris, January 4–February 9; *Andy Warhol Disaster Paintings 1963,* Dia Art Foundation, New York, March 13–mid-June; *Andy Warhol,* Anthony d'Offay Gallery, London, July 9–August 22 (Self-Portraits); *Hand-Painted Images, Andy Warhol 1960–62,* Dia Art Foundation, New York, November 5, 1986–June 13, 1987; and *Oxidation Paintings,* Larry Gagosian Gallery, New York, November 7–December 24.

## 1987

Beethovens, Rado Watches. Begins work on The History of American TV.

Travels to Milan and Paris.

February 22, dies following gall-bladder surgery, at New York Hospital–Cornell Medical Center, New York. His funeral takes place in Pittsburgh, where he is buried.

April 1, a memorial service for Warhol is held at St. Patrick's Cathedral, New York (figure 65). More than two thousand people attend.

The Andy Warhol Foundation for the Visual Arts is established to support cultural organizations working in the plastic arts, with Frederick Hughes as President, John Warhola as Vice President, and Vincent Fremont as Secretary/Treasurer.

Individual exhibition: *Andy Warhol Photographs,* Robert Miller Gallery, New York, January 6–31.

# A COLLECTIVE PORTRAIT OF ANDY WARHOL

### PHILIP PEARLSTEIN

I can think of Andy Warhol only as Andy Warhola. For about three critical years we were very close. I didn't realize just how close until many years later when I took my fifteen-year-old son to West Berlin, where I had a museum exhibition, and then to Paris. We roamed around both cities rather aimlessly, sightseeing, not always in agreement: my son was not interested in going to the Louvre, and we went to the zoo instead. The evening he returned alone to New York, I suddenly could not remember my son's face or form. I could only recall Andy as the youngster he was when we first came to live in New York, angry with me one evening when we got lost, telling me he knew we should have gone a different way but he hadn't said anything because he had trusted me.

We had gone to New York together a week after we had graduated from Carnegie Tech, and shared a summer sublet apartment on the Lower East Side. I was four or five years older than Andy. We had met when I returned from the army and entered Carnegie Tech's painting and design program.

Andy, one of the handful of youngsters in the class, obviously quite talented, was at first totally unaware of European modernism. While I pursued intellectual aspirations, Andy discovered a way of drawing that took off from the artificial naiveté of American illustrators like Ben Shahn. We all became aware of modernism in our junior and senior years, primarily through informal discussion groups in the cafeteria, at a gallery in downtown Pittsburgh called Outlines that brought representatives of the New York avant-garde to lecture and exhibit, and in the living room of Balcomb Greene and his wife, Gertrude, who called herself Peter. Balcomb taught art history and was very influential. Andy, while taking it all in, remained unspoiled. He got a job at a department store and completed his education by studying the display department's collection of fashion magazines, which were reflected in the portfolio he took to advertising and magazine offices to get freelance work in New York.

He was an immediate success; my portfolio was too full of serious ideas, and I floundered. Although I did production work for eight

Philip Pearlstein. *Portrait of Andy Warhola*. 1950.
Oil on composition board, 10 × 8″ (25.4 × 20.3 cm).
Whitney Museum of American Art, New York. Gift of Andy Warhol

years, I went to New York University to study art history, discovered the exciting world of painting centered on East Tenth Street, and became an expressionist painter. Andy's move into the painting scene of the sixties and on to world prominence could not have been foreseen in the mid-fifties, when our close tie came undone simply because our lives became so complicated.

### GERALDINE STUTZ

Starry-eyed and straight from school, Andy and I came from the hinterlands to conquer Manhattan almost at the same moment—and our professional fortunes were firmly linked all through the fifties. First, at Condé Nast's *Glamour,* art editor Tina Fredericks coaxed fresh, vivid illustrations of shoes and other fashion accessories from a young Andy who was endearingly shy, but very sure of his talent. Then in the mid-fifties, under the aegis of the brilliant art director Peter Palazzo, Andy turned out the dazzling run of drawings for an I. Miller advertising campaign, which made his reputation as *the* commercial artist of the decade.

From the beginning, Andy was a master draftsman, with astonishing drawing skills. His concepts had wit and surprise. His blotted line and quirky perspective were hallmarks of a style that was both sophisticated and whimsical. Whatever he did was stamped with unmistakable character—unique, looking like no one else, changing how we look at the world, altering the way our eyes see.

### DIANA VREELAND

I must be Andy's oldest friend. Long before anyone had heard of him, he used to hang out at *Harper's Bazaar.* We all loved him but were a bit mystified. He never seemed to have much to say or do, although he always sniffed out tomorrow's news.

That's how I always think of Andy, as someone who was in the heart of what was happening—a creative force in a turbulent era. That's why his work will always keep its immediacy, its power.

### DUANE MICHALS

Duane Michals. *Andy Warhol and Julia Warhola.* 1958

## GENE MOORE

What Andy wanted most in the world was to be recognized. Glamor meant everything to him.

Andy was not like other people; there was something about him that was almost magical—like a leprechaun.

I liked his work in the fifties and sixties very much because it really had an essence to it similar to that which Colette had as a writer. Andy saw things in a different way from most people—in a slightly pixilated fashion—and with great humor.

## NATHAN GLUCK

Andy! Now that he is not among us, it will almost seem as though there were two Andys. The one I knew in the early fifties to 1965 was not the Pop celebrity the public has come to know. When I first saw his work, about 1950, I thought it possessed charm and sly wit. It was the product of a shy guy with salt-and-pepper hair in grungy clothes with shoes scrunched down at the heels, and a naiveté (feigned or otherwise) about the ways of the world. He once passed out birdseed to friends and art directors with instructions to plant them and watch the birds grow; self-promotion, but with great originality. His early self-promotional books and drawings may have been full of borrowings, but in Andy's hands they became his alone, through the use of his flowing line or his blotted-line technique.

About 1955 Andy's commercial work had increased to the point where he needed someone to help him. His first assistant, Vito Giallo, after several months suggested I take over. My work involved creating layouts and realistic drawings from a morass of fashion accessories. Andy would take these and make adjustments, corrections, or simplify them to suit his purpose. Sometimes it was shoes; other times Andy would ask me to think of an idea for Christmas cards or some other project.

The delightful Mrs. Warhola would give me a soup-and-sandwich lunch and regale me with stories of her youth in Czechoslovakia. Because Andy liked his mother's penmanship he one day asked her to sign his name to a drawing. This became a regular routine except when Mrs. Warhola did not feel well or was asleep, in which case I was asked to fake her writing! If the drawing needed a caption, Mrs. Warhola would painstakingly copy it out letter-by-letter, but sometimes she mistook one letter for another and would write *Marlyn Monore* for *Marilyn Monroe,* for example. Andy loved these errors.

## SUZIE FRANKFURT

I met Andy under the guise of art, after admiring some butterfly drawings at Serendipity. We quickly became "best friends" and spent endless days puttering around New York "getting ideas." I was about to become a mother and Andy seemed genuinely fascinated with my domestic role. I was a dunce in the kitchen, which was the reason for our joint cookbook *Wild Raspberries.* He

was quite taken with my simplistic recipes and lavished on them marvelously fanciful illustrations. We hand-colored all of them with Dr. Martin's dyes, collated them ourselves, and had them bound downtown by some rabbis Andy knew. Andy loved collaborations, so no sooner was the cookbook distributed than we decided to do a "Drinkbook." Sadly, it never got any further than a White Russian.

## FAIRFIELD PORTER

Fairfield Porter. *Portrait of Ted Carey and Andy Warhol.* 1960.
Oil on canvas, 40 × 40″ (101.6 × 101.6 cm).
Whitney Museum of American Art, New York. Gift of Andy Warhol

## WALTER HOPPS

In 1960, no one I knew, either within or at the fringes of the vanguard art world of the day, had ever mentioned Andy Warhol. Pop art existed in America then, but wasn't really exposed until 1962; artists like Lichtenstein, Rosenquist, and Warhol didn't yet know of each other. So it was a surprise, while Irving Blum and I were visiting New York late that year, when our host, David Herbert, a perspicacious young art dealer, strongly urged us to meet Andy Warhol. Herbert owned no Warhol work, gave us no description, and we had no idea what we might see. Blum somehow knew of Warhol as a curious, if chic, fashion illustrator. This did not hold out a great deal of promise for me. Herbert suggested that Warhol could be contacted through the proprietor of Serendipity, an East Side emporium whose endearing decor further pointed my expectations in the wrong direction for a serious art encounter.

But a studio meeting was arranged. It turned out that Warhol worked at home, in an imposing Lexington Avenue building, formerly some kind of lodge hall or private club. This setting in no way resembled any New York artist's loft or studio that I had ever seen. As Warhol escorted us back through shadowy recesses, we glimpsed a congested array of Americana—barber poles, carousel horses, assorted oddments. We ended up in a large, high-ceilinged, paneled room, like an austere meeting chamber. The room was a shock: it seemed bare, except for a sea of magazines covering the entire floor, ankle-deep, wall-to-wall—an obsessive, casual array of magazines of every sort, with a heavy emphasis on entertainment. There seemed to be nowhere to sit down, except to mound up a pile of fan magazines and squat.

Warhol himself appeared every bit a night person: drained white skin and white hair, yet alert and intense. And, what in retrospect seems amazing, immediately talkative, to a degree that I never found to be the case throughout the rest of his life. Here was an artist our own age, under thirty, who began to ask more pointed questions at this first encounter than any other artist I'd ever met, or ever have since. (Whom did we know in the art world? What did we think was happening? As Californians, what was it like working in Los Angeles? What did we think of Hollywood? Did we know Rauschenberg? What did we think of his Combines? His drawings? Did we know Jasper Johns? Did we think what he was up to was really good?) Back then, this was all novel, oddly flattering and, yes, lively.

We finally asked if he had some art of his own to show us. Warhol diffidently consented to bring in from an adjoining room some stretched canvases that absolutely amazed us—among them, a loosely painted cartoon view of Dick Tracy and Sam Ketchum; a large, stark black-on-white image of an Underwood typewriter; an even larger black-on-white image of an old-fashioned telephone. More by looks than words, Blum and I communicated to each other that we'd never seen any art like this. Warhol had grown conspicuously quiet during the viewing phase of our visit; we tried to convey our interest and excitement, but at the same time were at somewhat of a loss to know quite how to praise these clearly assured, yet puzzling, works. With six or seven of them on view, I asked if there was anything else that he'd like to show us.

After a certain hesitation, Warhol disappeared through a closet door and came out with a large, tightly rolled linen canvas, and unrolled a five- or six-foot-square work that proved to be the most memorable of them all: a comic-book frame of Superman flying through a tumultuous sky with Lois Lane in his arms, all neatly painted in flat, bright, cartoon-strip colors. Notwithstanding the painting's exhilarating impact, it had one curious feature that I questioned Warhol about: the figures of Superman and Lois Lane were done in markedly different scales, Lois being half-size next to the full-scale superhero. I felt badly to have made a point of mentioning this, especially since Warhol himself somehow expressed uncertainty about it. He rolled the painting up; we departed in the flourish of exchanged addresses, good wishes, promises to keep in touch; and then everything ensued.

### JANE WILSON

Jane Wilson. *Andy and Lilacs*. 1960. Oil on canvas, 30 × 42″ (76.2 × 106.7 cm).
Whitney Museum of American Art, New York. Gift of Andy Warhol

## WILLIAM S. BURROUGHS

I had known Andy Warhol for twenty-three years at the time
of his death, and it came as a surprise to me to learn that he
was a devout Catholic—a surprise that, when considered, is not a
surprise but somehow appropriate. He was a very private person who
was able to maintain reserve without any trace of chilliness or *hauteur*.

Andy was as easy to talk to as anyone I have ever known, always
interested and receptive. The English say a well-dressed man
is one whose clothes you never notice, and the really well-
mannered person is someone whose manners you never notice.

Andy Warhol's influence on the art world cannot be overstated. He
shattered the whole existing hierarchy of "artistic" image, and wiped
away the arbitrary lines that had delineated and confined "art."
A soup tin, seen with a clear eye, can be portentous as a comet; the
way any image is seen alters the entire field of perception.
Andy was himself a portentous, perhaps a saintly figure.

## MARISOL

Marisol. *Andy*. 1962–63. Mixed mediums, 55 × 17″
(139.7 × 43.2 cm). Private collection

## JOHN CAGE

didn't have to do it

one thing to sAy i've said it
ofteN
iDea for film
from roof in brooklYn no need to move the camera

dusk to daWn
lights of lower mAnhattan
scRapers color
pictures come to it nigHt divided frame by frame
a shOrt
his Long ones did it for me

## HENRY GELDZAHLER

There were at least three Andy Warhols, and confusing them
has led to apparently contrary evaluations of his
achievement. Each aspect of his public persona deserves attention,
though not equal weight.

First was the least known—Andrew Warhola, who conversed with his
mother in a kind of pidgin Czech-English, and who attended church
with her, often several times a week. The facts of his
biography were deliberately obscured by his extreme reluctance
to reveal his own system of values. He wanted *not* to be known,
in the biographer's sense. An amusing paradox with Andy is that for
all his love of gossip and stardom he remained coy in the face of
publicity, protecting his privacy, and the private meaning of his work.

Second, we had Andy Warhol the international spokesman
for a Pop response to a world dominated by new
technologies. One of his key insights was that we live in the first age
cursed with total recall. It was through his unselfconscious use of
cameras and recording devices that Andy captured archetypal images
of his time. Later, we experienced a fleeting sense of dislocation when
Andy dropped the know-nothing dumb-blond persona and
cunningly emerged as a philosopher. In *POPism* and *The
Philosophy of Andy Warhol (From A to B and Back Again),*
he married straight depiction with outrageous anecdotes and good
advice, all wrapped in a literate and immensely readable style. In detail
and scope, Andy's as yet unpublished diaries and journals promise to
rival those of Pepys and Boswell as a social chronicle.

The third aspect was, quite simply, Andy Warhol the artist: a painter
who was able to hold multiple and contradictory meanings in balance.
In addition to a brilliant eye for subject matter, he was concerned
with the *package,* the ways in which the public is addressed as
consumer. Out of this he invented a fresh way of picturing the urban
landscape, with verve and good humor. He respected the trembling
halo of spirituality that he saw in the lives around him, the factual
description of a world alight with his own brand of phosphorescence.

Dennis Hopper. *Andy Warhol, Henry Geldzahler, David Hockney, and Geoffrey Goodman.* 1963

## JOHN CHAMBERLAIN

HENRY GELDZAHLER INTRODUCED ME TO ANDY WARHOL
IN 1960
WE GOT ALONG QUITE WELL
WE WERE AT HIS STUDIO LOOKING
AT ALL THOSE DICK TRACY AND NANCY PAINTINGS
AND PAINTINGS OF ADVERTISEMENTS
WE DISCUSSED THE PAINTING OF A HUNDRED SOUP CANS
WHICH I JUST MARVELED AT
HE WAS SO GLAD THAT SOMEONE LIKED THEM
WE MADE A TRADE
I WAS QUITE DELIGHTED
I HAD A HUNDRED CANS OF BEEF AND NOODLE
WHICH I KEPT FOR MANY YEARS
SOMEONE DIDN'T LIKE THE PAINTING
I SPENT AN HOUR TRYING
TO FIND OUT WHAT IT WAS
THIS PERSON DIDN'T LIKE ABOUT THIS PAINTING
I CLEARED MY HEAD
OF ALL THE THINGS I LIKED AND HAD LEARNED ABOUT THE PAINTING
WHICH SURPRISED EVEN ME
I GUESS HE JUST DIDN'T LIKE CAMPBELL'S SOUP
WE WERE FRIENDS FOR A LIFETIME, ANDY AND I.

## GERARD MALANGA

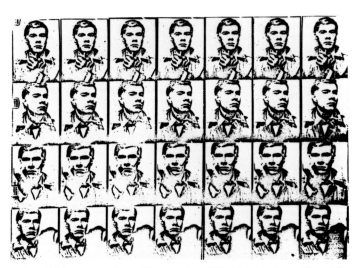

Gerard Malanga. *Andy Warhol Photomation*. 1965. Mixed mediums, 30 × 40″
(76.2 × 101.6 cm). Collection the artist

## ROBERT RAUSCHENBERG

To write about Andy is no simple matter. He never relinquished his
innocence and yet in his short life managed to move from
speechless (sic) to creating a universal communication network. In his
stardom he became capable, as his own shadow, to control his mass.

A good Warhol may not be a Warhol. A bad one can't exist. He
befuddles critical history. Whether he sacrificed this or didn't give a
damn doesn't make a damn. His impact on our lives remains explosive.

## EDWARD RUSCHA

I first met Andy Warhol in June of 1963 after Joe Goode and I
had hitchhiked to New York from L.A. We were invited by
Andy to have lunch with him and Gerard Malanga and walked to a
luncheonette on Seventy-second Street. He was wearing a pair of
British walker shoes that looked expensive and had been spotted with
little drips of paint. Gerard was the more serious of the two, while
Andy was more off in the clouds and asked if we knew any
movie stars and seemed to be content with art gossip. We
walked to his studio in an old firehouse, then to a brownstone on
Lexington Avenue where he was living. Right away, he asked Joe and
me to kneel together behind a couch and began shooting Polaroid
pictures of us. While all this was going on, a 45-rpm record player sat
on the floor of the dark living room repeatedly playing
"I Will Follow Him," by Little Peggy March, for over an hour.

Most artists are born to be opinionated, but he was like no artist I had
ever met because he was for everything and nothing at the same time.

## LITA HORNICK

I first met Andy Warhol in 1963 when Gerard Malanga took me
over to his house on Lexington Avenue to talk about a cover and
picture portfolio for my magazine *Kulchur*. There I saw the Brillo
Boxes, soon to be displayed at the Stable Gallery. I didn't know what to
make of them. I also saw some of the Disaster paintings, which I loved.

In 1966 he did my portrait, first taking me down to a
photo-booth on Forty-second Street and taking five dollars'
worth of three-for-a-quarter photos. From these he selected one image,
blew it up, silkscreened it onto canvas and painted over it. There are
eight twenty-four-by-twenty-four-inch canvases, each with the same
image but all painted in different colors.

A few years after that, I lost contact with Andy, but surprisingly he
agreed to allow me to interview him in 1981 about my portrait.
I asked him if he had chosen the photograph for psychological or
purely visual reasons. He replied, "It was just the right photograph."
I asked, "Just visually right or also psychologically right?" Rather
reluctantly he said, "Well, both." He went on to say that as in his
other paintings the repetition of colors was the most important factor.

## MARK LANCASTER

The first telephone call I made in America, on July 6, 1964,
was to Andy Warhol. A female voice answered, "Andy
Warhol." It was his answering service. Next day I called back. "This is
Andy Warhol," said that inimitable voice. I told him that I was a
student from England, that Richard Hamilton, who had met him at the

Pasadena Duchamp exhibition, had said I should say hello. "Oh, come by the Factory tomorrow, we're making a movie," he said. The Factory then was on Forty-seventh Street, above a garage, opposite the Y.M.C.A., up the silver elevator. After my first visit, I found Andy to thank him. "Oh, see you tomorrow," was his answer.

After about a week, with many comings and goings, and a never-completed Dracula movie being shot, Andy was one day found kneeling on the floor with tubes of acrylic paint, bits of canvas, brushes, and a can of water, complaining that he had to make this picture. He spent several hours mixing paints—yellow, brown, ochre, white—making a vaguely off-white creamy color, hardly a color at all, one thought. But he would not stop until it was "right." This was the background, as it were, for the silkscreened image to be added. He had the silkscreen of the head of a very conventional-looking middle-aged man. (The painting is called *The American Man—Watson Powell*.) I was very impressed by the way Andy worked—not at all in the way he presented himself as working. I helped out for several weeks that summer when a number of Marilyns, Lizes, Jackies, and the first Flowers were made. I also put onto stretchers the Most Wanted Men paintings, the images of which had been rejected and painted over at the New York World's Fair, which had just opened. The stretchers were of slightly different dimensions from the images, so I asked Andy how he wanted the margins. He said to do what I thought looked good, but when he saw them he asked for two to be done over—he thought them a bit "too like Art."

### MICK JAGGER

I first met Andy in 1964 on my first visit to the United States. He introduced the Rolling Stones to the New York art and underground scene, and we stayed in touch until his death.

Doing the lithographs and portraits with Andy was a very painless exercise for me. It was fun staying up all night signing the lithographs. I thought that the album cover he did for the Rolling Stones' *Sticky Fingers* was the most original, sexy, and amusing package that I have ever been involved with.

### BILLY KLÜVER

In the summer of 1964, Andy asked me if I could make a floating light bulb for him. I went back to Bell Labs and discussed the problem with my colleagues. We looked into batteries, lights, a material to contain helium, etc. We did some calculations and tests and decided it could not be done without the bulb being very large, because of the weight of the batteries, lights, etc. Meanwhile, Harold Hodges found a material that was highly impermeable to helium and could be heat-sealed easily. Made by 3M, it was called Scotchpak and, we were told, was used by the army to wrap sandwiches. A friendly local salesman for 3M supplied us with several hundred feet of the four-foot-wide metalized polyester film. This all took many months, not because it was complicated, but because both of us were doing a lot of other things.

### FRED McDARRAH

Fred McDarrah. *Andy Warhol*. 1964

We told Andy we couldn't make the light bulb but showed him the material we had found. When Andy saw it he said, "Let's make clouds." Back to Bell Labs to figure out how to heat-seal irregular rounded surfaces. During this time we had left some of the Scotchpak with Andy; we built him a makeshift heat-sealing machine and brought him a bottle of helium. One day in the spring or summer of 1965 I came to the Factory. Andy had simply folded the material over and heat-sealed it on three sides and filled it with helium. Warhol's "pillows" were born. We added a valve so they could be refilled, and Andy found someone to make a lot of them. A roomful of the pillows were shown at the Leo Castelli Gallery in April 1966; they were called Silver Clouds.

### DOMINIQUE DE MENIL

My first recollection of Andy Warhol: his apparition at the Metropolitan Museum. He arrived accompanied by two or three lovely girls in outlandish clothes. They were his avant-garde as well as rampart. The looks of his entourage corresponded to his reputation—frivolous and amoral. Later, talking with Andy, I discovered how serious and moral he was. I never heard him talk ill of anybody, and I was struck by the generosity of his judgment; he had only kind words for irritating people.

The exhibition, *Raid the Icebox,* taught me a lot about Andy. The museum of the Rhode Island School of Design had volunteered to let an artist select what pleased him from a basement packed with applied as well as fine art. Andy, whom we had asked to prepare the exhibition, made an amazing selection. He did not miss the Cézanne nor the Guy Pène du Bois, but he also decided to exhibit in its present condition a partially cleaned anonymous portrait and an entire closet of shoes. He even insisted on bundles of old magazines, which had to remain tied as they were and be placed casually on a table. As a finishing touch he had a tree, still balled, dropped in front of the door of the museum.

### SAMUEL ADAMS GREEN

Andy was, well, passive about the arrangements being made for his first museum retrospective. As the director of Philadelphia's Institute of Contemporary Art, it was my job to get the new institution notices. Invitations to the preview were printed on the backs of real Campbell's soup-can labels. Thousands of poster-sized S&H Green Stamp announcements were sent. S&H Green Stamp fabric was printed to make a dress for Mrs. H. Gates Lloyd, the Institute's chairman, and a tie for me. These thoughtful details were to give the press something to write about in case they couldn't deal with the art. Andy went along with everything as he usually did. It was too late when he realized that it was him, not his art, that was on exhibition.

Hardly anybody in those days went to art openings to see the

art anyway: they went to see other people and to be seen. Because so many people were expected, there were almost no pictures hanging in the galleries when six thousand voyeurs arrived. There were, instead, TV cameras, lights, reporters, "superstars," and Andy Warhol himself.

The crowd became unruly, and changed from crowd to mob. Andy, Edie, a few other superstars, and I were engulfed by a frightening surge of people trying to get interviews, autographs, souvenirs, even clothing. Buoyed along by this crush we reached an unused staircase in one of the galleries. The staircase led to a ceiling that sealed it from the library on the floor above. We scrambled to the top, as four armed campus police held the fans at bay. "Andy! Edie! Andy! Edie!" the crowd screamed. Andy, whiter than ever, cowered; Edie baited the crowd, egging them on by posing, shrieking, and waving. The crowd screamed for more. We were trapped! Eventually, I spotted a familiar architecture student in the crowd; he was permitted past the guards, accompanied by cheers from the crowd. "Get us out of here," I hissed. "Get the security guards to let you into the floor above. Bring a fire ax, anything, rip up the floor. Just get us out of here, this is dangerous!"

Meanwhile, three people had been pushed out of one of the gallery windows by the sheer volume of the crowd. Ambulances came. Philadelphia police came. Finally, somebody chopped through the ceiling over our heads, and up we scrambled into the dimly lit library. We were ushered toward a fire exit, which led to the roof: we hurried onto another roof and down a fire escape into waiting squad cars. We'd been saved. It had been a success. Andy was pleased because, without his art, he'd become a superstar on his own.

### PETER LUDWIG

It was love at first sight: when I first encountered Warhol's work in the Leo Castelli Gallery in the mid-sixties, I made an immediate purchase. And, as it is with love, there was something shocking about his art; I was smitten, even disturbed. Warhol's pictures—they *were* my own time, my generation, my experience of the world. But also, love adores what is Other, what is unfamiliar, denied to oneself. Warhol's art is the art of America: a young art, without all the looks backward at other centuries and millennia, without all the skepticism that feeds itself on ancient events. And yet, it is profound and serious; it deals continually with death.

Warhol's creations are absolutely new and direct, the opposite of flowery. His work scrupulously mirrors his lifetime: an industrial society with its phenomenal material production; the mass media with their constantly fluctuating catastrophes, violence, and death machines, and with their gossip and stars. The stars, above all, are needed, and are produced in order to entertain the public. Andy Warhol, the child of poor, immigrant parents, wanted to become, and did become a star, and from the beginning was a superstar. He did it with a creativity that was compelling, a creativity that led to images that had never been seen before. Warhol was one of the most remarkable artists of the United States in the second half of our century. And he, who always created so emphatically for the moment, will endure in the history of art.

I fell in love with Warhol's art spontaneously, and right away I purchased his pictures by the dozens. I showed them in my hometown and then in Cologne's major museum and was thrilled by the response. His works have found a permanent home in Cologne and in other European cities. How powerfully, willfully, and exquisitely this art exists in the company of famous works of European art history.

In the delirium of acquiring his art, I knew from the beginning that it was truly important, and that it would very soon be very expensive. And, in fact, that is what has happened. I would like to have continued buying Warhols, but they became prohibitively expensive for me. Yet they are worth any price. Andy Warhol gave expression to his (and my) generation's way of looking at the world, and presented his country with an art that will remain characteristic of the United States. The shy introvert who turned so completely inward, who in conversation withdrew verbally and physically, who never spoke of his Christian faith, and who loved his mother so extremely, affected the world as practically no one else has. He was lonely and he was contemplative. What he created became a mirror of the world of his time. His work is loved by the masses; his life stands as a synonym for artistic genius.

### ARMAN

From the beginning we were close, in terms of the serial image and in the use of the common object, so close that in 1962 during the *New Realists* show at the Sidney Janis Gallery, European friends such as Martial Raysse, Rottrôut Klein, and Niki de St.-Phalle wrote to me to tell me of an artist in New York who was doing accumulations of objects on canvas, very bright, colorful, and that maybe I should consider translating my own accumulation images onto canvas as well!

Well, Andy's works are quite different, and I never felt threatened or competitive with his works. The more successful paintings by Andy deal with common images of our civilization. Furthermore, it is the work of a painter in the way it deals with color and scale.

The Andy I knew as a friend was always very nice and charming—but behind a facade of shiny superficiality. I always found him extremely attentive. I think he had a very compartmental brain and could function simultaneously on different registers of his complex personality: artist, director of a permanent show, sociologist, collector, and philosopher.

It is difficult to characterize Andy as an artist only; like Marcel Duchamp he originated an artistic and cultural closed system.

### RICHARD ARTSCHWAGER

Everybody has their own Warhol. For me he was a model of diligence. The job was, first, to fill in all the space between the works of art. He became more thorough and ingenious as time went on (as the remaining spaces actually became fewer). First he filled in some space by making art on commission (commercial art); then by making more than just one by employing assistants and copying devices; and then by making sub-versions by using different colors and/or sizes.

It still wasn't full, so then he invited some friends and strangers to stand in the gaps, with himself filling in the remaining one, appearing to have been there all the time.

Others have struggled, dabbled, speculated, but he did it so thoroughly that the whole enterprise is thrown open to question. And there you are.

### ALLAN KAPROW

Warhol, when he appeared in the art world, seemed to have signaled the repudiation of serious art and its replacement by commercial stereotypes. "Trash art," someone said. But there was a compelling simplicity in his imagery, despite its crassness, which was like some nagging old tune you couldn't shake off.

There was in Warhol an intuitive ability to appropriate for his paintings just the right mass-media photographs and emblems from literally millions of options. His only equal in this regard was Roy Lichtenstein. Furthermore, he had an old-master sense of the placement of images on a field: think of the forward tilt of Jacqueline Kennedy's head and the precise amount of framing around it, just enough to crowd its silhouette for expressive emphasis. The early Nolde and Kirchner come to mind.

More radically for Western traditions of composition, Warhol revived some of the Cubist, Futurist, Constructivist, and Dada experiments with mechanical repetition. Using gridded repeats within a single field, he suggested more than a comment on modern mechanical life. It was a persistent reexamination of the temporal aspects of the visual arts. Warhol also introduced to serious art a panoply of new decorator colors. Mixed or applied straight, it is startling for traditional eyes to see how consistently Warhol could "fine-tune" their vibrations, contrasts, and tones, especially in figure-ground interactions. While such professional observations only scratch the surface of Warhol's considerable artistry, it is important to touch upon them, if only to dispel any notions of him as a mere commercial hack. But, then, neither was Warhol an authentic fine artist.

Warhol had an undeniable taste for chic. Chic pervaded everything he did; his choice of friends and his lifestyle. The fragility of chic, the dying inherent in all that's fashionable, drew him to it from the

Cecil Beaton. *Andy Warhol and Candy Darling.* 1969

beginning. For Warhol, the outsider, turning to high art was hardly to embrace its idealism. He took for granted the commodity status of all fine and commercial work: each simply had different consumers. Warhol never left commerce at all; the domain was only shifted to a more self-conscious and educated context. In offering for sale endlessly reproducible images of Campbell's Soup Cans or Brillo Boxes, he underlined art's mercantile role and implicitly undermined the traditional artist's romance of spiritual purity.

### ALLEN GINSBERG

Despite the coolness of Warhol's art attitudes, surface unemotionality, advertising texture, and multiples method, there was (as in Burroughs's cut-up procedure for prose composition) an advantage: an almost spiritual nonattachment, or appearance of nonattachment, since ultimately Warhol's private mortal reference was to the supreme kitsch of the Catholic Church.

Yet in practice Warhol provided an opportunity to review archetypal U.S. images, grocery containers, movie stars, and most-wanted-criminal posters, etc.; and see them isolated epiphanous with new eyes, "the doors of perception" cleansed of associations or with associations rememberable but oddly irrelevant to the actual images enlarged for inspection.

His autobiography presents also an almost Zen-like nonattachment—except for crucial instances where Warhol's preferences and straightforward predilections are declared. His method of relating to film censorship was Taoist—let go of one banned film and produce another, faster than censors could catch up.

Kerouac, Corso, Orlovsky, and myself cavorted and talked on his *Couch;* he didn't participate much in the moment, simply left the camera turned on, and I've never managed to see the picture. Yet it's the only existing picture with all four of us in the frame on Earth.

Was his enormous wealth, by-product of his own genius and communal effort, recycled in any large part back to the artistic community he inhabited?

In the long run, effort to evade egocentric subjectivity by making cool anonymous art is unnecessary. Friendly relationship to a tamed transparent ego encourages more passionate intensity without disillusioning backfires. Some Marxists aimed at puritanically egoless aesthetics, often with suicidal or secret power-mad consequences.

### BILLY NAME

Billy Name. *Andy Warhol / Iconic Divisionist.* 1964

## LOU REED

Andy Warhol was an inspiration to me. I learned a lot from him. I watched everything he did and how he did it. Some of these things serve me well to this day. For example, how to handle interviews, the press . . . or the juxtaposition of odd things. I loved watching Andy work with colors. I found his use of colors to be very beautiful—beautiful colors on odd subject matter: Cows, Electric Chairs. I remember walking into Castelli's gallery with Andy and finding the room lined with resplendent Cow Wallpaper and filled with floating Silver Clouds. We released one "pillow" for photographers on Lexington Avenue. It soared over some buildings and disappeared, a balloon for adults. It was, as Andy would say, "Fabulous."

Andy said, "Why don't you write a song called 'Viscous.'" And I said, "What kind of viscous?" And he said, "You know, viscous, I hit you with a flower." So I did. I tried to follow most of his suggestions.

He was incredibly generous and hard-working. He was the first to arrive for work at the Factory and the last to leave. And then he would take us all to dinner. He gave everyone a chance. When he told me I should start making decisions about the future and what could be a career, I decided to leave him. He did not try to stop me, legally or otherwise. He did, however, tell me I was a rat. It was the worst word he could think of.

Andy's movies helped consolidate and make clearer the approach I wanted to take in song-writing and poetry. I found his movies galvanizing beyond their content, specifically in their philosophical stance. He had one of the most exciting minds of anyone I've met to this day. Andy was brilliant, and I miss him and his ideas.

Sometimes, when I got to the Factory early, there would be Andy hard at work on a silkscreen. I'd ask him why he was working so hard and he'd say, "Somebody's got to bring home the bacon." Then he'd look at me and say, "How many songs have you written today?" I'd lie and say, "Two."

He'd say, "You're really lazy. You should be writing more. Five. And if you write five you should be writing ten. Ohhhh Lou, don't you know work is everything, the most important thing." I do know that today and I try to carry, if not all of it, some small piece of it, some fragment of Andy with me at all times. I find myself asking, what would Andy do?

He was, dare I say it, "Fabulous!"

## PAUL MORRISSEY

Andy's artwork came easily to him and never caused any strain or insecurity in him. Possibly because it wasn't in any way difficult for him, he never really trusted it to become "the goose that laid the golden egg"—his own expression, which he used occasionally in regard to other enterprises that he hoped one day might "strike it rich." His ever-present positivism was not on display when it came to his own artwork, but that was the only thing he did entirely on his own. Although he was polite and occasionally asked others how something might look, he seemed secure in his own judgment, and he paid little attention to other people's appraisals. But whether it was an artwork, a film, or an interview, the element he looked for was spontaneity. Deliberation, anxiety, reworking, or changing things was alien to him.

I'll be surprised if any of the many biographies supposedly being written of Andy are able to capture his peculiar temperament; but if any do, I think they would define him best by his special attitude toward the art world itself. So much of what he was involved in elsewhere derived, I think, from his feelings and his approach to modern art. But just exactly what those feelings were, Andy made sure, remained elusive. In any event, it was fun to do things with and for Andy. He was never pretentious, always positive, and always looked for humor in any subject or situation. Introspection was not his thing, and he was not quite like anyone else. But although he kept his reserve and his distance, you felt you knew who you were dealing with, and it was not hard to like him.

## TAYLOR MEAD

Andy was a "piece of cake" behind the camera—it was like no one was there, and our self-consciousness melted away. Occasionally he might say, "Say something dirty," or, "Ask her about her boyfriend," or, "Get personal."

The Factory was always exciting and unpredictable, sometimes dangerous, but generally our home away from home. The phone was always ringing, the music was always playing (in the sixties), Andy was always doing something and never took a breather. When he started to clean up (sweeping and arranging) we knew it was closing time. Let's hope he invites us to a party!

## JOHN GIORNO

In 1963 Andy and I used to see a lot of underground movies. We went a couple of times a week to the Bleecker Street Cinema or the Gramercy Arts Theater or wherever they were playing. It was the beginning of the phenomenon of the underground movie. There were Jack Smith's *Flaming Creatures,* Ron Rice's *Chumlum,* Taylor Mead's *The Queen of Sheba Meets the Atom Man,* and Kenneth Anger's *Scorpio Rising.* They were great, but most of the others were horrible. "They're so terrible," said Andy. "Why doesn't somebody make a beautiful movie! There are so many beautiful things!"

A week later he bought his first Bolex 16mm camera. He didn't know how to use it, so he would ask a lot of dumb questions like "How do you focus it?" to filmmakers or whoever he happened to be with.

A week after that we were in Old Lyme, Connecticut, visiting Wynn

Chamberlain for the weekend. We were up late one night to 4:30 in the morning. It was one of those ninety-degree, sweltering June nights. I got really drunk on 150-proof black rum. I just passed out when my head hit the pillow. I woke up to take a piss as the sun was coming up. I looked over and there was Andy in bed next to me, his head propped up on his arm, wide-eyed awake, looking at me. "What are you doing?" I said with a rubber tongue.
"Watching you," said Andy.

I awoke again and Andy was still looking at me with Bette Davis eyes. "What are you doing?"

"Watching you sleep!"

I went back to sleep, and awoke every once in a while to see if he was still doing it. I woke up again to take a piss and Andy was sitting in a chair alongside the front of the bed in the morning light. The next time I woke up, he was lying with his cheek on the pillow drowsily looking at me. It was 11:30 in the morning, boiling hot; my body was steaming with sweat, and did I have a hangover. "Why are you looking at me?"

"What do you want to know for?" Andy laughed cynically.

When I awoke the next time, Andy was gone. It was 1:30 in the afternoon and he had watched me sleep for eight hours.

From this was born the idea for Andy Warhol's first movie, *Sleep*. On the crowded New Haven railroad back to New York, Andy said, "I want to make a movie. Do you want to be the star?"

"Absolutely," I said, getting closer to him in the jam-packed, sweating train. "What do I have to do?"

"I want to make a movie of you sleeping," said Andy.

"I want to be a movie star!" I said enthusiastically. "I want to be like Marilyn Monroe." This was before the word *superstar* was invented by Jack Smith, and before Andy expropriated it.

Andy just laughed and said, "Oh, John!"

In July 1963 Andy started shooting. It was an easy shoot. I loved to sleep. I slept all the time, twelve hours a day, every day. It was the only place that felt good. Everything else was so horrible. I was so unhappy: a nap in the afternoon at 4:00 P.M., see a few more people, another little nap before Andy and I met and went out. Every time Andy telephoned—morning, afternoon, or night—I would be asleep. He would say "What are you doing?" and I would say "Sleeping." Or he would say "What are your doing? Don't tell me, I know!"

We would get back to my place around 1:00 or 2:00 A.M. I'd have another drink and take off my clothes as Andy set up the tripod and the camera and messed around with the lights. Two minutes after my head hit the pillow, I was asleep. When I woke up the next morning, Andy would be gone, the lights still on, and the floor littered with scraps of film and empty yellow boxes.

Andy would shoot for about three hours, until about 5:00 A.M., all by himself. The Bolex was an early model. The camera had to be reloaded every three minutes, and every twenty seconds he had to rewind it. When he had the film developed he discovered there was a jerk every twenty seconds—two weeks' shooting down the drain. Then someone told him there was a gadget that you plug into the camera and plug into the wall that rewinds the camera automatically. We started over again. The shoot lasted for a month. We stopped when he had taken thousands of rolls of film. He tried to think what he could do with them to make it into a film. Andy would look at them on the hand-cranked movie viewer and say, "Oh, they're so beautiful!"

### EMILE DE ANTONIO

Andy wrote his history as he needed it, not unlike any other artist, shaping and reshaping his times and experience. What Andy said is not factual but it is true. At a point in his life when I first met him, Andy was troubled and tentative about entering the art world. The problem was not that he was a commercial artist but that he was a *successful* commercial artist of reputation.

### IVAN C. KARP

In the aftermath of Andy Warhol's death, his career was frantically and methodically examined by the popular press, and his achievement as an artist grossly distorted by commercial activity: the public and private sales of his paintings and prints. Indeed, some of the inflated values put upon his minor work have served to distort the entire art market and have created a kind of hysterical focus on the importance of an artwork as a commodity rather than as a cultural artifact. Warhol preferred his fame as an artist to his commercial success, which he certainly pursued and thoroughly enjoyed. Perhaps the passage of time will remedy some of the excesses.

Warhol's significant work was produced between 1961 and 1968. Aside from the voluminous body of portraiture, the best of its kind in this century, there is little the artist produced after 1968 that warrants the attention it receives. Warhol at his finest was an innovator of consequence and it is incumbent upon those members of the fine-arts community who possess the requisite perceptual ability to sort out and identify what part of his production should enter the visual-arts culture.

### CARL ANDRE

Andy Warhol was the perfect glass and mirror of his age and certainly the artist we deserved.

**UGO MULAS**

Ugo Mulas. *Andy Warhol*. c. 1964–65

### BRIGID BERLIN AND VINCENT FREMONT

B.B.: What kind of boss was Andy?

V.F.: He wasn't like a normal boss, who would give you a specific job; you just kind of made a niche for yourself. You swept the floor, answered phones, and then he asked you to do something else. And then pretty soon . . .

B.B.: . . . You made a job for yourself.

V.F.: As the years went on, Andy let me get involved in more creative and business decisions. He was more personal than

just a boss. Andy took an interest in your life. He'd want you to go places with him, he'd take you to parties. In my early twenties I remember being a kind of "walking stick" for Andy. I'd pick him up at his house, he'd give his philosophies about life and things, mostly like, "Oh well, gee, wouldn't it be great to be young and rich?" — as we were walking by Bloomingdale's. And he'd look into stores. He would have ongoing conversations like, "Isn't it great if we could do this? Oh, wouldn't it be great if we could do that?" Later, I read his diaries so we could do the business-expense breakdowns, so I knew what he was saying: funny things like what people had said about other people, or even about me sometimes, which he put in because he knew I'd be reading them. We used to talk about his opinions of people and gossip.

B.B.: And remember how he used to sit on the windowsill and read the *Post*. Andy would be quoting lines of murders that happened, and you'd be sitting there not knowing a thing about what he was talking about, "Gee, why do you think they did this?"

V.F.: That's like when he would call in the mornings and you'd be talking to him on the phone and he would go into an abstract conversation for an hour. "Wh, why do you think they did that? I mean really . . . oh, really." Those were actually really wonderful moments, spending a lot of time on the phone with him, in the mornings or on weekends. I think working with him on Saturdays was the most fun.

B.B.: I always felt that Andy was very close to you. He really trusted you.

V.F.: I felt very close to him too. When he was at the Factory alone he would call me to say he was leaving, and then I would have to wait an hour to make sure he didn't get stuck in the elevator. So I'd call him again to see if he arrived home, because if I didn't hear from him, he might be caught in the elevator.

B.B.: What was it like picking up Andy at the Factory?

V.F.: I always stayed with him until he locked up. It started at 33 Union Square West. We'd have to go up to his little studio on the eighth floor and he'd put his hand under the faucet and he'd say, "Is the water off? Is the water off?" He'd say it six times. Then we'd look at it and we'd look at it again. He'd scrutinize everything. He'd make sure the paints were in a certain order. Then we'd go down to the sixth floor and we'd look for lit cigarettes: "Are they lit? Are they lit? Brigid was here smoking." I had to be there until the end of everything for years. I was the last person to leave. A lot of times Andy would stay because he was afraid of fire. He did all the same things at 860 Broadway. It became a ritual. I'll have that ingrained in me forever.

B.B.: I remember nothing was plugged in on Monday mornings; the typewriter never worked. And remember Andy's cranky mood when you took a vacation?

V.F.: He always used to tell me how much he missed me when I left, because he liked to know that everyone was there working on a certain project or area for him. He really wanted you to work, think of ideas. It would get him crazy just seeing people sitting around, except at those times at the end of the day. I remember that around 5:00 or 6:00, we would all be standing around. Fred [Hughes] would become Frederick of Union Square and do face-lifts with Scotch tape on people's faces. Friends dropped by and things relaxed before the evening activities.

B.B.: What did you do with Andy that was really fun?

V.F.: Just going out. I had been a great fan of his in high school. When I was with him I got to meet just about everybody I wanted to meet as a

kid. Lunch with Alfred Hitchcock was great. Jim Morrison came by the office. He was the first person I met through Andy who had been an idol; that was in 1969. The first time I was invited to Montauk, I was kind of nervous, I had never been with everybody on a weekend. That was in '72. It was Andy, Fred, Jed [Johnson], and me. Those were fun times out in Montauk. Lee Radziwill had the main house; Peter Beard was there, Mick Jagger. We would go down to the beach and videotape.

B.B.: I did my going out with Andy during the sixties and early seventies; then my life changed and I could no longer keep up with him, I was doing other things.

V.F.: I went out with him for four or five years before I got married, meeting and getting to know an amazing array of people. With the first money I ever made from Andy, I went to Fred's great tailor and had three suits made, a black one, a gray one, and a three-piece navy-blue one. So at least if I didn't have any money I looked good. Andy could look any way he wanted. I learned very quickly that he never would tell you where we would be going. I'd show up in these brown jackets that looked ridiculous at very fancy dinners, until I figured it out.

B.B.: What about some of the Christmas parties at 860 Broadway?

V.F.: I remember the first Christmas party at 33 Union Square West: Dumas cookies and William Poll food. A few people would come by and there would be champagne. We put everything out on the balcony because we didn't have a refrigerator. People would come by and we'd set up one camera, like a bank-vault camera, just to catch people as they were coming in, a static shot. It got a bit bigger each year, and Andy would give things to people: drawings, little things. So, by the time we got to 860 Broadway, we had a big one there, and Andy got really mad because people were demanding presents, they weren't even waiting to be given one, they just asked for a present. So we decided, with Fred, not to give a Christmas party anymore.

B.B.: Remember when the luncheons got really fancy at 860 Broadway? The guests would arrive, and I was supposed to be typing. We had the entire room filled with people holding wineglasses at 1:00 in the afternoon, and everybody would be waiting for Andy. Andy would waltz in late loaded down with shopping bags.

V.F.: Remember he used to carry Brownies [health food] shopping bags? He started that fad. He was in English *Vogue* with a Brownies plastic shopping bag. He was wearing jeans with a jacket and tie. I think he was one of the first people to do that that I'm aware of. We all used to wear that. It was the Factory uniform.

B.B.: Then he'd wear the same jacket every day. It was filthy, all of his marker pens leaking through the pockets. . . .

V.F.: He had his tape recorder, camera, everything, stuffed into those pockets. He'd wear the same jacket until it almost fell off his back.

B.B.: It was a nightmare to give Andy presents: what were you ever

Stephen Shore. *Andy Warhol.* 1965

going to get him and how long would it remain unopened?

V.F.: That's the thing, if you got him something he could wear, like all-cotton black turtlenecks, then it was a success. Otherwise, he would just put it away. And it was very important for Andy to have everything in its original box. When you bought him crackers, you bought them in the tin.

B.B.: I remember how I used to have to go shopping for him. He'd always hand me a hundred-dollar bill, tear the corner from it, and tell me not to forget to bring back the receipt. I think of Andy every time I ask for a receipt.

V.F.: I always went to buy him tons of batteries and tape recorders, because he always dropped them. He also had a knack of walking in just as we were trying to get rid of junk. He'd always think of a reason for saving it.

B.B.: Talk about the "time capsules" and how they started.

V.F.: I know exactly when they started. I was upstairs on the eighth floor of 33 Union Square West helping him, actually bringing bills up because he liked to have someone to talk to while working. I was watching him stretch small Mao paintings. The first thing I ever helped him with was to locate a photograph of Richard Nixon to do the *Vote McGovern* print. I had called different offices, and we finally settled on that photograph. In the back he had big, big boxes where he threw everything. They were huge. We started thinking about moving out of that little floor. I said, why don't we call them "time capsules"

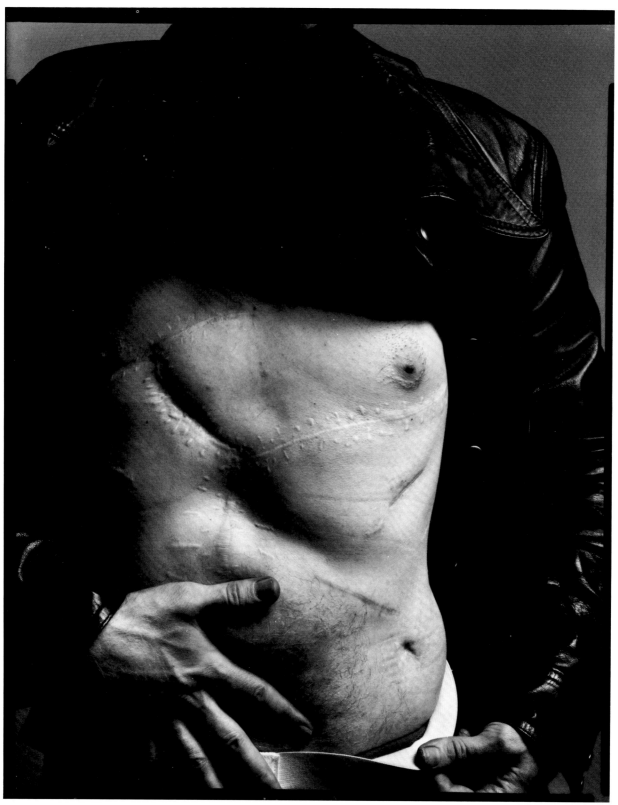

Richard Avedon. *Andy Warhol, Artist, New York City, 8/20/69.* 1969

and make them smaller so we can carry them? So I found the F-42 box, which was about the right size, and we had shelving made that Ronnie Cutrone measured out to that specification. It was the right box, you could carry it. He could increase his volume and make it neat. He liked it neat and labeled. Andy, Ronnie, and I would label all those boxes. He liked volume. He literally would have liked me to videotape constantly, for twenty-four hours. He loved the idea of that. Lots of tapes, lots of things.

B.B.: I remember at "860" how exasperated I'd get with him when he'd give me tapes to type and they weren't even marked. I'd listen to them, and I didn't know who was talking or where they were. I'd have to wait for him to come in so I could ask who they were.

V.F.: Andy would say, "I mean, Brigid, I mean, could you just do it!"

B.B.: "Just make it up, I don't care!" He didn't care where you began and where you ended. That didn't make any sense to me. I would have rather typed the whole thing. Then I'd go ahead and type it all, and he'd say, "That's not what I asked you to do." When I told him I'd done thirty pages in a morning, he'd say, "That's great, well, tomorrow you can do thirty-five." He loved stacks. Everything was stacked; if you touched anything in his office it would fall.

V.F.: He couldn't get to the desk anymore. The hallway was full of double rows of "time capsule" boxes.

Do you remember meeting me?

B.B.: I don't remember meeting you, I just remember you always being there. I remember your long hair.

V.F.: The first time I saw you was in the back of Max's in 1969, slapping Candy Darling's manager on camera for German television and threatening to knock Candy Darling's wig off for ten dollars. Paul Morrissey first brought me up to the Factory. I had long hair, and I was with two other friends from Los Angeles. We started staying at Paul's house, which I called "Paul Morrissey's Boys' Town." My friends and I were called "the Babies"; Danny Fields called us "the group that came from nowhere and did nothing." While we were staying there, Tom Hompertz was in the basement making a surfboard sculpture, and Paul was stripping doors all night long. I worked in the Paradox restaurant in the back. I held the microphone for Paul's film *Trash*, and I ran around with Joe Dallesandro and his brother Bobby. Oh, remember when Bobby was Andy's chauffeur in the filthy station wagon, and he used to drive like a maniac? Remember that funny story about him being with Jackie Onassis and Lee Radziwill. . .

B.B.: . . . Going to The Brooklyn Museum, wasn't it?

V.F.: Isn't it in one of the books, the story? I think it's in *Exposures*. That car was filthy. Andy never hired limousines, he never liked to. He always took a cab. I remember the time he took a bus in a blizzard.

B.B.: Gee, I miss him.

V.F.: Me too.

B.B.: I guess we're "lifers."

### LIZA MINNELLI

As a friend he was fabulous, as a force he was formidable.

### EDMUND WHITE

Andy Warhol was a death's-head full of life, a brilliant dumbbell, a Taoist master of passivity as American as Astroturf. Back in the sixties, when his hair was still his own and not yet a patented wig, he taught us that art could be at once shocking and banal, idiotic and luminously cerebral. Most arty Americans in the fifties hated America, dreaded the herd, and daydreamed of classy ol' Europe. Warhol led us, for better or for worse, into the sixties, and blurred the distinction between art and junk.

He did it as a philosopher might (as the philosopher-artist Marcel Duchamp had already done in a less deadpan way). Andy took every conceivable definition of the word *art* and challenged it. Art reveals the trace of the artist's hand: Andy resorted to silkscreening. A work of art is a unique object: Andy came up with multiples. A painter paints: Andy made movies. Art is divorced from the commercial and the utilitarian: Andy specialized in Campbell's Soup Cans and Dollar Bills. Painting can be defined in contrast to photography: Andy recycled snapshots. A work of art is what an artist signs, proof of his creative choice, his intentions: for a small fee, Andy signed any object whatsoever. Art is an expression of the artist's personality, congruent with his discourse: Andy sent in his stead a look-alike on the lecture tour.

All of these precise abnegations were performed under the guise of humor and self-advancing cynicism, as though a chemist were to conduct the most delicate experiments at the target end of a shooting gallery. Now, as the smoke clears, we see that distinctions must be made. The Disaster paintings and the Electric Chairs are enduring images, whereas the later portraits are forced and forgettable. Most of the films are unsalvageable, whereas the books are as witty as those of Gertrude Stein and far more readable. His acceptance of mass culture turns out, paradoxically, to have been the last gasp of mandarin aestheticism, whereas his know-nothing admiration of rich fascists can only suggest moral collapse.

"Pop art is a way of liking things," he once said—a valuable break with tradition-bound elitism in the arts but a deplorable slogan for the politically lazy and passive. Which is all just another way of saying that even Andy's failures are symptomatic and disturbing.

### RICHARD BERNSTEIN

Sometime around 1970 Andy asked me to do the posters for his movies *Women in Revolt* and *L'Amour*. Andy had been publishing *Interview* magazine since 1968—but inexpensively—so the covers were usually nothing more than black-and-white film stills. Then, in 1972, he decided to put more money into it and make the covers full-color, and he asked me to design the first one. I used a picture of Donna Jordan (she had starred in *L'Amour*), and instead of the original type logo, I took a grease pencil and wrote the name "Andy Warhol's Interview."

For the next sixteen years I designed the covers for the magazine. When I'd bring them over to show Andy each month, he'd let me know in gestures or just a few words if he liked them or not. Painterly qualities were more important to him than being able to recognize who the person was. With Andy's guidance and encouragement, my style for the covers evolved from more-or-less tinted photographs to the full-blown lush portraits that became the instantly recognizable face of *Interview*.

### ALICE NEEL

Alice Neel. *Andy Warhol*. 1970. Oil on canvas, 60 × 40″
(152.4 × 101.6 cm). Whitney Museum of American Art, New York.
Gift of Timothy Collins

### ROBERT WILSON

I always loved Andy's drawings

Two memories: In 1970 Andy gave me five large drawings of poet–art critic Gene Swenson's lips. These drawings were sold to pay for the Paris performances of *Deafman Glance,* my first major work. I was unknown then, but after the Paris presentation my career in the theater was established. It was an extremely generous gift.

Upon my return from Europe, Andy and I had dinner. Andy made a drawing of an apple on the tablecloth. After he completed it, I said, "Oh, Andy, how beautiful your drawings are." Andy looked at me and, in his soft-spoken voice, said, "Oh, I just trace."

### JED JOHNSON

When I decorated Andy's house on East Sixty-sixth Street, naturally I wanted to hang some of *his* paintings in it. "No," he said when I suggested a Natalie for one of the walls; and from the decisive way he vetoed the idea, I realized it wasn't the Natalie he was objecting to but the whole idea of hanging his own art on his own walls. Later he mumbled something about it being "too corny" to put up your own work and whether that was the reason, or whether he just didn't like the thought of looking back every day at paintings he'd done years earlier, I don't know. Anyway, his canvases stayed rolled up in his closets.

He felt an artist should keep a neutral expression on his face when he showed his work to other people, that to betray pleasure or displeasure was, again, "corny." I'd watched him at many museum and gallery openings of his shows and he followed that policy consistently.

### WILLIAM WEGMAN

I met Andy and Mick [Jagger] at my show with Ileana [Sonnabend] in 1971. "I really like your work," I said, trying to shake their hands. Ileana told me not to worry about it.

### GILBERT & GEORGE

Andy Warhol was a very, very good artist and an extremely nice person.

## GIANFRANCO GORGONI

Gianfranco Gorgoni. *Andy Warhol and de Chirico, N.Y.C.* c. 1974

## LAWRENCE WEINER

FORM, THEN, FOR ANDY WARHOL WAS A FOLLOWER OF FUNCTION.
TO BE ABLE TO ACCEPT THAT ALL OBJECTS, ALL MATERIALS HAVE MEANING
AND IGNORE (OR SEEMING TO IGNORE) THE QUESTIONS OF MORALITY
INVOLVED IN THE OBJECTIFICATION OF THAT MEANING.
THE INEVITABLE LAPSES IN TASTE OF THE SOCIETY AS A WHOLE AND OF
THE INDIVIDUAL ARTIST WITHIN THAT SOCIETY RECALL THE CATHOLIC EXISTENTIALISM
OF THE CATHOLIC WORKER.
THE BODY OF WORK DID NOT COMMAND ADMIRATION.
AS AN ARTIST I FOUND MYSELF BECOMING A FAN OF WARHOL.
TCH-TCHING AT LAPSES AND USING HIS SUCCESSES TO HELP ACCOMMODATE WORK
OF ONE'S OWN THAT DIDN'T SEEM TO PLACE WITHIN THE SOCIETY.
WARHOL HELPED US TO BE ABLE TO ACCEPT THE HISTORY OF ART AS JUST THAT:
THE HISTORY OF ART.
HE, OFTEN IN COLLABORATION WITH OTHERS, PRODUCED A COHESIVE BODY OF MEANING
AND A SET OF IMAGES THAT TRANSCEND JOURNALISM IN BOTH ITS USE AND IN ITS MANNER OF PRODUCTION.
GOOD ARTISTS DON'T HAVE TO BE NICE PEOPLE.
IT WOULD HAVE HELPED THOUGH.
FAR BE IT FROM ME TO TRY AND DETERMINE AESTHETIC ASCENDANCY BETWEEN
A PAINTED UKRAINIAN EASTER EGG AND ONE FROM FABERGÉ.

Helmut Newton. *Andy Warhol, Paris.* 1974

**DAVID HOCKNEY**

David Hockney. *Andy, Paris 1974*. 1974. Colored pencil and pencil on paper, 25⅝ × 19¾″ (65.1 × 50.2 cm). Collection Steve Martin

## CAMILLA McGRATH

Camilla McGrath. *Paul Morrissey, Maxime McKendry, Alexander Hesketh, Warhol, Steven Paley, Diana Vreeland, Earl McGrath, and Jonathan Lieberson.* 1976

### RUPERT JASEN SMITH

Something I really loved about Andy was his art-by-committee philosophy. He was very receptive to other people's ideas and a great listener.

In 1980, Andy asked me to find some shoes for him to photograph. I was living on Duane Street, which was the old Jewish wholesale shoe district. Shoe businesses were going bankrupt because the old buildings were being converted into lofts. The shoe businesses would have sidewalk sales. I bought two thousand pairs of shoes for Andy. They were all really odd old ones from the forties and fifties and sixties. They were either size 4, quadruple-A, the Cinderella-size shoes, or they were size 13, triple-D, like boats for Divine. Andy wanted to make sure that he got the boxes and the wrappings, so he had a complete package. He said, make sure you get the boxes, and the paper that goes inside. I bought all the shoes for two dollars a pair. We had piles and piles of shoes, and Andy started photographing them.

Another time he asked me to find a picture of Leonardo da Vinci's *Last Supper.* We couldn't get a photograph from an art book because they were all too dark and you couldn't see any detail. So I found a sculpture of the painting one day on the New Jersey Turnpike in a gas station. It was made to look like marble but it was really white plastic. I paid thirteen dollars for it. Andy found another one in Times Square. It was a big enameled sculpture. He actually had to pay a couple of thousand for it. But the one we ended up using I found in a Korean store next to the Factory, and it was a copy of a nineteenth-century version that had been redone, like one you would buy in Woolworth's. It became the basis for the painting, and we blew up the picture to the size of the canvas, twelve yards long and ten feet high. Andy wanted it really big so that it would take up a whole wall in Alexander Iolas's gigantic exhibition space in Milan.

446

## JAMIE WYETH

Jamie Wyeth. *Portrait of Andy Warhol*. 1976. Oil on panel, 30 × 24″ (76.2 × 61 cm). Cheekwood Fine Arts Center, Nashville

## JOHN BALDESSARI

I felt a closeness to Andy Warhol—he helped to bring photo-imagery under the umbrella of art, to "deghettoize" it. I value him for his love of the banal and the ordinary, plus his blurring of high and low culture. I admire his adroitness at balancing idea and execution in the making of his art. At this he was a master.

On the other hand, he was a bit like Dr. Frankenstein and the monster gone amuck in the state of current art, that is, the emphasis on art as product (quality detached from price as a result of clever P.R.) and the confusion of artist-as-art (the artist as star).

But, in sum, he was certainly a model to young artists. The model of the artist as sufferer wielding his brush heroically against the world is no more. For me there is no pre-Warhol and post-Warhol, for better or worse (richer or poorer). B.W. and A.D.

## FRANCESCO CLEMENTE

I first met Andy Warhol at the Factory in 1981. The way he moved about the room seemed like he was making things occur in an effortless, oblique way. We talked very little. When two shy people meet, nothing much happens.

He said to me, "I'm only a graphic artist, you're so lucky you can invent things." Being told this by someone whom I knew to be such a great talent always made me a little amused and uneasy.

Andy Warhol found his subject matter in common places and asked the questions that everybody was too intelligent to ask. He was the exemplary mediator between the meaningful and meaningless.

Warhol sought a democratic approach to the image, but ideas of liberty and democracy rely on an unlimited space in which to expand. The only unlimited space we have is not the West or the planet but the space of the imagination. Warhol's work is an open-ended list of possible images approached and left behind in total freedom. Is that modern art?

## RAINER FETTING

After Picasso Andy Warhol is my favorite artist.

Andy appeared very easy in his interviews, but the result of his work is very great. Andy made beautiful pictures.

Some time ago, when I went to the Factory with Bruno Bischofberger, Andy asked me, "Where did you get your boots?"

## KOMAR AND MELAMID

Komar and Melamid. *Post Art No. 1 (Warhol)*. 1973. Oil on canvas, 48 × 36″ (121.9 × 91.4 cm). Collection Frayda and Ronald Feldman, New York

## ROBERT LONGO

Warhol was never "Andy" to me. The person or personality never seemed that important, it was always the work: the Maos, the Marilyns, the Skulls, the Dollar Signs. Shortly after his death, I saw a two-paneled, orange car crash from 1963 in a small group show at Castelli's—it was so fresh, simple, and sublime, as if no one had actually made it and it had always existed. In this age of the shrug, when our civilization could well die of indifference from within, Warhol took that sense of decay and numbness and gave it a new passion, a new picture, a new hope.

At times when I look at his work, I feel that he was creating with a heart that was near dead, and that he was being loyal to things he once might have felt, heard, or read about.

I never met Warhol and I'm not sure I really ever wanted to, just like I believe I wouldn't have wanted to meet Marilyn Monroe. What would I have said, "I really like your pictures"?

## JOHN WATERS

Andy Warhol, Walt Disney, Russ Meyer, and the Kuchar Brothers made me want to make movies.

Andy was always a big help. He first invited us to the Factory to screen *Pink Flamingos* because he didn't want to go to a crazed midnight show. Since he wasn't sure if he'd like it, he hid in the back until it was over and then came out. "You should make the exact same movie over again, exactly the same way," he told me. He later took Fellini to see it.

Through the years Andy went out of his way to help promote my films in his magazine. He was always especially sweet to Edith Massey, a star of many of my movies. He always tried to make me gossip about Tab Hunter but I never would.

I think Andy Warhol was really handsome. His obvious wig was the perfect answer to balding. Andy was just the best.

## CHRISTOPHER MAKOS

Christopher Makos. *Andy Warhol, Paris.* 1986

### C. O. PAEFFGEN

C. O. Paeffgen. *Andy Warhol*. 1985. Synthetic polymer paint on
photo-silkscreen on canvas, 55 × 45¼″ (139.7 × 114.9 cm).
Private collection

### DEBORAH HARRY

Andy Warhol was a great artist, a magnetic and kindred
spirit, and an influence on me. He collected people and
objects. Andy was like a performer through whom things pass and
to whom they return. He was not a cold and abstract person,
but a truly passionate one.

Andy made the act of creating Art into an art.

### BARBARA KRUGER

Throughout all his work, Warhol functioned as a kind of
engineer of retention: a withholder who became the doorkeeper
at the floodgates of someone else's expurgatory inclinations. His
acuity can be construed as a kind of coolness: an ability to collapse the
complexities and nuances of language and experience into the chilled
silences of the frozen gesture. He elevated the reductivism of myth
and mute iconography to new heights of "incommunicado."
Like any good voyeur, he had a knack for defining sex
as nostalgia for sex, and he understood the cool hum of power
that resides not in hot expulsions of verbiage, but in the elegantly
mute thrall of sign language.

### LOUISE LAWLER

Whose Conscious?

"What do you want from me? I did the best I could."
The constant screams, repeated as she shuffles, of a disheveled, fortyish
inmate of Bellevue.
You thought this was going to be about Warhol, or shall I call him Andy?
Who says it isn't.
What is your interest in what I have to say? He's shown us what
"rubbernecking" is all about.
Would it have worked if he had been less vigorous with his limp wrist?
Was the *Vote McGovern* poster (green-faced Nixon) a slip?
He can easily be blamed.
As a leading figure in the pageant, is it necessary to believe he truly
believed in BRILLO?
What would you do?

NEW SHOES
BLUE SHOES
RED & PINK & BLUE SHOES
TELL ME WHAT WOULD YOU CHOOSE
IF YOU WERE TO BUY

HE MADE NO ATTEMPT TO
RESCUE ART FROM RITUAL
☐          ☐
YES       NO

### JULIAN SCHNABEL

There are the rocks, the sea, and the sky; the days, the hours,
the minutes; pain; the temperature of a particular day—all
permutations of reality—and there is Andy Warhol.

All these are matters of fact, part of life. Any description is just a
description. We can only talk about how they affect us. There is no
personal language, just a personal selection of it. What Andy chose to
select is as impossible to decipher as any of the great
unfathomable mysteries, like the sky, the sand, or the wind.

Unendingly unexplainable, cold and succinct, the realness of his
mystery has confounded as many people as it has informed. There is
something unexplainable in the way Andy decided to paint, the
way he decided a painting was finished, and what he chose to paint.
His work is dramatic, epic, poetic, soulful, funny, depressing,
inspired, not sentimental. The radicality of his vision has
done more for the mental health of art than any other artist has
since Picasso—even Joseph Beuys. He presented the horror
of our time with the thoroughness of Goya in his time. His use
of color has given us new vision.

In 1977 I saw Andy's Shadow paintings in New York and

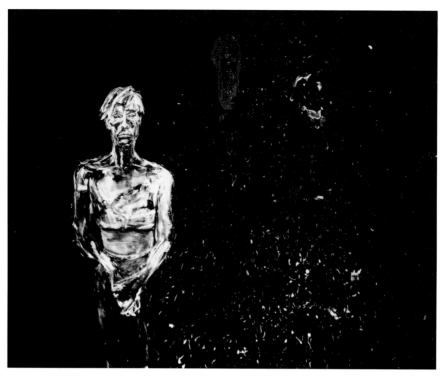

Julian Schnabel. *Portrait of Andy Warhol*. 1982. Oil on velvet, 9 × 10′ (274.3 × 304.8 cm).
The Estate of Andy Warhol

thought they were decorative displays of Andy Warhol on automatic pilot, almost images in decorator colors. I didn't get it. Ten years later I saw the same paintings in Houston, and realized I was seeing them for the first time. In 1977 I wasn't ready. There are a lot of people who aren't ready to see what he has done. They will get there or they won't; the work will be there waiting for them. Andy's last paintings are as essential to our understanding of modern art as is his work from the sixties.

In 1988 I saw his Skull paintings. I thought, boy, this guy can paint. There was a large yellow painting that made my eyes pop out of my head. I love Andy Warhol.

### THOMAS LAWSON

A few years ago Dior ran a creepily knowing ad campaign in the glossies—three characters called Oliver, the Wizard, and the Mouth in a ghoulish *ménage à trois*. As the campaign developed, a variety of sexual and social combinations were coyly suggested, although never acted out. In one of the last of the series the trio visit Andy Warhol. The artist, sitting sphinxlike in front of a white canvas, appears in white wig and white clothes, a ghostly apparition at the side of the picture. It's an image I return to, fascinated.

There is a succinct elegance in the way in which Warhol's poses suggests a critical intervention in the seamless world of advertising, but ultimately withholds that, simply offering nothing. His simultaneous acceptance and refusal of the madcap creativity represented by the Dior campaign highlights the near-impossible position in which artists have found themselves in postmodernist culture: marginal entertainers and interior decorators. His glamorous negativity in the face of the self-consciously fake imaginings of consumerism came to be understood as the appropriate stance: artists became phantoms, lost souls denying the very idea of purpose. Joseph Beuys may have wanted to be art-world shaman, healer of wounds, but Warhol countered that fey optimism with the cool of schlock horror; he replayed, continuously, the melodrama of the living dead. And over the years the juice he generated kept many of the undead moving on.

Now that both Beuys and Warhol are gone it is perhaps time to rethink how we want to continue as working artists in this culture, which threatens to stifle us with insignificance.

### EDWARD W. HAYES

If Andy Warhol is not the American Dream, then there is no American Dream.

Marcus Leatherdale. *Andy Warhol at the Factory.* 1981

Jean-Michel Basquiat. *Dos Cabezas*. 1982. Synthetic polymer paint on canvas with wood supports,
60½ × 61″ (153.7 × 154.9 cm). Private collection

## MICHAEL HALSBAND

Michael Halsband. *Area, New York*. 1986. From left to right: Back row—Michael Heizer, Arman, LeRoy Neiman, Dennis Oppenheim (partially obscured), Julian Schnabel, William Wegman, Tony Shafrazi (obscured); fourth row—Warhol, David Hockney, Stefano, Keith Haring, Red Grooms; third row—John Chamberlain, Kenny Scharf, Ronnie Cutrone; second row—Jean-Michel Basquiat, Francesco Clemente, Robert Mapplethorpe, Sandro Chia; front row (kneeling)—Chris Goode, Darius Azari, Shawn Hausman, Eric Goode

## DAVID McDERMOTT AND PETER McGOUGH

David McDermott and Peter McGough. *High School Portrait.* 1986
(dated 1947). Oil on canvas, 23¾ × 18″ (60.3 × 45.7 cm).
Private collection

## JOHN RICHARDSON

Eulogy for Andy Warhol

Besides celebrating Andy Warhol as the quintessential artist of his time
and place—the artist who held the most revealing mirror up to his
generation—I'd like to recall a side of his character that he hid from all
but closest friends: his spiritual side. Those who knew him in
circumstances that were the antithesis of spiritual may be
surprised that such a side existed. But exist it did, and it's the
key to the artist's psyche.

Never forget that Andy was born into a fervently Catholic family and
brought up in the fervently Catholic *Ruska dolina,* the Ruthenian
section of Pittsburgh. As a youth, he was withdrawn and reclusive,
devout and celibate; and beneath the disingenuous public

mask that is what he at heart remained. Thanks largely to the
example of his adored mother, Julia, Andy never lost the habit of going
to mass more often than is obligatory. As fellow parishioners will
remember, he made a point of dropping in on his local church,
St. Vincent Ferrer, several days a week until shortly before he died.

Although Andy was perceived—with some justice—as a
passive observer who never imposed his beliefs on other people, he
could on occasion be an effective proselytizer. To my certain
knowledge, he was responsible for at least one conversion. He also took
considerable pride in financing a nephew's studies for the priesthood.
He regularly helped out at a shelter serving meals to the homeless and
hungry. Trust Andy to keep these activities very, very dark.

The knowledge of this secret piety inevitably changes our
perception of an artist who fooled the world into believing that his only
obsessions were money, fame, and glamor, and that he was cool to the
point of callousness. Never take Andy at face value. The callous
observer was in fact a recording angel. And Andy's detachment—the
distance he established between the world and himself—was
above all a matter of innocence and of art. Isn't an artist
usually obliged to step back from things? In his impregnable innocence
and humility Andy always struck me as a *yurodstvo*—one of those
saintly simpletons who haunt Russian fiction and Slavic villages, such
as Mikova in Ruthenia, whence the Warhols stemmed. Hence his
peculiar, passive power over people; his ability to remain
uncorrupted, no matter what activities he chose to film or
tape or scrutinize. The saintly simpleton side, likewise, explains
Andy's ever increasing obsession with folklore and mysticism. He
became more and more like a medieval alchemist searching not so
much for the philosopher's stone as the elixir of youth.

If in the sixties some of the hangers-on at the Factory were
hell-bent on destroying themselves, Andy was *not* to blame.
He did what he could to help, but nothing in the world was going to
deter those lemmings from their fate. In any case, Andy was not cut out
to be his brother's keeper. That would hardly have been compatible
with the existent detachment which was his special gift. However,
Andy *did* feel compassion, and he *did,* in his Prince Myshkin
way, save many of his entourage from burn-out.

Although ever in his thoughts, Andy's religion didn't surface in his
work until two or three Christmases ago, when he embarked on his
series of Last Suppers, many of them inspired by the cheap plaster
mockup of Leonardo's masterpiece he bought in Times Square.
Andy's use of a Pop concept to energize sacred subjects
constitutes a major breakthrough in religious art. He even managed to
give a slogan like "Jesus saves" an uncanny new urgency. And how
awesomely prophetic is Andy's painting—one of his very
last—which announces, "Heaven and Hell are just one breath away."

Robert Mapplethorpe. *Andy Warhol*. 1986

# WARHOL IN HIS OWN WORDS

**SELECTED BY NEIL PRINTZ**

*If you want to know all about Andy Warhol, just look at the surface: of my paintings and films
and me, and there I am. There's nothing behind it.*[1]

● ● ● ● ● ● ● ● ● ● ● ●

*I see everything that way, the surface of things, a kind of mental Braille,
I just pass my hands over the surface of things.*[2]

★ ★ ★ ★ ★ ★ ★ ★ ★

*I never wanted to be a painter. I wanted to be a tap dancer.*[3]

● ● ● ● ● ● ● ● ● ● ● ●

*The reason I'm painting this way is that I want to be a machine, and I feel that
whatever I do and do machine-like is what I want to do.*[4]

★ ★ ★ ★ ★ ★ ★ ★ ★

*I like boring things. I like things to be exactly the same over and over again.*[5]

● ● ● ● ● ● ● ● ● ● ● ●

*I've been quoted a lot as saying, "I like boring things." Well, I said it and I meant it. But that
doesn't mean I'm not bored by them. Of course, what I think is boring must not be
the same as what other people think is, since I could never stand to watch all the most popular
action shows on TV, because they're essentially the same plots and the same shots and
the same cuts over and over again. Apparently, most people love watching the same basic thing,
as long as the details are different. But I'm just the opposite: if I'm going to sit
and watch the same thing I saw the night before, I don't want it to be essentially the same—
I want it to be* exactly *the same. Because the more you look at the same exact thing,
the more the meaning goes away, and the better and emptier you feel.*[6]

★ ★ ★ ★ ★ ★ ★ ★

*I think everybody should be a machine.
I think everybody should like everybody.*[7]

● ● ● ● ● ● ● ● ● ● ● ●

*I think of myself as an American artist; I like it here, I think it's so great. It's fantastic. I'd like to work in Europe but I wouldn't do the same things, I'd do different things. I feel I represent the U.S. in my art but I'm not a social critic. I just paint those objects in my paintings because those are the things I know best. I'm not trying to criticize the U.S. in any way, not trying to show up any ugliness at all. I'm just a pure artist, I guess. But I can't say if I take myself seriously as an artist. I just hadn't thought about it. I don't know how they consider me in print, though.* [8]

*Everybody has their own America, and then they have pieces of a fantasy America that they think is out there but they can't see. When I was little, I never left Pennsylvania, and I used to have fantasies about things that I thought were happening in the Midwest, or down South, or in Texas, that I felt I was missing out on. But you can only live life in one place at a time. And your own life while it's happening to you never has any atmosphere until it's a memory. So the fantasy corners of America seem so atmospheric because you've pieced them together from scenes in movies and music and lines from books. And you live in your dream America that you've custom-made from art and schmaltz and emotions just as much as you live in your real one.* [9]

★★★★★★★★

*I adore America and these are some comments on it. My image [Storm Door, 1960] is a statement of the symbols of the harsh, impersonal products and brash materialistic objects on which America is built today. It is a projection of everything that can be bought and sold, the practical but impermanent symbols that sustain us.* [10]

*What's great about this country is that America started the tradition where the richest consumers buy essentially the same things as the poorest. You can be watching TV and see Coca-Cola, and you can know that the President drinks Coke, Liz Taylor drinks Coke, and just think, you can drink Coke, too. A Coke is a Coke and no amount of money can get you a better Coke than the one the bum on the corner is drinking. All the Cokes are the same and all the Cokes are good. Liz Taylor knows it, the President knows it, the bum knows it, and you know it.* [11]

★★★★★★★★

*History books are being rewritten all the time. It doesn't matter what you do. Everybody just goes on thinking the same thing, and every year it gets more and more alike. Those who talk about individuality the most are the ones who most object to deviation, and in a few years it may be the other way around. Some day everybody will think just what they want to think, and then everybody will probably be thinking alike; that seems to be what is happening.* [12]

●● ●●●● ●●●● ●●

*Someone said that Brecht wanted everybody to think alike. I want everybody to think alike. But Brecht wanted to do it through Communism, in a way. Russia is doing it under government. It's happening here all by itself without being under a strict government; so if it's working without trying, why can't it work without being Communist? Everybody looks alike and acts alike, and we're getting more and more that way.* [13]

•••• •• ••••• ••

*Business art is the step that comes after Art. I started as a commercial artist, and I want to finish as a business artist. After I did the thing called "art" or whatever it's called, I went into business art. I wanted to be an Art Businessman or a Business Artist. Being good in business is the most fascinating kind of art. During the hippie era people put down the idea of business—they'd say "Money is bad," and "Working is bad," but making money is art and working is art and good business is the best art.* [14]

✶✶✶✶✶✶✶✶

*[On commercial art:] I was getting paid for it, and did anything they told me to do. If they told me to draw a shoe, I'd do it, and if they told me to correct it, I would—I'd do anything they told me to do, correct it and do it right. I'd have to invent and now I don't; after all that "correction," those commercial drawings would have feelings, they would have a style. The attitude of those who hired me had feeling or something to it; they knew what they wanted, they insisted; sometimes they got very emotional. The process of doing work in commercial art was machine-like, but the attitude had feeling to it.* [15]

••••• •• •••• ••

*I tried doing them by hand, but I find it easier to use a screen. This way, I don't have to work on my objects at all. One of my assistants or anyone else, for that matter, can reproduce the design as well as I could.* [16]

✶✶✶✶✶✶✶✶

*My paintings never turn out the way I expect them to, but I'm never surprised.* [17]

*When I have to think about it, I know the picture is wrong. And sizing is a form of thinking, and coloring is too. My instinct about painting says, "If you don't think about it, it's right." As soon as you have to decide and choose, it's wrong. And the more you decide about, the more wrong it gets. Some people, they paint abstract, so they sit there thinking about it because their thinking makes them feel they're doing something. But my thinking never makes me feel I'm doing anything. Leonardo da Vinci used to convince his patrons that his thinking time was worth something—worth even more than his painting time—and that may have been true for him, but I know that my thinking time isn't worth anything. I only expect to get paid for my "doing" time.* [18]

✶✶✶✶✶✶✶✶

*I still care about people but it would be so much easier not to care. I don't want to get too close; I don't like to touch things, that's why my work is so distant from myself.* [19]

•••• •• ••••• ••

*You should always have a product that has nothing to do with who you are, or what people think about you. An actress should count up her plays, a model should count up her photographs, and a writer should count up his words, and an artist should count up his pictures so that you never start thinking that your product is you, or your fame, or your aura.* [20]

✶✶✶✶✶✶✶✶

*If everybody's not a beauty, then nobody is.*[21]

✦✦✦✦✦✦✦✦

*In the future everybody will be world famous for fifteen minutes.*[22]

•• •• ••• •• •• ••

*I don't feel I'm representing the main sex symbols of our time in some of my pictures, such as Marilyn Monroe or Elizabeth Taylor. I just see Monroe as just another person. As for whether it's symbolical to paint Monroe in such violent colors: it's beauty, and she's beautiful and if something's beautiful it's pretty colors, that's all. Or something. The Monroe picture was part of a death series I was doing, of people who had died by different ways. There was no profound reason for doing a death series, no victims of their time; there was no reason for doing it all, just a surface reason.*[23]

✦✦✦✦✦✦✦✦

[On beginning the "death series":] *I guess it was the big plane crash picture, the front page of a newspaper: 129 DIE. I was also painting the* Marilyns. *I realized that everything I was doing must have been Death. It was Christmas or Labor Day—a holiday—and every time you turned on the radio they said something like "4 million are going to die." That started it. But when you see a gruesome picture over and over again, it doesn't really have any effect.*[24]

•• •• •• •• •• ••

*I started those* [pictures of Elizabeth Taylor] *a long time ago, when she was so sick and everybody said she was going to die. Now I'm doing them all over, putting bright colors on her lips and eyes.*[25]

✦✦✦✦✦✦✦✦

*I used to drink it* [Campbell's soup]. *I used to have the same lunch every day, for twenty years, I guess, the same thing over and over again. Someone said my life has dominated me; I liked that idea. I used to want to live at the Waldorf Towers and have soup and a sandwich, like that scene in the restaurant in* Naked Lunch. . . .[26]

•• •• •• •• •• ••

[On making Brillo boxes]: *I did all the* [Campbell's soup] *cans in a row on a canvas, and then I got a box made to do them on a box, and then it looked funny because it didn't look real. I have one of the boxes here. I did the cans on the box, but it came out looking funny. I had the boxes already made up. They were brown and looked just like boxes, so I thought it would be great just to do an ordinary box.*[27]

✦✦✦✦✦✦✦✦

*The farther west we drove* [to California, fall 1963], *the more Pop everything looked on the highways. Suddenly we all felt like insiders because even though Pop was everywhere— that was the thing about it, most people still took it for granted, whereas we were dazzled by it—*

*to us, it was the new Art. Once you "got" Pop, you could never see a sign the same way again.
And once you thought Pop, you could never see America the same way again.
The moment you label something, you take a step—I mean, you can never go back again to
seeing it unlabeled. We were seeing the future and we knew it for sure. We saw people walking
around in it without knowing it, because they were still thinking in the past, in the references of
the past. But all you had to do was* know *you were in the future, and that's what put you there.
The mystery was gone, but the amazement was just starting.*[28]

*The Pop artists did images that anybody walking down Broadway could recognize
in a split second—comics, picnic tables, men's trousers, celebrities, shower curtains,
refrigerators, Coke bottles—all the great modern things that the Abstract Expressionists
tried so hard not to notice at all.*[29]

★ ★ ★ ★ ★ ★ ★ ★

*When you think about it, department stores are kind of like museums.*[30]

●● ●● ●● ●● ●● ●●

*I don't think Pop Art is on the way out; people are still going to it and buying it but I can't tell
you what Pop Art is, it's too involved. It's just taking the outside and putting it on the inside
or taking the inside and putting it on the outside, bring the ordinary objects into
the home. Pop Art is for everyone. I don't think art should be only for the select few,
I think it should be for the mass of American people and they usually accept art anyway. I think
Pop Art is a legitimate form of art like any other, Impressionism, etc. It's not just a put-on,
I'm not the High Priest of Pop Art, I'm just one of the workers in it. I'm neither bothered by
what is written about me or what people may think of me reading it.*[31]

★ ★ ★ ★ ★ ★ ★ ★

*The best atmosphere I can think of is film, because it's three-dimensional physically
and two-dimensional emotionally.*[32]

*All my films are artificial, but then everything is sort of artificial. I don't know
where the artificial stops and the real starts.*[33]

★ ★ ★ ★ ★ ★ ★ ★

*All the movies with Edie were so innocent when I think back on them, they had more
of a pajama-party atmosphere than anything else.
Edie was incredible on camera—just the way she moved. And she never stopped moving
for a second—even when she was sleeping, her hands were wide awake. She was all energy—
she didn't know what to do with it when it came to living her life, but it was wonderful to film.
The great stars are the ones who are doing something you can watch every second,
even if it's just a movement inside their eye.
I always wanted to do a movie of a whole day in Edie's life. But then, that was what I wanted*

*to do with most people. I never liked the idea of picking out certain scenes and pieces of time and putting them together, because then it ends up being different from what really happened— it's just not like life, it seems so corny. What I liked was chunks of time all together, every real moment. . . . I only wanted to find great people and let them be themselves and talk about what they usually talked about and I'd film them for a certain length of time and that would be the movie. . . . To play the poor little rich girl in the movie, Edie didn't need a script— if she'd needed a script, she wouldn't have been right for the part.*[34]

●●●● ●● ●●●● ●●

*"Good performers," I think, are all-inclusive recorders, because they can mimic emotions as well as speech and looks and atmosphere—they're more inclusive than tape recordings or videotapes or novels. Good performers can somehow record complete experiences and people and situations and then pull out these recordings when they need them. They can repeat a line exactly the way it should sound and look exactly the way they should look when they repeat it because they've seen the scene before somewhere and they've shelved it away. So they know what the lines should be and the way the lines should come out of them. Or stay in them. I can only understand really amateur performers or really bad performers, because whatever they do never really comes off, so therefore it can't be phoney. But I can never understand really good, professional performers.*[35]

★★★★★ ★✦ ★★

*If I ever have to cast an acting role, I want the wrong person for the part. I can never visualize the right person in a part. The right person for the right part would be too much. Besides, no person is ever completely right for any part, because a part in a role is never real, so if you can't get someone who's perfectly right, it's more satisfying to get someone who's perfectly wrong. Then you know you've really got something.*[36]

●●●● ●● ●●●● ●●

*What I was actually trying to do in my early movies was show how people can meet other people and what they can do and what they can say to each other. That was the whole idea: two people getting acquainted. And then when you saw it and you saw the sheer simplicity of it, you learned what it was all about. Those movies showed you how some people act and react with other people. They were like actual sociological "For instance"s. They were like documentaries, and if you thought it could apply to you, it was an example, and if it didn't apply to you, at least it was a documentary, it could apply to somebody you knew and it could clear up some questions you had about them.*[37]

★✦★★★★★✦

*What we'd had to offer—originally, I mean—was a new, freer content and a look at real people, and even though our films weren't technically polished, right up through '76 the underground was one of the only places people could hear about forbidden subjects and see realistic scenes of modern life.*[38]

●● ●●●● ●● ●●●●

*I think movies should appeal to prurient interests. I mean, the way things are going now—people are alienated from one another. Movies should—uh—arouse you. Hollywood films are just planned-out commercials.* Blue Movie *was* real. *But it wasn't done as pornography—it was an exercise, an experiment. But I really do think movies* should *arouse you, should get you excited about people, should be prurient.*[39]

★★★★★★★★

*When you read Genet you get all hot, and that makes some people say this is not art. The thing I like about it is that it makes you forget about style and that sort of thing; style isn't really important.*[40]

*I think movies are becoming novels and it's terrific that people like Norman Mailer and Susan Sontag are doing movies now too. That's the new novel. Nobody's going to read anymore. It's easier to make movies. The kind of movies that we're doing are like paperbacks. They're cheaper than big books. The kids at college don't have to read anymore. They can look at movies, or make them.*[41]

★★★★★★★★

*I never read, I just look at pictures.*[42]

●●●●●●●●●●●●

*Before I was shot, I always thought that I was more half-there than all-there—I always suspected that I was watching TV instead of living life. People sometimes say the way things happen in movies is unreal, but actually it's the way things happen to you in life that's unreal. The movies make emotions look so strong and real, whereas when things really do happen to you, it's like watching television—you don't feel anything.*
*Right when I was being shot and ever since, I knew that I was watching television. The channels switch, but it's all television. When you're really involved with something, you're usually thinking about something else. When something's happening, you fantasize about other things. When I woke up somewhere—I didn't know it was at the hospital and that Bobby Kennedy had been shot the day after I was—I heard fantasy words about thousands of people being in St. Patrick's Cathedral praying and carrying on, and then I heard the word "Kennedy" and that brought me back to the television world again because then I realized, well, here I was, in pain.*[43]

★★★★★★★★

*The acquisition of my tape recorder really finished whatever emotional life I might have had, but I was glad to see it go. Nothing was ever a problem again, because a problem just meant a good tape, and when a problem transforms itself into a good tape it's not a problem any more. An interesting problem was an interesting tape. Everybody knew that and performed for the tape. You couldn't tell which problems were real and which problems were exaggerated for the tape. Better yet, the people telling you the problems couldn't decide any more if they were really having the problems or if they were just performing.*
*During the 60s, I think, people forgot what emotions were supposed to be. And I don't think they've ever remembered. I think that once you see emotions from a certain angle you can never think of them as real again. That's what more or less has happened to me.*[44]

●●●●●●●●●●●●

★★★★★ ★★ ★★

*Interviews are like sitting in those Ford machines at the World's Fair that toured around while someone spoke a commentary. I always feel that my words are coming from behind me, not from me. The interviewer should just tell me the words he wants me to say and I'll repeat them after him. I think that would be so great because I'm so empty I just can't think of anything to say.*[45]

•• •••• •• ••••

*The thing is to think of nothing. . . . Look, nothing is exciting, nothing is sexy, nothing is not embarrassing. The only time I ever want to be something is outside a party so I can get in.*[46]

★★★★★★★★

*But I always say, one's company, two's a crowd, three's a party.*[47]

•• •• •• ••• •• ••

*You should have contact with your closest friends through the most intimate and exclusive of all media—the telephone.*[48]

★★ ★★ ★★★★

*Before media there used to be a physical limit on how much space one person could take up by themselves. People, I think, are the only things that know how to take up more space than the space they're actually in, because with media you can sit back and still let yourself fill up space on records, in the movies, most exclusively on the telephone and least exclusively on television.*[49]

•••• •• •••• ••

*I like to be the right thing in the wrong space and the wrong thing in the right space. But when you hit one of the two, people turn the lights out on you, or spit on you, or write bad reviews of you, or beat you up, or mug you, or say you're "climbing." But usually being the right thing in the wrong space and the wrong thing in the right space is worth it, because something funny always happens. Believe me, because I've made a career out of being the right thing in the wrong space and the wrong thing in the right space. That's one thing I really do know about.*[50]

★★★★★ ★★ ★★

*I've always had a conflict because I'm shy and yet I like to take up a lot of personal space. Mom always said, "Don't be pushy, but let everybody know you're around." I wanted to command more space than I was commanding, but then I knew I was too shy to know what to do with the attention if I did manage to get it. That's why I love television. That's why I feel that television is the media I'd most like to shine in. I'm really jealous of everybody who's got their own show on television. As I said, I want a show of my own—called* Nothing Special.[51]

•• •• •• •••• ••

*I never fall apart because I never fall together.*[52]

★★★★★★★★

●● ●●●●● ●●●●● ●●

*I don't know if I was ever capable of love, but after the 60s I never thought in terms of "love" again. However, I became what you might call* fascinated *by certain people. One person in the 60s fascinated me more than anybody I had ever known. And the fascination I experienced was probably very close to a certain kind of love. Fantasy love is much better than reality love. Never doing it is very exciting. The most exciting attractions are between two opposites that never meet.*[53]

✦✦✦✦✦✦✦✦

*Truman says he can get anyone he wants. I don't want anyone I can get.*[54]

●●●●● ●● ●●●●● ●●

*Sex is nostalgia for when you used to want it, sometimes.
Sex is nostalgia for sex.*[55]

✦✦✦✦✦✦✦✦

*When I'm really impressed I get so nervous I can't talk. Fortunately most of the people who work for me get so nervous they can't stop talking.*[56]

●● ●● ●● ●● ●●● ●●

*I think we're a vacuum here at the Factory, it's great. I like being a vacuum; it leaves me alone to work. We are bothered though, we have cops coming up here all the time. They think we're doing awful things and we aren't.*[57]

✦✦ ✦✦ ✦✦✦✦

*Now and then someone would accuse me of being evil—of letting people destroy themselves while I watched, just so I could film them and tape record them. But I don't think of myself as evil—just realistic. I learned when I was little that whenever I got aggressive and tried to tell someone what to do, nothing happened—I just couldn't carry it off. I learned that you actually have more power when you shut up, because at least that way people will start to maybe doubt themselves. When people are ready to, they change. They never do it before then, and sometimes they die before they get around to it. You can't make them change if they don't want to, just like when they do want to, you can't stop them.*[58]

●●●●● ●● ●●●●● ●●

*A lot of people thought it was me everyone at the Factory was hanging around, that I was some kind of big attraction that everyone came to see, but that's absolutely backward: it was me who was hanging around everyone else. I just paid the rent, and the crowds came simply because the door was open. People weren't particularly interested in seeing me, they were interested in seeing each other. They came to see who came.*[59]

✦✦✦✦✦✦✦✦

*You really have Social Disease when you make all play work. The only reason to play hard is to work hard, not the other way around like most people think.*[60]

●● ●●●●● ●● ●●●●

*There are so many people here* [in New York City] *to compete with that changing your tastes to what other people don't want is your only hope of getting anything.*[61]

•• •• •• •• •• ••

*I don't think I have an image, favorable or unfavorable.*[62]

★★★★★★★★

*Publicity is like eating peanuts. Once you start you can't stop.*[63]

•••• •• •••• ••

*I'm not more intelligent than I appear. . . .   I never have time to think about the real Andy Warhol, we're just so busy here. . .not working, busy playing because work is play when it's something you like. My philosophy is: every day's a new day. I don't worry about art or life. I mean, the war and the bomb worry me but usually there's not much you can do about them. I've represented it in some of my films and I'm going to try to do more. Money doesn't worry me, either, though I sometimes wonder where is it? Somebody's got it all!*[64]

★★★★★★★★

*I suppose I have a really loose interpretation of "work," because I think that just being alive is so much work at something you don't always want to do. Being born is like being kidnapped. And then sold into slavery. People are working every minute. The machinery is always going. Even when you sleep.*[65]

•• •• •• •• •• ••

*I don't like big moments, weddings, anniversaries, funerals; I like to play things all at the same level. When you run into somebody you haven't seen in 20 years, the best thing is when you both play it cool, very American, don't get excited, don't try to catch up. Maybe mention you're on your way to a movie, they'll tell you they're on their way to dinner, but just be offhand; just play it like it's no big deal. Like you just saw them yesterday and like you'll be seeing them all again tomorrow.*[66]

★★ ★★ ★★★★

*When I die I don't want to leave any leftovers. I'd like to disappear. People wouldn't say he died today, they'd say he disappeared. But I do like the idea of people turning into dust or sand, and it would be very glamorous to be reincarnated as a big ring on Elizabeth Taylor's finger.*[67]

•••• •• •••• ••

*I never understood why when you died, you didn't just vanish, and everything could just keep going the way it was only you just wouldn't be there.*
*I always thought I'd like my own tombstone to be blank. No epitaph, and no name.*
*Well, actually, I'd like it to say "figment."*[68]

★ ★ ★★ ★★★★

*I went to China. I didn't want to go, and I went to see the Great Wall. You know, you read about it for years. And actually it was great. It was really really really great.*[69]

Andy Warhol at the Great Wall, 1982

# NOTES

1. Gretchen Berg, "Andy: My True Story," *Los Angeles Free Press* (March 17, 1967), p. 3. (Reprinted from *East Village Other*.)
2. Ibid.
3. Andy Warhol, Kasper König, Pontus Hultén, and Olle Granath eds., *Andy Warhol* (Stockholm: Moderna Museet, 1968), n.p.
4. G. R. Swenson, "What Is Pop Art?: Answers from 8 Painters, Part I," *Artnews* 62 (November 1963), p. 26.
5. Read by Nicholas Love at Memorial Mass for Andy Warhol, St. Patrick's Cathedral, New York, April 1, 1987.
6. Andy Warhol and Pat Hackett, *POPism: The Warhol '60s* (New York: Harcourt Brace Jovanovich, 1980), p. 50.
7. Swenson, "What Is Pop Art?" p. 26.
8. Berg, "Andy: My True Story," p. 3.
9. Andy Warhol, *America* (New York: Harper & Row, 1985), p. 8.
10. "New Talent U.S.A.," *Art in America* 50, no. 1 (1960), p. 42.
11. Andy Warhol, *The Philosophy of Andy Warhol (From A to B and Back Again)* (New York: Harcourt Brace Jovanovich), 1975, pp. 100–101.
12. Swenson, "What Is Pop Art?" p. 61.
13. Ibid., p. 26.
14. *Philosophy of Andy Warhol*, p. 92.
15. Swenson, "What Is Pop Art?" p. 26.
16. Warhol, König, et al., *Andy Warhol*.
17. Read by Nicholas Love (April 1, 1987).

18. *Philosophy of Andy Warhol*, p. 149.
19. Read by Nicholas Love (April 1, 1987).
20. Ibid.
21. *Philosophy of Andy Warhol*, p. 62.
22. Warhol, König, et al., *Andy Warhol*.
23. Berg, "Andy: My True Story," p. 3.
24. Swenson, "What Is Pop Art?" p. 60.
25. Ibid.
26. Ibid., p. 26.
27. Glenn O'Brien, "Interview: Andy Warhol," *High Times* 24 (August 1977), p. 34.
28. *POPism*, pp. 39–40.
29. Ibid., p. 3.
30. *America*, p. 22.
31. Berg, "Andy: My True Story," p. 3.
32. *Philosophy of Andy Warhol*, p. 160.
33. Read by Nicholas Love (April 1, 1987).
34. *POPism*, pp. 109–110.
35. *Philosophy of Andy Warhol*, p. 82.
36. Ibid., p. 83.
37. Ibid., p. 48.
38. *POPism*, p. 280.
39. Letitia Kent, "Andy Warhol, Movieman: 'It's Hard to Be Your Own Script,'" *Vogue* 155 (March 1970), p. 204.
40. Swenson, "What Is Pop Art?" p. 62.
41. Joseph Gelmis, [interview with Andy Warhol, in] *The Film Director as Superstar* (New York: Doubleday and Co., 1970), p. 72.
42. Warhol, König, et al., *Andy Warhol*.
43. *Philosophy of Andy Warhol*, p. 91.

44. Ibid., pp. 26–27.
45. Berg, "Andy: My True Story," p. 3.
46. *Philosophy of Andy Warhol*, p. 9.
47. *Andy Warhol's Exposures* (New York: Andy Warhol Books/Grosset & Dunlap, 1979), p. 176.
48. *Philosophy of Andy Warhol*, p. 147.
49. Ibid., p. 146.
50. Ibid., p. 158.
51. Ibid., p. 147.
52. Ibid., p. 81.
53. Ibid., pp. 27, 44.
54. *Exposures*, p. 145.
55. *Philosophy of Andy Warhol*, p. 53.
56. *Exposures*, p. 26.
57. Berg, "Andy: My True Story," p. 3.
58. *POPism*, p. 108.
59. Ibid., p. 74.
60. *Exposures*, p. 19.
61. *Philosophy of Andy Warhol*, p. 93.
62. Read by Nicholas Love (April 1, 1987).
63. *Exposures*, p. 176.
64. Berg, "Andy: My True Story," p. 3.
65. *Philosophy of Andy Warhol*, p. 96.
66. Read by Nicholas Love (April 1, 1987).
67. Ibid.
68. *America*, pp. 128–29.
69. Paul Taylor, "Andy Warhol: The Last Interview," *Flash Art* (International Edition) 133 (April 1987), p. 44.

# SELECTED BIBLIOGRAPHY

PREPARED BY DANIEL STARR

The Selected Bibliography is divided into four sections. The first section consists of works by the artist, and within it are listed books Warhol illustrated, books he wrote, and interviews with and statements by the artist. The second section comprises books and catalogues about Warhol, and the third section is made up of books and catalogues that include Warhol. Articles about the artist are listed in the fourth section.

## I. BY THE ARTIST

(Listed chronologically)

### ILLUSTRATED BOOKS

Vanderbilt, Amy. *Amy Vanderbilt's Complete Book of Etiquette*. Garden City, N.Y.: Doubleday, 1952. Illustrated by Warhol, Fred McCarroll, and Mary Suzuki. Reprinted 1954–72.

*A Is an Alphabet*. [New York, 1953]. By Corkie and Andy (Ralph T. Ward and Warhol).

*Love Is a Pink Cake*. [New York, 1953]. By Corkie and Andy (Ralph T. Ward and Warhol).

*25 Cats Name Sam and One Blue Pussy*. [New York: Printed by Seymour Berlin, 1954]. Reprinted (with *Holy Cats by Andy Warhol's Mother*) New York: Panache Press at Random House, 1987. Text by Charles Lisanby.

*A la Recherche du Shoe Perdu*. [New York, 1955]. Shoe poems by Ralph Pomeroy.

*In the Bottom of My Garden*. [New York, 1955].

*A Gold Book*. [New York, 1957].

*Wild Raspberries*. [New York, 1959]. By Warhol and Suzie Frankfurt.

Vanderbilt, Amy. *Amy Vanderbilt's Complete Cookbook*. Garden City, N.Y.: Doubleday, 1961. Drawings credited to Warhol but actually done by Ted Carey.

*Andy Warhol's Children's Book*. Küsnacht/Zürich: Bruno Bischofberger, 1983.

Benirschke, Kurt. *Vanishing Animals*. New York: Springer-Verlag, 1986. Illustrations by Warhol.

The illustrations from many of the above books are reproduced in *Andy Warhol: A Picture Show by the Artist* by Rainer Crone (New York: Rizzoli, 1987). *See* Crone in Books and Catalogues About the Artist for more information.

### BOOK-LENGTH WRITINGS

*Andy Warhol's Index (Book)*. New York: Random House, 1967. With the assistance of Stephen Shore and others, particularly David Paul. Several photographs by Nat Finkelstein; Factory photographs by Billy Name. Includes "An Interview with Andy Warhol at the Balloon Farm."

*Screen Tests: A Diary*. New York: Kulchur Press, 1967. By Warhol and Gerard Malanga.

*A: A Novel*. New York: Grove Press, 1968.

*Blue Movie: A Film*. New York: Grove Press, 1970. Complete dialogue plus photographs.

*The Philosophy of Andy Warhol (From A to B and Back Again)*. New York: Harcourt Brace Jovanovich, 1975.

*Andy Warhol's Exposures*. New York: Andy Warhol Books/Grosset & Dunlap, 1979. Photographs by Warhol; text by Warhol and Bob Colacello.

*POPism: The Warhol '60s*. New York: Harcourt Brace Jovanovich, 1980. Reprinted New York: Harper & Row, 1983. By Warhol and Pat Hackett.

*America*. New York: Harper & Row, 1985. Texts and photographs by Warhol.

*Andy Warhol's Party Book*. New York: Crown, 1988. Text and photographs by Warhol and Pat Hackett, with additional photographs by Edit de Ak, Jan Bolton, Paige Powell, Wilfredo Rosado, Jeffrey Slonim, and C. J. Zumwalt.

### INTERVIEWS AND STATEMENTS

[Statement. In] "New Talent USA." *Art in America* 50, no. 1 (1960): 42.

Swenson, G. R. "What Is Pop Art?: Answers from 8 Painters, Part I." *Artnews* 62 (November 1963): 24–27, 60–63. Reprinted in *Pop Art Redefined* by John Russell and Suzi Gablik (New York: Praeger, 1969) [N.B. The last three questions and answers attributed to Warhol are actually from the interview with Tom Wesselmann originally printed in Part II of the article (*Artnews* 62 [February 1964]: 40–43, 62–67)]; excerpts reprinted in *Readings in American Art, 1900–1975*, edited by Barbara Rose (New York: Praeger, 1975).

Malanga, Gerard. "Andy Warhol: Interviewed by Gerard Malanga." *Kulchur* 16 (Winter 1964/65): 37–39.

Lyon, Ninette. "Robert Indiana, Andy Warhol: A Second Fame—Good Food." *Vogue* 145 (March 1, 1965): 184–86. Interview.

Glaser, Bruce. "Oldenburg, Lichtenstein, Warhol: A Discussion." *Artforum* 4 (February 1966): 20–24. Reprinted in *Roy Lichtenstein*, edited by John Coplans (New York: Praeger, 1972). Transcript of a radio broadcast that took place in June 1964.

Ehrenstein, David. "Interview with Andy Warhol." *Film Culture* 40 (Spring 1966): 41.

Weinraub, Bernard. "Andy Warhol's Mother." *Esquire* 66 (November 1966): 99, 101, 158. Interview with Warhol's mother.

Powers, J. G. "12 Paintings from the Powers Collection: Pop Art, Op Art." *Aspen* 1 (December 1966). "Fab issue" designed by Warhol; includes his *Kiss: Underground Movie Flip Book* and an interview by Gerard Malanga.

Malanga, Gerard. "My Favorite Superstar: Notes on My Epic, 'Chelsea Girls.'" *Arts Magazine* 41 (February 1967): 26. Interview.

Berg, Gretchen. "Nothing to Lose: Interview with Andy Warhol." *Cahiers du Cinema in English* 10 (May 1967): 38–43. Excerpts translated in *Il Cinema Underground Americano* by Raffaele Milani (Messina: Casa Editrice G. D'Anna, 1978).

Goldberger, Clem, Joanna Romer, and Jan Lavasseur. "We Talk to Warhol." *Mademoiselle* 65 (August 1967): 325.

*Intransit: The Andy Warhol–Gerard Malanga Monster Issue*. Eugene, Oreg.: Toad Press, 1968. Includes Warhol's "From Cock" (pp. 3–12).

Castle, Frederick. "Occurrences: Cab Ride with Andy Warhol." *Artnews* 66 (February 1968): 46–47, 52. Transcription of a conversation that took place in June 1967.

Kent, Letitia. "Andy Warhol, Movieman: 'It's Hard to Be Your Own Script.'" *Vogue* 155 (March 1970): 167, 204. Interview.

Pomeroy, Ralph. "An Interview with Andy Warhol, June 1970." *Afterimage* 2 (Fall 1970): 34–39.

Malanga, Gerard. "A Conversation with Andy Warhol." *Print Collector's Newsletter* 1 (January/February 1971): 125–27.

"Sunday with Mister C.: An Audio-Documentary by Andy Warhol Starring Truman Capote." *Rolling Stone* 132 (April 12, 1973): 28–54. Translated in *Hollywood aujourd'hui: Une Legende americaine* by Guy Abitan (Paris: La Table Ronde, 1976), pp. 235–45.

Tuchman, Phyllis. "Pop!: Interviews with George Segal, Andy Warhol, Roy Lichtenstein, James Rosenquist, and Robert Indiana." *Artnews* 73 (May 1974): 24–29.

"Painter Hangs Own Paintings." *New York Magazine* 52 (February 5, 1979): 9–10. Reprinted in *Warhol Shadows* (Houston: Menil Foundation, 1987).

Shapiro, David. "Polvere di diamanti." In *Pop Art: Evoluzione di una generazione*, edited by Attilio Codognato (Milan: Electa, 1980), pp. 133–48. Interview.

Wolf, Reinhart. *New York in Photographs.* New York: Vendome Press, 1981. Includes an interview conducted by Warhol on April 30, 1980.

Kayser, Alex. *Artists' Portraits.* New York: Harry N. Abrams, 1981. Includes "An Andy Warhol Interview with Alex Kayser," an interview conducted by Warhol.

Blinderman, Barry. "Modern 'Myths': An Interview with Andy Warhol." *Arts Magazine* 56 (October 1981): 144–47.

Stein, Jean, with George Plimpton, editors. *Edie: An American Biography.* New York: Alfred A. Knopf, 1982. Statements.

"A Warhol Portrait Gallery." *The Paris Review* 94 (Winter 1984): 100–112. Text by Warhol and Robert Becker.

Ervin, Wilma. *On the Edge: The East Village.* New York: Times Books, 1985. Includes an interview conducted by Warhol.

Nickas, Robert. "Andy Warhol's *Rorschach Test.*" *Arts Magazine* 61 (October 1986): 28–29. Interview.

Fairbrother, Trevor J. "Warhol Meets Sargent at Whitney." *Arts Magazine* 61 (February 1987): 64–71. Interview taped at the John Singer Sargent exhibition at the Whitney Museum of American Art, New York, October 10, 1986.

Taylor, Paul. "Andy Warhol: The Last Interview." *Flash Art* (International Edition) 133 (April 1987): 40–44.

## II. BOOKS AND CATALOGUES ABOUT THE ARTIST

*Andy Warhol.* Berlin: Deutsche Gesellschaft für Bildende Kunst e.V. (Kunstverein Berlin) and the Nationalgalerie, 1969. Foreword by Werner Haftmann and Eberhard Roters.

*Andy Warhol: Arbeiten/Works, 1962–1986.* Salzburg: Galerie Thaddaeus Ropac, 1987. Includes essays by Anton Gugg, William Milié, and Stuart Morgan, and reminiscences by Glenn O'Brien, David Hockney, Leo Castelli, and Dennis Hopper.

*Andy Warhol: Death and Disasters.* Houston: Menil Collection and Houston Fine Arts Press, 1988. Includes essays by Neil Printz and Remo Guidieri.

*Andy Warhol: Guns, Knives, Crosses.* Madrid: Galeria Fernando Vijande, 1982. Includes an interview by Rodrigo Vijande and Alfred Nadaff (in English and Spanish) that took place on November 20, 1980, at the "New" Factory, New York; originally published in *El Pais*, February 7, 1981, Arts Supplement, no. 66, pp. 1–8.

*The Andy Warhol Collection: Sold for the Benefit of the Andy Warhol Foundation for the Visual Arts.* New York: Sotheby's, 1988. 6 vols.

*Andy Warhol in the 1980's.* Ridgefield, Conn.: Aldrich Museum of Contemporary Art, 1983.

*Andy Warhol in Venice.* Milan: Mazzotta, 1988. Introductions by Carlo Monzino and Leo Castelli; texts by Pier Paolo Pasolini (reprint) and Lola Bonora.

Aprà, Adriano, and Enzo Ungari. *Il cinema di Andy Warhol.* Rome: Arcana, 1978. Includes a bibliography.

Bailey, David. *Andy Warhol: Transcript of David Bailey's ATV Documentary.* London: Bailey Litchfield/Mathews Miller Dunbar Ltd., 1972. Reprinted Paris: Giraudin Import Disques, 1973. Includes interviews with Warhol.

Barozzi, Paolo. *Voglio essere una macchina (La fotografia in Andy Warhol).* Milan: All'insegna del pesce d'oro, 1979. Includes four photographs of Warhol printing by Ugo Mulas.

Barthes, Roland. *Wilhelm von Gloeden: Interventi di Joseph Beuys, Michelangelo Pistoletto, Andy Warhol.* Naples: Amelio, 1978. Introductory text in English, French, and Italian.

Bastian, Heiner. *Joseph Beuys, Robert Rauschenberg, Cy Twombly, Andy Warhol: Sammlung Marx.* Munich: Prestel-Verlag, 1982. Second edition Berlin: Arkadien Verlag, 1983.

Billeter, Erika, editor. *Andy Warhol: Ein Buch zur Ausstellung 1978 im Kunsthaus Zürich.* Zürich: Kunsthaus, 1978. Includes essays by David Bourdon, John Coplans, Hans Heinz Holz, Jonas Mekas, Barbara Rose, Helmut Salzinger, and Wolfgang Siano. Includes a filmography and a bibliography of interviews.

Bonito Oliva, Achille. *Warhol verso de Chirico.* Milan: Electa, 1982. Includes "Una metafisica industriale," an interview of Warhol by Bonito Oliva, translated in *Warhol verso De Chirico* (New York: Marisa del Re Gallery, 1985).

Bowman, Russell. *Warhol/Beuys/Polke.* Milwaukee: Milwaukee Art Museum, 1987. Includes "Prophecy and Legacy: The Work of Andy Warhol" by Linda L. Cathcart.

Bonuomo, Michele, editor. *Vesuvius by Warhol.* Naples: Electa Napoli, 1985. Includes texts by Giuseppe Galasso, Nicola Spinosa, Angele Tecce, Francesco Durante, and Bonuomo and an interview by Bonuomo in English and Italian.

Börjeson, Per-Olov. *Portraits of Ingrid Bergman by Andy Warhol.* Malmö: Galerie Börjeson, [1986?].

Brant, Sandra, and Elissa Cullman. *Andy Warhol's "Folk and Funk."* New York: Museum of American Folk Art, 1977. Accompanied an exhibition of works from Warhol's collection.

Brest, Jorge Romero. *Andy Warhol.* Buenos Aires: Galeria Rubbers, 1965.

Brown, Andreas, compiler. *Andy Warhol: His Early Works, 1947–1959.* New York: Gotham Book Mart Gallery, 1971. Gives Warhol's birthdate as August 6, 1928, "confirmed from 1945 school records in Pittsburgh."

Carluccio, Luigi. *Warhol.* Turin: Gian Carlo Sperone Arte Moderna, 1965.

Chiaretti, Maria. *Andy Warhol.* Turin: Galleria Galatea, 1972.

*Collaborations: Jean-Michel Basquiat, Francesco Clemente, Andy Warhol.* Küsnacht/Zürich: Edition Galerie Bruno Bischofberger, 1984.

Coplans, John. *Andy Warhol.* Greenwich, Conn.: New York Graphic Society, 1970. With contributions by Jonas Mekas and Calvin Tomkins. Includes a filmography and a bibliography.

Crone, Rainer. *Andy Warhol.* New York: Praeger, 1970. Includes a bibliography of 649 entries.

———. *Andy Warhol: A Picture Show by the Artist.* New York: Rizzoli, 1987. Translation and elaboration of *Andy Warhol: Das zeichnerische Werk, 1942–1975.* Includes reprints of *Love Is a Pink Cake, 25 Cats Name Sam and One Blue Pussy, A Is an Alphabet, In the Bottom of My Garden, A Gold Book,* and the illustrations for *A la Recherche du Shoe Perdu* and *Wild Raspberries.*

———. *Andy Warhol: Das zeichnerische Werk, 1942–1975.* Stuttgart: Württembergischer Kunstverein, 1976. Translated as *Andy Warhol: A Picture Show by the Artist* (New York: Rizzoli, 1987).

———. *Das bildnerische Werk Andy Warhols.* Berlin: Kommissionsvertrieb Wasmuth, 1976. Includes a bibliography of 658 entries through May 1, 1974.

Crone, Rainer, and Winifred Wiegand. *Die revolutionäre Ästhetik Andy Warhols.* Darmstadt: Melzer Verlag, 1972.

Dolezal, Georg J. *Andy Warhol: Schweizer Portraits.* Thun: Kunstsammlung der Stadt Thun, 1982.

Feldman, Frayda, and Jörg Schellmann, editors. *Andy Warhol Prints: A Catalogue Raisonné.* New York: Ronald Feldman Fine Arts, Editions Schellmann, and Abbeville Press, 1985. Introduction by Henry Geldzahler; essay by Roberta Bernstein.

Fournet, Claude. *Warhol au plus juste/Warhol in Close-Up.* Nice: Galerie des Ponchettes, 1982.

Gablik, Suzi. "Andy Warhol." In *Andy Warhol: Portrait Screenprints, 1965–80.* London: Arts Council of Great Britain, 1981.

Geldzahler, Henry. *Andy Warhol.* Bogotá: Galeria Fernando Quintana, 1988.

———. *Andy Warhol: A Memorial*. Bridgehampton, N.Y.: Dia Art Foundation, 1987.

Gidal, Peter: *Andy Warhol: Films and Paintings*. New York: Studio Vista, 1971.

Green, Samuel Adams. *Andy Warhol*. New York: Wittenborn, 1966. Reprinted in *The New Art*, edited by Gregory Battcock (New York: Dutton, 1966), pp. 229–34.

———. *Andy Warhol*. Philadelphia: Institute of Contemporary Art, University of Pennsylvania, 1965.

Haenlein, Carl. *Andy Warhol: Bilder 1961 bis 1981*. Hannover: Kestner-Gesellschaft, 1981.

Hahn, Otto. *Andy Warhol*. Paris: Galerie Ileana Sonnabend, 1965.

———. "Rembrandt vidé de Rembrandt." In *Andy Warhol—The Thirteen Most Wanted Men*. Paris: Galerie Ileana Sonnabend, 1967.

———. *Warhol*. Paris: Fernand Hazan Éditeur, 1972.

Hanhardt, John G., and Jon Gartenberg. *The Films of Andy Warhol: An Introduction*. New York: Whitney Museum of American Art, 1988.

Janus, editor. *Andy Warhol: Ladies and Gentlemen*. Milan: Mazzotta, 1975.

Koch, Stephen. *Andy Warhol Photographs*. New York: Robert Miller Gallery, 1986.

———. *Stargazer: Andy Warhol's World and His Films*. New York: Praeger, 1973. Second edition, New York: M. Boyars, 1985. With a new introductory chapter.

Kornbluth, Jesse. *Pre-Pop Warhol*. New York: Panache Press at Random House, forthcoming.

Kramer, Margia. *Andy Warhol et al.: The FBI File on Andy Warhol*. New York: UnSub Press, 1988.

Krohg, Morten. *Andy Warhol*. Oslo: Kunstnernes Hus, 1968.

Kulturmann, Udo. *Andy Warhols Blumen*. Essen: Galerie M. E. Thelen, 1965.

*Lenin by Warhol*. Munich: Galerie Bernd Klüser, 1987. Includes essays by Katharina Hegewisch and Achille Bonito Oliva in English and German.

Levi, Marcello. *Andy Warhol: 1974–1976*. Boissano, Italy: Centro Internazionale di Sperimentazioni Artistiche Marie-Louise Jeanneret, 1976.

Licht, Ira. *Andy Warhol: Ten Portraits of Jews of the Twentieth Century*. Coral Gables, Fla.: Lowe Art Museum, University of Miami, 1980.

Makos, Christopher. *Warhol: A Personal Photographic Memoir*. London: W. H. Allen, 1988. Foreword by Henry Geldzahler; introduction by Glenn Albin.

Mason, Rainer Michael, editor. *The American Indian: Une série de six dessins et onze peintures d'Andy Warhol*. Geneva: Musée d'Art et d'Histoire, 1977. Second edition, Geneva: Association Musée d'Art Moderne, 1978.

Morphet, Richard. "Andy Warhol." In *Warhol*. London: Tate Gallery, 1971.

Ostrow, Stephen E. *Raid the Icebox I with Andy Warhol: An Exhibition Selected from the Storage Vaults of the Museum of Art, Rhode Island School of Design*. Providence: Museum of Art, Rhode Island School of Design, 1969. Includes "Confessions of a Museum Director" by Daniel Robbins and "Andy's Dish" by David Bourdon.

Pacquement, Alfred. *Andy Warhol*. Paris: Musée d'Art Moderne de la Ville de Paris, 1971. Preface by Gilbert Brownstone.

Paoletti, John. *Andy Warhol*. Hartford: Wadsworth Atheneum, 1979. Number 50 in the museum's Matrix series.

Pasolini, Pier Paolo. *Warhol*. Milan: Luciano Anselmino, 1976.

Patalas, Enno. *Andy Warhol und seine Filme: Eine Dokumentation*. Munich, 1971.

Ratcliff, Carter. *Andy Warhol*. New York: Abbeville Press, 1983. Includes a bibliography.

*Remembering Andy: Warhol's Recent Works*. Tokyo: Galerie Watari, 1987. Text in Japanese.

Rosebush, Judson, editor. *Studies for Warhol's Marilyns, Beuys' Actions and Objects, Duchamp's Etc., Including Film*. Syracuse, N.Y.: Everson Museum of Art, 1973. Concept and design by Elaine Sturtevant.

Salzano, Giancarlo. *Andy Warhol*. Rome: Magna, 1976.

Salzmann, Siegfried. *Kultstar—Warhol—Starkult*. Duisburg: Horst E. Visser Verlag, 1972.

Schrage, Dieter. *Warhol '80: Serie Reversal*. Vienna: Museum moderner Kunst, Museum des 20. Jahrhunderts, 1981. Text by Dieter Ronte.

Serrano, Eduardo. *Andy Warhol*. Bogotá: Museo de Arte Moderno, 1974.

Smith, Patrick S. *Andy Warhol's Art and Films*. Ann Arbor: UMI Research Press, 1986. Revision of his Ph.D. dissertation "Art in Extremis: Andy Warhol and His Art," Northwestern University, 1981.

———. *Warhol: Conversations About the Artist*. Ann Arbor: UMI Research Press, 1988.

Smith, Robert L. *LeRoy Neiman, Andy Warhol: An Exhibition of Sports Paintings*. Los Angeles: Los Angeles Institute of Contemporary Art, 1981. Includes "Healthy Suicides" by Jeff Perrone and "Pentimenti/Partial Portraits" by Lynn Thorpe McAllister.

Solomon, Alan. *Andy Warhol*. Boston: Institute of Contemporary Art, 1966.

Spies, Werner. *Andy Warhol Cars: Die letzten Bilder*. Tübingen: Kunsthalle, 1988.

Stanton, Suzy. "On Warhol's 'Campbell's Soup Can.'" In *Andy Warhol*. New York: Stable Gallery, 1962.

Thorpe, Lynn Teresa. "Andy Warhol: Critical Evaluation of His Images and Books." Ph.D. dissertation, Cornell University, 1980. Includes a bibliography.

Vester, Karl-Egon, editor. *Andy Warhol*. Hamburg: Verlag Michael Kellner, 1988. Includes an interview with Warhol by Eva Windmöller.

Warhol, Andy, Kasper König, Pontus Hultén, and Olle Granath, editors. *Andy Warhol*. Stockholm: Moderna Museet, 1968. Photographs by Rudolph Burckhardt, Eric Pollitzer, and John D. Schiff.

*Warhol*. Paris: Ileana Sonnabend, 1964. Essays by Jean-Jacques Lebel (an extract from his *La Perception de l'image*), Alain Jouffroy, and John Ashbery.

*Warhol*. Milan: Galleria Il Fauno, 1974.

*Warhol: Campbell's Soup Boxes*. Van Nuys, Calif.: Martin Lawrence Limited Editions, 1986. Introduction by Martin S. Blinder. Includes "From Can to Box" by Michael Kohn and an interview with Warhol by Blinder and Kohn that took place in June and September 1986.

*Warhol Maos: Zehn Bildnisse von Mao Tse-Tung*. Basel: Kunstmuseum Basel, 1972.

*Warhol Shadows*. Houston: Menil Foundation, 1987. Includes text by Walter Hopps and "Painter Hangs His Own Paintings" by Warhol, originally published in *New York Magazine* 52 (February 5, 1979): 9–10.

*Warhol verso De Chirico*. New York: Marisa del Re Gallery, 1985. Includes "Warhol Salutes De Chirico" by Claudio Bruni Sakraischik and "Industrial Metaphysics," an interview with Warhol by Achille Bonito Oliva, originally published in his *Warhol verso de Chirico* (Milan: Electa, 1982).

Whitney, David. *Johns, Stella, Warhol: Works in Series*. Corpus Christi: Art Museum of South Texas, 1972.

Whitney, David, editor. *Andy Warhol: Portraits of the 70s*. New York: Random House in association with the Whitney Museum of American Art, 1979. Includes an essay by Robert Rosenblum.

Wilcock, John. *The Autobiography & Sex Life of Andy Warhol*. New York: Other Scenes, 1971. Photos by Shunk-Kender. Interviews.

Williams, Ron G. "Andy Warhol's Faces." In *Andy Warhol at Colorado State University*. Fort Collins: Department of Art, Colorado State University, 1981.

Wünsche, Hermann. *Andy Warhol: Das graphische Werk, 1962–1980*. N.p., n.d. Catalogue raisonné in English, French, and German, with essays by Gerd Tuchel and Carl Vogel.

## III. BOOKS AND CATALOGUES INCLUDING THE ARTIST

Alloway, Lawrence. *American Pop Art*. New York: Collier Books in association with the Whitney Museum of American Art, 1974. Includes a bibliography.

———. *The Photographic Image*. New York: The Solomon R. Guggenheim Museum, 1966.

———. *Six Painters and the Object*. New York: The Solomon R. Guggenheim Museum, 1963.

Amaya, Mario. *Pop Art . . . and After*. New York: Viking, 1966. Originally published as *Pop as Art: A Survey of the New Super-Realism* (London: Studio Vista, 1965).

Battcock, Gregory, editor. *The New Art*. New York: Dutton, 1966. Includes reprints of "Andy Warhol" by Samuel Adams Green and "Humanism and Reality: Thek and Warhol" by Battcock.

Beck, Heinz, and Johannes Cladders. *Pop—Sammlung Beck*. Düsseldorf: Rheinland-Verlag, 1970. Includes biographies and bibliographies by Hannelore Grimmig.

Boatto, Alberto. *Pop Art in USA*. Milan: Lerici, 1967. Revised edition: *Pop Art* (Milan: Editori Laterza, 1983).

Bockris, Victor, and Gerard Malanga. *Up-Tight: The Velvet Underground Story*. New York: Quill, 1983.

Calas, Nicolas, and Elena Calas. *Icons and Images of the Sixties*. New York: Dutton, 1971. Includes "Andy Warhol's One-Dimensional Mind" by Nicolas Calas.

Codognato, Attilio, editor. *Pop Art: Evoluzione di una generazione*. Milan: Electa, 1980. With contributions by Roland Barthes, Achille Bonito Oliva, David Bourdon, Germano Celant, and David Shapiro.

Compton, Michael. *Pop Art*. London: Hamlyn, 1970.

Coplans, John. *Pop Art USA*. Oakland, Calif.: Oakland Art Museum, 1963.

———. *Serial Imagery*. Pasadena, Calif.: Pasadena Art Museum, 1968.

Dypréau, Jean, and Pierre Restany. *Pop Art, nouveau réalisme, etc. . . .* Brussels: Palais des Beaux-Arts, 1965.

Finch, Christopher. *Pop Art: Object and Image*. London: Studio Vista; New York: Dutton, 1968.

Geldzahler, Henry. *New York Painting and Sculpture, 1940–1970*. New York: Dutton in association with The Metropolitan Museum of Art, 1969.

———. *Pop Art, 1955–70*. [Sydney]: International Cultural Corporation of Australia Limited, 1985. Includes a bibliography by Paula Baxter.

Glauber, Robert. *Violence in Recent American Art*. Chicago: Museum of Contemporary Art, 1968.

Haskell, Barbara. *Blam!: The Explosion of Pop, Minimalism, and Performance, 1958–1964*. New York: Whitney Museum of American Art in association with W. W. Norton, 1984. Includes an essay on the American independent cinema by John G. Hanhardt.

Lipman, Jean, and Richard Marshall. *Art About Art*. New York: Dutton in association with the Whitney Museum of American Art, 1978.

Lippard, Lucy R., editor. *Pop Art*. New York: Praeger, 1966.

Pierre, José. *Pop Art: An Illustrated Dictionary*. London: Methuen, 1977.

Rose, Barbara. *American Painting: The Twentieth Century*. Geneva: Skira, 1969.

Rublowsky, John. *Pop Art*. New York: Basic Books, 1965. Photography by Ken Heyman.

Russell, John, and Suzi Gablik. *Pop Art Redefined*. New York: Praeger, 1969. Includes "Andy Warhol" by Larry Bell and "Andy Warhol," an interview with G. R. Swenson.

*Sammlung 1968 Karl Ströher*. Munich: Galerieverein München, 1968.

Sandler, Irving. *American Art of the 1960s*. New York: Harper & Row, 1988.

———. *The New York School: The Painters and Sculptors of the Fifties*. New York: Harper & Row, 1978.

Scheugl, Hans. *Sexualität und Neurose im Film: Die Kinomythen von Griffith bis Warhol*. Munich: W. Heyne Verlag, 1978.

Solomon, Alan R. *New York: The Second Breakthrough, 1959–1964*. Irvine: University of California, 1969.

———. *Painting in New York: 1944 to 1969*. Pasadena, Calif.: Pasadena Art Museum, 1969.

Wilson, Simon. *Pop*. London: Thames & Hudson, 1974.

## IV. PERIODICAL ARTICLES ABOUT THE ARTIST

"Andy Warhol, 1928–87: A Collage of Appreciations from the Artist's Colleagues, Critics and Friends." *Art in America* 75 (May 1987): 137–43. Contributions by Peter Schjeldahl, Philip Pearlstein, Lawrence Alloway, David Bourdon, Scott Burton, Kenneth E. Silver, Larry Rivers, John Coplans, Charles F. Stuckey, and Martin Filler.

*Artstudio* 8 (Spring 1988). Special number devoted to Warhol. Includes "De la marchandise absolue" by Jean Baudrillard, "Sweet Andy" by Stephen Koch, "Andy Warhol et la photographie" by Gabriel Bauret, "Trente Warhol valent mieux qu'un" by Luc Lang, "Warhol et la culture populaire" by Eric Valentin, "La duplicité" by Bruno Paradis, "Saturday Disasters: Trace et référence de la première période de Warhol" by Thomas Crow, "Andy Warhol à Paris dans les années 60" by Michel Bourel, "Andy Warhol: Un hymne à la mort" by Démosthènes Davvetas, "Andy Warhol, Quelques grands témoins: Sidney Janis, Leo Castelli, Robert Rosenblum, Clement Greenberg" by Ann Hindry (a group of interviews), "Andy Warhol, Moraliste de l'image" by Bernard Marcadé, a list of exhibitions, a selected bibliography, and a filmography.

Battcock, Gregory. "Andy Warhol: New Predictions for Art." *Arts Magazine* 48 (May 1974): 34–37.

———. "An Art Your Mother Could Understand." *Art & Artists* (London) 5 (February 1971): 12–13.

Bergin, Paul. "Andy Warhol: The Artist as Machine." *Art Journal* 26 (Summer 1967): 359–63.

Betsch, Carolyn. "Catalogue Raisonné of Warhol's Gestures." *Art in America* 59 (May/June 1971): 47.

Bourdon, David. "Andy Warhol and the Society Icon." *Art in America* 63 (January/February 1975): 42–45.

———. "Warhol as Filmmaker." *Art in America* 59 (May/June 1971): 48–53.

Chanan, Michael. "Pasolini and Warhol: The Calculating and the Nonchalant." *Art International* 14 (April 20, 1970): 25–27.

Cipnic, Dennis J. "Andy Warhol: Iconographer." *Sight and Sound* 41 (Summer 1972): 158–61.

Collins, Bradford R. "The Metaphysical Nosejob: The Remaking of Warhola, 1960–1968." *Arts Magazine* 62 (February 1988): 47–55.

Coplans, John. "Andy Warhol and Elvis Presley: Social and Cultural Predictions of Warhol's Serial Images." *Studio International* 181 (February 1971): 49–56.

———. "Early Warhol: The Systematic Evolution of the Impersonal Style." *Artforum* 8 (March 1970): 52–59.

Crow, Thomas. "Saturday Disasters: Trace and Reference in Early Warhol." *Art in America* 75 (May 1987): 128–36. Discussion in 75 (October 1987): 21.

Danto, Arthur. "Who Was Andy Warhol?" *Artnews* 86 (May 1987): 128–32.

Deitch, Jeffrey. "The Warhol Product." *Art in America* 68 (May 1980): 9, 11, 13.

Finch, Christopher. "Warhol Stroke Poussin." *Art & Artists* (London) 1 (February 1967): 8–11.

Gardner, Paul. "Gee, What's Happened to Andy Warhol?" *Artnews* 79 (November 1980): 72–77.

Geelhaar, Christian. "Zeit im Schaffen von Andy Warhol." *Pantheon* 32 (October/December 1974): 390–98.

Geldzahler, Henry. "Andy Warhol." *Art International* 8 (April 25, 1964): 34–35.

Gidal, Peter. "Problems 'Relating to' Andy Warhol's 'Still Life 1976.'" *Artforum* 16 (May 1978): 38–40.

Hancock, Marianne. "Soup's On." *Arts Magazine* 39 (May/June 1965): 16–18.

Hilberry, Susanne F. "Two Andy Warhol Self-Portraits." *Bulletin of the Detroit Institute of Arts* 50, no. 4 (1971): 63–69.

Hoberman, J. "Andy Warhol: Top Gun and Brancusi." *Artforum* 25 (December 1986): 70–77.

Johnson, Ellen H. "The Image Duplicators—Lichtenstein, Rauschenberg, and Warhol." *Canadian Art* 23 (January 1966): 12–19.

Josephson, Mary. "Warhol: The Medium as Cultural Artifact." *Art in America* 59 (May/June 1971): 40–46.

Kagan, Andrew. "Most Wanted Men: Andy Warhol

and the Anti-Culture of Punk." *Arts Magazine* 53 (September 1978): 119–21.

Kozloff, Max. "Andy Warhol and Ad Reinhardt: The Great Accepter and the Great Demurrer." *Studio International* 181 (March 1971): 113–17. Reply by Jeanne Siegel in 182 (July 1971): 4.

Kuspit, Donald. "Andy's Feelings." *Artscribe International* 64 (Summer 1987): 32–35.

Leff, Leonard. "Warhol's 'Pork.'" *Art in America* 60 (January 1972): 112–13.

Leider, Philip. "Saint Andy: Some Notes on an Artist Who, for a Large Section of a Younger Generation, Can Do No Wrong." *Artforum* 3 (February 1965): 26–28.

Lurie, David. "Andy Warhol/'Disaster Paintings.'" *Arts Magazine* 60 (Summer 1986): 117–18.

Mascheck, Joseph. "Warhol as Illustrator: Early Manipulations of the Mundane." *Art in America* 59 (May/June 1971): 54–59.

Meyer, Jean-Claude. "Andy Warhol et l'arrêt du monde." *XXe Siècle* 41 (December 1973): 61, 83–87.

Morgan, Stuart, Glenn O'Brien, Remo Guidieri, and Robert Becker. "Collaboration Andy Warhol." *Parkett* 12 (1987): 32–103.

Perreault, John. "Andy Warhola, This Is Your Life." *Artnews* 69 (May 1970): 52–53, 79–80. Reply by John Coplans in 69 (September 1970): 6.

Pluchard, François. "Andy Warhol." *Connaissance des arts* 290 (April 1976): 36–41.

Pomeroy, Ralph. "The Importance of Being Andy Andy Andy Andy Andy." *Art & Artists* (London) 5 (February 1971): 14–19.

Porter, B. "Andy Warhol (1928–1987): Anti-Obit." *Start Interacting with Art* 1 (1987): 10–11. Interview with Trevor J. Fairbrother.

Ratcliff, Carter. "Andy Warhol: Inflation Artist." *Artforum* 23 (March 1985): 68–75.

———. "Starlust: Andy's Photos." *Art in America* 68 (May 1980): 120–22.

Restany, Pierre. "Andy Warhol: A Mauve-Tinged Platinum Wig." *Cimaise* 34 (June/August 1987): 69–72.

Schjeldahl, Peter. "Warhol and Class Content." *Art in America* 68 (May 1980): 112–19.

Steiner, Reinhard A. "Die Frage nach der Person: Zum Realitätscharakter von Andy Warhols Bildern." *Pantheon* 42 (April/June 1984): 151–57.

Stuckey, Charles F. "Andy Warhol's Painted Faces." *Art in America* 68 (May 1980): 102–11.

Wilson, William. "'Prince of Boredom': The Repetitions and Passivities of Andy Warhol." *Art & Artists* (London) 2 (March 1968): 12–15.

# *LENDERS TO THE EXHIBITION*

Stedelijk Museum, Amsterdam
Oeffentliche Kunstsammlung Basel
Museum of Contemporary Art, Chicago
Museum Ludwig, Cologne
The Detroit Institute of Arts
Kunstsammlung Nordrhein-Westfalen,
    Düsseldorf
Museum für Moderne Kunst, Frankfurt
The Menil Collection, Houston
The Nelson-Atkins Museum of Art,
    Kansas City, Missouri
La Jolla Museum of Contemporary Art
Saatchi Collection, London
The Trustees of the Tate Gallery, London
Los Angeles County Museum of Art
Landesmuseum Mainz
Städtisches Museum Abteiberg,
    Mönchengladbach
Dia Art Foundation, New York
The Solomon R. Guggenheim Museum,
    New York
The Metropolitan Museum of Art, New York
The Museum of Modern Art, New York
Whitney Museum of American Art, New York
Musée National d'Art Moderne,
    Centre Georges Pompidou, Paris
The Art Museum, Princeton University,
    Princeton, New Jersey
Virginia Museum of Fine Arts, Richmond
Moderna Museet, Stockholm
Staatsgalerie Stuttgart
Museum moderner Kunst, Vienna
Rose Art Museum, Brandeis University,
    Waltham, Massachusetts

Hirshhorn Museum and Sculpture Garden,
    Smithsonian Institution, Washington, D.C.
Kunsthaus Zürich

Michael D. Abrams
American Republic Insurance Company,
    Des Moines, Iowa
Mr. and Mrs. Harry W. Anderson
Betty Asher
Mr. and Mrs. S. Brooks Barron
Martin and Janet Blinder
Irving Blum
Peder Bonnier
Leo Castelli
Douglas S. Cramer
Mr. and Mrs. Asher B. Edelman
Stefan T. Edlis
Tom Eliasson
Louise Ferrari
Gerald S. Fineberg
Shirley and Miles Fiterman
J. W. Froehlich
Henry Geldzahler
Mrs. Raymond Goetz
Joni and Monte Gordon
Goldie Heller
Stellan Holm
Jasper Johns
Jed Johnson
Philip Johnson
Miriam and Erwin Kelen
Mr. and Mrs. Richard S. Lane
Roy and Dorothy Lichtenstein
Robert Mapplethorpe
Georges Marciano

Dr. Erich Marx
Robert and Meryl Meltzer
Adelaide de Menil
Adrian and Robert Mnuchin
J. Y. Mock
Morton G. Neumann Family Collection
Mr. and Mrs. S. I. Newhouse, Jr.
PaineWebber Group Inc.
Francesco Pellizzi
John and Kimiko Powers
Mr. and Mrs. Joseph Pulitzer, Jr.
Elizabeth and Michael Rea
Mr. and Mrs. John N. Rosekrans, Jr.
Noreen and Jack A. Rounick
Gunter Sachs
Mrs. Irma S. Seitz
Mr. and Mrs. Harold Siegel
The Sonnabend Collection
Emily and Jerry Spiegel
The Estate of Andy Warhol
David Whitney
Windsor, Inc.
Anonymous lenders

Thomas Ammann Fine Art, Zürich
Galerie Bruno Bischofberger, Zürich
Blum Helman Gallery, New York
Ronald Feldman Fine Arts, Inc., New York
Gagosian Gallery, New York
Nigel Greenwood Gallery, London
Robert Miller Gallery, New York
Holly Solomon Gallery, New York
Sperone Westwater Gallery, New York

# PHOTOGRAPH CREDITS

Photographs of works of art reproduced in this volume have been provided in most cases by the owners or custodians of the works, identified in the captions. The photographers of these works are listed alphabetically below, along with the sources and photographers of the documentary illustrations. Illustrations in the plate section are cited by plate number; reference illustrations in the text are cited by page number. Unless otherwise indicated, a page number refers to all of the illustrations on that page.

Courtesy Abbeville Press: pl. 226
Jon Abbot: pls. 216 (© Dia Art Foundation), 351, 380
Noel Allum: pls. 256, 261, 272, 274, 364
© The Art Institute of Chicago, all rights reserved: pl. 361
Peppe Avallone: pl. 386
© Richard Avedon, all rights reserved: p. 440
© John Back: pls. 109, 191, 211
Ch. Bahier & Ph. Migeat: pl. 231
David Bailey: p. 480
Courtesy Galerie Bruno Bischofberger, Zürich: pl. 384
Courtesy Blum Helman Gallery, New York: pl. 164
Rudolph Burckhardt: pls. 302, 305 (both courtesy Leo Castelli Gallery, New York); pp. 45, 49 bottom right, 52 bottom, 73 top
Barney Burstein, courtesy Institute of Contemporary Art, Boston: pl. 184
Courtesy Leo Castelli Gallery, New York: pl. 277
Powey Chang: pl. 255
Courtesy Christie's, New York: pls. 91, 151
© Geoffrey Clements, Inc.: pls. 79, 214, 325; pp. 68 left, 415 bottom right, 425, 426, 442
Ken Cohen: p. 47
Courtesy Paula Cooper Gallery, New York: p. 30 bottom
Courtesy Rainer Crone Archive: pls. 77, 301
Prudence Cuming Associates Limited, London: pl. 223
Bevan Davies, New York: pl. 224; p. 48
© The Dayton Art Institute: pl. 138
D. James Dee: pls. 16 (courtesy Souyun Yi Gallery, New York), 178, 247–249, 303, 304, 313–315, 318, 401, 402, 413 (BLACKGLAMA® and WHAT BECOMES A LEGEND MOST® with its pictorial representation are trademarked and copyrighted by the Great Lakes Mink Association), 414 (© Andy Warhol; this interpretation created by Andy Warhol is derived from an original version of a James Dean poster copyrighted by Warner Bros., Inc.), 415, 459; p. 74

© The Detroit Institute of Arts: pl. 5
eeva-inkeri: pls. 387 (courtesy Ronald Feldman Fine Arts, Inc., New York), 388 (© Andy Warhol, D.C. Comics), 389 (Feldman; this interpretation created and copyrighted by Andy Warhol is derived from an original version of Mickey Mouse © Walt Disney Productions); p. 447 right
Susan Einstein, courtesy Newspace Gallery, Los Angeles: pl. 353
M. Lee Fatherree: pl. 8
Courtesy Ronald Feldman Fine Arts, Inc., New York: pls. 212, 311, 316
Clem Fiori: pls. 156, 207
Courtesy Gagosian Gallery, New York: pl. 270
Ron Galella, courtesy Sotheby's, New York: p. 412 bottom right
Lynton Gardiner: pl. 460
Gianfranco Gorgoni: p. 443
Courtesy Samuel Adams Green: p. 411 top left, bottom left, top right
John M. Hall: pl. 143
© Howard Halma: p. 404 top left
Michael Halsband: p. 453
Robert Hausser GDL, Mannheim: pl. 262
David Heald: pl. 279
Paul Hester: pls. 12, 15, 88, 94, 127, 139 (courtesy The Menil Collection), 266 (Menil), 273, 307, 381
© Ken Heyman, courtesy Archive Pictures Inc.: pp. 73 bottom left, 404 top right, 409 top left
Hickey and Robertson, Houston: pls. 235, 281, 285
© Hans Hinz: pl. 256
Courtesy Hirschl & Adler Modern, New York: p. 15 top left
© David Hockney, photographed by Lynton Gardiner: p. 445
Courtesy Vivian Horan Fine Art, New York: pl. 225
Susan Horwitz: p. 31
Jacqueline Hyde, courtesy Leo Castelli Gallery, New York: pl. 347
Courtesy The Institute of Contemporary Art, University of Pennsylvania: pl. 183
© Ruth Kaiser: pl. 165
George Klauber: p. 404 bottom right
James Klosty, courtesy Cunningham Dance Foundation, Inc.: p. 414 top left
Bob Kolbrener: pls. 9, 173
Rolf Lauter, Frankfurt: pl. 135
Marcus Leatherdale: p. 451
The Limon Studio: pl. 195
Tord Lund, The National Art Museums of Sweden: pl. 283

© Christopher Makos: pp. 418 bottom, 419 top left, 448
Archives Malanga: p. 429
© Robert Mapplethorpe: frontispiece; p. 455
Marburg/Art Resource, New York: p. 22 top
© Fred W. McDarrah: pl. 182; p. 430
Camilla McGrath: p. 446
R. McKeever: pl. 175
Patrick McMullan: p. 419 bottom right
Edward Meneeley: p. 43 top right
Courtesy The Menil Collection, Houston: pl. 282; p. 428
© The Metropolitan Museum of Art, New York, all rights reserved: pls. 85, 236
© Duane Michals: pp. 23, 404 second from top at left, 424
Courtesy Robert Miller Gallery, New York: pls. 39, 46, 50, 51, 52, 59, 120
Ugo Mulas, Milan: pp. 71, 437
Muldoon Studios: pl. 271
© Museum Associates, Los Angeles County Museum of Art, all rights reserved: pl. 268
© Museum of Fine Arts, Boston, all rights reserved: pl. 278
The Museum of Modern Art, New York: pls. 13, 21–31, 32 (except top image), 34–36, 38, 41, 44, 45, 47–49, 53–58, 60, 67–72, 74, 81, 83, 84, 87, 95–99, 102–107, 121, 128–132, 141, 160–163, 168, 179–181, 185–188, 190, 196, 197, 199, 200, 212, 217–220, 222, 228, 229, 243, 244, 309, 312, 316, 319, 320, 322, 330, 331, 346, 359, 360, 363, 376, 377, 420, 424, 430, 437, 442, 443, 447–449, 453; pp. 13, 14, 17, 20 center, 21 right, 41 bottom, 43 top left and bottom, 46, 53, 54 bottom right, 63, 67 bottom, 401 bottom, 402 left, 403 top left and center left, 404 bottom center, 407 top, 414 top right, 418 top, 420
The Museum of Modern Art, New York; Film Stills Archive: pp. 409 bottom left, 414 top center, 416 center and bottom
Billy Name; Factory Foto: pp. 73 bottom right, 409 bottom right, 410 top left, top center, and bottom left, 411 center right and bottom right, 412 (except center right and bottom right), 413 top right, 415 bottom left, 434
Courtesy National Gallery of Art, Washington, D.C.: p. 44 bottom
© W. R. Nelson Trust, all reproduction rights reserved: pl. 198
Helmut Newton: p. 444
Bill Orcutt: pls. 37, 275
© Douglas M. Parker: pl. 230

475

# *INDEX OF PLATES*

DOCUMENTARY PLATES